Understanding Children's Literature

Blackburn
College

Libra

This book introduces the study of children's literature, addressing theoretical questions as well as the most relevant critical approaches to the field.

The fourteen chapters draw on insights from academic disciplines ranging from cultural and literary studies to education and psychology, and include an essay on what writers for children think about their craft. This results in a fascinating range of perspectives on key topics in children's literature and an introduction to such diverse concerns as literacy, ideology, stylistics, feminism, history and culture, and bibliotherapy. An extensive general bibliography is complemented by lists of further reading for every chapter and a glossary defines critical and technical terms, making the book accessible to those coming to the field or to a particular approach for the first time.

In this second edition there are four entirely new chapters; contributors have revisited and revised or rewritten seven of the chapters to reflect new thinking, while the remaining three are classic essays, widely acknowledged to be definitive. The glossary, further reading lists and general bibliography have also been thoroughly updated.

Understanding Children's Literature is an invaluable guide for students of literature or education and it will also inform and enrich the practice of teachers and librarians.

Peter Hunt is Professor Emeritus in Children's Literature at Cardiff University.

Understanding Children's Literature

Second Edition

Edited by Peter Hunt

Key essays from the second edition of *The International Companion Encyclopedia of Children's Literature*

Routledge
Taylor & Francis Group

LONDON AND NEW YORK

First published 1999
by Routledge
2 Park Square, Milton Park, Abingdon, Oxon, OX14 4RN

Simultaneously published in the USA and Canada
by Routledge
270 Madison Ave., New York, NY 10016

Reprinted 2003 (twice), 2006

Second edition first published 2005

Reprinted 2006 (twice), 2007 (three times), 2008

Routledge is an imprint of the Taylor & Francis Group, an informa business

Typeset in Galliard and GillSans by
Taylor & Francis Books
Printed and bound in Great Britain by
MPG Books Ltd, Bodmin

British Library Cataloguing in Publication Data
A catalogue record for this book is available from the British
Library

Library of Congress Cataloging in Publication Data
A catalog record for this book has been requested

ISBN 10: 0-415-37547-9 (HBK)
ISBN 10: 0-415-37546-0 (PBK)
ISBN 13: 978-0-415-37547-4 (HBK)
ISBN 13: 978-0-415-37546-7 (PBK)

Contents

Note on the second edition

The key difference between the first and second editions of *Understanding Children's Literature* is the acknowledgement of the shift in the humanities away from 'high theory' over the past ten years. Theory remains essential to an understanding of how and why children's literature works, but the four new essays included here move the emphasis of the book more towards applications, and towards a broader audience. Seven of the essays have been extensively revised or rewritten to reflect new thinking, while the remaining three are classic essays, widely acknowledged to be definitive, and these have been given updated bibliographies.

Contributors

Michael Benton is Professor Emeritus in Education, University of Southampton. His books include work focused on reader-response in the classroom, for example, *Teaching Literature 9–14* (with Geoff Fox) (1985), and *Young Readers Responding to Poems* (with John Teasey, Ray Bell, and Keith Hurst) (1988); classroom anthologies, for example *Picture Poems* (with Peter Benton) (1997); and *Studies in the Spectator Role: Literature, Painting, and Pedagogy* (2000).

Hamida Bosmajian is a Professor of English at Seattle University. Her books include *Metaphors of Evil: Contemporary German Literature and the Shadow of Nazism* (1977) and *Sparing the Child: Grief and the Unspeakable in Youth Literature about the Holocaust* (2002), which won the Children's Literature Association Book Award.

Hugh Crago is co-editor, with Maureen Crago, of *The Australian and New Zealand Journal of Family Therapy*. He was co-author, with Maureen, of the ground-breaking study of their daughter's interaction with texts, *Prelude to Literacy* (1983). His latest book is *A Circle Unbroken: the Hidden Emotional Patterns that Shape our Lives* (1999).

Matthew Grenby is Reader in Children's Literature in the School of English Literature, Language and Linguistics at the University of Newcastle upon Tyne. While at de Montfort University, he was Director of the Hockliffe Project, a pioneering venture in digitising 18th- and 19th-century texts. His work focuses on eighteenth-century and Romantic-era British cultural history, and the emergence of the children's book industry.

Peter Hunt is Professor Emeritus in Children's Literature, Cardiff University. He has written or edited 23 books in the field, including *Children's Literature: A Guide* (2001) and *Children's Literature: An Anthology 1801-1902* (2001). He won the Brothers Grimm Award for services to Children's Literature from the International Institute for Children's Literature in Osaka, in 2003. He is co-editor of *The Norton Anthology of Children's Literature* (2005).

Perry Nodelman is a Professor of English at the University of Winnipeg. He was editor of the *Children's Literature Association Quarterly* for five years, and has published over a hundred articles. His *Words about Pictures: the Narrative Art of Children's Picture Books* (1988) is a pioneering work, and his handbook *The Pleasures of Children's Literature*

(1992) is in its third edition (with Mavis Reimer, 2003). His children's books include *The Same Place But Different* (1993), *Behaving Bradley* (1998) and, with Carol Matas, *A Meeting of Minds* (1999).

Lissa Paul is a Professor in the Faculty of Education at the University of New Brunswick. She has written widely on education, gender, and on Ted Hughes. Her books include *Reading Otherways* (1998), and she is Associate General Editor of *The Norton Anthology of Children's Literature* (2005).

David Rudd lectures in literature and education at the University of Bolton. He has written two books on Children's Literature, *A Communication Studies Approach to Children's Literature* (1992) and *Enid Blyton and the Mystery of Children's Literature* (2000), and over seventy articles. He is on the editorial boards of three journals in the field, including *Children's Literature in Education*.

Charles Sarland was a Senior Lecturer in Education at John Moores University. His books include *Young People Reading: Culture and Response* (1991) and *Teaching English, Language and Literacy* (with Dominic Wyse, Russell Jones and Roger Bainbridge) (2000).

John Stephens is Professor and Head of the Department of English at Macquarie University. He is the author of *Language and Ideology in Children's Fiction* (1992), two books on discourse analysis, and around a hundred articles on children's (and other) literature. His latest books are *Retelling Stories, Framing Culture: Traditional Stories and Metanarratives in Children's Literature* (with Robyn McCallum) (1998), and *Ways of Being Male: Representing Masculinities in Children's Literature and Film* (2002). In 2004, he was Visiting Fellow at the University of Surrey.

Tony Watkins founded and directed the first British MA in Children's Literature, and the Centre for International Research in Childhood: Literature, Culture, Media, at the University of Reading. He lectures each year at Children's Literature New England, and has been a Fellow at the International Institute for Children's Literature in Osaka. His latest book is *A Necessary Fantasy: the Heroic Figure in Children's Popular Culture* (with Dudley Jones) (2000).

Christine Wilkie-Stibbs lectures in English at the Institute of Education of the University of Warwick, where for several years she developed and was Director of the MA in Children's Literature Studies. Her books include *Through the Narrow Gate* (1989) on Russell Hoban, and *The Feminine Subject in Children's Literature* (2002).

Sally Yates is Head of Primary Education at University College Chichester, where she lectures in literacy and children's literature. She is the author (with Nikki Gamble) of *Exploring Children's Literature – Teaching the Language and Reading of Fiction* (with Nikki Gamble) (2002) and is currently researching the social and cultural factors impacting on children's responses to reading.

1 Introduction

The expanding world of Children's Literature Studies

Peter Hunt

So what good is literary theory? Will it keep our children singing? Well perhaps not. But understanding something of literary theory will give us some understanding of how the literature we give to our children works. It might also keep us engaged with the texts that surround us, keep us singing even if it is a more mature song than we sang as youthful readers of texts. As long as we keep singing, we have a chance of passing along our singing spirit to those we teach.

(McGillis 1996: 206)

Children's literature

'Children's literature' sounds like an enticing field of study; because children's books have been largely beneath the notice of intellectual and cultural gurus, they are (apparently) blissfully free of the 'oughts': what we ought to think and say about them. More than that, to many readers, children's books are a matter of private delight, which means, perhaps, that they are real literature – if 'literature' consists of texts which engage, change, and provoke intense responses in readers.

But if private delight seems a somewhat indefensible justification for a study, then we can reflect on the direct or indirect influence that children's books have, and have had, socially, culturally, and historically. They are overtly important educationally and commercially – with consequences across the culture, from language to politics: most adults, and almost certainly the vast majority of those in positions of power and influence, read children's books as children, and it is inconceivable that the ideologies permeating those books had no influence on their development.

The books have, none the less, been marginalised. Childhood is, after all, a state we grow away from, while children's books – from writing to publication to interaction with children – are the province of that culturally marginalised group, females. But this marginalisation has had certain advantages; because it has been culturally low-profile, 'children's literature' has not become the 'property' of any group or discipline: it does not 'belong' to the Department of Literature or the Library School, or the local parents' organisation. It is attractive and interesting to students (official or unofficial) of literature, education, library studies, history, psychology, art, popular culture, media, the caring professions, and so on, and it can be approached from any specialist viewpoint. Its nature, both as a group of texts and as a subject for study, has been to break down barriers between disciplines, and between types of readers. And as a group of texts it is at once one of the liveliest and most original of the arts, and the site of the crudest commercial exploitation.

This means that, just as children's books do not exist in a vacuum (they have real, argumentative readers and visible, practical, consequential uses), so the theory of children's literature constantly blends into the practice of bringing books and readers together.

The slightly uncomfortable (or very inspiring) corollary of this is that we have to accept that children's books are complex, and the study of them infinitely varied. Many students around the world who have been enticed onto children's literature courses at all 'levels' rapidly find that things are more complicated than they had assumed. There cannot be many teachers of children's literature who have not been greeted with a querulous 'But it's only a children's book', 'Children won't see that in it', or 'You're making it more difficult than it should be'. But the complexities are not mere problematising by academics eager to secure their meal tickets; the most apparently straightforward act of communication is amazingly intricate – and we are dealing here with fundamental questions of communication and understanding between adults and children, or, more exactly, between individuals.

If children's literature is more complex than it seems, even more complex, perhaps, is the position it finds itself in, between adult writers, readers, critics and practitioners, and child readers. Children's literature is an obvious point at which theory encounters real life, where we are forced to ask: what can we say about a book, why should we say it, how can we say it, and what effect will what we say have? We are also forced to confront our preconceptions. Many people will deny that they were influenced by their childhood reading ('I read *xyz* when I was a child, and it didn't do *me* any harm'), and yet these may be the same people who accept that childhood is an important phase in our lives (as is almost universally acknowledged), and that children are vulnerable, susceptible, and must be protected from manipulation. Children's literature is important – and yet it is not.

Consequently, before setting off to explore the somewhat tangled jungle that is 'children's literature', we need to establish some basic concepts, ideas, and methods: to work through fundamental arguments, to look at which techniques of criticism, which discourses, and which strategies are appropriate to – or even unique to – our subject. It can be argued that we can (and should) harness the considerable theoretical and analytical apparatus of every discipline from philosophy to psychotherapy; or that we should evolve a critical theory and practice tailored to the precise needs of 'children's literature'.

This book, which selects key essays from the second edition of the *International Companion Encyclopedia of Children's Literature*, provides the essential theory for any adventure into 'children's literature', outlines some practical approaches, suggests areas of research, and provides up-to-date bibliographies to help readers to find their own, individual, appropriate paths.

Literature and children

All the writers in this book share an unspoken conviction that children's literature is worth reading, worth discussing, and worth thinking about for adults. Aidan Chambers has summed up the motivation of many 'liberal humanist' teachers and writers:

> I belong to the demotic tradition; I believe literature belongs to all the people all the time, that it ought to be cheaply and easily available, that it ought to be fun to read as well as challenging, subversive, refreshing, comforting, and all the other qualities we claim for it. Finally, I hold that in literature we find the best expression of the human imagination, and the most useful means by which we come to grips with our ideas about ourselves and what we are.
>
> (Chambers 1985: 16)

Such a faith in literature underlies a great deal of day-to-day teaching and thinking about children and books; it lies behind the connection between literature and literacy, whether or not children's books are seen as valuable in themselves, or as stepping-stones to higher things (to 'adult' or 'great' literature).

Chambers's statement is, however, clearly not neutral: it embodies some very obvious (and some not-so-obvious) ideology (aspects of ideology are considered in Chapter 3), and it brings us up against the question of what is 'literature'. Oceans of ink have been spilt on this matter, but it is essential to recognise that there is no such thing as 'literary' quality or value inherent in any set of words on a page. As Jonathan Culler sums it up, 'Literature … is a speech act or textual event that elicits certain kinds of attention' (1997: 27) – or, better, which is accorded a certain value by those members of the culture who are in a position to accord values.

This is fundamental to children's literature, where practitioners (those who work with books and children, and who generally have more pressing concerns than subtle theoretical nuances) want to know – as simply as possible – what is good? The shadow of what they 'ought' to value lies over them, and it is difficult to convince many people that 'good' doesn't belong to somebody else – to the great 'they'. Outside academia, arguments about what is 'good' very often collapse into a rather weary 'well, it's all a matter of taste'. But people are usually a little uneasy – or defiant – about that, as if somebody, somewhere, knows better than they do what is 'good' (and they don't necessarily like it) (see Hunt 1997).

This leads to the common situation that people will privately like, or value, one type of book, while publicly recommending something else. Books which would have low status on some cosmic value-scale (and which are highly successful commercially, notably J. K. Rowling's 'Harry Potter' series) are excluded from serious consideration (see Hunt 2001: 122–4; Zipes 2001: 170–89). Others – the 'classics', perhaps – are taught and prescribed and written about. In primary and secondary education, this can lead to a backlash against reading: if children read one kind of book in school, and another kind outside school, then certain books may be regarded by them as 'other' (see Chapter 11).

This division leads to inappropriate critical approaches being taken to the books. Children's books are different from adults' books: they are written for a different audience, with different skills, different needs, and different ways of reading; equally, children experience texts in ways which are often unknowable, but which many of us strongly suspect to be very rich and complex. If we judge children's books (even if we do it unconsciously) by the same value systems as we use for adult books – in comparison with which they are bound *by definition* to emerge as *lesser* – then we give ourselves unnecessary problems. To say that, for example, Judy Blume is not as good a writer as Jane Austen is not to compare like with like, and presupposes an innate superiority in the latter. 'Literature', then, is only a useful concept if we want to educate children into a particular kind of culture: but it can be misleading or pernicious if we are 'using' the texts in other ways.

If the word 'literature' presents obvious problems, the word 'children' proves to be equally slippery. The notion of childhood changes from place to place, from time to time, and the history, definition, and study of childhood as a concept has burgeoned in recent years, as in Chris Jenks's *Childhood* (1996), Colin Heywood's *A History of Childhood* (2001), and Carol Garhart Mooney's *Theories of Childhood* (2000) (and see also Cunningham 1995, and, in a lighter but no less revealing vein, Hardyment 1995). In non-Western countries, the relationships between story and storyteller, adult and child, can be radically different from those in the West (see, for example, Pellowski 2004). Consequently, making judgements on behalf of present or past children – as those adults who work with children and books are inclined (or bound) to do – is fraught with difficulty. This in itself draws our attention to the gross simplifications made about peer readers in very many critical texts: with the 'child' reader in children's literature, the problem of talking about 'the reader', or a specific 'reader', should be much more obvious (see Chapter 2).

A central example of these kinds of confusion may be seen in the discussion of poetry for children. Surely such a thing cannot exist, if we assume that 'poetry' is a kind of literature which is structured so as to invite or require a special kind of reading – a kind of reading that 'children' (it is widely assumed) cannot provide. Neil Philip effectively demolishes this proposition in his 'Introduction' to *The New Oxford Book of Children's Verse*:

> Some would argue that the very notion of poetry for children is a nonsense.... Yet there is a recognisable tradition of children's verse. It is, most crucially, a tradition of immediate apprehension. There is in the best children's poetry a sense of the world being seen as if for the first time, and of language being plucked from the air to describe it. ... This does not necessarily mean that children's poems are 'simple' in any reductive sense. I would argue that no poem can be called a poem that does not have at its heart some unknowable mystery.
>
> (Philip 1996: xxv)

History, ideology, politics

It will be clear by now that both the range of children's books and the ways in which they can be studied are very extensive. Just as children's books are part of the ideological structures of the cultures of the world, so their history is constructed ideologically (some of these issues are dealt with in Chapters 3, 4, and 8). The two most obvious constructions of history are from an Anglocentric viewpoint, and from a male viewpoint (although, of course, those 'viewpoints' are far from stable). Other constructions of history – such as a feminist, gay, or 'childist' approach – wait to be written, although much progress has been made in the first of these with books such as Lynne Vallone's *Disciplines of Virtue. Girls' Culture in the Eighteenth and Nineteenth Centuries* (1995), Roberta Seelinger Trites's evangelical *Waking Sleeping Beauty: Feminist Voices in Children's Novels* (1997), Christine Wilkie-Stibbs's *The Feminine Subject in Children's Literature* (2002), and Beverly Lyon Clark and Margaret Higonnet's *Girls, Boys, Books, Toys: Gender in Children's Literature and Culture* (1999) (and see Chapter 8).

Children's books have a long history around the world, and they have absorbed into themselves elements of folk, fairy tale, and the oral tradition. In many places, such as parts of Africa, they have a post-colonial tinge, and an uneasy relationship with indigenous culture; elsewhere, they have seemed sufficiently important to totalitarian states as to suffer severe censorship. It is also possible to perceive similar patterns throughout the world – although it is clearly possible to challenge a wide-ranging view such as this, by Sheila Ray:

> In the early stages of a printed literature, there are few or no books published specifically for children. There are perhaps a few books intended for broadly educational purposes, such as the courtesy or behaviour books printed in the fifteenth or sixteenth centuries in European countries, or the twentieth-century text books published to support the formal school curriculum in developing countries. In this situation, children, as they learn to read, also take over adult books which appeal to them, a process helped by the fact that the early printed literature in any society is likely to draw on traditional stories which contain elements which appeal to every age group. Religion

is also an important factor ... Gradually stories written specially for children begin to appear ... [and eventually] demands for books to meet a variety of interests and special needs emerge. One of the problems which face developing countries in the twenty-first century is that they are expected to go through all the stages in a relatively short space of time – thirty or forty years at most – whereas European countries have taken five hundred years over the same process.

(Ray 2004: II, 850)

If a recognisable children's literature requires a recognisable childhood, and should not be totally shared with adults, then we might argue that English-language children's books only emerged in the eighteenth century, with British publishers such as Mary Cooper and John Newbery. The first book 'especially prepared for North American youth', John Cotton's *Spiritual Milk for Boston Babes*, was printed in London in 1646 (Griswold 2004: II, 1270); in India, children's books began in Calcutta with the establishment of the School Book Society by missionaries in 1817 (Jafa 2004: II, 1078), and the earliest children's book in Malayalam (spoken in Kerala), *Cherupaithangalkku Upakaratham Kathakal* (c. 1824), contained stories translated from English (Jafa 2004: II, 1083). This dominance by the English language has continued: in 1988, half the children's books published in France were translations from English (Bouvaist 1990: 30). (In contrast, France was the dominant influence upon German children's books.) Today, the traffic between English and other languages remains virtually one-way (Hunt 2000: 107–11).

The earliest books for children were, as in Ray's formulation, based on traditional materials, or overtly didactic; children's literature in its modern form is largely a nineteenth-century phenomenon. For example, at the end of the eighteenth century in the Netherlands there was a rapid growth in fiction for children; whereas in Spain, despite translations of Grimm, Andersen, and Perrault, 'true' children's books did not emerge until the end of the nineteenth century.

Thereafter, histories of children's books worldwide demonstrate tensions between the exercise of educational, religious, and political power on the one hand, and various concepts associated with 'freedom' (notably fantasy and the imagination) on the other. The literatures that result demonstrate very clearly those societies' concepts of childhood and its power-relationship to adults. Notable English-language histories include Avery 1994 (USA); Darton 1932/1982 (England); Gilderdale 1982 (New Zealand); Hunt 1995 (England); Saxby 1969, 1971, 1993 (Australia); Townsend 1965/1990 (England).

History, as constructed, generally shows us (obviously enough) that adults can and do control the production of children's literature – however subversive the child's reading might be (see Chapter 6). Censorship permeates the process, operating both before and after the texts are produced, and often in bizarre circumstances. As Mark West has observed:

Throughout the history of children's literature, the people who have tried to censor children's books, for all their ideological differences, share a rather romantic view about the power of books. They believe, or at least profess to believe, that books are such a major influence in the formation of children's values and attitudes that adults need to monitor nearly every word that children read.

(West 2004: II, 689)

Censorship is relative: if books are withdrawn from classrooms, as they have often been, is that being protective, or restrictive? Many of the most forceful actions taken against books, publishers, libraries, and teachers have been in the USA by right-wing organisations, usually fundamentalist-Christian in origin. Perhaps the most famous instance has been Educational Research Analysts, a Texas-based organisation run by Mel and Norma Gabler, which analyses texts, has provided 'evidence' for local campaigners, and has sought to influence publishers (sometimes through state textbook-buying boards). Books which have been banned locally have included *The Diary of Anne Frank*, *The Wizard of Oz*, and adult books widely read by children and young adults such as *The Catcher in the Rye* – and, of course, Rowling's 'Harry Potter' books (West 2004: II, 686).

The fact that children may well (or must inevitably) read 'against' the text (making simple cause-and-effect arguments very questionable) means that children's books have been potentially highly subversive. One, ironic, example of their power is that, although they were tightly controlled in Nazi Germany as part of the *Gleichschaltung*, Erich Kästner's classic *Emil and the Detectives* (1929) remained available – even though his other books had been burned by the Nazis.

Censorship tends to characterise children as impressionable and simple-minded, unable to take a balanced view of, for example, sexual or racial issues, unless the balance is explicitly stated. Judy Blume's books, which in *Forever* (1975) include the first example of explicitly described sexual intercourse in a children's book, have been widely condemned, but have been bought in huge numbers by adolescents. Attempts have been made to censor or influence writers as diverse as Beatrix Potter (undressed kittens in *The Tale of Tom Kitten* (1907)) or Alan Garner (unsupervised sledging in *Tom Fobble's Day* (1977)). Difficulties have arisen over books which contain attitudes that were quite acceptable to the majority in their day. British examples include the racial caricatures in, for example, Hugh Lofting's *The Story of Dr Dolittle* (1922), or the gender bias in Enid Blyton's work; new editions of these books have been modified, as Britain has become increasingly multicultural and politically correct – or at least, more aware of such issues. Different cultures exercise 'censorship' in different ways. In Britain, it operates through selection, notably by large booksellers and wholesalers; in the USA, direct and vocal action is more the norm; elsewhere, just as totalitarian states 'manufactured' politically acceptable texts, so post-totalitarian (and post-colonial) societies have reacted against their previous masters.

Children's literature, then, has its own histories, and immense influence, but this has not until recently been reflected in serious study of the form. Perhaps the most neglected area has been bibliography – the history of the books as books. As Brian Alderson has observed, 'there can be no doubt that scientific bibliography is able to play as important a role in supporting the very varied activity which is taking place among children's books as it does in the field of literary studies elsewhere' (1977: 203; see also Chapter 10). However, because the study of children's literature has been skewed towards the reader and affect, rather than towards the book as artefact, we are in the position of having a great deal of speculative and theoretical criticism but relatively little 'solid' bibliographical backup. How far such backup is necessary will remain a matter of debate, but with vast collections of children's literature in libraries across the world, most of them very little used, there is immense potential for bibliographic and historical research.

Reading children's literature

Because it is unwise to assume that reading and interpreting children's books is a simple process, one of the recurrent themes in this volume is the relationship between reader and text. How far can the writer, by implying a reader (that is, a type of reader or a reader with certain knowledge, skills, and attitudes), control what is understood from a text? How can we discover what has been understood? What are the mechanisms by which understanding is produced?

Chapter 5 of this book, 'Analysing texts: linguistics and stylistics', and Chapter 9, 'Decoding the images: how picture books work', take us to the basics of textual analysis. It is clearly important to have an understanding of text as both verbal and visual language, and this is particularly true of children's literature – given that the primary audience is still learning about language as it uses it. The detailed and careful analyses suggested in these chapters also militate against the temptation to see children's literature (and its readers) as an amorphous mass; what we are dealing with is individual readings and 'literary' readings which are not to be judged in terms of an external scale of values. As Nodelman and Reimer have noted:

> Unfortunately, many readers approach texts with the idea that their themes or messages can be easily identified and stated in a few words … Reading in this way directs attention away from the more immediate pleasures of a text … away from other, deeper kinds of meaning the text might imply.
>
> (Nodelman and Reimer 2003: 66)

Children's literature studies fall between the extremes of 'literary' and 'cultural' studies. The first, as Jonathan Culler has pointed out, tends to encourage 'close reading', a type of reading that is 'alert to the details of narrative structure and attends to complexities of meaning'. In contrast, cultural studies (which usually deals with 'non-literary' texts, such as television and children's books) tends 'towards "symptomatic interpretation" – that is, identifying broad, portable themes' (Culler 1997: 52). In the context of child readers, and the power structures within children's books that pivot on the idea that adult writers attempt to influence child readers, we might feel the need to challenge the assumptions behind both these positions. Similarly, we should look very carefully at the philosophical problem at the root of understanding reading; to take the most pragmatic and perhaps conservative viewpoint:

> It is known that the reader's understanding of a text will be conditioned by what he [sic] already knows, and by the availability of that knowledge during the reading process. Given that different purposes and motivations for reading result in different levels of processing and outcome … it is likely that different readers will to some extent interpret different texts in varied ways. This, indeed, is notoriously the case for literary texts, where it is often said that there are as many interpretations as there are readers to interpret. Yet it is intuitively unsatisfying to claim that a text can mean anything to any reader. The text itself must to some extent condition the nature of the understanding that the reader constructs.
>
> (Alderson and Short 1989: 72)

The complexities of how the text 'conditions … understanding' are no more obvious than in the case of the picture-book – where it is often assumed that pictures are in some way 'easier' to interpret than words. As Scott McCloud points out in his revolutionary *Understanding Comics: the Invisible Art*, it is 'nothing short of incredible' that the human mind can understand icons – symbolic representations or abstractions from reality – as readily as it does (1993: 31, and see pp. 30–45). Picture-books cannot help but be polyphonic; even the 'simplest' of them requires complex interpretative skills. What is missing is as complex an interpretative vocabulary as exists for words, although this is rapidly being supplied through the work of Nodelman (1988), Doonan (1993), Nikolajeva and Scott (2001), Anstey and Bull (2000), and others.

Underestimating the power of the picture-book (or the comic book) is tantamount to underestimating the 'child' as reader – which, as I hope I have demonstrated, is a central error. Jane Doonan, for example, is concerned less with the complex mechanics of reading pictures than with aesthetics:

> A less common view, and the one I believe honours the picture-book most fully, holds that pictures, through their expressive powers, enable the book to function as an art object. ... The value lies ... in the aesthetic experience and the contribution the picture book can make to our aesthetic development. In an aesthetic experience we are engaged in play of the most enjoyable and demanding kind ... And in that play we have ... to deal with abstract concepts logically, intuitively and imaginatively.
>
> (Doonan 1993: 7)

Of course, the experience of a book starts before – and goes beyond – the words or the pictures on the page. The total book-as-object is an experience, one that has become increasingly the province of the book designer: 'each book is different and none so elementary as not to benefit from considered design. ... The designer sometimes has to take the initiative for presenting the author's material visually and thereby transforming it into a marketable product' (Martin 2004: II, 638).

Although we have been focusing on texts, it is obvious that the study of children's literature involves the audience: the child, the reader, and the circumstance of reading. Text is also a context; readers are made, or un-made, by the 'reading environment', as Aidan Chambers has called it. Nor do 'texts' need to be written. As Chambers observes: 'Storytelling is indispensable in enabling people to become literary readers' (Chambers 1991: 46), and the study of how stories are told orally contributes to our understanding of how stories – and communication – work.

Storytelling (to return to questions of ideology, which are never very far away) also has a political axis. Jack Zipes, a distinguished American expert on children's literature, folk-lore, and storytelling, believes passionately in the subversive virtues of storytelling. Schools in the West (with the collusion of society in general), he notes:

> ... are geared towards making children into successful consumers and competitors in a 'free' world dictated by market conditions. ... If storytellers are to be effective on behalf of children in schools ... it is important to try to instil a sense of community, self-reflecting and self-critical community, in the children to demonstrate how the ordinary can become extraordinary. ... Schools are an ideal setting for this 'subversive' type of storytelling ... if schools want ... to show that they can be other than the institutions of correction, discipline, and distraction that they tend to be.
>
> (Zipes 1995: 6)

How a story is communicated, then, by spoken word or written word, by picture or symbol, and through whatever medium (for a discussion of film see Wojcik-Andrews (2000), Whyte (2004); and for television, Buckingham (2002)), the circumstances of that communication and the possible effects have all become an integral part of the study of children's literature. This means that the concerns of what might broadly be called 'criticism' extend beyond the traditional bounds of literary criticism, and present a singularly eclectic challenge.

Criticising children's literature

There is a happy irony that people involved with the apparently simple subject of children's literature have (often unwittingly) been at the forefront of literary and critical theory.

It has been widely argued that practitioners of children's literature studies should not ghettoise themselves, but make use of all appropriate critical techniques. There is no shortage, as a sceptic might remark, of schools of criticism, nor of books which will outline their principles. But the fact that the work of such schools can be productively applied to children's literature is demonstrated by Roderick McGillis's *The Nimble Reader* (1996), which shows the relevance of schools of thought from formalism to feminism.

In the present book, five chapters (Chapter 2 and Chapters 5–8) cover the major general areas of literary theory and practice; other particularly fruitful approaches for children's literature are those concerned with the analysis of narrative (see, for example, Nikolajeva 2004), discourse in general, and the cultural structures reflected in texts (notably those affected by colonialism and post-colonialism, see McGillis 2000).

'Structuralism', for example, although perhaps somewhat outmoded as a critical fashion, may well provide a starting point for the study of myth, legend, folk- and fairy-tales – but only a starting point. It is a sociological and historical oddity that children's literature (perceived to be innocent) has come to include and absorb these (initially) crude, violent, and sexually-charged texts, but by understanding their structures, and then relating them to broader cultural movements, as well as to historical moments, they may be seen as other than they are generally supposed to be. The idea that folk-tales and myths contain archetypal patterns, for example, may be valuable; the idea that these archetypes are appropriate to childhood because of their 'simple' form leads us back to debates about perception, understanding, acculturalisation, and concepts of childhood. Jack Zipes's *The Trials and Tribulations of Little Red Riding Hood* (1993) is an excellent example of the way in which structural analyses can be combined with psychological, sociological, and historical studies. 'Little Red Riding Hood' may seem to the casual observer to be merely a simple children's story. Zipes rejects such a view:

> It is impossible to exaggerate the impact and importance of the Little Red Riding Hood syndrome as a dominant cultural pattern in Western societies. [One reading is that] Little Red Riding Hood reflects men's fear of women's sexuality – and of their own as well. The curbing and regulation of sexual drives is fully portrayed in this bourgeois literary fairy tale of the basis of deprived male needs. [Alternatively,] given the conditions of Western society where women have been prey for men, there is a positive feature to the tale: its warning about the possibility of sexual molestation continues to serve a useful purpose.
>
> (Zipes 1993: 80–1; see also Zipes 1997, and Griswold 2000)

The uses of children's literature

When academics are born, a good fairy at the christening promises them that when they grow up they will be able to read and understand books. Hardly has she finished speaking, however, when a bad fairy interrupts to say, with a threatening gesture, 'but you must never, never look out of the window'.

(Joan Rockwell, quoted in Parker 1994: 194)

As we have seen, the study of children's literature brings us back to some very fundamental concerns: why are we reading? what are books *for*? The answers may be, as in the case of Chambers, a general liberal-humanist faith in the book and in human civilisation; but very often, children's literature is seen as the last repository of the *dulcis et utile* philosophy: the books may be pleasant, yes, but essentially they have to be *useful*. Children's books are of the world, and one of the features of critical theory which has made it unattractive to many children's book practitioners has been its solipsistic turn.

In the judgement of children's books, then, *for* is often the key word. Books are not just 'good', but 'good *for*'. Children's books are used for different purposes at different times – for more things than most books are. Some are 'good' time-fillers; others 'good' for acquiring literacy; others 'good' for expanding the imagination or 'good' for inculcating general (or specific) social attitudes, or 'good' for dealing with issues or coping with problems, or 'good' for reading in that 'literary' way which is a small part of adult culture, or 'good' for dealing with racism … and most books do several of these things. This is not a scale where some purposes stand higher than others; it is a matrix where hundreds of subtle meanings are generated. What you think is good depends on you, the children, and on what you're using the book for – and every reading is different.

The two chapters of this book which address practical outcomes of reading children's books, 'Understanding reading and literacy' (Chapter 11) and 'Healing texts: bibliotherapy and psychology' (Chapter 13), demonstrate how theory and practice, psychological probability and practical outcome, and awareness of words, people, and their environments, are all inextricably linked. But the same could be said of other 'practical' applications of children's literature, notably the mediation of story to children with special needs (Mathias 2004).

It is the awareness that the study of children's literature encompasses not only subtle textual distinctions but practical, life-affecting actions which holds the 'subject' of children's literature together. The phenomenal range of prizes for 'the best' children's books awarded each year covers books which are not just abstractly 'the best', but which portray minorities, or promote peace – or which are chosen by children (Allen 2004).

Thus, while writers, publishers, librarians, teachers, parents, and children, and very many others, discuss the applications of children's literature, they are talking about the same interactive area as those who look into the books themselves. This seems to me to be the source, potentially, of immense strength and of immense innovation. In 1997, an issue of the prestigious annual journal, *Children's Literature*, was devoted to 'cross-writing', based on the idea that 'a dialogic mix of older and younger voices occurs in texts too often read as univocal. Authors who write for children inevitably create a colloquy between past and present selves'. This, the editors concluded, involves 'interplay and cross-fertilisation' (Knoepflmacher and Myers 1997: vii). That image could stand for much of Children's Literature Studies, and it is an understanding of the meanings behind those many voices that this book addresses.

The future of Children's Literature Studies

We are living in a period of unprecedented production and sales of children's books, which in turn has generated an unprecedented level of general interest in the field. There has been a steady consolidation of 'children's literature' as an accepted subject in universities across the world, and it seems likely that (despite widespread economic pressures on education systems) this will continue. However, this development has come at a time when there has also been a steady erosion of the established divisions between academic subjects, both in the humanities and the sciences, and in some ways the interdisciplinary nature of children's literature provides a model for this process.

It may seem that the competing elements will pull the subject apart, rather than give it any coherence. As McGillis has pointed out:

> ... lots of people in lots of places talk about and even study something called children's literature, but more often than not these various groups do not speak to each other. The rarefied theorising of the literary academic strikes the practising teacher as arid beyond tolerance, whereas the practical aims of the educationalist seem too limited and limiting to the theorist and historian of children's literature. The interest in bibliotherapy, sometimes expressed by the psychologically oriented critic ... is often dismissed as lacking the formalist rigor of serious literary analysis. And the interest in accumulating data, the purview of the librarian/media specialist, some [regard as] interesting but hardly intellectually stimulating or socially engaged.
>
> (McGillis 1999: 203)

But this should not discourage us. In 1981 Harold Rosen described the discipline of 'English' as:

> ... the least subject-like of subjects, the least susceptible to definition by reference to the accumulation of wisdom within a single academic discipline. No single set of informing ideas dominates its heartland. No one can confidently map its frontiers: it colonises and is colonised. When we inspect the practices which cluster together uncomfortably under its banner, they appear so diverse, contradictory, arbitrary and random as to defy analysis and explanation.
>
> (Quoted in Eaglestone 2000: 7)

Children's Literature Studies has as its core a concern – however distant – with children and the concept of childhood, and a natural way forward may be its association with the rapidly developing meta-discipline of Childhood Studies. Here, children's literature can be placed in the context of real and theoretical childhoods, and in the context of (adult) literary constructions and portrayals of childhood (see Travisano 2000, and Lesnik-Oberstein 1998). Bereavement can be linked to bibliotherapy, commodification of childhood to literary archetypes. A recent series of books on childhood, published by the British Open University, sums up the field:

> The growing field of childhood and youth studies provides an integrative framework for interdisciplinary research and teaching, as well as analysis of contemporary policy and practice in, for instance, education, health and social work. Childhood is now a global issue, forcing a reconsideration of conventional approaches to study. Childhood is also a very personal issue for each and every one of us – scholars, policy-makers, parents and children.
>
> (Kehily and Swann 2003: ii)

Diversity, then, is basic to children's literature. Thus the Fall 2004 edition of the *Children's Literature Association Quarterly* (29.3) contains a close literary analysis of the work of Noel Streatfeild, beside an examination of lesbian dolls and the place of the dog in child literature and sexuality. The *International Companion Encyclopedia*, from which the essays in this volume are taken, ranges from critical theory to publishing for special needs, and from 'texts' written in 4500BC to postmodern metafiction. It is this diversity of concerns, expressed through a diversity of voices, that makes the study of children's literature so complex and fascinating.

References

Alderson, B. (1977) *Bibliography and Children's Books: The Present Position*, London: The Bibliographical Society. Reprinted from *The Library* 32, 3: 203–13.

Alderson, J. C. and Short, M. (1989) 'Reading Literature', in Short, M. (ed.) *Reading, Analysing and Teaching Literature*, London: Longman.

Allen, R. (2004) *Winning Books*, Lichfield: Pied Piper.

Anstey, M. and Bull, G. (2000) *Reading the Visual*, Sydney: Harcourt.

Avery, G. (1994) *Behold the Child. American Children and their Books, 1621–1922*, London: The Bodley Head.

Bouvaist, J. M. (1990) *Les Enjeux de l'édition – jeunesse à la veille de 1992*, Montreuil: Salon du Livre de jeunesse.

Buckingham, D. (ed.) (2002) *Small Screens. Television for Children*, London: Leicester University Press.

Chambers, A. (1985) *Booktalk. Occasional Writing on Literature and Children*, London: The Bodley Head.

—— (1991) *The Reading Environment. How Adults Help Children Enjoy Books*, South Woodchester: Thimble Press

Clark, B. L. and Higonnet, M. (1999) *Girls, Boys, Books, Toys: Gender in Children's Literature and Culture*, Baltimore: Johns Hopkins University Press.

Culler, J. (1997) *Literary Theory: A Very Short Introduction*, Oxford: Oxford University Press.

Cunningham, H. (1995) *Children and Childhood in Western Society since 1500*, London: Longman.

Darton, F. J. H. (1932/1982) *Children's Books in England: Five Centuries of Social Life*, 3rd edn, rev. Alderson, B., Cambridge: Cambridge University Press.

Doonan, J. (1993), *Looking at Pictures in Picture-Books*, South Woodchester: Thimble Press.

Eaglestone, Robert (2000) 'Undoing English', *CCUE News* 13: 6–8.

Gilderdale, B. (1982) *A Sea Change: 145 Years of New Zealand Junior Fiction*, Auckland: Longman Paul.

Griswold, J. (2000) *Is History Real? A Multimedia Meditation on 'Sleeping Beauty'*, San Diego: Campanile Press.

—— (2004) 'The U.S.A.: A Historical Overview', in Hunt, P. (ed.) *International Companion Encyclopedia of Children's Literature*, 2nd edn, London and New York: Routledge.

Hardyment, C. (1995) *Perfect Parents. Baby-Care Advice Past and Present*, Oxford: Oxford University Press.

Heywood, C. (2001) *A History of Childhood: Children and Childhood in the West from Medieval to Modern Times*, Oxford: Polity Press.

Hunt, P. (ed.) (1995) *Children's Literature: An Illustrated History*, Oxford: Oxford University Press.

—— (1997) 'Good? Good as? Good for?', *Books for Keeps* 103: 8–9.

—— (2000) 'Children's Literature', in France, P. (ed.) *The Oxford Guide to Literature in English Translation*, Oxford: Oxford University Press.

—— (2001) *Children's Literature: A Guide*, Oxford: Blackwell.

Jafa, M. (2004) 'The Indian Sub-continent', in Hunt, P. (ed.) *International Companion Encyclopedia of Children's Literature*, 2nd edn, London and New York: Routledge.

Jenks, C. (1996) *Childhood*, London: Routledge.

Kehily, M. J. and Swann, J. (2003) *Children's Cultural Worlds*, Milton Keynes/Chichester: Open University Press/John Wiley.

Knoepflmacher, U. C. and Myers, M. (1997) 'From the editors: "Cross-writing" and the Reconceptualizing of Children's Literary Studies', *Children's Literature* 25, New Haven, CT: Yale University Press, vii–xvii.

Lesnik-Oberstein, K. (ed.) (1998) *Children in Culture. Approaches to Childhood*, Basingstoke and London: Macmillan.

Martin, D. (2004) 'Children's Book Design', in Hunt, P. (ed.) *International Companion Encyclopedia of Children's Literature*, 2nd edn, London and New York: Routledge.

Mathias, B. (2004) 'Publishing for Special Needs', in Hunt, P. (ed.) *International Companion Encyclopedia of Children's Literature*, 2nd edn, London and New York: Routledge.

McCloud, S. (1993) *Understanding Comics: the Invisible Art*, Northampton, MA: Tundra.

McGillis, R. (1996) *The Nimble Reader*, New York: Twayne.

—— (1999) 'The Delights of Impossibility: No Children, No Books, Only Theory', *Children's Literature Association Quarterly*, 23, 4: 202–8.

—— (ed.) (2000) *Voices of the Other. Children's Literature and the Postcolonial Context*, New York: Garland.

Mooney, C. G. (2000) *Theories of Childhood: An Introduction to Dewey, Montessori, Piaget and Vygotski*, St Paul, MN: Redleaf Press.

Nikolajeva, M. (2004) 'Narrative Theory and Children's Literature', in Hunt, P. (ed.) *International Companion Encyclopedia of Children's Literature*, 2nd edn, London and New York: Routledge.

Nikolajeva, M. and Scott, C. (2001) *How Picturebooks Work*, New York: Garland.

Nodelman, P. (1988) *Words About Pictures*, Athens, GA: University of Georgia Press.

Nodelman, P. and Reimer, M. (2003) *The Pleasures of Children's Literature*, 3rd edn, Boston: Allyn and Bacon.

Parker, J. (1994) 'Unravelling the Romance: Strategies for Understanding Textual Ideology', in Corcoran, B., Hayhoe, M. and Pradl, G. M. (eds) *Knowledge in the Making. Challenging the Text in the Classroom*, Portsmouth, NH: Boynton/Cook, Heinemann.

Pellowski, A. (2004) 'Culture and Developing Countries', in Hunt, P. (ed.) *International Companion Encyclopedia of Children's Literature*, 2nd edn, London and New York: Routledge.

Philip, N. (ed.) (1996) *The New Oxford Book of Children's Verse*, Oxford: Oxford University Press.

Ray, S. (2004) 'The world of children's literature: An introduction', in Hunt, P. (ed.) *International Companion Encyclopedia of Children's Literature*, 2nd edn, London and New York: Routledge.

Saxby, H. M. (1969) *A History of Australian Children's Literature 1841–1941*, Sydney: Wentworth Books.

—— (1971) *A History of Australian Children's Literature 1941–1970*, Sydney: Wentworth Books.

—— (1993) *The Proof of the Puddin': Australian Children's Literature 1970–1990*, Gosford, NSW: Ashton Scholastic.

Townsend, J. R. (1965/1990) *Written for Children: An Outline of English-Language Children's Literature*, London: Penguin.

Travisano, T. (2000) 'Of Dialectic and Divided Consciousness: Intersections Between Children's Literature and Childhood Studies', *Children's Literature* 28: 22–9.

Trites, R. S. (1997) *Waking Sleeping Beauty: Feminist Voices in Children's Novels*, Iowa City, IA: University of Iowa Press.

Vallone, L. (1995) *Disciplines of Virtue. Girls' Culture in the Eighteenth and Nineteenth Centuries*, New Haven, CT: Yale University Press.

West, M. (1988) *Trust Your Children: Voices Against Censorship in Children's Literature*, New York: Neal-Schuman.

—— (2004) 'Censorship', in Hunt, P. (ed.) *International Companion Encyclopedia of Children's Literature*, 2nd edn, London and New York: Routledge.

Whyte, P. (2004) 'Adaptation and Authenticity. Filming Children's Literature', *Inis* [Children's Books Ireland], 9: 6–9.

Wilkie-Stibbs, C. (2002) *The Feminine Subject in Children's Literature*, New York and London: Routledge.

Wojcik-Andrews, I. (2000) *Children's Films: History, Ideology, Pedagogy*, New York: Garland.

Zipes, J. (ed.) (1993) *The Trials and Tribulations of Little Red Riding Hood*, 2nd edn, New York: Routledge.

—— (1995) *Storytelling. Building Community, Changing Lives*, New York: Routledge.

—— (1997) *Happily Ever After. Fairy Tales, Children, and the Culture Industry*, New York: Routledge.

—— (2001) *Sticks and Stones: The Troublesome Success of Children's Literature from Slovenly Peter to Harry Potter*, New York and London: Routledge.

2 Theorising and theories

How does children's literature exist?

David Rudd

Editor's Introduction

The study of children's literature involves three elements – the texts, the children, and the adult critics. The relationship between these is more complex than might be supposed, and there have been extensive debates as to the place of the 'child' – actual or conceptual – in both the texts and the criticism of children's literature. It has been argued that the 'child' implied in texts 'for children' is inevitably a construction by writers, and therefore, far from 'owning' the literature, its readers are only manipulated by it. Similarly, criticism of children's literature can be seen as resting on the idea that children's literature is 'good for' a generalised child. David Rudd explores many approaches to these problems and suggests ways of balancing extreme opinions.

P.H.

> 'What – is – this?' [the Unicorn] said at last.
> 'This is a child!' Haigha replied eagerly … 'We only found it to-day. It's as large as life, and twice as natural!'
> 'I always thought they were fabulous monsters!' said the Unicorn. 'Is it alive?'
> 'It can talk,' said Haigha solemnly.
>
> (Carroll 1970: 287)

Competing critical histories and the status of the child

Just as there are competing histories of children's literature, so there are of children's literature criticism – and the two are interlinked. Most of these histories set the beginnings of children's literature in the eighteenth century – sometimes dated as precisely as 1744 with John Newbery's *A Little Pretty Pocket-Book*, as it is in Harvey Darton (1982: 1) – and most draw on the tension between instruction and entertainment, often explicitly (for example, *From Primer to Pleasure* (Thwaite 1964), *Fantasy and Reason* (Summerfield 1984)), which is seen as a battle eventually won by entertainment. Harvey Darton, again, dates this precisely, to Carroll's *Alice* (1865), which he speaks of as the first appearance 'in print … of liberty of thought in children's books' (1982: 260), instigating a golden age in children's literature (Carpenter 1985). However, we need to be aware that such 'grand narratives' about the area's development are only that. Through them children's literature critics frequently construct a 'story' of a movement from darkness to light – just as developmental psychologists, like Piaget, envisage the child growing from an original, autistic state to adult rationality. The notion of a *Bildungsroman* is, therefore, often implicit, celebrating the discipline as having recently 'come of age' (for example, Broadbent *et al.* 1994; Nikolajeva 1996). But there are other stories, querying this. At one extreme, Gillian

Adams (1986) takes children's literature texts back some 4,000 years, to Sumer; at the other, Jacqueline Rose (1984) argues that the whole enterprise is impossible anyway – something that Karín Lesnik-Oberstein (1994) extends to its criticism. In this chapter, I shall try to get behind these various stories, to see what 'regimes of truth' they draw on, in order to tease out what I shall term the conditions of possibility of children's literature and its criticism – and, particularly, to revisit those who see it as impossible.

This will involve steering a course between, on the one hand, notions that there is an underlying 'essential' child whose nature and needs we can know and, on the other, the notion that the child is nothing but the product of adult discourse (as some social constructionists argue). I shall suggest that neither of these positions is tenable: that the problematic of children's literature lies in the gap between the 'constructed' and the 'constructive' child, in what I shall term a 'hybrid', or border area.

Let me begin with Jacqueline Rose's provocative suggestion that, despite the possessive apostrophe in the phrase 'children's literature', it has never really been owned by children:

> Children's fiction rests on the idea that there is a child who is simply there to be addressed and that speaking to it might be simple ... If children's fiction builds an image of the child inside the book, it does so in order to secure the child who is outside the book, the one who does not come so easily within its grasp.
>
> (Rose 1984: 1–2)

Adults, she argues, evoke this child for their own purposes (desires, in fact), as a site of plenitude to conceal the fractures that trouble us all: concerns over a lack of coherent subjectivity, over the instabilities of language and, ultimately, existence itself (Rose 1984: 16). Barrie's *Peter Pan* texts are seen as perfect examples of this, purporting to be about the eternal child, but actually acknowledging the problems of such a construction, especially in the way that Barrie himself had problems producing a final, definitive version of his text.

Rose's book remains a revolutionary work, opening up children's literature to wider debates in cultural studies. However, her insight into the power of the child as a cultural trope (standing for innocence, the natural, the primitive, and so on) has led to a neglect of the child as a social being, with a voice. Rose herself does not deny the existence of the child 'outside the book', on whom she actually draws at times, conceding that things are indeed different 'at the point of readership' (1984: 84); her emphasis is simply elsewhere, just as is James Kincaid's in his related work, *Child-Loving* (1992), which details how the figure of the child, constructed as innocent, a site of purity, thereby became, in the Victorian period, an erotic lure for adults. However, Kincaid's work has been misread in similar ways to that of Rose; Carolyn Steedman thus laments that

> James Kincaid's conclusion ... that the child 'is not, in itself, anything', is very easy to reach (and quite irresponsible proposals may follow on it) ... children were *both* the repositories of adults' desires (or a text, to be 'written' and 'rewritten', to use a newer language), *and* social beings who lived in social worlds.
>
> (Steedman 1995: 96–7)

Like Rose, Kincaid does not deny the child as a social being; indeed, he too draws on what he terms 'children with quite ordinary child needs' (1992: 388). But Steedman's point is still valid: that the thrust of much of this criticism has tended to make the child appear voiceless. Lesnik-Oberstein goes further, arguing that this must be so for, unlike other disempowered groups such as women, who can speak for themselves, 'Children, in culture and history, have no such voice' (1994: 26).

Ironically, even to make such a claim is to have already separated out 'the child' as a special being, subject to its own rules, distinct from other social groups. Furthermore, such a universal claim effectively adulterates (forgive the pun) a social constructionist perspective; for if children are merely constructions, social conditions might construct them otherwise. In effect, in order to make such a wide-sweeping claim, it would seem that Lesnik-Oberstein is, tacitly at least, invoking more enduring qualities, such as, to quote Allison James and Alan Prout, the 'different physical size of children and their relative muscular weakness compared to adults'; however, as they continue, it would be absurd were it otherwise, exempting 'human beings from the rest of the animal kingdom by denying *any* effects of our biological and physical being'. This, as they say, is 'cultural determinism' (1990: 26), as problematic as its opposite: a humanistic essentialism.

The claim, therefore, 'that the "child" has no "voice" within the hierarchies of our society, because "adults" either silence or create that voice' (Lesnik-Oberstein 1994: 187), actually helps construct the child as a helpless, powerless being, and contributes to the culturally hegemonic norm. As Rex and Wendy Stainton Rogers put it, 'To model the child as construct*ed* but not as construct*ive* … permits us to see the young person as having their identity constructed by outside forces but not the young person constructing their identity out of the culturally available.' They, therefore, are of the opinion that the child's voice 'should be heard' (1992: 84).

The doubleness of discourse: constructed/constructive

The Stainton Rogers' more Foucauldian notion of power, seen as not only repressive but productive, too, allows us to overcome what is otherwise a problematic shift; that is, from the spoken-for child to the controlling adult. In Foucault's (1980, 1981) model, power is not held by one particular group over another, powerless one; rather, power is conceived of as immanent in all encounters, through which certain discursive relations are possible.

So, while children can be construed as the powerless objects of adult discourse, they also have subject positions available to them that resist such a move. Valerie Walkerdine, also known for her work on girls' comics, illustrates this process in action. In one instance she records a nursery class in which a group of three- to four-year-old boys undermine a female teacher's authority with a barrage of comments like 'Miss Baxter, show your knickers your bum off' (Walkerdine 1990: 4). By effecting a sexist discourse they disempower her while empowering themselves.

As this more dynamic notion of discourse is crucial to much that follows, let me spend some time clarifying its implications before I move on to broader issues about the conditions of the discipline's existence. First, it should be noted that the boys, above, are not free agents; they are simply positioned in another discourse: that of sexism. Children, in other words, become subjects through multiple discourses, which is to reject earlier notions of the process, like Althusser's, where one is more summarily subjected.

This leads to a second point: that for many of these other discursive positions, 'childhood' *per se* is irrelevant; thus the sexist discourse above can be seen to upset the adult–child binary. But there is still a tendency – among constructionists as well as those more biologically inclined – to overextend the term 'child', such that 'childhood' is seen to ground their entire being. A more familiar example might make this clear: the position of 'women' in the nineteenth century, who were automatically opposed to 'men' on all counts, as 'frail vessels', 'emotional', 'unstable', 'spontaneous', 'weak', 'irrational', and so on. With childhood, overextension of the term persists, being applied to discourses where, in fact, children are often as competent as adults.

Looking at children 'in culture and history', then, we find that in some cultures they *are* regarded as having more of a voice. Among the Tonga, for example, children are 'accorded positions of dignity and worth … They are valued for themselves and … as companions and workers. They are accorded rights and these are upheld at public forums such as during court cases' (Pamela Reynolds, quoted in Scheper-Hughes and Sargent 1998: 11; see also Hoyles 1979). As James *et al.* (1998: 120–1) have noted, in societies where children work alongside adults, they are often seen in more egalitarian terms. In contrast, the more economically 'useless' children become, as in America towards the end of the nineteenth century, the more emotionally priceless seems their value (Zelizer 1994) – and the more pervasive a restrictive, overextended notion of childhood. Most recently, the anonymity of cyberspace has opened up a particularly powerful area where age is irrelevant, expertise among the young being legendary (Katz 1997; Kincheloe 1998) – although, with adults 'passing' as children, it has raised opposing worries. But the key issue is that cyberspace effectively disembodies the child, removing many markers that often produce more condescending responses – of being 'talked down to'.

The third point also relates to the above for, though the world is constructed through discourse – language being 'the ultimate prosthesis' (Braidotti 1994: 44) – not everything is thereby discursive. The body itself influences how we speak, not only through the metaphors it tends to generate (Johnson 1987; Bakhtin 1968), but in the simple fact that discourse itself 'is the product of a speaking or writing body located at a point in space and a moment in time' (Burkitt 1999: 37). Moreover, the body, being part of social relations, can itself resist certain discursive shaping (inappropriately breaking wind, and so on). Children are, therefore, seen as playing a key role in 'the civilising process' (Elias 1978: 53–4) and are, hence, a source of worry, of disturbance (as I'll discuss later).

Unfortunately, an exclusive emphasis on discourse has led to a neglect of the role of bodily comportment and action in producing 'the child', 'the model pupil', 'the girl' – or whatever. A good example of the latter is 'throwing like a girl', as detailed by Iris Marion Young (1990), referencing Mark Twain's *Huckleberry Finn*. 'Bodily conduct' – part of what Pierre Bourdieu terms 'habitus', the cultural dispositions that influence our social behaviour – is, therefore, a crucial, non-discursive aspect of childhood (James *et al.* 1998: 161), albeit discursively constructed. With some notable exceptions – for example, Engel (1995), Grainger (1999), Paley (1981), Wolf and Heath (1992) – this embodied component of children's discourse has been neglected. In the latter, for example, Shelby Wolf's daughter, Lindsey, is shown enacting texts using role play and costume, and delighting in the sound and 'musicality' of words; on one occasion she is observed leaping on to the kitchen counter to hasten her breakfast, bellowing 'Fee Fi Fo Fum …'. As the authors comment, 'The giant, with his all-encompassing power, would never have had to wait, and neither should she. Motion takes the mind to action, and action brings results' (Wolf and Heath 1992: 97). Given earlier comments on the perceived relation between power and physical size, Lindsey's enaction of the giant's discourse is particularly interesting.

To recap, then: not only are there problems with each model – an authentic, essential child and a voiceless, discursive construction – but the two notions are, in fact, impossible to keep apart (just like adult and child), the essential child still being tacitly evoked by constructionists, in that a perennially voiceless child is juxtaposed to a dominating adult, though no similar questions are raised about, say, a fifty-year-old writing for a twenty-something. However, it is surely unacceptable for either side to argue that one must *be* a child in order to write genuine children's fiction, or to read it, for the simple fact that language cannot ground authenticity, language itself being a construction or, in a Lacanian version of development, a misrepresentation. Moreover, as Spivak notes, 'The position that only the subaltern can know the subaltern, only women can know women and so on ... predicates the possibility of knowledge on identity' (1988: 253–4). Were one to accept such an 'identity politics', then, the ramifications would be ultimately self-defeating: not only would class, gender and ethnicity delimit reading and writing, but one would end up with only a boy of thirteen and three-quarters from a working-class broken home being able to appreciate the exploits of an Adrian Mole (Townsend 1982).

But, as I've also suggested, this cannot relegate the child to a discursive effect. Many feminists have already trodden this ground, moving away from essentialist notions of an authentic women's experience to a discursive position which then permitted men to emulate their voice, both in writing as a woman (Cixous 1976: 878) and reading as one (Culler 1983: 43–64). Elaine Showalter describes this disparagingly as 'male cross-dressing' (Showalter 1987; also Braidotti 1994; Young 1990). What seems missing here is, again, some notion of embodiment, of discourse having a concrete location. The same applies to children, who, as the Stainton Rogers put it (1998: 184), must be granted legitimacy in 'the *practically real* (that which passes for "real" in practice)'.

In terms of children's literature, though, it might still be argued that, unlike women and other minority groups, children still have no voice, their literature being created for them, rather than creating their own. But this is a nonsense. Children produce literature in vast quantities, oral and written, both individually wrought and through collaborative effort (sometimes diachronically), and in a variety of forms: rhymes, jokes, songs, incantations, tall tales, plays, stories and more. Yet, apart from a few collections and studies (for example, Fox 1993; Opie and Opie 1959; Rosen and Steele 1982; Steedman 1982; Sutton-Smith *et al.* 1999; Turner *et al.* 1978), plus the isolated publishing exceptions (such as nine-year-old Jayne Fisher's (1980) Garden Gang series), it goes largely unrecognised – though some of it does feed back, intertextually, into subsequently published works (as, for example, did material that 'Lewis Carroll' wrote in his own magazines, as a juvenile). And, of course, it should be emphasised that all this literature comes from reworking the discourses around them, through which children negotiate their social and embodied positioning.

The fact that children are seen *not* to have a stake in this is, once again, a product of the way children's literature (in its texts and its criticism) has become institutionalised, such that – ironically – only commercially published work is seen to count; or, to put it another way, only adults are seen to 'authorise' proper children's literature. Certainly, more work needs doing on this, but it does not help when scholars underwrite this culturally dominant version of events.

Origins and the genealogy of children's literature

Foucault's 'genealogical' approach is helpful here. Rather than engage in internal disputes about origins, such an approach asks, more broadly, what makes children's literature possible – or, to pursue the metaphor used earlier, how it has been 'storied' in a particular way (Stainton Rogers and Stainton Rogers 1992), and how certain other stories become 'disqualified' (Foucault 1980: 81). Of singular note is Foucault's rejection of any simple social constructionism. Thus, in looking at madness, he rejects the notion that the term is just a label, recognising that, certainly, there were 'mad' people before the advent of psychiatry; however, rather than being seen as a uniform category, they were 'read' in different ways (Foucault 1967). Turning to children's literature, we can similarly point to a range of elements existing in separate discursive spaces (books of manners, folk tales, children's Bibles, nursery rhymes, chapbooks – even Sumerian instructional texts!), some of which purport to address 'children' specifically, others of which do not. The point is, these constituent elements were not considered a separate cultural entity until the eighteenth century (when the figure of the child in its modern form was also increasingly being shaped as an 'essence'), only to be fully consolidated late in the nineteenth, when the various institutional apparatuses of children's literature were in place – including an educational system promoting literacy (Morgenstern 2001). As Jack Zipes puts it, 'until the system of production, distribution and reception was instituted' it was simply not possible 'for a broad range of books to be approved and to reach children in specific ways' (Zipes 2001: 46).

However, the more that children's literature became institutionalised (in its texts and its criticism), the more it filtered out, or ignored, that which didn't fit, 'in the name of some true knowledge' (Foucault 1980: 83). Thus 'folklore, nursery rhyme and nonsense', as Rose (1984: 139) notes, became sidelined as mere 'rhythm and play', for fear of their disruptive potential (interestingly, these literary forms are also those linked more closely to the body and to performance – to, in fact, the semiotic order, which Kristeva (1984) theorises as disruptive of the Symbolic). Likewise, the standard '*his*-story' of how male Romantics (featuring Locke and Rousseau as progenitors) fathered modern children's literature, with fantasy emerging victorious over the instructional writings of the matriarchal 'cursed Barbauld crew', goes mostly unchallenged; though scholars like Mitzi Myers (1995) have consistently attacked such a patrimony and, along with discoveries like the material that Jane Johnson devised for her own children (Hilton *et al.* 1997), there are attempts at telling a new 'story'. Folk and fairy tale (Harries 2001; Warner 1994), nursery rhyme and nonsense (Rollin 1992; Warner 2000) are similarly being retold.

So, although children's literature might be seen as 'impossible' in some ways (ideologically, in inscribing an 'eternal child' to suture problematic cultural issues), there is no question of its social and economic reality. It is part of the 'practically real', which warrants attention, and will not go away (any more than madness) just because it is shown to be a social construction. A similar point can be made about the uncritical recycling of Philippe Ariès's claim that, 'In medieval society the idea of childhood did not exist' (Ariès 1973: 125); it was, rather, '*our* concept of childhood' that medieval society lacked (Archard 1993: 19); other constructions of childhood there certainly were, and Ariès himself was later to express remorse at not being better informed about this period (Alexandre-Bidon and Lett 1999: 1). Given children's literature's social, cultural and economic reality, then, it is hard to comprehend how Rose 'closes down the field of children's fiction, and therefore, by implication, children's literature criticism', as Lesnik-Oberstein claims (1994: 158–9). For, powerful as the universal child is – lingering in many constructionist accounts too – the literature's criticism is not dependent on it. Rose's commendable work itself demonstrates this, marking a shift in paradigm towards a more culturally nuanced analysis. And much other work published around this time (for example, Barker 1989; Hunt 1991; Kincaid 1992; McGillis 1996; Nikolajeva 1996; Nodelman 1992; Sarland

1991; Shavit 1986; Stephens 1992; Wolf and Heath 1992; Zipes 1983) contributed to this widening of perspectives, albeit from – healthily – differing theoretical stances. This said, all would probably be united in signing up to Lesnik-Oberstein's provocative statement – though without her intended irony – that 'Children's fiction criticism ... cannot do without some "child"' (1994: 140). While society cannot do without it, it would certainly be a mistake for criticism to do so (cf. Meek 1995; Nodelman 1996).

Hybridity

The above, more culturally sensitive notion of the constructed child and its literature, however, should not allow us to lose sight of the constructive child, for, as suggested earlier, it is in the gap between the two that a way forward lies. Language, of course, is central to this, for the move from 'infant' (literally, one incapable of speech) to a discursively situated being is fraught with anxiety – as this statement from a fictional children's writer captures:

> Each new generation of children has to be told: 'This is a world, this is what one does, one lives like this.' Maybe our constant fear is that a generation of children will come along and say, 'This is not a world, this is nothing, there's no way to live at all.'
>
> (Hoban 1975: 100)

Accepting the proviso that 'People do not "accept" their native language – it is in their native language that they first reach awareness' (Vološinov 1973: 81), the fear is no less valid. Which is why children are so central to the 'civilising process':

> children necessarily touch again and again on the adult threshold of delicacy, and – since they are not yet adapted – they infringe the taboos of society, cross the adult shame frontier, and penetrate emotional danger zones which the adult himself can only control with difficulty.
>
> (Elias 1978: 167)

The concept of hybridity, originally meaning 'the offspring of a tame sow and a wild boar' (Young 1995: 6), imaginatively encapsulates this ambivalence surrounding child- and adulthood noted by numerous commentators (for example, Banerjee 1984; Lesnik-Oberstein 1994: 28; Morrison 1997; Rollin 1992; Shavit 1986; Stahl 1996: 46; Taylor 1998: 91). The term is expressive of that uneasy transaction along borders, in which something other is gradually brought within, melded into adulthood. So, while Rose is surely right about 'writers for children' leaving undisturbed any 'psychic barriers ... the most important of which is the barrier between adult and child' (Rose 1984: 70), her emphasis, I would argue, needs shifting; for it seems to me that there is a disturbing recognition of the frailty of such barriers. As the British children's writer John Gordon puts it, 'The boundary between imagination and reality, and the boundary between being a child and being an adult are border country, a passionate place in which to work. Laws in that country are lifelines' (Gordon 1975: 35). The ever-present speech tags, the instances of telling rather than showing, the intrusive narrators (Hunt 1991; Knowles and Malmkjær 1996), the 'have to' tone that Rose detects (1984: 141), are all examples of such 'lifelines', masking a relationship that is often disturbing.

Homi Bhabha (1994) has explored this troubling hybrid relationship in the colonial situation, arguing, similarly, that those who effectively wield power – adults, in this case – are never secure in their position. As detailed earlier, this is because power is not an abstract possession, but an effect of discursive relations which are productive as well as repressive (as we saw with Walkerdine's boys, and with Lindsey, above).

The construct*ed* child, as *tabula rasa* – an 'empty' being on which society attempts to inscribe a particular identity – becomes, in that very process, the construct*ive* child, and sameness is disrupted. Traces of otherness, of difference, creep into children's repertoires as they learn language, 'sense' being shown to emerge from non-sense, words being stripped down to bare – and, indeed, to bear – signifiers in parent–child interactions, and in children's own crib monologues (Weir 1960; Nelson 1985, 1989). Moreover, the fact that the sign is itself 'multi-accented' produces increasing slippage, as songs, stories and dialogue are forever reworked (Bruner 1987; Fox 1993; Kimberley *et al.* 1992; Wolf and Heath 1992). Staying with Shelby Wolf's study, her son, Ashley (aged three; 1992: 11), amusingly reworked 'Max stepped into his private boat' (Sendak 1967) as 'Max stepped onto their private parts' (Wolf and Heath 1992: 44). In learning language, then, the child is also inadvertently learning 'how to curse', in Caliban's phrase (*The Tempest*, I ii; see also Dunn 1988: 157).

Children's speech is hybrid, therefore, in that official, adult language is responded to from a new social and physical location (it is discursively situated), with different nuances and inflections and, often, with intentional revision and intertextuality – as children both disentangle and interweave discursive threads (Rudd 1992, 2000). Bhabha (1994: 126) describes this process of 'mimicry' as inherently unstable. Adult behaviour, being emulated, becomes unoriginal, excessive, comic – which, in turn, undermines what it is to be an 'adult', self-contained and rational. Michael Rosen captures this eloquently in his poem, 'Mind Your Own Business', where we are told what 'Father says' as he upbraids his sons (the civilising process, again). Then, in the last two lines, the tables are turned, the mimicry made overt:

> My brother knows all his phrases off by heart
> So we practise them in bed at night.
> (Rosen 1974: 72)

The father's authority is effectively undermined, seen to be located in nothing more than his 'say so', and it happens by the adult's 'look of surveillance' being turned back on him, as 'the observer becomes the observed' (Bhabha 1994: 89). Peter Pan does the same with Hook, such that his adult adversary finds his own authority, and identity, undone, 'his ego is slipping from him' (Barrie 1995: 122). Eventually, of course, Hook loses more than this to Pan, who replaces him 'on the poop in Hook's hat and cigars, and with a small iron claw' (Barrie 1995: 146).

Bhabha (1994: 92) notes similar slippages when 'the English Book' (the Bible) was introduced to the colonised subjects of India. Its 'representational authority' was displaced by more utilitarian needs – becoming, for example, a natty tear-off dispenser of wrapping paper for snuff! Children's physical mistreatment of their books is, likewise, a perennial concern for adults, often being thematised in the texts themselves; to cite Max again (an obvious hybrid), he is depicted provocatively standing on some worthy tomes, foreshadowing his later dismissal of 'the Word' in the Wild Rumpus. There is no notion of the child as an innately subversive being here, though. The child is simply positioned as not yet adult (one of the civilised) and, as an apprentice, is coming to terms with the differential relations of power involved, themselves negotiated through discourse and its embodied practices.

We can thus see how a hybrid and always contested area of childhood is dialogically engendered in the 'practically real'. As Bakhtin puts it (writing under the name Vološinov):

> Utterance ... is constructed between two socially organized persons, and in the absence of a real addressee, an addressee is presupposed ... The *word is oriented toward an addressee,* toward *who* that addressee might be.
>
> (Vološinov 1973: 85)

Exactly what a representative of that amorphous, socially constructed group – children – does with the word depends on the addressee (their situatedness in relation to other discourses). But the key point is that the word is not *owned* by either party, lodged in neither the child's nor the adult's inner-being. Rather, the word constitutes a 'border zone' (Vološinov 1973: 86), in which the addressees – children, in this case – orient themselves precisely in the way that they 'lay down' their own set of 'answering words' (Vološinov 1973: 102); in this process they – the children – can only ever be construct*ive*.

In the 'practically real', then, there can only ever be constructed positions: the child constructed by the text, and the response (itself constructed) from the constructive child, the product being necessarily co-authored. Just as an adult initially talks on behalf of an infant, 'scaffolding' its meaning (Bruner 1987), so it is in that very address that 'the child' becomes constituted as a social category – as what Diana Fuss (1989: 4) terms, following John Locke, 'a nominal essence ... a classificatory fiction we need to categorize and label'. The child has nowhere else to be. This said, the process is anything but mechanical, given the multiple subject positions available, and the way language itself is multi-accented. Moreover, as mentioned earlier, the process is not simply top down: the habitus of childhood has its own performative dimensions (learned from peers, books, playground folklore, the media, and so on, as mentioned in the last section). In practice, this means that, while it is almost impossible for adults to *avoid* addressing children, their success in doing so will vary remarkably. But even when judged successful, there is no notion of 'identification' by the child, only of 'talkings to' and 'responses from' different social locations.

Conditions of possibility

It has been argued, then, that children's literature occurs in the space between the constructed and the constructive – and that this must be so, given the nature of language and our positioning within a variety of discourses. The attempt to prevent such slippage, to keep language 'single-voiced', tolerating 'no play with its borders' (Bakhtin 1981: 343), is doomed; such a 'sealed-off and impermeable monoglossia' (Bakhtin 1981: 61) is elegantly figured in the unyielding shell of Humpty Dumpty, who, of course, also foreshadows the fate of such intransigence: 'When *I* use a word ... it means just what I choose it to mean – neither more nor less' (Carroll 1970: 269). Unfortunately, he never was master of his words, perilously ignoring the discursive chain in which he was positioned – the nursery rhyme – as a consequence of which, he has a great fall.

In early children's literature this monological, authoritarian voice is quite popular, often bolstered by 'the English Book' (the Bible), but even this does not obviate the anxiety mentioned earlier: the fact that, however much such work directs the reader down the path of righteousness, it inevitably sketches in the surrounding landscape, the delights just beyond the path, the grass that must be kept off (Caliban's curse, again).

Of course, it is only from records of children's reading that we can interpret how such works may have been received. So that when Victor Watson (1992: 14–15) says of Mrs Sherwood's heavily didactic *History of the Fairchild Family* (1818–47) that the children in it 'are voiceless. It is a coercive text', we can point to some readers, at least, who were not coerced, and who did voice their views: 'I liked the book notwithstanding. There was plenty about eating and drinking; one could always skip the prayers and there were three or four very brightly written accounts of funerals in it', as the young Lord Frederick Hamilton commented (quoted in Lochhead 1956: 51).

Because the word is always half someone else's, as Bakhtin notes, the attempt to avoid hybrid contamination is fated: it refuses to mean just what the author intends, 'neither more nor less'. This means that, though Lesnik-Oberstein rightly points out that children's literature can never escape 'the didactic impulse' (1994: 38), neither can the didactic impulse escape this hybrid relation, the excess and play of the signifier, such that an entertaining surplus is ever present. Partly in recognition of this lack of control, children's texts have become increasingly explicit in their hybridity. Even in Victorian times, Knoepflmacher (1983) notes an increasing number of 'childlike' adult characters in the books, besides more amorphous creations like E. Nesbit's Psammead. Clearly, as this corpus of targeted 'children's books' burgeoned, children could more readily draw on a larger body of texts, and intertextually comment on them – as, most famously, does Lewis Carroll's work, with its savage reworking of earlier homiletic verses, such as the Duchess's 'sort of lullaby' in *Alice*: 'Speak roughly to your little boy,/And beat him when he sneezes', revoking the sentiments of Isaac Watts's original, 'Speak gently! It is better far/To rule by love than fear' (Carroll 1970: 85). (Carroll, of course, also points up the ambivalence between adult and child in the lullaby itself, in which care of the child goes hand in hand with fantasies of its destruction: 'down will come baby, cradle and all' (Parker 1995; Warner 2000).) It was also in the nineteenth century that the fairy tale became a popular form for staging hybrid relations (Auerbach and Knoepflmacher 1992; Zipes 1987), especially as it became more directly aimed at children. And today this hybrid relation has been foregrounded to the extent that many see a blurring of boundaries between adult and child literatures, theorised as 'cross-writing' (Knoepflmacher and Myers 1997) or writing for 'dual audiences' (Beckett 1999).

However, although the hybridity has recently become more explicit, my main point is that it has always been there: a product of the differential power relations and signifying latitude of language. So, without wishing to diminish the importance of the works that speak about how the child is constructed – or 'implied' – in its literature, it would be a mistake to see them as the whole story: they miss, precisely, half of it, in neglecting the constructive powers of the child.

Naturally, this also makes children's literature studies far more messy and complex, and challenges traditional forms of scholarship. The oral roots of much children's literature make it particularly problematic, with published work often taking shape in stories told to specific children, either privately or in small groups (famous examples being Barrie, Blyton, Carroll and Grahame; see also Hilton *et al.* 1997). In such a context, the dialogic negotiation of the 'children's text' is far more explicit, and no doubt involves both verbal and non-verbal elements. Furthermore, even after publication, children are renowned for feeding back their views to their authors, influencing subsequent works (for example, Enid Blyton, through her *Sunny Stories* magazine).

But the physical response of a child is not necessary. The dialogic process of anticipating answering words must still occur, as authors construct notional readers – even if only to coerce them into voicelessness! Often the addressees will be younger, or idealised versions of themselves, as so many writers attest, for, as Rose (1984: 12) notes, following Freud, childhood is never really left behind; it 'persists as something which we endlessly rework in our attempt to build an image of our own history'. Ursula Le Guin (1975: 91) expresses something similar, if more poetically: 'an adult is not a dead child, but a child who survived'. Thus many of the imagined concerns of childhood live on, inflecting later discourses, and feeding back into what Nina Bawden (1975: 62) terms 'the emotional landscape' of authors' writings about childhood – which will either have a resonance for certain children, or not. But it should not be thought that the adults are secure in their status. Bawden herself is quite outspoken about her wish to '*expose*' adults, those 'uncertain, awkward, quirky, *dangerous* creatures', who, she says, wrote books in which 'they didn't want to give themselves away; show themselves to us children, to their *enemies*, as they really were' (Bawden 1995: 110). Again, this example is not used to point to the truth of adults or children, but a concern over the hybrid relation.

All these approaches to the subject are obviously fallible: whether we look at what *the writers* say in, or about, their work; or whether we explore what *the readership* says – but this is the nature of the subject: exploring the 'practically real', which is forever open to dialogic revision in that contested space between the respective parties.

Conclusion

Drawing on a Foucauldian notion of power as both repressive and productive, I have tried to steer a course between biological essentialism and a cultural determinism, arguing that the child is necessarily both constructed and constructive, and that this hybrid border country is worthy of exploration. Here the tired verities about the child and its literature are seen to be less secure – but more revealing. As Bhabha (1994: 38) puts it, 'it is the "inter" – the cutting edge of translation and negotiation, the *in-between* space – that carries the burden of the meaning of culture'. The children's writer C. Walter Hodges (1975: 57) uses different terms, but invokes the same space: 'if in every child there is an adult trying to get out, equally in every adult there is a child trying to get back. On the overlapping of those two, *there* is the common ground.' One thing is certain, though. Without recognition of this 'someone else' who half-owns the words, then, by fiat, children's literature *will* be impossible, a generic plaything for adults, satisfying their desires for a point of stability, with the child as indeed but an 'empty' category, effectively muted. As Patricia Holland says, 'the trap of recurring childish*ness* is only escaped by attention to actual child*ren*' (1996: 170).

Where, finally, does this leave us in terms of a definition? Clearly, it cannot rest on an essential child, nor an essential children's book (as impossible as an essential 'Orient' (Said 1978)) – which means that an essential definition is equally impossible. However, it is not enough to declare that children's literature is just 'a Boojum' (Carroll 1967: 96) – a meaningless construction – and leave it at that. So here, finally, is an attempt to depict its nominal essence:

Children's literature consists of texts that consciously or unconsciously address particular constructions of the child, or metaphorical equivalents in terms of character or situation (for example, animals, puppets, undersized or underprivileged grown-ups), the commonality being that such texts display an awareness of children's disempowered status (whether containing or controlling it, questioning or overturning it). Adults are as caught up in this discourse as children, engaging dialogically with it (writing/reading it), just as children themselves engage with many 'adult' discourses. But it is how these texts are read and used that will determine their success as 'children's literature'; how fruitfully they are seen to negotiate this hybrid, or border country.

References

Adams, G. (1986) 'The First Children's Literature? The Case for Sumer', *Children's Literature* 14: 1–30.

Alexandre-Bidon, Daniele and Lett, Didier (1999) *Children in the Middle Ages: Fifth–Fifteenth Centuries*, Notre Dame, IN: University of Notre Dame Press.

Archard, D. (1993) *Children: Rights and Childhood*, London: Routledge.

Ariès, P. (1973) *Centuries of Childhood*, Harmondsworth: Penguin.

Auerbach, N. and Knoepflmacher, U. (1992) *Forbidden Journeys: Fairy Tales and Fantasies by Victorian Women Writers*, Chicago, IL and London: University of Chicago Press.

Bakhtin, M. M. (1968) *Rabelais and His World*, Cambridge, MA: Massachusetts Institute of Technology Press.

—— (1981) *The Dialogic Imagination: Four Essays*, Austin, TX: University of Texas Press.

Banerjee, J. (1984) 'Ambivalence and Contradiction: The Child in Victorian Fiction', *English Studies* 65: 481–94.

Barker, M. (1989) *Comics: Ideology, Power and the Critics*, Manchester: Manchester University Press.

Barrie, J. M. (1995) *Peter Pan and Other Plays*, ed. Hollindale, P., Oxford: Oxford University Press.

Bawden, N. (1975) 'The Imprisoned Child', in Blishen, E. (ed.) *The Thorny Paradise: Writers on Writing for Children*, Harmondsworth: Kestrel.

—— (1995) 'A Dead Pig and My Father', in Fox, G. (ed.) *Celebrating Children's Literature in Education*, London: Hodder and Stoughton.

Beckett, S. L. (ed.) (1999) *Transcending Boundaries: Writing for a Dual Audience of Children and Adults*, New York and London: Garland.

Bhabha, H. K. (1994) *The Location of Culture*, London and New York: Routledge.

Braidotti, R. (1994) *Nomadic Subjects: Embodiment and Sexual Difference in Contemporary Feminist Theory*, New York: Columbia University Press.

Broadbent, N., Hogan, A., Inkson, G. and Miller, M. (eds) (1994) *Researching Children's Literature: A Coming of Age?*, Southampton: LSU.

Bruner, J. (1987) *Making Sense: The Child's Construction of the World*, New York: Methuen.

Burkitt, I. (1999) *Bodies of Thought: Embodiment, Identity and Modernity*, London and Thousand Oaks, CA: Sage.

Carpenter, H. (1985) *The Secret Garden: The Golden Age of Children's Literature*, London: Allen and Unwin.

Carroll, L. (1967) *The Annotated Snark,* ed. Gardner, M., Harmondsworth: Penguin.

—— (1970) *The Annotated Alice*, ed. Gardner, M., rev. edn, Harmondsworth: Penguin.

Cixous, H. (1976) 'The Laugh of the Medusa', trans. Cohen, K. and Cohen, P., *Signs* 1: 875–93.

Culler, J. (1983) *On Deconstruction: Theory and Criticism after Structuralism*, London: Routledge and Kegan Paul.

Darton, F. J. H. (1982) *Children's Books in England: Five Centuries of Social Life*, 3rd edn, rev. Alderson, B., Cambridge: Cambridge University Press.

Dunn, J. (1988) *The Beginnings of Social Understanding*, Oxford: Blackwell.

Elias, N. (1978) *The Civilizing Process: The History of Manners*, trans. Jephcott, E., Oxford: Blackwell; New York: Urizen.

Engel, S. (1995) *The Stories Children Tell: Making Sense of the Narratives of Childhood*, New York: W. H. Freeman

Fisher, J. (1980) *Peter Potato and Alice Apple: Two Stories from the Garden Gang*, Loughborough: Ladybird.

Foucault, M. (1967) *Madness and Civilization: A History of Insanity in the Age of Reason*, London: Tavistock.

—— (1980) *Power/Knowledge: Selected Interviews and Other Writings, 1972–1977*, London: Harvester Wheatsheaf.

—— (1981) *The History of Sexuality: An Introduction*, trans. Hurley, R., London and New York: Penguin.

Fox, C. (1993) *At the Very Edge of the Forest: The Influence of Literature on Storytelling by Children*, London: Cassell.

Fuss, D. (1989) *Essentially Speaking: Feminism, Nature and Difference*, London: Routledge.

Gordon, J. (1975) 'On Firm Ground', in Blishen, E. (ed.) *The Thorny Paradise: Writers on Writing for Children*, Harmondsworth: Kestrel.

Grainger, T. (1999) 'Physical Poetry?', paper presented at 'Odysseys of the Mind – the Future of Reading' conference, Homerton College, Cambridge, September.

Harries, E. W. (2001) *Twice upon a Time: Women Writers and the History of the Fairy Tale*, Woodstock, NY: Princeton University Press.

Hilton, M., Styles, M. and Watson, V. (1997) *Opening the Nursery Door: Reading, Writing and Childhood, 1600–1900*, London and New York: Routledge.

Hoban, R. (1975) *Turtle Diary*, London: Jonathan Cape; New York: Random House.

Hodges, C. W. (1975) 'Children? What Children?', in Blishen, E. (ed.) *The Thorny Paradise: Writers on Writing for Children*, Harmondsworth: Kestrel.

Holland, P. (1996) ' "I've Just Seen a Hole in the Reality Barrier!": Children, Childishness and the Media in the Ruins of the Twentieth Century', in Pilcher, J. and Wagg, S. (eds) *Thatcher's Children? Politics, Childhood and Society in the 1980s and 1990s*, London and Washington, DC: Falmer Press.

Hoyles, M. (ed.) (1979) *Changing Childhood*, London: Writers and Readers Publishing Cooperative.

Hunt, P. (1991) *Criticism, Theory and Children's Literature*, Oxford: Blackwell.

James, A. and Prout, A. (eds) (1990) *Constructing and Reconstructing Childhood: Contemporary Issues in the Sociological Study of Childhood*, London: Falmer Press.

James, A., Jenks, C. and Prout, A. (1998) *Theorizing Childhood*, Cambridge: Polity Press.

Jenkins, H. (ed.) (1998) *The Children's Culture Reader*, New York and London: New York University Press.

Johnson, M. (1987) *The Body in the Mind: The Bodily Basis of Meaning, Imagination, and Reason*, Chicago, IL: Chicago University Press.

Katz, Jon (1997) *Virtuous Reality*, New York: Random House.

Kimberley, K., Meek, M. and Miller, J. (eds) (1992) *New Readings: Contributions to an Understanding of Literacy*, London: A. and C. Black.

Kincaid, J. R. (1992) *Child-Loving: The Erotic Child and Victorian Culture*, London: Routledge.

Kincheloe, J. L. (1998) 'The New Childhood: Home Alone as a Way of Life', in Jenkins, H. (ed.) *The Children's Culture Reader*, New York: New York University Press.

Knoepflmacher, U. C. (1983) 'The Balancing of Child and Adult: An Approach to Victorian Fantasies for Children', *Nineteenth Century Fiction* 37: 497–530.

Knoepflmacher, U. C. and Myers, M. (eds) (1997) ' "Cross-Writing" and the Reconceptualizing of Children's Literature Studies', *Children's Literature* 25 (special edition).

Knowles, M. and Malmkjær, K. (1996) *Language and Control in Children's Literature*, London: Routledge.

Kristeva, J. (1984) *Revolution in Poetic Language*, trans. Waller, M., New York: Columbia University Press.

Le Guin, U. (1975) 'This Fear of Dragons', in Blishen, E. (ed.) *The Thorny Paradise: Writers on Writing for Children*, Harmondsworth: Kestrel.

Lesnik-Oberstein, K. (1998) (ed.) *Children in Culture: Approaches to Childhood*, Basingstoke: Macmillan.

Lochhead, M. (1956) *Their First Ten Years: Victorian Childhood*, London: John Murray.

McGillis, R. (1996) *The Nimble Reader: Literary Theory and Children's Literature*, New York: Twayne.

Meek, M. (1995) 'The Constructedness of Children', *Signal* 76: 5–19.

Morgenstern, J. (2001) 'The Rise of Children's Literature Reconsidered', *Children's Literature Association Quarterly* 26: 64–73.

Morrison, B. (1997) *As If*, London: Granta.

Myers, M. (1995) 'De-Romanticizing the Subject: Maria Edgeworth's "The Bracelets", Mythologies of Origin, and the Daughter's Coming to Writing', in Feldman, P. and Kelley, T. M. (eds) *Romantic Women Writers: Voices and Countervoices*, Hanover and London: University Press of New England.

Nelson, K. (1985) *Making Sense: The Acquisition of Shared Meaning*, New York: Academic Press.

—— (ed.) (1989) *Narratives from the Crib*, Cambridge, MA: Harvard University Press.

Nikolajeva, M. (1996) *Children's Literature Comes of Age: Towards a New Aesthetic*, London and New York: Garland.

Nodelman, P. (1992) 'The Other: Orientalism, Colonialism, and Children's Literature', *Children's Literature Association Quarterly* 17: 29–35.

—— (1996) 'Hatchet Job', *Children's Literature Association Quarterly* 21: 42–5.

Opie, I. and Opie, P. (1959) *The Lore and Language of Schoolchildren*, Oxford: Clarendon Press.

Paley, V. (1981) *Wally's Stories*, Cambridge, MA: Harvard University Press.

Parker, R. (1995) *Torn in Two: The Experience of Maternal Ambivalence*, London: Virago.

Rollin, L. (1992) *Cradle and All: A Cultural and Psychoanalytic Reading of Nursery Rhymes*, Jackson, MS and London: University Press of Mississippi.

Rose, J. (1984) *The Case of Peter Pan or The Impossibility of Children's Fiction*, Basingstoke: Macmillan.

Rosen, M. (1974) *Mind Your Own Business*, London: André Deutsch.

Rosen, M. and Steele, S. (1982) *Inky, Pinky, Ponky: Children's Playground Rhymes*, London: Granada.

Rudd, D. (1992) *A Communication Studies Approach to Children's Literature*, Sheffield: Pavic/Sheffield Hallam University Press.

—— (2000) *Enid Blyton and the Mystery of Children's Literature*, Basingstoke: Macmillan/Palgrave.

Said, E. (1978) *Orientalism*, Harmondsworth: Penguin; New York: Vintage.

Sarland, C. (1991) *Young People Reading: Culture and Response*, Milton Keynes: Open University Press.

Scheper-Hughes, N. and Sargent, C. (eds) (1998) *Small Wars: The Cultural Politics of Childhood*, Berkeley, CA and London: University of California Press.

Sendak, M. (1967) *Where the Wild Things Are*, London: Bodley Head.

Shavit, Z. (1986) *Poetics of Children's Literature*, Athens, GA: University of Georgia Press.

Showalter, E. (1987) 'Critical Cross-Dressing: Male Feminists and the Woman of the Year', in Jardine, A. and Smith, P. (eds) *Men in Feminism*, New York: Routledge and Kegan Paul.

Spivak, G. C. (1988) *In Other Worlds: Essays in Cultural Politics*, New York and London: Routledge.

Stahl, J. D. (1996) 'The Imaginative Uses of Secrecy in Children's Literature', in Egoff, S., Stubbs, G., Ashley, R. and Sutton, W. (eds) *Only Connect: Readings on Children's Literature*, 3rd edn, Toronto: Oxford University Press.

Stainton Rogers, R. and Stainton Rogers, W. (1992) *Stories of Childhood: Shifting Agendas of Child Concern*, London: Simon and Schuster.

—— (1998) 'Word Children', in Lesnik-Oberstein, K. (ed.) *Children in Culture: Approaches to Childhood*, Basingstoke: Macmillan.

Steedman, C. (1982) *The Tidy House: Little Girls Writing*, London: Virago.

—— (1995) *Strange Dislocations: Childhood and the Idea of Human Interiority, 1780–1930*, London: Virago Press.

Stephens, J. (1992) *Language and Ideology in Children's Fiction*, London: Longman.

Summerfield, G. (1984) *Fantasy and Reason: Children's Literature in the Eighteenth Century*, London: Methuen.

Sutton-Smith, B., Mechling, J., Johnson, T. W. and McMahon, F. R. (eds) (1999) *Children's Folklore: A Source Book*, Logan, UT: Utah State University Press.

Taylor, J. B. (1998) 'Between Atavism and Altruism: The Child on the Threshold in Victorian Psychology and Edwardian Children's Fiction', in Lesnik-Oberstein, K. (ed.) *Children in Culture: Approaches to Childhood*, Basingstoke: Macmillan.

Thwaite, M. F. (1964) *From Primer to Pleasure in Reading: An Introduction to the History of Children's Books in England from the Invention of Printing to 1914 with an Outline of Some Developments in Other Countries*, London: Library Association.

Townsend, S. (1982) *The Secret Diary of Adrian Mole, Aged 13¾*, London: Methuen.

Turner, I., Factor, J. and Lowenstein, W. (1978) *Cinderella Dressed in Yella*, 2nd edn, Richmond, Australia: Heinemann Educational.

Vološinov, V. (1973) *Marxism and the Philosophy of Language*, New York: Seminar Press.

Walkerdine, V. (1990) *Schoolgirl Fictions*, London: Verso.

Warner, M. (1994) *From the Beast to the Blonde: On Fairy Tales and Their Tellers*, London: Chatto and Windus.

—— (2000) *No Go the Bogeyman: Lulling, Scaring and Making Mock*, London: Vintage Press.

Watson, V. (1992) 'The Possibilities of Children's Fiction', in Styles, M., Bearne, E. and Watson, V. (eds) *After Alice: Exploring Children's Literature*, London: Cassell.

Weir, R. (1960) *Language in the Crib*, Mouton: The Hague.

Wolf, S. A. and Heath, S. B. (1992) *The Braid of Literature: Children's Worlds of Reading*, Cambridge, MA: Harvard University Press.

Young, I. M. (1990) *Throwing Like a Girl and Other Essays in Feminist Philosophy and Social Theory*, Bloomington, IN: Indiana University Press.

Young, R. J. C. (1995) *Colonial Desire: Hybridity in Theory, Culture and Race*, London and New York: Routledge.

Zelizer, V. A. (1994) *Pricing the Priceless Child: The Changing Social Value of Children*, Princeton, NJ: Princeton University Press.

Zipes, J. (1983) *Fairy Tales and the Art of Subversion: The Classical Genre for Children and the Process of Civilization*, London: Heinemann Educational.

—— (1987) *Victorian Fairy Tales: The Revolt of the Fairies and Elves*, London: Routledge and Kegan Paul.

—— (2001) *The Troublesome Success of Children's Literature from Slovenly Peter to Harry Potter*, New York and London: Routledge.

3 Critical tradition and ideological positioning

Charles Sarland

Editor's Introduction

One of the fundamental changes in critical thinking and teaching over the past twenty years has been the acceptance that ideology is not a separate concept 'carried by' texts, but that all texts are inevitably infused by ideologies. This has been particularly difficult to accept in the case of children's literature, which is still widely assumed to be 'innocent' of concerns of gender, race, power, and so on – or to carry transparently manipulative messages. Charles Sarland surveys the development of ideas about ideology, and their relationship to the distinctive power-balances which exist within children's literature.

P. H.

Introduction

There is a problem for this chapter to be noted at the very start, which is that as an English person writing in English for an English-reading audience, and with limited skills in other languages, I do not have access to wider world literatures unless they have been translated into English. Both Penni Cotton and Margaret Meek note the shortage of English translations of foreign children's books, and until recently there has been a similar shortage of commentary in English upon such books, though that is beginning to change (Cotton 2000; Meek 2001; and e.g. Nikolajeva 1996). We are thus at the very start faced with an ideological issue which relates to the political domination by English as a world language; and there is an ideological bias already written into this chapter, a bias that I hope at least to make explicit where it arises.

Discourse on children's fiction sits at the crossroads of a number of other discourses. At the start of the twenty-first century the most important among these, for the purposes of this chapter, are the discourses that surround the subject of 'literature' itself and the discourses that surround the rearing, socialisation and education of the young. Thus discussion of ideology in children's literature requires the consideration of a number of issues (see, for example, Zipes 2001). The very use of the expression 'children's litera-ture', for instance, brings with it a whole set of value judgements which have been variously espoused, attacked, defended and counterattacked over the years. In addition, discussion of children's fiction – my preferred term in this chapter – has always been characterised by arguments about its purposes. These purposes, or in some cases these denials of purpose, stem from the particular characteristics of its intended readership, and are invariably a product of the views held within the adult population about children and young people themselves and about their place in society. Since there is an imbalance of power between the children and young people who read the books, and the adults who write, publish and review the books, or who are otherwise engaged in commentary upon or dissemination of the books, either as parents, or teachers, or librarians, or booksellers, or academics, there is here immediately a question of politics, a politics first and foremost of age differential.

But wider than this, the books themselves and the social practices that surround them will raise ideological issues. These issues will be related to specific debates in adult society, to do for instance with class, gender, sexuality, ethnicity; or they will be instances of more general debate about the role of liberal humanist values in a capitalist democracy; or, particularly at times of increasing international tension, they will be to do with questions of international identity and international roles. In addition, there is a continuing debate about reader response, which also impacts upon considerations of ideology in children's fiction. Finally, we must consider the fact that children's fiction has become a commodity in a global market, controlled by a relatively small number of international publishers.

Ideology

Ideology is itself a problematic notion. In the general discourse of the electronic media, for instance, it is often considered that ideology and bias are one and the same thing, and that ideology and 'common sense' can be set against each other. This distinction continues into (particularly British) party political debate: 'ideology' is what the other side is motivated by while 'our' side is again merely applying common sense. In the history of Marxist thought there has been a convoluted development of usage of the term, not unre-lated to the distinction just outlined. For the purposes of this chapter, however, ideology will be taken to refer to all espousal, assumption, consideration and discussion of social- *ideology* and cultural values, whether overt or covert. In that sense it will include common sense itself, for common sense is always concerned with the values and underlying assumptions of our everyday lives.

Vološinov (1929/1986) encapsulates the position when he argues that all language is ideological. All sign systems, including language, he argues, have not only a simple deno-tative role, they are also evaluative, and thus ideological: 'The domain of ideology coincides with the domain of signs' (10). From this perspective it will thus be seen that all writing is ideological since all writing either assumes values even when not overtly espousing them, or is produced and also read within a social and cultural framework which is itself inevitably suffused with values – that is to say, suffused with ideology. In addition, in Marxist terms, considerations of ideology can be divorced neither from considerations of the economic base nor from considerations of power (that is, of politics), and that too is the position taken here.

Moral purpose and didacticism

At the heart of any consideration of ideology will be a consideration of moral purpose and didacticism and it is useful, I think, to recognise the historical nature of the debate. My examples are largely British. In the Preface to *The Governess, or Little Female Academy* in 1749, Sarah Fielding wrote:

> Before you begin the following sheets, I beg you will stop a Moment at this Preface, to consider with me, what is the true Use of reading: and if you can once fix this

Truth in your Minds, namely that the true Use of Books is to make you wiser and better, you will then have both Profit and Pleasure from what you read.

(Fielding 1749/1968: 91)

Contrary views have almost as long a history; Elizabeth Rigby, for instance, writing in 1844 in *The Quarterly Review*, while admitting that no one would deliberately put what she calls 'offensive' books in the way of children, goes on:

but, should they fall in their way, we firmly believe no risk to exist – if they will read them at one time or another, the earlier, perhaps, the better. Such works are like the viper – they have a wholesome flesh as well as a poisonous sting; and children are perhaps the only class of readers which can partake of one without suffering from the other.

(Hunt 1990: 21)

The debate was lively in the eighteenth and nineteenth centuries, and has continued on and off ever since. So far as Britain was concerned, at one stage it looked as if it had been settled, Harvey Darton having introduced his 1932 history of *Children's Books in England* with the words: 'By "children's books" I mean printed works produced ostensibly to give children spontaneous pleasure, and not primarily to teach them, not solely to make them good, nor to keep them *profitably* quiet' (Darton 1932/1982: 1; his emphasis).

For some while after that, explicit discussion of values was left in abeyance. There was discussion both about how to write for children in ways that were not condescending – an ideological formulation in itself, of course – and about what the differences might be between fiction written for children and fiction written for adults, but considerations either of moral purpose or of didacticism did not appear to be at issue. In fact the debate had never gone away: it had rather gone underground, as my discussion of the Leavisite paradigm below demonstrates, or recoded itself in educational terms. The debate re-emerged more overtly with Fred Inglis in 1981:

Only a monster would not want to give a child books she will delight in and which will teach her to be good. It is the ancient and proper justification of reading and teaching literature that it helps you to live well.

(Inglis 1981: 4)

Pat Pinsent makes similar claims: 'I would go so far as to claim that sustained experience of literature from an early age can be a means of combining pleasure with the acquisition of tolerance, a combination less readily available from other sources' (Pinsent 1997: 21).

Elsewhere, the picture is mixed. Karín Lesnik-Oberstein (1999) and Cotton (2000) both suggest that the same historical distinction as that described by Darton between writing for moral purpose in the nineteenth century and writing for pleasure in the twentieth can be found in a number of European countries – France, Germany, Italy, Norway, Sweden, Switzerland – and in North America. Large numbers of children's books were published, but in European countries that remained as dictatorships after the Second World War – Cotton quotes Spain as an example – the production of children's books remained very much under state control and did not flourish (Cotton 2000: 16). Similarly, Peter Hunt draws on various sources to note that, in newly emergent children's literatures in newly emergent postcolonial countries, moral purpose and didacticism are also high on the agenda (Hunt 1992b).

In fact, as John Stephens (1992: 3) has observed, writing for children has almost always had a purpose over and beyond that of just giving children pleasure and, as Lesnik-Oberstein points out (1999: 15), a central question has always been and will always be the question of which books are 'best for children' – however one wants to define 'best'.

In the British context the *educational* purposes of literature have also always been an issue, with official reports and curriculum documents from the 1920s to the 1990s emphasising the importance of the role of literature, and by implication children's literature, in the personal and moral development of school students (Board of Education 1921; DES 1975; DFE 1995). In addition, the English National Curriculum has spawned a market for books aimed at particular niches within it: Franklin Watts's Sparks series, aimed at primary schools, is marketed as 'Stories linking with the History National Curriculum Key Stage 2'. In the member states of the European Union, with the dishonourable exception of Britain itself, the dissemination of translated books is seen to have an important educational and hence ideological function, fostering mutual understanding and European unity.

The recognition that the question of values had in fact always been there had actually re-emerged in Britain in the late 1940s (Trease 1949/1964) but the debate grew more intense in the 1970s, and it was at this point that ideological considerations came to be labelled as such.

Representation: gender, minority groups and bias: the debate from the 1970s until the present day

In eighteenth- and nineteenth-century didacticism the promotion of values in children's books had often taken the overt form of direct preaching, and the values to be promoted were an issue. By the 1970s the focus of the debate in Britain and the United States had changed to questions of character representation and character role, and analysis consisted in showing how children's fiction represented some groups at the expense of others, or how some groups were negatively represented in stereotypical terms. The argument was that, by representing certain groups in certain ways, children's books were promoting certain values – essentially white, male and middle-class – and that the books were thus class-biased, racist and sexist. The fact that the protagonists of most children's books tended to be white middle-class boys was adduced in evidence. Working-class characters were portrayed either as respectful to their middle-class 'betters', or as stupid – or they had the villain's role in the story. Black characters suffered a similar fate. Girls tended to be represented in traditional female roles.

Trease (1949/1964) had led the way in drawing attention to the politically conservative bias of historical fiction, and had attempted to offer alternative points of view in his own writing. From the United States, Nat Hentoff drew attention to the under-representation of teenagers in children's books, and saw the need to make 'contact with the sizeable number of the young who never read anything for pleasure because they are not in it' (Hentoff 1969: 400). Bob Dixon's work (1974) was characteristic of many attacks on that most prolific of British authors, Enid Blyton. Zimet (1976), from the USA, drew attention to the exclusion or the stereotypical presentation of ethnic minorities and women in children's fiction, and incidentally also in school textbooks, and espoused the use of positive images of girls and of ethnic minorities. Dixon (1977), in a comprehensive survey, demonstrated the almost universally reactionary views on race, gender and class, together with a political conservatism, that informed most British children's books of the time, and Robert Leeson (1977) came up with similar findings. The Writers and Readers Publishing Co-operative (1979) drew attention to the racism inherent in a number of children's classics and one or two highly rated more modern books, and examined sex roles and other stereotyping.

In order to promote working-class, anti-racist and anti-sexist values, it was argued that books should be written with working-class, or female, or black protagonists. Thus in 1982 Dixon drew up what was essentially an annotated book list of 'stories which show a positive overall attitude with regard to sex roles, race and social class' (Dixon 1982: 3), although he also insisted that the books should meet 'literary' standards that were essentially Leavisite. Such initiatives have multiplied in the later years of the twentieth century, and the practical outcome was a proliferation of series aimed particularly at the teenage market and the emergence of writers like Petronella Breinburg, Robert Leeson and Jan Needle in Britain, and Rosa Guy, Julius Lester, Louise Fitzhugh and Virginia Hamilton in the USA.

It is worth noting, however, that the current publication life of any given title can be very short and this can result in the fairly rapid silencing of work that challenges prevailing norms and values. Jan Needle's *Albeson and the Germans* (1977), which both challenges British xenophobia and contains a pretty devastating attack upon a benevolently intentioned primary school teacher, is out of print, while much of Needle's other work is still available. More recently Adele Geras's *A Candle in the Dark* (1995), which portrays anti-semitism in its just pre-Second World War primary-school child characters, had a shelf life of only five years (two years in its paperback format).

The debate has been revisited in recent years, particularly by Pinsent (1997), Cedric Cullingford (1998) and Margery Hourihan (1997). Pinsent writes for teachers in an English context in which many of the texts criticised in the 1970s are still enshrined in the English National Curriculum (DFE 1995) and/or are still to be found being taught in English classrooms. She debates the desirability of using such texts and the need to handle them sensitively, and touches on issues of sexuality. Cullingford, in a much bolder foray, seems largely unconcerned by the ideological debate, but offers in passing fascinating insights into the work of popular English authors such as Herbert Strang and Percy F. Westerman from the first half of the twentieth century, noting their chauvinism with regard to the rest of Europe, their wholehearted espousal of the imperialist, essentially racist values of their day, and their assumptions about the natural superiority of 'British gentlemen' over the rest of the English characters who populated their books. When it comes to Blyton's notorious characterisations of travellers and gypsies he sees them as 'so absurdly innocent that they are beside the point' (Cullingford 1998: 100), a worrying observation both in light of the fact that, around the same time as Blyton was writing, over 200,000 gypsies were either being killed or had recently been killed in the Nazi death camps, and in light of the fact that Blyton is still promoted in school and very widely read by children while Strang and Westerman are not.

Finally, Hourihan, in a much more systematically theorised approach, explores the role of the hero in a range of literature including, alongside children's books themselves, those authors such as Homer, Defoe, Dickens and Tolkien whose adult work often gets offered to children in some sort of abbreviated form. She too notes the tradition of the young white male European protagonists and, in the specifically British context, the importance of the notion of the gentleman.

As has been indicated, with the exception of Hourihan's work, the debate has been essentially about representation, and 'literary standards' *per se* have not generally been challenged. Thus more complex considerations of the ways in which ideology is inscribed in texts did not enter into the discussion, nor did considerations of the complexity of reader response. What such a debate has done, however, is to point out that all texts incorporated value positions. It was therefore not long before questions were raised about the grounds for the judgements made on the quality of children's books, and that debate in turn relates to a wider consideration of such questions with regard to literary criticism as a whole.

The development of criticism of children's fiction: the Leavisite paradigm

The criticism of children's fiction has been something of a poor relation in English and American critical studies. For the first two-thirds of the twentieth century there was little written that addressed the subject, and Felicity Hughes (1978/1990) offers some analysis as to why this was the case. She argues that, at the end of the nineteenth century and the beginning of the twentieth, Henry James and others encapsulated the view that, for the novel to fully come of age as an art form, it had to break free of its family audience. Since then the tendency has increased to view writing for children as a 'mere' craft, not worthy of serious critical attention. Reviewing and commentary focused on advising parents, librarians and other interested adults on what to buy for children, or on advising teachers on how to encourage and develop the reading habits of their pupils. While critical judgements were offered about the quality of the books, the criteria for such critical judgements were assumed rather than debated. When surveys of the field were published they also tended to sacrifice discussion of critical criteria to the need for comprehensive coverage.

However, a developing body of work did start to emerge in the 1960s and 1970s which was directly concerned with confronting the problem and trying to establish criteria for judgement. Such work drew on two traditions, the Leavisite tradition in Britain and New Criticism in the USA. Foremost among such initiatives was a collection of papers edited by Egoff *et al.* (1969); Rosenheim (1969) and Travers (1969), both from that collection, look specifically to New Critic Northrop Frye's mythic archetypes, as do Ted Hughes (1976) and Peter Hunt (1980). Wallace Hildick (1970) and Myles McDowell (1973) both address the question of the difference in writing for children and writing for adults, but both resort to Leavisite criteria for evaluating the quality of children's books. The Leavisite tradition perhaps reaches its apogee with Inglis's *The Promise of Happiness*. Inglis's opening sentence directly quotes the opening of Leavis's *The Great Tradition* (1948): 'The great children's novelists are Lewis Carroll, Rudyard Kipling, Frances Hodgson Burnett, Arthur Ransome, William Mayne, and Philippa Pearce – to stop for a moment at that comparatively safe point on an uncertain list' (Inglis 1981: 1).

The tradition is not dead. Margery Fisher (1986), for instance, assumes that the definition of a children's classic is still essentially unproblematic. William Moebius (1986/1990) brings similar assumptions to bear upon picture books, and Hunt's book on Arthur Ransome is still largely rooted in Leavisite practice in its judgements of quality and value (Hunt 1992a).

One of the features of the tradition is its refusal to address questions of value at a theoretical level. Here is Townsend exemplifying the point:

> We find in fact that the literary critics, both modern and not-so-modern, are reluctant to pin themselves down to theoretical statements. In the introduction to *Determinations* (1934), F. R. Leavis expresses the belief that 'the way to forward true appreciation of literature and art is to examine and discuss it'; and again, 'out of agreement or disagreement with particular judgements of value a sense of relative value in the concrete will define itself, and without this, no amount of talk in the abstract is worth anything'.
>
> (Townsend 1971/1990: 66)

The values in question can be culled from a variety of sources. F. R. Leavis (1955) talks of 'intelligence', 'vitality', 'sensibility', 'depth, range and subtlety in the presentment of human experience', 'achieved creation', 'representative significance'. Inglis (1981) talks of 'sincerity', 'dignity', 'integrity', 'honesty', 'authenticity', 'fulfilment', 'freedom', 'innocence', 'nation', 'intelligence', 'home', 'heroism', 'friendship', 'history'. And Hunt tells us that the virtues of Arthur Ransome are 'family, honour, skill, good sense, responsibility and mutual respect', and 'the idea of place' (Hunt 1992a: 86). All of these terms and formulations are offered by their various authors as if they are essentially unproblematic, and they are thus rendered as common sense, naturalised and hidden in the discourse, and not raised for examination. We may have little difficulty, however, in recognising a liberal humanist consensus which runs through them, even if one or two of Inglis's choices are somewhat idiosyncratic. Nowhere, however, are we able to raise the question of the role that this liberal humanist discourse plays ideologically in a late capitalist or postcolonial world, and it is such a challenge that an ideological critique inevitably raises.

However, before moving on to such considerations, it is necessary to add that Inglis's book also marks a peak in the *educational* debate, which filled the pages of such journals as *English in Education* throughout the 1980s and into the 1990s, and which is also a debate between the Leavisites and the exponents of newer developments in structuralism and semiotics. As I have indicated above, the discourses of children's literature and education continuously overlap. Hughes (1978/1990) highlights Henry James's concern that the universal literacy that would follow from universal schooling would endanger the future of the novel as an art form, leading to inevitable vulgarisation, as the novel itself catered to popular taste – and children's literature itself catered to an even lower common denominator. As a result, and in order to try to return some status to children's literature, it was, and often still is, seen as the training ground of adult literary taste. From such a perspective the distinction conferred by the term 'literature' is crucial, since by that means the Jamesian distinctions between the novel as an art form and other fiction as *commercial* entertainment is promoted.

It is perhaps ironic that the criticism of children's fiction should have come of age at precisely the point when the newer perspectives of structuralism, semiotics and Marxism were beginning to make their mark in literary criticism in Britain, and to undermine those very certainties after which Inglis was searching. In the 1990s things did indeed move on, with Nikolajeva (1996) drawing on structuralism and in particular semiotics to demonstrate the ways in which children's literature itself has come of age as it takes on board the structures, processes and techniques of the modern adult novel.

The ideological debate in literary studies

Character and action: structuralist insights

As already noted, the work of New Critic Northrop Frye (1957) had been influential in establishing a structuralist tradition in the criticism of children's fiction in the USA in the early 1970s. From Europe a different tradition began to make its influence felt in Britain in the later 1970s and 1980s, particularly with regard to the treatment of character and action. The Russian formalist Vladimir Propp (1928/1968) suggested in his study of the Russian folk tale that character was not the source of action, rather it was the product of plot. The hero was the hero because of his or her role in the plot. One can go back to Aristotle for similar insistence that it was not character but action that was important in tragedy (Aristotle 1965: 39) and such views were echoed by the pre-war critic Walter Benjamin (1970) and in Tzvetan Todorov's work (1971/1977).

In Britain the Leavisite tradition had, by contrast, tended to emphasise the importance of psychological insight in characterisation, and had seen characters themselves as the source of the action of the story, and it is easy to see how the work of authors writing in English such as Philippa Pearce, Nina Bawden, William Mayne, Maurice Sendak, Anthony Browne or Aidan Chambers, to take a list not entirely at random, lends itself to such approaches. By contrast the work of popular authors, such as Enid Blyton or Roald Dahl, more easily lends itself to structuralist analysis: their protagonists are heroines and heroes primarily because that is their plot role, not because there is anything in their psychological make-up that makes them inherently 'heroic'.

Such structuralist approaches need not be limited to popular texts, and can be applied with equal usefulness to the work of authors at what is often regarded as the 'quality' end of the market. To take an example, the character of Toad in Kenneth Grahame's *The Wind in the Willows* (1908) could be seen on the one hand as a rounded psychological creation, by turns blustering and repentant, selfish, self-seeking and replete with hubris. His exploits can then be seen entirely in terms of his personality. Structuralist analysis, on the other hand, might see him as comic hero, archetypal overreacher, functioning as the disruptive element in the social order that is necessary for the book's main plot to develop, and thus acting as a pivotal point for the articulation of the conflict between the uncertainties of the newer machine age and the more settled life of the rural idyll, a conflict which is one of the major themes of the book.

Robert Leeson (1975/1980) led the attack on the application to children's fiction of the then prevailing British tradition of adult literary criticism. He writes: 'these days, turning to adult lit-crit is like asking to be rescued by the *Titanic*' (209). He locates the debate about characterisation in a specifically ideological context, suggesting that enthusiasm for psychological characterisation is a bourgeois trait. The old tales, he argues, echoing Propp, didn't need psychology, they had action and moral. The claims made by traditional 'lit-crit' for such characterisation are elitist, and have little application for the general reader. J. S. Bratton, too, rejected the Leavisite tradition in her study of Victorian children's books: 'the liberal humanist tradition of literary criticism offers no effective approach to the material' (Bratton 1981: 19), although she draws on Frye as well as Propp in her resort to structuralism (see also Sarland 1991: 142).

The critique of the position which sees character as the source of meaning and action comes from a wider and more ideological perspective than that of structuralism alone, and structuralism itself has more to offer than insights about character and action. More widely, structuralism draws on semiotics to explore the whole range of codes that operate in texts and by which they construct their meanings; it also takes a lead from Lévi-Strauss (1963), who related structural elements in myths to structural elements in the society that gave rise to them. This becomes a central tool of ideological critique, allowing parallels to be drawn between ideological structures in the works and those in society at large.

The underlying ground of ideological value

Marxist literary criticism analyses literature in the light of prevailing economic class conflict in capitalist society. This conflict is not slavishly reproduced in the ideological superstructure, of which literature is a part, but it is always possible to trace it in some form in individual work. The liberal humanist tradition, by contrast, is not so much concerned with class conflict as with materialism itself. The ideological conflict then becomes materialism versus humanism and the paradigm distinction to be made about the work, *pace* Henry James, is that between art and commerce. Terry Eagleton (1976) and Catherine Belsey (1980) are among the major critics of the Leavisite tradition, identifying its liberal humanist roots and analysing its escapist response to the materialism of bourgeois capitalism. Furthermore, they argue, by 'naturalising' its values as common sense, liberal humanism conceals its reactionary political role, although the idealist nature of its position is often clear enough in its claim of transcendent status for those same values and for a universal 'human nature' in which they inhere.

To take an example, a liberal humanist reading of *The Wind in the Willows* might see it as celebrating the values enshrined in notions of home and good fellowship, in opposition to the threatening materialism of the wide world with its dominant symbol of the motor car. A case might be made that the recurrent plots and sub-plots, all of which involve explorations away from and successive returns to warm secure homes, culminating in the retaking of Toad Hall from the marauding weasels and stoats, have a 'universal' appeal, since such explorations and returns are the very condition of childhood itself. An ideological perspective might note, by contrast, the resemblance of those secure warm homes to the Victorian middle-class nursery, and comment upon the escapism of the response to the materialism of the wide world. Such an approach might further recognise the underlying feudalist presuppositions that are hidden within the 'common sense' assumptions of the book, and might identify in the weasels and stoats the emergence of an organised working class challenging the privileges of property and upper-middle-class idleness. Jan Needle's re-working of the book, *Wild Wood* (1981), starts from just such a premise. In addition, the celebration of fellowship is an entirely male affair: the only women in *The Wind in the Willows* – the gaoler's daughter and the barge-woman – have distinctly subservient roles, and claims for universality just in terms of gender alone begin to look decidedly suspect.

Belsey also suggests that from the liberal humanist perspective people are seen as the sole authors of their own actions, and hence of their own history, and meaning is the product of their individual intentions. In fact, she argues, the reverse is true: people are not the authors of their own history, they are rather the products of history itself or, less deterministically, engaged in a dialectical relationship with their history – both product and producer. The grounds for Leeson's argument, above, are now clear, for a criticism that espouses psychological characterisation as a central tenet of 'quality', and that insists that the stories in which those characters find themselves should be rooted in the intentionality of those characters' psyches, is liberal humanist in assumption, and will fail to expose the ideological nature both of the fiction to which it is giving attention, and of the fiction that it is ignoring.

In liberal humanist criticism it is the author who takes centre-stage, and Belsey identifies 'expressive realism' as literature's dominant form over the past 150 years: reality, as experienced by a single gifted individual, is expressed in such a way that the rest of us spontaneously perceive it as being the case. Grahame's intention is assumed to be that readers should see childhood as a time and place of adventure within a secure framework, and readers are to take his word for it. The resort to the author's intention as the source of meaning in the work, known to its critics as the 'intentional fallacy', had already come under attack for circularity from the New Critics, since the primary evidence for the author's intention was usually the work itself. Belsey takes the argument one step further, suggesting that expressive realism operates to support liberal humanism, and thus, effectively, to support capitalism itself. Ideological perspectives insist, in contrast, that texts are constructions in and of ideology, generally operating unconsciously, and it is the job of the critic to deconstruct the work in order to expose its underlying ideological nature and role. Thus, far from being the unique insight of an individual with a privileged understanding of the world, *The Wind in the Willows* can be seen as resting securely within a continuum of escapist response to developing bourgeois capitalism that stretches all the way from *Hard Times* to *Lady Chatterley's Lover*.

Peter Hollindale (1988) takes on a number of the perspectives outlined above, and applies them to his discussion of ideology in children's books. He distinguishes three levels of ideology. There is first of all an overt, often proselytising or didactic level, as in books like Gene Kemp's *The Turbulent Term of Tyke Tyler* (1977). Then there is a second, more passive level, where views of the world are put into characters' mouths or otherwise incorporated into the narrative with no overt ironic distancing. (There is a famous example of this from Enid Blyton's *Five Run Away Together* (1944), analysed by Ken Watson (1992: 31), in which the reader is implicitly invited to side with the obnoxious middle-class Julian putting down a member of the 'lower orders'.) Finally, there is what Hollindale calls an 'underlying climate of belief' which he identifies as being inscribed in the basic material from which fiction is built. It is possible to detect a hankering after the old transcendent certainties in Hollindale's work; nonetheless, he does substantially shift the ground of the debate in regard to children's fiction, recognising the complexity of the issues.

Postcolonialism and 'othering'

To these debates may be added the perspectives of postcolonial studies. The work of Edward Said (1993) draws our attention to the ways in which the assumptions of imperialism are often buried so deep in the dominant culture as to be invisible to those who live within it. It was only after the successful resistance of the colonised which led to the throwing off of the imperialist yoke that such perspectives began to penetrate the discourses of the dominant culture, leading us to look anew at the ideological assumptions of much of our cultural product.

Within that product a number of things can occur. The first is that imperialist assumptions are built into the text quite overtly, with imperialist and racist sentiments put explicitly into the mouths of the characters (see Cullingford 1998).

Second, the ground of ideological assumption can mean that the evidence is there in the text, but that commentary has not noted it. Said's own expositions of Conrad's *Heart of Darkness* and Austen's *Mansfield Park* are cases in point. In children's fiction a glance at the work of some of the canonical names provides obvious examples. Arthur Ransome's *Secret Water* (1939) comes replete with the language of imperialism: 'natives' and 'savages' abound, 'natives' being adults, and 'savages' being other children with whom the central characters enter into a war game. When 'the savages' embark upon a raid the descriptions are explicit enough: 'Except for their faces all three were shiny and black. All three were in bathing things, but it was hard to see where bathing things ended and mud began. The savages. There was no doubt about it' (Ransome 1939: 220). *Secret Water* operates as an imperialist text at a more structural level, too, since the whole book is about the central family's and in particular John the oldest boy's agenda, given him by his father, to explore the estuary upon which they are camped. As Said suggests: 'The main battle in imperialism is over land' (Said 1993: xiii), and in the course of the book *Secret Water* the central invading family maps and names the land; they even recruit a local boy as a 'native guide'.

The operation of imperialism does not occur just at the material level of physical occupation and subsequent economic annexation. It also, Said suggests, operates at a cultural and ideological level. This is exemplified in *The Story of Dr Dolittle* (Hugh Lofting 1922): in line with the characterisation of the Africans as both primitive and stupid, Lofting's story also offers us an almost prophetic narrative of colonisation, cultural hegemony, de-colonisation and postcolonial influence. The arrival of the white man in the form of the good doctor and his animal helpers plays out the initial colonisation of imperialism (his ostensible reason for being there is to cure the monkeys of some mysterious disease which is decimating the population – the eeriest of pre-echoes of the AIDS story of the final years of the twentieth century). The next stage, in which Prince Bumpo wishes to be like the hero of *The Sleeping Beauty*, then demonstrates the operation of European cultural hegemony, as, in order to become such a hero, Bumpo himself has to turn white. Dolittle, with some misgivings it has to be said, for it is to be a painful process, bleaches his face, but does not even attempt to sort out problems that might ensue. Instead he appropriates the natural resources of the country in the form of the pushmi-pullyou and, in a classic trope of de-colonising irresponsibility, sails away leaving Bumpo to his fate, commenting only that the whiteness will probably wear off in time. He does, however, promise to send Bumpo some candy, hence prefiguring precisely the ways in which the former imperial nations have continued to exercise neo-imperialist economic hegemony over their former colonies through the operation of economic aid with all its concomitant controlling mechanisms, and through the direct supply of arms to any of them that looked as if they were on 'our' side, no matter how dubious their governments or how appalling their human rights records.

In both the above examples, imperialism was encapsulated in both the language of the text and the structures of the narratives. In other examples imperialism is silenced. In *The Wind in the Willows*, for instance, the Rat silences the Mole's interest in the Wide World, while later the Mole physically restrains the Rat from going to explore it, re-establishing English domestic order in order to erase the threat of the 'other', the 'out there'.

Finally there are those texts which raise the issues of xenophobia, racism and imperialism and succeed in challenging prevailing ideological assumption. Bradford (2001) suggests that it is in particular those books that are about boundaries that bring out such issues, and offers an analysis of some Australian and New Zealand fiction to make her point. Garry Disher's *The Divine Wind* (1998) and Gaye Hiçyilmaz's *The Frozen Waterfall* (1993) do just that, the former looking at relationships between Australians and the immigrant Japanese community during the Second World War, and the latter looking at the contemporary experience of Turkish immigrants in Switzerland. Hiçyilmaz's earlier

Against the Storm (1990) is perhaps even more challenging for English readers since it portrays in uncompromising terms what it is like to be young and living on the streets of Ankara, a far cry from the standard fare of most children's books in English.

Both Said and Hourihan suggest that the discourse of imperialism is structured around a process of 'othering', a process that it shares with the discourses of racism, of xenophobia, of class distinction, of paternalism, of homophobia. Each of these have their particular ideological formulations which can be identified in terms of the particular group that is othered. In current neo-imperialism, terms such as civilisation, freedom, democracy are set against terms such as terrorism and fundamentalism and formulations such as 'the evil empire', all of which are designed to preclude understanding and debate. As postcolonial readings can help us to understand the imperialist ideologies that characterise particular texts, so anti-racist readings, class-conscious readings, feminist readings and queer readings can help us to understand the racist, paternalist, class-biased and homophobic ideologies that also characterise texts. Such readings, however, also have the ability to penetrate the surface of the text to demonstrate the ambiguity underneath, as I have attempted to do in my readings of popular literature (Sarland 1991).

As a further example and in an area that is continuously re-erased in children's literature, a queer reading of *The Wind in the Willows* might note that the central relationship of the book, that between Mole and Ratty, is very much one of two men living together in domestic bliss. Indeed, Philip Hoare quotes Peter Burton to the effect that the appearance of Pan in the 'Piper at the Gates of Dawn' chapter would have lent itself to just such a queer reading at the time of the book's original publication (Hoare 1997: 80).

Circumstances of production

Within the Marxist tradition it has long been recognised that literature is a product of the particular historical and social formations that prevail at the time of its production (see, for example, Lenin 1908, 1910, 1911/1978; Plekhanov 1913/1957; Trotsky 1924/1974). Children's books have not received such attention until comparatively recently. Bratton (1981) traced the relationship between British Victorian children's fiction and its various markets – stories for girls to teach them the domestic virtues, stories for boys to teach them the virtues of military Christianity, stories for the newly literate poor, to teach them religion and morality. Leeson, in his history of children's fiction (1985), suggests that there has always been a conflict between middle-class literature and popular literature, a distinction which can be traced in the content of the material and related to the market that it found. He draws attention to the roots of popular fiction in folk tale, which had political content which survived (somewhat subdued) into the written forms. Leeson thus raises a question-mark over the perhaps somewhat more determinist analysis offered by Belsey and Eagleton.

More thorough exploration of the issues in contemporary children's fiction has come from feminist perspectives, with a collection of studies from Australia of popular teen romance fiction edited by Linda Christian-Smith (1993a). Christian-Smith herself (1993b) provides a particularly powerful analysis of the economic, political and ideological circumstances of the growth in production of romances for teenagers and/or 'young adults', which is now a global industry, with most of the publishing houses based in the USA. She traces the relationship between the imperatives of 'Reaganomics', the emphasis on family values in the rise of the New Right in the 1980s, and the need to enculture young women into the gendered roles that serve such interests.

The construction of the reader

The initiatives of the 1970s to redress the balance in the bias of children's fiction took a straightforward view about the relationship between the text and the reader. At its simplest an almost directly didactic relationship was assumed. If you wrote books with positive characterisations of, and roles for, girls, ethnic minorities and the working class, then readers' attitudes would be changed and all would be well with the world. I do not suggest that anyone, even then, thought it would be quite that simple, and since the 1970s there has been something of a revolution in our understandings of how readers are constructed by texts. The insights of reader-response theoreticians like Wolfgang Iser (1978), applied to children's books most notably by Aidan Chambers (1980), had alerted us to some of the textual devices by which an implied reader is written into the text. Iser had also drawn attention to the fact that texts brought with them a cultural repertoire which had to be matched by the reader. Macherey (1978) brought Freudian perspectives to bear on ways in which ideology operated in hidden ways in the text, and by extension also in the reader, and Belsey drew insights from Althusser, Derrida and Lacan to further explore the ways in which the subjectivity of the reader is ideologically constructed.

It is Jacqueline Rose (1984/1994) who offers the most thoroughgoing exposition of this view with respect to children's fiction. She argues that, by a combination of textual devices, characterisation and assumptions of value position, children's books construct children, both as characters and as readers, as without sexuality, innocent and denied politics, either a politics between themselves or within wider society. As such they are seen as beings with a privileged perception, untainted by culture. John Stephens (1992) engages in a detailed analysis of a number of books to show how they produce ideological constructions of implied child readers. He concentrates particularly on narrative focalisation and the shifts, moves and gaps of narrative viewpoint and attitude, showing how such techniques imply certain ideological assumptions and formulations, and construct implied readers who must be expected to share them.

Implied readers and real readers

When real readers are introduced into the equation, however, the picture becomes more complicated, and it is here that the educational discourse overlaps with the discourse about fiction *per se*, for it is almost always within school that evidence is gathered and intervention is proposed. The introduction of real readers has another effect, for it throws into relief some of the more determinist assumptions of the analysis offered above. The evidence comes under three headings: identification, the polysemous text, and contradictory readings.

Identification

The notion of identification has been a contentious issue for some time. The assumption is that readers 'identify with' the protagonists, and thus take on their particular value positions. Readers are thus ideologically constructed by their identification with the character. D. W. Harding (1977) offered an alternative formulation of the reader as an observer in a more detached and evaluative spectator role, and both Geoff Fox (1979) and Robert Protherough (1983) suggest that such a straightforward notion as identification does not account for the evidence that they collected from children and young people. It is clear from their evidence that readers take up a range of positions of greater or lesser involvement, and of varied focalisation. The ideological initiatives of the 1970s presupposed an identification model of response, and subsequent commentators are still most fearful of what happens should a young person engage in unmediated identification with characters constructed within ideologically undesirable formulations. Such fears underlie Stephens's analysis (1992) and the work of Christian-Smith and her co-contributors (1993a).

The polysemous text

Roland Barthes (1974) alerted us to the notion that texts operated through a plurality of codes that left them open to a plurality of readings, and Umberto Eco (1981) offers the most extensive analysis of that plurality. Specifically, with regard to ideology, Eco agrees that all texts carry ideological assumptions, whether overt or covert, but readers have three options: they can assume the ideology of the text and subsume it into their own reading; they can miss or ignore the ideology of the text and import their own, thus producing 'aberrant' readings – 'where "aberrant" means only different from the ones envisaged by the sender' (22); or they can question the text in order to reveal the underlying ideology. This third option is the project that ideological critique undertakes, but when real readers, other than critics, are questioned about their readings, it is clear that the second option is often taken up, and that 'aberrant' readings abound (Sarland 1991; Christian-Smith 1993a) though consensual readings also occur. Texts, it seems, are contradictory, and so evidently are readings.

Contradictory readings

Macherey (1977, 1978) and Eagleton (1976) both assume that the world is riven with ideological conflict. To expect texts to resolve that conflict is mistaken, and the ideological contradictions that inform the world will also be found to inform the fictional texts that are part of that world. Some texts, Eagleton argues, are particularly good at revealing ideological conflict, in that they sit athwart the dominant ideology of the times in which they were written. Eagleton looks to examples from the traditional adult canon to make his point.

Jack Zipes (1979) takes the argument one stage further and suggests that popular work too will be found to be contradictory. He links popular literature and film with its precursors in folk tale and romance, and suggests that it offers the hope of autonomy and self-determination, in admittedly utopian forms, while at the same time affirming dominant capitalist ideology. In other words, while the closure of popular texts almost always reinforces dominant ideology, in the unfolding narratives there are always countering moves in which it is challenged. Zipes, then, denies the implications of Eagleton's work that only texts that sit athwart the prevailing ideology can be open to countervailing readings, and he denies too the implications of Belsey's work that popular forms sit within the classic expressive realist tradition and as such demand readings that are congruent with the dominant ideology.

For example, in Enid Blyton's *Famous Five* books, many of the plots are predicated on the refusal of the central female character, George, to accept her role as subservient, domesticated and non-adventurous, despite repeated exhortations to 'behave like a girl'. She even refuses to accept her 'real' name, which is Georgina. Countering this is the fact that Blyton only offers her the alternative of 'tomboy', an alternative that is itself determined by a predominantly male discourse; and the closures of the books re-establish traditional domestic order with the sexes acting according to conventional gender stereo-type. (Zipes himself later turned his attention to children's fiction (Zipes 1983), and see also Sarland 1983.)

While this analysis is still essentially theoretical, supporting evidence emerges from studies that have been done of readers themselves. The focus has been on popular fiction and on teenagers. Popular fiction causes liberal educationalists particular concern since it appears to reinforce the more reactionary values in society, particularly so far as girls and young women are concerned. The research evidence, however, uncovers a complex picture of the young seeking ways to take control over their own lives, and using the fiction that they enjoy as one element in that negotiation of cultural meaning and value. Gemma Moss showed how teenage girls and boys were able to turn the popular forms of, respectively, the romance and the thriller to their own ends. She found unhelpful some of the more determinist ideological analysis that suggested that, by their reading of romance, girls were constructed as passive victims of a patriarchal society. The girls who liked the romances were tough, worldly-wise working-class girls who were not subservient to their male counterparts. 'Girls didn't need to be told about male power, they were dealing with it every day of their lives' (Moss 1989: 7). The traditional assessment of 'teen romance' by most teachers as stereotypical drivel was applied to the girls' writing, too, when they chose to write in that form. However, Moss shows how the teenage girls she was working with were able to take the form into their own writing and use it to negotiate and dramatise their concerns with and experience of femininity and oppression. Romance offered them a form for this activity that was not necessarily limiting at all.

In *Young People Reading: Culture and Response* (Sarland 1991) I argued that young people engaged in 'aberrant' readings of pulp violence and horror, readings which ran against the reactionary closure of such material, and they thus were able to explore aspirations of being in control of their own lives, and I further argued that the official school literature as often as not offered them negative perspectives on those same aspirations. Christian-Smith and her colleagues (1993a) explore similar dualities and demonstrate the complexity of the problem. For instance, in her analysis of the Baby-Sitters Club books, Meredith Rogers Cherland shows how the characters are placed securely within feminine roles and functions, being prepared for domestic life and work in lowly paid 'caring' jobs. The eleven-year-old girls who are reading them, however,

> saw the baby-sitters making money that they then used to achieve their own ends. They saw the baby-sitters shaping the action around them so that things worked out the way they wanted them to. They saw girls their age acting as agents in their own right.
>
> (Cherland with Edelsky 1993: 32)

By contrast, horror, Cherland argues, which these girls were also beginning to read, casts women in increasingly helpless roles. In its association of sexuality with violence it seemed to offer the girls in Cherland's study a position of increasing powerlessness, living in fear and thus denied agency.

Research into the meanings that young people actually make of the books they are reading demonstrates the plural nature of the texts we are dealing with. While it was often claimed that texts within the canon had complexity and ambiguity, it was always thought that popular texts pandered to the lowest common denominator, and offered no purchase on complex ideological formulations. The evidence does not bear that out. Popular texts too are discovered to be open to more than one reading, and the deconstruction of those texts, and the readings young people bring to them, prove be a productive tool of analysis for exploring the ideological formulations which constitute them. There is yet to be a large mainstream study of what readers make of the more traditional central canon of children's fiction, though John Stephens and Susan Taylor's exploration of readings of two retellings of the Seal Wife legend (Stephens and Taylor 1992) is a useful start.

Ideology and children's fiction

We have learned from the more international debate in literary studies that ideology is inscribed in texts much more deeply and in much more subtle ways than we thought in Britain in the 1970s. The initial emphasis in the criticism of children's books was on the characters, and addressed questions of representation. The relationship between reader and text was assumed to be one of simple identification. Literary merit was an unproblematic notion built upon Leavisite assumptions. This was set in question by reconsideration of characterisation itself, and then by the revolution in literary studies. Hollindale (1988) made an initial attempt to explore the complexity of the problem, and Stephens (1992) has taken it further. Stephens brings powerful ideological perspectives to bear upon the themes of children's fiction, the ways in which the stories are shaped, as well as the ways in which implied readers are constructed by the texts. He looks at a range of texts, including picture books written for the youngest readers, and examines specific titles by a number of writers in the central canon – Judy Blume, Anthony Browne, Leon Garfield, Jan Mark, William Mayne, Jan Needle, Rosemary Sutcliff, Maurice Sendak and others. The debate has been informed by a re-recognition of the moral/didactic role of children's fiction, now recoded as its ideological role. Newer perspectives from postcolonial studies are now suggesting further avenues of pursuit, though there is, as yet, no substantial postcolonial study of children's fiction (see McGillis 2000).

What the work of Said (1993) also does is re-alert us to the relationship between fiction and the wider world. From such a perspective we may note that in the last ten years we have seen a substantial electoral challenge from extreme right-wing parties across Europe echoed by a major shift to the right of an ostensibly left-wing British Labour government. At an international level, there has been the development of neo-imperialist rhetoric from the USA, supported by Britain, all of which has also been accompanied at the ideological level by what has been described as the total collapse of liberalism (e.g. Hutton 2002).

More parochially, within the English schooling system the anti-racist and anti-sexist initiatives of the 1970s have virtually sunk without trace (Jones 1999; Mac an Ghaill 1994) and Máirtín Mac an Ghaill documents in passing the virtual death of what used to be referred to as liberal educational values. Henry Giroux traces the increasing commercialisation and commodification of children, of education and of culture itself in the USA in recent years, quoting in support of his argument a definition of democracy that came from a poll of the young as 'the freedom to buy and consume whatever they wish without government restriction' (Giroux 2000: 99), a formulation that might make us pause and revisit the underlying ideological consumerist assumptions of series such as Point Horror. In England many of the books that were criticised in the 1970s are still being promoted in school in official curriculum documentation and elsewhere. The British response to the growth of cross-fertilisation of European literatures has been one of increasing rather than decreasing isolation and xenophobia. Cotton (2000: 22), for instance, quotes Brennan to the effect that although other European countries publish up to 35 per cent of picture books in translation from fellow European states, Britain translates only about 1 per cent. In the midst of all this, unresolved conflicts remain between those who want to retain or re-negotiate some literary criteria for judging the quality of children's fiction and those who are more sceptical of such judgements. There is clearly, then, plenty of scope for adding the newer theoretical critical perspectives to the proselytising debate of the 1970s in order to re-examine the texts themselves in relation to wider current social, political and cultural change.

The overlap of the discourses of commentary upon children's fiction with the discourse of child rearing, and in particular education, reveals another conflict, that between determinism and agency. One view of fiction is that it constructs readers in specific ideological formations, and thus enculturates them into the dominant discourses of capitalism – class division, paternalism, racism. Such views are not totally fatalistic, but do require of readers a very conscious effort to read against texts, to deconstruct them in order to reveal their underlying ideology. This then becomes the educational project. The opposing view is that readers are not nearly such victims of fiction as has been assumed, and that the fictions that are responsible for the transmission of such values are more complex than was at first thought. Evidence from the children and young people themselves is beginning to be collected in order to explore this complexity. The argument is that readers are not simply determined by what they read; rather, there is a dialectical relationship between determinism and agency. With reference to her discussions of girls' reading, Cherland quotes J. M. Anyon:

> The dialectic of accommodation and resistance is a part of all human beings' response to contradiction and oppression. Most females engage in daily conscious and unconscious attempts to resist the psychological degradation and low self-esteem that would result from the total application of the cultural ideology of femininity: submissiveness, dependency, domesticity and passivity.
>
> (Cherland with Edelsky 1993: 30)

Applied to language itself, this analysis of a dialectic between individual identity and the ideological formulations of the culture within which it finds itself can be traced back to Vološinov. Within children's literature the dialectic will be found within the texts, and between the texts and the reader.

In Christian-Smith's collection *Texts of Desire: Essays on Fiction, Femininity and Schooling* (1993a), ideological criticism of children's fiction came of age. The collection as a whole addresses the complexity of the debate, analysing the ideologies of the texts themselves, the economic and political circumstances of their production, dissemination and distribution, the ideological features of the meanings their young readers make of them, and the political and economic circumstances of those young readers themselves. The focus of attention is the mass-produced material aimed at the female teen and just preteen market, but their study offers a paradigm for future exploration of children's fiction generally, if we are to fully understand its ideological construction within society.

References

Aristotle (1965) 'On the Art of Poetry', in Aristotle, Horace and Longinus, *Classical Literary Criticism*, trans. Dorsch, T., Harmondsworth: Penguin.

Barthes, R. (1974) *S/Z*, New York: Hill and Wang.

Belsey, C. (1980) *Critical Practice*, London: Methuen.

Benjamin, W. (1970) *Illuminations*, Glasgow: Collins Fontana.

Board of Education (1921) *The Teaching of English in England (The Newbolt Report)*, London: HMSO.

Bradford, C. (2001) 'The End of Empire? Colonial and Post-colonial Journeys in Children's Books', *Children's Literature* 29: 196–218.

Bratton, J. S. (1981) *The Impact of Victorian Children's Fiction*, London: Croom Helm.

Chambers, A. (1980) 'The Reader in the Book', in Chambers, N. (ed.) *The Signal Approach to Children's Books*, Harmondsworth: Kestrel.

Cherland, M. R., with Edelsky, C. (1993) 'Girls Reading: The Desire for Agency and the Horror of Helplessness in Fictional Encounters', in Christian-Smith, L. K. (ed.) *Texts of Desire: Essays on Fiction, Femininity and Schooling*, London: Falmer Press, 28–44.

Christian-Smith, L. K. (ed.) (1993a) *Texts of Desire: Essays on Fiction, Femininity and Schooling*, London: Falmer Press.

——(1993b) 'Sweet Dreams: Gender and Desire in Teen Romance Novels', in Christian-Smith, L. K. (ed.) *Texts of Desire: Essays on Fiction, Femininity and Schooling*, London: Falmer Press.

Cotton, P. (2000) *Picture Books sans Frontières*, Stoke on Trent: Trentham Books.

Cullingford, C. (1998) *Children's Literature and Its Effects: The Formative Years*, London: Cassell.

Darton, F. J. H. (1932/1982) *Children's Books in England: Five Centuries of Social Life*, 3rd edn, rev. Alderson, B., Cambridge: Cambridge University Press.

DES (Department of Education and Science) (1975) *A Language for Life (The Bullock Report)*, London: HMSO.

DFE (Department for Education) (1995) *English in the National Curriculum*, London: HMSO.

Dixon, B. (1974) 'The Nice, the Naughty and the Nasty: The Tiny World of Enid Blyton', *Children's Literature in Education* 15: 43–62.

——(1977) *Catching Them Young*, London: Pluto Press.

——(1982) *Now Read On*, London: Pluto Press.

Eagleton, T. (1976) *Criticism and Ideology*, London: Verso.

Eco, U. (1981) *The Role of the Reader*, London: Hutchinson.

Egoff, S., Stubbs, G. T. and Ashley, L. F. (eds) (1969) *Only Connect*, Toronto: Oxford University Press.

Fielding, S. (1749/1968) *The Governess, or Little Female Academy*, London: Oxford University Press.

Fisher, M. (1986) *Classics for Children and Young People*, South Woodchester: Thimble Press.

Fox, G. (1979) 'Dark Watchers: Young Readers and Their Fiction', *English in Education* 13, 1: 32–5.

Frye, N. (1957) *Anatomy of Criticism*, Princeton, NJ: Princeton University Press.

Giroux, H. (2000) *Stealing Innocence: Youth, Corporate Power, and the Politics of Culture*, New York: St Martin's Press.

Harding, D. W. (1977) 'Psychological Processes in the Reading of Fiction', in Meek, M., Warlow, A. and Barton, G. (eds) *The Cool Web*, London: Bodley Head.

Hentoff, N. (1969) 'Fiction for Teenagers', in Egoff, S., Stubbs, G. T. and Ashley, L. F. (eds) *Only Connect*, Toronto: Oxford University Press.

Hildick, W. (1970) *Children and Fiction*, London: Evans.

Hoare, P. (1997) *Wilde's Last Stand*, London: Duckworth.

Hollindale, P. (1988) 'Ideology and the Children's Book', *Signal* 55: 3–22.

Hourihan, M. (1997) *Deconstructing the Hero*, London: Routledge.

Hughes, F. (1978/1990) 'Children's Literature: Theory and Practice', in Hunt, P. (ed.) *Children's Literature: The Development of Criticism*, London: Routledge.

Hughes, T. (1976) 'Myth and Education', in Fox, G., Hammond, G., Jones, T. and Sterk, K. (eds) *Writers, Critics and Children*, London: Heinemann.

Hunt, P. (1980) 'Children's Books, Children's Literature, Criticism and Research', in Benton, M. (ed.) *Approaches to Research in Children's Literature*, Southampton: University of Southampton Department of Education.

——(ed.) (1990) *Children's Literature: The Development of Criticism*, London: Routledge.

——(1992a) *Approaching Arthur Ransome*, London: Cape.

——(1992b) 'Internationalism', in Hunt, P. (ed.) *Literature for Children: Contemporary Criticism*, London: Routledge.

Hutton, W. (2002) *The World We're In*, London: Little, Brown.

Inglis, F. (1981) *The Promise of Happiness*, Cambridge: Cambridge University Press.

Iser, W. (1978) *The Act of Reading*, London: Routledge and Kegan Paul.

Jones, R. (1999) *Teaching Racism or Tackling It*, Stoke on Trent: Trentham Books.

Leavis, F. R. (1948) *The Great Tradition*, Harmondsworth: Penguin.

——(1955) *D. H. Lawrence: Novelist*, Harmondsworth: Penguin.

Leeson, R. (1975/1980) 'To the Toyland Frontier', in Chambers, N. (ed.) *The Signal Approach to Children's Books*, Harmondsworth: Kestrel.

——(1977) *Children's Books and Class Society*, London: Writers and Readers Publishing Co-operative.

——(1985) *Reading and Righting*, London: Collins.

Lenin, V. (1908, 1910, 1911/1978) 'Lenin's Articles on Tolstoy', in Macherey, P. (ed.) *A Theory of Literary Production*, London: Routledge and Kegan Paul.

——(1999) 'Essentials: What is Children's Literature? What is Childhood?', in Hunt, P. (ed.) *Understanding Children's Literature*, London: Routledge.

Lévi-Strauss, C. (1963) *The Structural Study of Myth*, Harmondsworth: Penguin.

Mac an Ghaill, M. (1994) *The Making of Men: Masculinities, Sexualities and Schooling*, Milton Keynes: Open University Press.

McDowell, M. (1973) 'Fiction for Children and Adults: Some Essential Differences', *Children's Literature in Education* 10: 50–63.

McGillis, R. (ed.) (2000) *Voices of the Other. Children's Literature and the Postcolonial Context*, New York: Garland.

Macherey, P. (1977) 'Problems of Reflection', in Barker, F., Coombes, J., Hulme, P., Musselwhite, D. and Osborne, R. (eds) *Literature, Society, and the Sociology of Literature*, Colchester: University of Essex.

——(1978) *A Theory of Literary Production*, London: Routledge and Kegan Paul.

Meek, M. (2001) 'Boundary Crossings', in Meek, M. (ed.) *Children's Literature and National Identity*, Stoke on Trent: Trentham Books.

Moebius, W. (1986/1990) 'Introduction to Picturebook Codes', in Hunt, P. (ed.) *Children's Literature: The Development of Criticism*, London: Routledge.

Moss, G. (1989) *Un/Popular Fictions*, London: Virago Press.

Nikolajeva, M. (1996) *Children's Literature Comes of Age: Toward a New Aesthetic*, New York: Garland.

Pinsent, P. (1997) *Children's Literature and the Politics of Equality*, London: David Fulton.

Plekhanov, G. V. (1913/1957) *Art and Social Life*, Moscow: Progress Publishers.

Propp, V. (1928/1968) *Morphology of the Folktale*, Austin: Texas University Press.

Protherough, R. (1983) *Developing Response to Fiction*, Milton Keynes: Open University Press.

Ransome, A. (1939) *Secret Water*, London: Cape.

Rose, J. (1984/1994) *The Case of Peter Pan or The Impossibility of Children's Fiction*, London: Macmillan.

Rosenheim, E. W. Jr (1969) 'Children's Reading and Adults' Values', in Egoff, S., Stubbs, G. T. and Ashley, L. F. (eds) *Only Connect*, Toronto: Oxford University Press.

Said, E. (1993) *Culture and Imperialism*, London: Vintage.

Sarland, C. (1983) 'The Secret Seven versus the Twits', *Signal* 42: 155–71.

——(1991) *Young People Reading: Culture and Response*, Milton Keynes: Open University Press.

Stephens, J. (1992) *Language and Ideology in Children's Fiction*, London: Longman.

Stephens, J. and Taylor, S. (1992) 'No Innocent Texts', in Evans, E. (ed.) *Young Readers, New Readings*, Hull: Hull University Press.

Todorov, T. (1971/1977) *The Poetics of Prose*, New York: Cornell University Press.

Townsend, J. R. (1971/1990) 'Standards of Criticism for Children's Literature', in Hunt, P. (ed.) *Children's Literature: The Development of Criticism*, London: Routledge.

Travers, P. (1969) 'Only Connect', in Egoff, S., Stubbs, G. T. and Ashley, L. F. (eds) *Only Connect*, Toronto: Oxford University Press.

Trease, G. (1949/1964) *Tales out of School*, London: Heinemann.

Trotsky, L. (1924/1974) *Class and Art*, London: New Park Publications.

Vološinov, V. N. (1929/1986) *Marxism and the Philosophy of Language*, Cambridge, MA: Harvard University Press.

Watson, K. (1992) 'Ideology in Novels for Young People', in Evans, E. (ed.) *Young Readers, New Readings*, Hull: Hull University Press.

Writers and Readers Publishing Co-operative (1979) *Racism and Sexism in Children's Books*, London: Writers and Readers Publishing Co-operative.

Zimet, S. G. (1976) *Print and Prejudice*, Sevenoaks: Hodder and Stoughton.

Zipes, J. (1979) *Breaking the Magic Spell: Radical Theories of Folk and Fairy Tales*, London: Heinemann.

——(1983) *Fairy Tales and the Art of Subversion*, London: Heinemann.

——(2001) *Sticks and Stones. The Troublesome Success of Children's Literature from Slovenly Peter to Harry Potter*, London and New York: Routledge.

Further reading

Clark, B. L. and Higgonet, M. (1999) *Girls, Boys, Books, Toys: Gender in Children's Literature and Culture*, Baltimore, MD: Johns Hopkins University Press.

Krips, V. (2000) *The Presence of the Past: Memory, Heritage, and Childhood*, New York: Routledge.

Marx, K. and Engels, F. (1859/1892/1971) *Historical Materialism*, London: Pluto Press.

4 Space, history and culture
The setting of children's literature

Tony Watkins

Editor's Introduction

The study of history and culture has changed radically; history is no longer seen as a fixed and ideologically neutral factual background to the study of literature. Rather, it is seen as a series of ideological constructs that constitute, are constituted by, and interact with texts and interpretations. Tony Watkins explores new concepts of history, the new historicism, cultural geography and national identity, and the inter-relationships between children's literature and cultural studies.

P. H.

In order to do justice to the important concepts which are implied by the title, this chapter will review developments in thinking about History, Culture and Cultural Geography before considering the relevance of such developments to the study of children's literature.

Until the late 1970s, there was (outside Marxist criticism) a generally accepted view of the nature of history and its place in literary studies. Perkins (1991) points out that, during most of the nineteenth century, literary history was popular and enjoyed prestige because it produced a more complete appreciation of the literary work than was otherwise possible. It functioned, too, as a form of historiography, revealing the ' "spirit", mentality or Weltanschauung of a time and place with unrivaled precision and intimacy' (Perkins 1991: 2). For much of the twentieth century, especially in Renaissance studies, history was seen as outside literature and as guaranteeing the truth of a literary interpretation: 'History ... was the single, unified, unproblematic, extra-textual, extra-discursive real that guaranteed our readings of the texts which constituted its cultural expression' (Belsey 1991: 26). In the traditional literary view of history and culture, there was no difficulty in relating text to context: history was singular and operated as a 'background' to the reading of a work of literature ('the foreground'); and culture was something which the work reproduced or expressed, or could be set against. Literary history was 'a hybrid but recognizable genre that co-ordinated literary criticism, biography, and intellectual/social background within a narrative of development' (Buell 1993: 216). Until about twenty years ago, such notions also remained the dominant ones behind the histories of children's literature.

In history studies itself, texts by Carr (*What Is History?*) and Elton (*The Practice of History*) would have represented the embodiment of thinking about the nature of history. But, as Keith Jenkins puts it,

over the last twenty to thirty years there has developed around and about this dominant academic discourse a range of theories (hermeneutics, phenomenology,
structuralism, post-structuralism, deconstructionism, new historicism, feminism and
post-feminism, post-Marxism, new pragmatism, postmodernism and so on) as articulated by a range of theorists (for example, Ricoeur, Foucault, Barthes, Althusser,
Derrida, Greenblatt, Kristeva, Bennett, Laclau, Fish, Lyotard *et al.*) which have
reached levels of reflexive sophistication and intellectual rigour with regard to the
question of historical representation, which one could not even hazard a guess at
from a reading of Carr and Elton's vintage texts.

(Jenkins 1995: 3)

The contributors to David Cannadine's collection, *What Is History Now?* (2002)
explore, in more detail, the various ways in which the discourse of historiography developed during the 1980s and 1990s. One of the most important was the rise of women's
history and gender history:

for many people today, both within academe and outside, the most significant development during recent decades has been the rise of women's history and gender
history: the recovery of the lives and experiences of one half of the world's population, based on the recognition that gender was not merely a useful, but arguably an
essential of historical analysis and comprehension.

(Cannadine 2002: x)

(Gender is discussed more fully below, within the section on cultural studies.)

But perhaps equally important was the influence of postmodernism and what some
historiographers call the 'linguistic turn' and 'narrative turn' to 'textualism', associated
with the work of such cultural theorists as Hayden White and Tony Bennett. White, says
Jenkins, views the historical work as a verbal artefact, a narrative prose discourse, the
content of which is as much invented – or as much imagined – as found (Jenkins 1995:
19). To see the past in story form

is to give it an imaginary series of narrative structures and coherences it never had. To
see the *content* of the past (i.e. what actually occurred) as if it were a series of stories
(of great men, of wars and treaties, of the rise of labour, the emancipation of women,
of 'Our Island Story', of the ultimate victory of the proletariat and so forth) is therefore a piece of 'fiction' caused by mistaking the narrative form in which historians
construct and communicate their knowledge of the past as actually being the past's
own ... the only stories the past has are those conferred on it by historians' interpretative emplotments.

(Jenkins 1995: 20)

Tony Bennett's arguments might be summarised by saying: 'the past as constituted by
its existing traces' is always apprehended and appropriated textually through the sedimented layers of previous interpretations and through the reading habits and categories
developed by previous/current methodological practices (Jenkins 1995: 18).

What such 'textualism' does is 'to draw attention to the "textual conditions" under
which *all* historical work is done and *all* historical knowledge is produced'. None of the
methodological approaches in history 'can continue to think that they gain direct access

to, or "ground" their textuality in a "reality" ' (Jenkins 1995: 32). White and Bennett are now regarded as influential theorists whose work embodies characteristics of the contemporary postmodern approach to history:

> History is arguably a verbal artifact, a narrative prose discourse of which ... the content is as much invented as found, and which is constructed by present-minded, ideologically positioned workers (historians and those acting as if they were historians) ... That past appropriated by historians, is never the past itself, but a past evidenced by its remaining and accessible traces and transformed into historiography through a series of theoretically and methodologically disparate procedures (ideological positionings, tropes, emplotments, argumentative modes) ... Understood in this way, as a rhetorical, metaphorical, textual practice governed by distinctive but never homogeneous procedures through which the maintenance/ transformation of the past is regulated ... by the public sphere, historical construction can be seen as taking place entirely in the present ... such that the cogency of historical work can be admitted without the past *per se* ever entering into it – except rhetorically. In this way histories are fabricated without 'real' foundations beyond the textual, and in this way one learns to always ask of such discursive and ideological regimes that hold in their orderings suasive intentions – *cui bono* – in whose interests?
>
> (Jenkins 1995: 178)

The blurring of the distinction between history and fiction works the other way too: if history could be regarded as forms of 'fiction' about the past, historical fiction could be regarded as proposals for understanding the present. Evans argues that several works of historical fiction (by authors such as Sebastian Faulks, Michael Ondaatje, Matthew Kneale, Zadie Smith)

> are not historical novels in the sense that their main purpose is to re-create a past world through the exercise of the fictional imagination; rather, they are novels which find it easiest to address present-day concerns by putting them in a past context.
>
> (Cannadine 2002: 10)

A second development was a shift from sociology to anthropology as the most fruitful subject from which historians could borrow with consequent interest in the work of such anthropologists as Clifford Geertz and his method of 'thick description'. There was also the concomitant interest in cultural history and cultural studies discussed below:

> just as social history seemed poised to sweep all before it in the 1960s, now cultural history seems to be in the ascendant: partly because it has been the most receptive to the insights of anthropology; partly because it makes very large claims about the terrain of the past which it encompasses; and partly because it has benefited most from the shift in interest from explanation to understanding.
>
> (Cannadine 2002: x)

Then there was the increasing 'democratisation' of history as a topic of study. Cannadine points to the revolution in information technology which transformed the popular study of history to focus on personal, cultural and national identity:

History as it is written and researched, and above all as it is presented to a popular audience, at the beginning of the twenty-first century, is about identity, about who we are and where we came from. At a time when other sources of identity such as class and region have declined, history is stepping in to fill the gap … Moreover, history is important once more in constructing national identity, and nowhere more so than in England, where the decline of the idea of British unity in the face of resurgent Welsh and Scottish nationalism on the one hand and growing integration into Europe on the other, have left the English wondering who on earth they are.

(Cannadine 2002: 12)

The exploration of national identity obviously ties in with another popular topic – heritage: 'Alongside so-called "family history", the sector known as "heritage" is now many people's main point of contact with history', argues Fernández-Arnesto (2002: 158). In turn, these aspects of history are taken up eagerly by media makers. All this is to be welcomed, argues David Cannadine:

The widespread pursuit of family history, the growing concern with defining and preserving the 'national heritage' and the unprecedented allure of history on television: all this betokens a burgeoning popular interest in the past as energetic and enthusiastic as that to be found within the walls of academe.

(Cannadine 2002: xi)

In literary studies, the reconceptualisation of history and its relationship to literature had its roots in the work of such theorists and critics as Michel Foucault, Raymond Williams, Edward Said and Frank Lentricchia. In the 1980s, new terms associated with literary history (including 'the New History', 'cultural poetics' and, especially, 'the new historicism') entered the critical vocabulary through the work of such critics as Stephen Greenblatt, Louis Montrose and Jerome McGann. The 'new historicism' is distinguished from the old by a lack of faith in the objectivity of historical study and replaced by an emphasis on the way the past is constructed or invented in the present. Felperin quotes the opening paragraph of Catherine Belsey's *The Subject of Tragedy* (1985):

History is always in practice a reading of the past. We make a narrative out of the available 'documents', the written texts (and maps and buildings and suits of armour) we interpret in order to produce a knowledge of a world which is no longer present. And yet it is always from the present that we produce this knowledge: from the present in the sense that it is only from what is still extant, still available that we make it; and from the present in the sense that we make it out of an understanding formed by the present. We bring what we know now to bear on what remains from the past to produce an intelligible history.

Felperin comments: '"history" is freely acknowledged to be a kind of story-telling towards the present, that is, a textual construct at once itself an interpretation and itself open to interpretation' (Felperin 1991: 89). The idea of a single 'History' is rejected in favour of the postmodern concept (Belsey 1991: 27) of 'histories', 'an ongoing series of human constructions, each representing the past at particular present moments for particular present purposes' (Cox and Reynolds 1993: 4).

The growth of radical alternative histories, such as women's history, oral history and postcolonial rewriting of Eurocentric and other imperialist viewpoints, together with the more general blurring of disciplinary boundaries between historiography, sociology, anthropology and cultural studies, have all cast doubt on the validity, relevance or accessibility of historical 'facts' (Barker *et al.* 1991: 4). Cultural history draws closer to the concerns of the humanities and anthropology: 'The deciphering of meaning ... is taken to be the central task of cultural history, just as it was posed by Geertz to be the central task of cultural anthropology' (Hunt 1989: 12). With the emergence of the postmodern concept of 'histories' several questions have been put on the agenda of theory: for example, what valid distinctions can be made between the 'narrative' of history and the 'fiction' of texts? (Montrose (1989: 20) called for the recognition of 'the historicity of texts and the textuality of history'; see also White (1973).) What are the implications of our construction of the past from our present situation? What is the relationship between 'histories' and power?

The rise of newer forms of literary historicism is connected, in part, with social change and the effort to recover histories for blacks, women and minority groups within society. In turn, these social aims are linked with the recuperation of forgotten texts, including texts that have never been considered worthy of academic study. Such changes have, of course, benefited the academic study of children's literature.

The major influence in all this is that of Michel Foucault. As David Perkins puts it,

> [Foucault] encouraged his readers to reject the traditional Romantic model of literary change as continuous development, to resituate literary texts by relating them to discourses and representations that were not literary, and to explore the ideological aspects of texts in order to intervene in the social struggles of the present, and these remain characteristic practices of present-day historical contextualism – of New Historicism, feminist historiography, and cultural criticism.
>
> (Perkins 1991: 4)

Not everyone, however, would agree with the implied radical political stance of the new historicist movements (see Veeser 1994). Felperin argues that there are two broad schools of new historicism, the American, sometimes called 'cultural poetics', and the British, often referred to as 'cultural materialism': 'Whereas cultural poetics inhabits a discursive field in which Marxism has never really been present, its British counterpart inhabits one from which Marxism has never really been absent' (Felperin 1991: 88).

The radical nature of cultural materialism is made clear in books such as Dollimore and Sinfield's collection of essays, *Political Shakespeare*. In their foreword, the editors define cultural materialism as 'a combination of historical context, theoretical method, political commitment and textual analysis' (Dollimore and Sinfield 1985: vii). The historical context

> undermines the transcendent significance traditionally accorded to the literary text and allows us to recover its histories; theoretical method detaches the text from immanent criticism which seeks only to reproduce it in its own terms; socialist and feminist commitment confronts the conservative categories in which most criticism has hitherto been conducted; textual analysis locates the critique of traditional approaches where it cannot be ignored. We call this 'cultural materialism'.
>
> (Dollimore and Sinfield 1985: vii)

Examples of how some of these new historicist ideas could be applied to children's literature are provided by the work of Mitzi Myers (Myers 1988, 1989, 1992). In a statement which blends something of the American and the British brands, Myers argues that a new historicism of children's literature would

> integrate text and socio-historic context, demonstrating on the one hand how extraliterary cultural formations shape literary discourse and on the other how literary practices are actions that make things happen – by shaping the psychic and moral consciousness of young readers but also by performing many more diverse kinds of cultural work, from satisfying authorial fantasies to legitimating or subverting dominant class and gender ideologies ... It would want to know how and why a tale or poem came to say what it does, what the environing circumstances were (including the uses a particular sort of children's literature served for its author, its child and adult readers, and its culture), and what kinds of cultural statements and questions the work was responding to. It would pay particular attention to the conceptual and symbolic fault lines denoting a text's time-, place-, gender-, and class-specific ideological mechanisms ... It would examine ... a book's material production, its publishing history, its audiences and their reading practices, its initial reception, and its critical history, including how it got inscribed in or deleted from the canon.
>
> (Myers 1988: 42)

Myers has also argued that 'Notions of the "child", "childhood" and "children's literature" are contingent, not essentialist; embodying the social construction of a particular historical context; they are useful fictions intended to redress reality as much as to reflect it' (Myers 1989: 52), and that such notions today are bound up with the language and ideology of Romantic literature and criticism (Myers 1992; see also McGann 1983).

These ideas have been applied by Myers to eighteenth-century children's authors such as Maria Edgeworth. The child constructed by Romantic ideology recurs as Wordsworth's 'child of nature' in such figures as Kipling's Mowgli and Frances Hodgson Burnett's Dickon in *The Secret Garden* (Knoepflmacher 1977; Richardson 1992) and, as one critic points out, 'many children's books that feature children obviously wiser than the adults they must deal with – like F. Anstey's *Vice Versa* or E. Nesbit's *Story of the Amulet* – would have been unthinkable without the Romantic revaluation of childhood' (Richardson 1992: 128).

Many of the changes outlined earlier on in this chapter in relation to *historiography* and history studies have appeared in literary *studies of historical fiction for children*. In 1992, as part of his discussion of the intellectual and ideological bases for the writing of historical fiction for children, John Stephens argued that the intellectual and ideological bases of the genre were no longer dominant within Western society because much of the historical fiction for children which had been published up to then had been shaped by humanistic ideas such as

> [that] there is an essential human nature which underlies all changing surface appearances; important human qualities, such as Reason, Love, Honour, Loyalty, Courage etc., are transhistorical; human desires are reasonably constant, and what differs are the social mechanisms evolved to express or contain them; individual experiences thus reflect constant, unchanging truths; history imparts 'lessons' because events, in a substantial sense, are repeatable and repeated. These assumptions inform the work of

most writers of historical fiction for children, and are overtly articulated in the writings of many, such as Lively and Rosemary Sutcliff.

(Stephens 1992: 203)

But, the postmodern 'challenge to the humanist position comes from cultural relativism', in which

> the individual subject is constructed as a point at which cultural systems and structures
> intersect and so determine the mode of being of the subject; there is no common
> ground between peoples of different places and times; the cultural assumptions of one
> society cannot be applied to another; events are not repeatable, but apparent analogies
> between different events are constructed from the point of view of a particular social
> formation in time and space; there is no transcendent truth.
>
> (Stephens 1992: 203)

Although Stephens does not pose the question, we might ask: how far do recent works
of children's historical fiction embody these new postmodern values? According to an
essay by Danielle Thaler in a recent collection, nothing much has changed. Thaler examined a group of historical novels for young people by French authors published during the
last thirty years. She concluded,

> Historical fiction for young people therefore follows in the footsteps of the adult
> historical novel, the only difference being that it often chooses a hero of its readers'
> age, who has a mentality and psychology close to those of our children and teenagers.
>
> (Thaler 2003: 10)

However, Deborah Stevenson, discussing 'shifting ideas of objective reality in
history and fiction', does point to changes in the treatment of 'non-fiction history' for
children: 'Non-fiction for children is beginning tentatively to examine the process of
history-making itself, to examine historiographic questions of objectivity and subjectivity and to call into question the existence of a completely knowable history'
(Stevenson 2003: 23–4).

Referring to the argument of Hayden White that 'histories gain part of their explanatory effect by their success in making stories out of mere chronicles' (White 1978 quoted
in Stevenson 2003: 25), Stevenson argues that newer histories for children 'overtly place
history into the category of narrative, emphasising the story in history'.

> These histories are not considering all viewpoints as equal ... they are merely
> suggesting that none of them possesses complete objective truth ... they offer written
> history as a metaphor for the past, as a self-aware representation of a kind of under-
> standing of another time.
>
> (Stevenson 2003: 25)

But, complexly and paradoxically, in historical *fiction* for children,

> The belief in historical fact *qua* fact is if anything stronger ... Historical fiction for chil-
> dren acts as history improved, a superior replacement for the real but flawed thing ...
> The genres are starting to trade places. History is offering possibilities, while fiction

offers certainty ... history is undercutting the authority of narrative while historical fiction still clings to it, asserting itself as more real than fact because it is a better story ... The change in historical fiction has been the embrace of relativity, the idea that someone else is going to see a different part of the past, but history begins to suggest the possibility of complete subjectivity – that no one is seeing the past quite right and that the stories will not match up.

(Stevenson 2003: 27–8)

Out of the many studies of children's historical fiction, two studies of post-war British novels may serve to illustrate the diversity of critical approaches now being employed and the way the new historiography feeds into studies of literary texts. Adrienne Gavin's essay (Gavin 2003) examines novels by Lucy M. Boston, Philippa Pearce, Penelope Farmer and Penelope Lively in which 'an ostensibly realist past is introduced into a realist present. Links to the past occur through quirks of fantasy or possible fantasy, by means of the supernatural, time-slips, dreams, or the power of the imagination' (Gavin 2003: 159).

She shows that the past presented in these novels is far from being realistic; rather, it is a metaphor for the imagination and for the creative act: 'The child protagonists, as "writers", re-create through their imaginations a history they have never experienced while in turn their creators ... necessarily rely on textualized narrativizations of history in order to create their own imagined versions of the past' (Gavin 2003: 161).

Valerie Krips's book *The Presence of the Past: Memory, Heritage and Childhood in Postwar Britain* (2000) is an important study which cannot easily be summarised here. It is a book which is grounded in the study of children's literature but moves well beyond the purely literary by the use of cultural theories by such figures as Pierre Nora. From an examination of post-war children's fiction (by writers such as Philippa Pearce, Rosemary Sutcliff, Susan Cooper and Alan Garner), in which she notes that a recurrent plot revolves around 'a child stumbling across an artefact from the past and over the course of the novel, trying to understand the relevance of the artefact to the present', she notes that this motif 'coincided with the appearance of the heritage movement in Britain' (Wojcik-Andrews 2002: 123).

Krips argues that the distinction between history and heritage is not much more than the lost and found of memory realised through objects that surround us: what we see as individuals and as nations is how we imagine ourselves to be. Country houses, books, and/or famous child characters such as Alice who function as representatives of a golden age of childhood are plucked from the past and presented in the present as symbolic reminders of a land of Hope and Glory long gone: the National Trust does it with the conservation of stately homes, children's writers do it with the construction of canonical fictions and ideal images of the child.

(Wojcik-Andrews 2002: 126)

The same crises in the humanities which resulted in radical questioning of the nature of history and the emergence of new historiographies of culture, including literary new historicism, also brought forth *cultural studies*. In *Keywords*, Raymond Williams describes culture as 'one of the two or three most complicated words in the English language' (Williams 1976: 76). Culture is an ambiguous term: a problem shared, perhaps, by all concepts which are concerned with totality, including history, ideology, society and myth. Disciplines such as cultural geography tend towards a mainly anthropological understanding of culture. But, in a book published in 2000, Don Mitchell argues for a more political understanding of culture: 'culture is politics by another name'. He selects six important ways of understanding the term 'culture':

> First, culture is the opposite of nature. It is what makes humans human. Second, 'culture' is the actual, perhaps unexamined, patterns and differentiations of a people (as in 'Aboriginal culture' or 'German culture' – culture is a way of life). Third, it is the processes by which these patterns developed ... Fourth, the term indicates a set of markers that set one people off from another and which indicate to us our member-ship in a group ... Fifth, culture is the way that all these patterns, processes, and markers are represented (that is, cultural activity, whether high, low, pop, or folk, that produces *meaning*). Finally, the idea of culture often indicates a hierarchical ordering of all these processes, activities, ways of life, and cultural production (as when people compare cultures or cultural activities against each other).
>
> (Mitchell 2000: 14)

'Cultural studies' is an equally ambiguous term, but most commentators would agree that cultural studies is 'concerned with the generation and circulation of meanings in industrial societies' (Fiske 1987: 254). It is difficult to define the field of cultural studies very precisely because, as Brantlinger argues, it has 'emerged from the current crises and contradictions of the humanities and social science disciplines not as a tightly coherent, unified movement with a fixed agenda, but as a loosely coherent group of tendencies, issues and questions' (1990: ix). An anthology published in 1992 suggests the following major categories of current work in the field:

> the history of cultural studies, gender and sexuality, nationhood and national identity, colonialism and post-colonialism, race and ethnicity, popular culture and its audi-ences, science and ecology, identity politics, pedagogy, the politics of aesthetics, cultural institutions, the politics of disciplinarity, discourse and textuality, history, and global culture in a postmodern age.
>
> (Grossberg *et al.* 1992: 1)

But the problem with trying to define cultural studies is that it is 'magnetic'. As Toby Miller, editor of a collection of essays published in 2001 entitled *A Companion to Cultural Studies,* explains:

> It accretes various tendencies that are splintering the human sciences: Marxism, femi-nism, queer theory, and the postcolonial. The 'cultural' has become a 'master-trope' in the humanities, blending and blurring textual analysis of popular culture with social theory, and focusing on the margins of power rather than reproducing established lines of force and authority.
>
> (Miller 2001: 1)

Unlike the traditional humanities, cultural studies focuses less on canonical works of art and more on popular media: 'The humanities' historic task of criticising entertainment is sidestepped and new commercial trends become part of cultural studies itself' (Miller 2001: 1). In spite of its diverse agenda of interests and approaches, Miller argues that cultural studies does have shared concerns and commitments:

Cultural studies is animated by subjectivity and power – how human subjects are formed and how they experience cultural and social space. It takes its agenda and mode of analysis from economics, politics, media and communication studies, sociology, literature, education, the law, science and technology studies, anthropology, and history, with a particular focus on gender, race, class, and sexuality in everyday life, commingling textual and social theory under the sign of a commitment to progressive social change.

(2001: 1)

The political commitment of cultural studies has been debated throughout its history, especially since 'the linguistic turn' of poststructuralism which has tended to place 'textualism', rather than politics, at its heart: 'Certain philosophical perspectives have gained a degree of currency in reading and interpreting cultural forms in a way that often obliterates the social context within which such practices are embedded' (Carrington 2001: 286), and an important figure in American cultural studies, Lawrence Grossberg, 'called on cultural studies to provide a dynamic way of "politicizing theory and theorizing politics" that combines abstraction and grounded analysis' (Miller 2001: 3).

Grossberg *et al.* (1992) stress the shapeless nature of the field and the variety of methodologies in use: '[cultural studies] remains a diverse and often contentious enterprise, encompassing different positions and trajectories in specific contexts, addressing many questions, drawing nourishment from multiple roots, and shaping itself within different institutions and locations' (1992: 2–3). There are, for example, distinctions to be made between the British and American traditions of cultural studies (just as there are between the two schools of 'new historicism' in literary studies – see above). The British tradition, which may be traced back to the pioneering work of F. R. Leavis and Denys Thompson in the 1930s (Leavis and Thompson 1933) but, more particularly, arises from the work of Raymond Williams (Williams 1958), believes that the study of culture involves both

> symbolic and material domains ... not privileging one domain over the other but interrogating the relation between the two ... Continually engaging with the political, economic, erotic, social, and ideological, cultural studies entails the study of all the relations between all the elements in a whole way of life.
>
> (Grossberg *et al.* 1992: 4, 14)

From the later work of Raymond Williams, from the work of Stuart Hall and others at the University of Birmingham's (UK) Centre for Contemporary Cultural Studies, and from major bodies of theory such as Marxism, feminism, psychoanalysis and poststructuralism, the British tradition derived the central theoretical concepts of articulation, conjuncture, hegemony, ideology, identity and representation. (See, for example, Williams 1975, 1976, 1977, 1989.) But even British cultural studies is not a coherent and homogeneous body of work: it is characterised by disagreements, 'divergencies in direction and concern, by conflict among theoretical commitments and political agendas' (Grossberg *et al.* 1992: 10) or, as Stuart Hall put it,

> Cultural studies has multiple discourses; it has a number of different histories. It is a whole set of formations, it has its own different conjunctures and moments in the past. It included many different kinds of work ... It always was a set of unstable formations.
>
> (Hall 1996: 26)

For example, Hall pointed to the revolutionary impact of feminism for the field of cultural studies: gender and sexuality had to be understood as central to the workings of power in society. In 1992, he wrote: 'It has forced a rethink in every major substantive area of work (Hall 1992: 282 quoted in Mitchell 2000: 54). As Mitchell comments,

> No longer was it possible to study the ... base – the workings of the economy – without also and at the same time studying what had been seen as epiphenomenal to that base (relations of family, ideologies of gender, social structures of sexuality, etc.).
>
> (Mitchell 2000: 55)

Although accepting Stuart Hall's words 'about continuities and breaks', Ben Carrington argues that it was 'the huge social, cultural, and economic changes that occurred in Britain during and immediately after the 1939–45 war' which provided the context within which cultural studies was to emerge around 1957:

> It is important to restate the fact that the formation of cultural studies was, first and foremost, a political project aimed at popular education for working-class adults. There was always a tension then with the provision of such education becoming incorporated – both ideologically and institutionally – within 'bourgeois' university departments, which, for the most part, is what did happen.
>
> (Carrington 2001: 277–8)

And he warns that 'there is danger of narrativising cultural studies' historical purpose ... into a depoliticised humanities discipline' (Carrington 2001: 279). He is anxious to emphasise that cultural studies is as much concerned with 'practice' as with texts, and he criticises earlier histories of British cultural studies for tending to

> highlight the publication of academic *texts* as 'producing' cultural studies as an academic discipline taught within universities, rather than seeing such texts themselves as being the outcome of a wider sociopolitical process of education from the 1930s and 1940s aimed at social transformation, situated within adult and workers' education colleges.
>
> (Carrington 2001: 277)

The radical aspect of British cultural studies has, unsurprisingly, drawn criticism from some quarters. Kenneth Minogue called cultural studies the 'politico-intellectual junkyard of the Western world' (Minogue 1994: 27 quoted in Miller 2001: 10); and Chris Patten, a former Conservative member of the UK Parliament, called it 'Disneyland for the weaker minded' (Miller 2001: 10).

In the USA, a somewhat different inflection has been given to cultural studies by the 'new ethnography', rooted primarily in anthropological theory and practice (a 'postdisciplinary anthropology') which is, in turn, linked to work by feminists and black and postcolonial theorists concerned with identity, history and social relations (Grossberg *et al.* 1992: 14).

In the work of some cultural studies theorists, one can detect the following characteristics: *first*, a belief that reality can only be made sense of through language or other cultural systems which are embedded within history. *Second*, a focus upon power and struggle. In cultural terms, the struggle is for meaning: dominant groups attempt to render as 'natural' meanings which serve their interests, whereas subordinate groups resist this process in various ways, trying to make meanings that serve *their* interests (Fiske 1987: 255). An obvious example is the cultural struggle between patriarchy and feminism and the impact that feminism had on cultural studies in Britain in the 1980s (Hall 1992: 282); but, of course, divisions into groups in society can be along lines of race, class, age and so on, as well as gender. However, British cultural studies was criticised for some years because of its relative neglect of race and colonialism. For example, in 1987, Paul Gilroy argued that it was essential to understand that histories of colonialism and Empire are 'central' to 'understanding how Britain's economy' has been constructed and 'its class relations mediated, and subsequently how this affected the formation of its culture more generally, and its sense of national identity' (Gilroy 1987: 12 quoted in Carrington 2001: 282). He deplored 'the invisibility of "race" within the field' of cultural studies in Britain and, most importantly, with the forms of nationalism endorsed by 'a discipline which, in spite of itself, tends towards a morbid celebration of England and Englishness from which blacks are systematically excluded' (Gilroy 1987: 12). *Third*, cultural studies has tried to theorise subjectivity as a socio-cultural construction. Some theorists, under the influence of poststructuralist psychoanalytical thinking and Althusserian notions of ideology, replace the idea of the individual by the concept of the 'subject'. The 'subject' and his or her 'subjectivity' is a social construction: 'Thus a biological female can have a masculine subjectivity (that is, she can make sense of the world and of her self and her place in that world through patriarchal ideology). Similarly, a black can have a white subjectivity' (Fiske 1987: 258).

But because subjectivity is a social construction, it is always open to change. All cultural systems, including language, literature and the products of mass communication, play a part in the construction and reconstruction of the subject. It is in this way, according to the Althusserian wing of cultural studies, that ideology is constantly reproduced in people.

This notion can be seen perhaps more clearly in the *fourth* characteristic of cultural studies – the way it views acts of communication, including the 'reading process'. As one theorist puts it, when talking about the 'reading' of a television programme as cultural text: 'Reading becomes a negotiation between the social sense inscribed in the program and the meanings of social experience made by its wide variety of viewers: this negotiation is a discursive one' (Fiske 1987: 268). The relevance of this notion to children's literature is not difficult to perceive.

The *fifth* characteristic is that cultural studies is not exclusively concerned with popular culture to the exclusion of 'high' culture, or vice versa:

> Cultural studies does not require us to repudiate elite cultural forms ... rather cultural studies requires us to identify the operation of specific practices, of how they continuously reinscribe the line between legitimate and popular culture, and of what they accomplish in specific contexts.
>
> (Grossberg *et al.* 1992: 13)

As a result, cultural studies does interest itself in the formation, continuation and changes in literary canons, including those of children's literature. For example, books originally denied inclusion in the canon of children's literature, such as Baum's *Oz* books, have later received recognition and have been included. Other books traditionally included in the canon of children's literature, such as Lewis's Narnia series, Tolkien's *The Hobbit* and Kipling's *Jungle Book*, have been criticised on the grounds that the values they contain are too exclusively male and white.

The *sixth* characteristic is the use of ideology as a central concept, either as a 'critical' concept or as a neutral concept. Materialist, political approaches deriving from Marxism and feminism obviously stress *power* as the major component of cultural text, power which is often hidden or rendered apparently 'natural' through the process of ideology. These approaches use what has been called the 'critical' concept of ideology which is 'essentially linked to the process of sustaining asymmetrical relations of power – that is, to the process of maintaining domination' (Thompson 1984: 4). If ideology is embodied in cultural text, the major task of the cultural critic is not only understanding the meaning of the text but also unmasking what appears as natural as a social construction which favours a particular class or group in society. This process of 'ideology critique' or ideological deconstruction is often carried out in literary studies using an approach, derived from Williams, involving a combination of textual analysis, theoretical method, study of historical context, and a political commitment to socialism and feminism.

However, ideology can also be used in a neutral sense (Ricoeur 1986) and this is reflected in the work of Fred Inglis, who has written at length on children's literature (for example, Inglis 1975, 1981). Inglis favours not cultural materialism but cultural hermeneutics. In *Cultural Studies* (1993), he argues in favour of making cultural studies 'synonymous with the study of values (and valuing)' (Inglis 1993: 190). The book is dedicated to the cultural anthropologist Clifford Geertz, with his influential view that 'man is an animal suspended in webs of significance he himself has spun' and that 'those webs are what we call culture'. For Geertz, the analysis of culture, therefore, will be 'an interpretive one in search of meaning', and culture itself is defined as 'an assemblage of texts' and 'a story they tell themselves about themselves' (Geertz 1975: 5, 448). So the model of cultural analysis Inglis favours is the interpretative one which aims not to *unmask* texts, using such critical concepts as ideology or hegemony which deconstruct and demystify ideologies, but to *understand* intersubjective meanings (Inglis 1993: 148). He argues against the tendency within cultural studies to collapse 'both aesthetics and morality into politics' so that 'the study of culture translates into politics without remainder' (1993: 175, 181). He quotes Dollimore and Sinfield's statement (see above) that cultural materialism 'registers its commitment to the transformation of a social order which exploits people on grounds of race, gender and class' (Dollimore and Sinfield 1985: viii) but asks, using the same phrase which formed the title of his book about children's literature (Inglis 1981), 'What about the promise of happiness held out by art? What about art itself?' (Inglis 1993: 181).

Following Geertz's concept, Inglis defines culture as 'an ensemble of *stories* we tell ourselves about ourselves' (Inglis 1993: 206) and argues that our historically changing identity is formed from experience and the 'narrative tradition' of which we are part. It is from this identity that we interpret the world. In a passage strongly relevant to the study of children's literature (see, for example, Watkins 1994), he goes on to argue that

> the stories we tell ourselves about ourselves are not just a help to moral education; they comprise the only moral education which can gain purchase on the modern world. They are not aids to sensitivity nor adjuncts to the cultivated life. They are theories with which to think forwards ... and understand backwards.
>
> (Inglis 1993: 214)

Although there are obviously major debates both within and outside cultural studies, nevertheless most scholars of children's literature would agree with the following statement:

> Cultural studies, at its best, has much of value to say about ... how discourse and imagery are organized in complex and shifting patterns of meaning and how these

meanings are reproduced, negotiated, and struggled over in the flow and flux of everyday life.

(Murdoch 1995: 94)

But, because of the variety within the cultural studies paradigm and the dynamic nature of the field, it is difficult to *generalise* about features which underlie such work in the study of children's literature and media. However, important work is being developed by Karín Lesnik-Oberstein on the cultural meanings of the child and childhood in children's literature and media (see Lesnik-Oberstein 1998). (For a collection of essays using different cultural studies approaches but focusing on important aspects of children's literature and media, see *A Necessary Fantasy? The Heroic Figure in Children's Popular Culture* (Jones and Watkins 2000): articles in the collection cover such topics as pony stories, Robin Hood films, comic-book heroes and superheroes, Action Man toys and Dr Who.)

Another area of investigation which could serve as a case study of work using a critical cultural studies perspective in the study of children's literature and media is what could be called 'childhood, media, the culture industries, and consumerism', concentrating on the cultural impact of the Disney Corporation. What Walt Disney discovered in the 1930s was that children will come to perceive themselves as part of a community 'based on their shared consumption of mass media and related merchandise'. Ellen Seiter, in her book *Sold Separately: Children and Parents in Consumer Culture*, points out that 'Consumer culture provides children with a shared repository of images, characters, plots and themes: it provides the basis for small talk and play, and it does this on a national, even global scale' (Seiter 1993: 7).

Similarly, Eric Smoodin, editor of *Disney Discourse*, a book critical of Disney's role in American culture, argues that we need to

gain a new sense of Disney's importance, because of the manner in which his work in film and television is connected to other projects in urban planning, ecological politics, product merchandising, United States domestic and global policy formation, technological innovation, and constructions of national character ... Disney constructs childhood so as to make it entirely compatible with consumerism.

(Smoodin 1994: 4–5, 18)

In the editorial to a special issue of *Children's Literature Association Quarterly* on 'Children's Media of the Twentieth Century', Anne Morey argues that, while social scientists have paid attention to the media for some years, scholars in children's literature need to 'bring their interest in textual meanings coupled with an increased sense of both historical context and the institutional matrices out of which children's texts are produced' (Morey 1997: 2). In the editorial to another special issue of *Children's Literature Association Quarterly*, this time on 'Children and Money', Judith Plotz refers to Stephen Kline's argument that, to an extent unprecedented in history, American children are no longer children but what trade professionals call a 'market': consumers with money to spend and the will and authority to spend it. Kline's argument is that in the age of marketing, toys 'serve a new function: they are the templates through which children are being introduced into the attitudes and social relations of consumerism' (Kline 1993: 349). Plotz adds that, according to a 1999 report, children now constitute the fastest growing consumer market in the USA and 'influence half a trillion dollars in consumer spending a year'. Plotz continues:

With children manipulated as never before by a seductive commercial rhetoric of make-believe choice and empowerment, scholars of children's culture are driven to examine both the systems of control and the possibilities of liberation in all the existing discourses of children's culture.

(Plotz 1999: 111)

The problem of arguing for change in public policy towards television, for example, is, according to Kline, that

as long as no 'harm' to children is proven, public policy makers have acceded to the marketers' view that television should now be governed by the principle of commercial speech ... Surely nobody can feign surprise anymore that commercial television fails to educate, inform or inspire our children ... Children are simply finding their place within consumer culture ... What the issue of proven harm obscures is the fact that we have granted to marketers enormous powers to meddle in the key realms of children's culture – the peer group, fantasy, stories and play.

(Kline 1993: 349–50)

However, Ellen Seiter offers a less pessimistic view when she points out that children are not simply passive consumers of goods and media:

children are creative in their appropriation of consumer goods and media, and the meanings they make of these are not necessarily and completely in line with a materialist ethos ... children create their own meanings from the stories and symbols of consumer culture.

(Seiter 1993: 299)

On the other hand, Henry Giroux argues that it is very important for us to analyse critically the power of the Disney Corporation. He focuses on the Disney films and argues:

these films appear to inspire at least as much cultural authority and legitimacy for teaching specific roles, values, and ideals as do the more traditional sites of learning such as the public schools, religious institutions, and the family ... Unlike the often hard-nosed, joyless reality of schooling, children's films provide a high-tech visual space where adventure and pleasure meet in a fantasy world of possibilities and a commercial sphere of consumption and commodification ... Disney's image as an icon of American culture is consistently reinforced through the penetration of the Disney empire into every aspect of social life. Children experience Disney's cultural influence through a maze of representations and products found in home videos, shopping malls, classroom instructional films, box offices, popular television programs and family restaurants ... Disney now produces prototypes for model schools, families, identities, communities, and the way the future is to be understood through a particular construction of the past ... But Disney does more than provide prototypes for upscale communities; it also makes a claim on the future through its nostalgic view of the past and its construction of public memory as a metonym for the magical kingdom.

(Giroux 1998: 53–5)

Nevertheless, Giroux thinks it is important not to be simplistic about Disney. He does not wish either to condemn

Disney as an ideological reactionary deceptively promoting a conservative worldview under the guise of entertainment or celebrate Disney as doing nothing more than providing sources of joy and happiness to children all over the world ... Critically analysing how Disney films work to construct meanings, induce pleasures, and reproduce ideologically loaded fantasies is not meant as an exercise in disparagement. On the contrary, as a \$4.7 billion company, Disney's corporate and cultural influence is so enormous and far-reaching that it should go neither unchecked nor unmediated.

(Giroux 1998: 56–7)

Giroux then proceeds to analyse the portrayal of girls and women in *The Little Mermaid*, *The Lion King* and *Beauty and the Beast*, and racial stereotyping in *Aladdin* and *Pocahontas*.

In the preface to his book *Sticks and Stones* (2001), Jack Zipes is provocatively critical of the way society regards and treats children:

Everything we do to, with, and for our children is influenced by capitalist market conditions and the hegemonic interests of ruling corporate elites. In simple terms, we calculate what is best for our children by regarding them as investments and turning them into commodities.

(Zipes 2001: xi)

In the past twenty years in America, argues Zipes, many diverse groups have been formed 'to do battle with the culture industry and government on behalf of children, including teenagers'. The first group are activists such as

media watch groups, family associations, religious institutions, and feminist organizations [which] place pressure on the government and mass media to alter shows, images and literature that they feel are destroying the moral health of our children. In their view children are innocent and passive victims and are at the mercy of outside forces.

(Zipes 2001: xi–xii)

The second group is made up largely of theorists 'who argue that children are much more creative and independent than we think' (Zipes 2001: xii). Later in the book, he argues, as others have done, that

The family, schools, and religious organizations have been the nodal points of socialization and acculturation, but their authority ... has yielded and been undercut by the force of the mass-mediated market ... Difference and otherness, rebellion and nonconformity have become commodities that children are encouraged to acquire because they can use them to defy parents and the community while furthering the same profit-oriented interests of corporate America.

(Zipes 2001: 12)

In recent years, there has been a growing interest in theme parks, in particular Disneyland, as examples of postmodern 'texts'. Suzanne Rahn analyses the 'narrative strategies' of some of Disneyland's rides. For example, she argues that Disneyland's 'dark rides' are 'conceived as narratives by the Imagineers'. Such rides resemble theatre:

In a traditional play, however, the audience sits motionless while the sequence of scenes is performed. In a theme park ride, the sequence of scenes is fixed in space – it is the audience that moves physically from scene to scene, literally *drawn into* the story.

(Rahn 2000: 19)

Other rides such as 'The Haunted Mansion' reflect the 'increasing presence of the post-modern, in American culture:

Postmodern literature abandons linear narrative for a randomly ordered sequence of events. It makes playful use of traditional elements removed from their original context and drained of meaning, as a way of escaping the burden of the past.

(Rahn 2000: 24)

Louis Marin uses Disneyland as an example of a 'degenerate utopia':

a supposedly happy, harmonious and non-conflictual space set aside from the 'real' world 'outside' in such a way as to soothe and mollify, to entertain, to invent history and to cultivate a nostalgia for some mythical past, to perpetuate the fetish of commodity culture rather than to critique it. Disneyland eliminates the troubles of actual travel by assembling the rest of the world, properly sanitized and mythologized, into one place of pure fantasy containing multiple spatial orders ... it offers no critique of the existing state of affairs on the outside. It merely perpetuates the fetish of commodity culture and tech-nological wizardry in a pure, sanitized and a-historical form.

(Harvey 2000: 167)

Disney theme parks are also connected with successful retailing:

The shopping mall was conceived of as a fantasy world in which commodity reigned supreme ... the whole environment seemed designed to induce nirvana rather than critical awareness. And many other cultural institutions – museums and heritage centers, arenas for spectacle, exhibitions and festivals – seem to have as their aim the cultivation of nostalgia, the production of sanitized collective memories, the nurturing of uncritical aesthetic sensibilities, and the absorption of future possibilities into a non-conflictual arena that is eternally present.

(Harvey 2000: 168)

Although this chapter cannot adequately cover the work of Karín Lesnik-Oberstein (Lesnik-Oberstein 1994, 1998; and Bradbury 2002), it is an important example of the contemporary postmodern challenge to liberal humanist and essentialist assumptions underlying approaches to the child in children's literature criticism. Referring to the work of Jacqueline Rose (1984), Lesnik-Oberstein explains that, in the constructivist approach,

Childhood, and children, are seen primarily as being constituted by, and constituting, sets of meanings in language ... Childhood is, as an identity, a mediator and reposi-tory of ideas in Western culture about consciousness and experience, morality and values, property and privacy, but perhaps most importantly, it has been assigned a crucial relationship to language itself.

(Lesnik-Oberstein 1998: 2, 6)

Cultural studies has affected many disciplines: for example, 'the new cultural geography' has grown considerably since its origins in the late 1980s. Peter Jackson (1989) was perhaps chief spokesperson for the early developments in recent cultural geography: Jackson and other cultural geographers built on British cultural studies but 'sought also to explicitly "spatialise" these studies', by showing how space and time are central to the 'maps of meaning' that constitute cultural experience (Mitchell 2000: 42). Jackson argued that culture 'is the level at which social groups develop distinct patterns of life' and hence 'are *maps of meaning* through which the world is made intelligible' (Jackson 1989: 2). The 'new cultural geography' is now associated with names such as David Harvey, who argues in his important book *The Condition of Postmodernity* that 'There has been a sea-change in cultural as well as in political–economic practices since around 1972. This sea-change is bound up with the emergence of new dominant ways in which we experience space and time' (Harvey 1989: vii).

There has been an amazing proliferation of work in cultural geography from the 1990s onwards, exploring ideas of landscape, spatiality, utopia, globalisation, heritage and national identity, and geographies of gender and of race, which could prove vital for the cultural study of children's literature and media. The field is already too vast to summarise adequately here, but Mitchell explains that the area that gained 'the earliest sustained criticism and reconstruction by new cultural geography' was landscape research (Mitchell 2000: 61). The research developed on four fronts. Some cultural geographers

> sought to connect the very idea of landscape to its historical development as part of the capitalist and Enlightenment transformation in the early modern period. That is to say, the goal of many studies has been to show how the land was made over in the image of 'landscape' – a particular and particularly ideological 'way of seeing' the land and people's relationship to that land. [In particular, see Cosgrove 1984.]

Second, 'other geographers reinvigorated the notion of "reading" the landscape ... to problematise the whole notion of exactly what constitutes the "text" to be read – and precisely how it is possible ... to read it.' That is, work began to focus 'on the interpretation of the *symbolic* aspects of landscapes' (for example, Daniels and Cosgrove 1988; Duncan and Duncan 1988). Third, 'where much traditional cultural geography had examined rural and past landscapes, some new work interested in landscape and culture focused on urban and contemporary scenes', and fourth, 'a sustained feminist critique of landscape studies – and of the very idea of landscape – has been launched' (for example, Rose 1993). What was new in these emphases was that they were 'infused with strong evaluations of the politics of class, gender, race, ethnicity ... and sexuality' and consequently 'the study of the spatiality of identity itself has become an issue of deep concern within cultural geography'. This explains, in part, the explosion of research on 'the cultural–geographic politics of sexuality, gender, race, and national identity' (Mitchell 2000: 61–2).

For scholars of children's literature and media, perhaps the most relevant research from cultural geography is that which involves 'reading the landscape'. For, as Mitchell explains,

> The degree to which landscapes are *made* (by hands and minds) and represented (by particular people and classes, and through the accretion of history and myth) indicates that landscapes are in some important senses 'authored'. Hence landscape can be understood to be a kind of text.
>
> (Mitchell 2000: 122)

But the reading of such texts is always a contested process and, moreover, the reading is linked to race and gender identities:

> Meaning is naturalised in the landscape, and only through concerted contestation are those sedimented meanings prised open ... By examining the various metaphors that govern our understanding of landscape (such as seeing the landscape as a text or a stage) and linking them to important axes of cultural differentiation (such as gender), [we can explore] how landscape functions both as a source of meaning and as a form of social regulation ... The production of cultural spaces ... [including landscape] is always the production of what Doreen Massey has identified as *power geometries:* the shape and structure of the space in which our lives are given meaning.
>
> (Mitchell 2000: xix–xxi)

Much of the landscape research, particularly on the representation of landscapes, is clearly of interest to children's literature studies. (Examples are Hunt 1987; Stevenson 1996; Thum 1992; Watkins 1992, 1994; Zitterkopf 1984–5.) It is possible to see such works as Grahame's *The Wind in the Willows* and Baum's *The Wizard of Oz* as not only operating as versions of the English and American national myth, with their landscapes representing the 'real' England and the 'real' America, but becoming sites for ideological struggle and appropriation by, for example, the 'culture industries' (Watkins 1992). Another important aspect of landscape is its connection with national identity and the power of some landscapes to be read as a national geography. But

> while landscape representation is an important aspect of nationalism, it is not so hegemonic as to preclude alternative readings or other forms of resistance. Instead, landscape representations are sites of contestation, just as are the landscapes they are meant to depict.
>
> (Mitchell 2000: 119)

National identity is obviously another very important topic which is being increasingly explored by scholars of children's literature (see, for example, Meek 2001).

This chapter has ranged very widely over developments in thinking about history, about the place of history in literary studies, about the complex developments in cultural studies and the way in which 'culture' has become 'a master trope' in the analysis of many kinds of text, including children's literature and media. It is appropriate to end by being reminded of the complexity of what is involved in thinking about history, culture and children's literature:

> Culture is a way people make sense of the world (the stories they tell themselves about themselves, in Clifford Geertz's formulation) but it is also a system of power and domination. Culture is a means of differentiating the world, but is also global and hegemonic. Culture is open and fluid, a 'text' ... always open to multiple readings and interpretations, but it is something with causative power ... Culture is clearly language – or 'text' or 'discourse' – but it is also the social, material construction of such things as 'race' or 'gender'. Culture is a point of political contact, it *is* politics; but it is also both ordinary and the best that has been thought and known.
>
> (Mitchell 2000: 64)

References

Barker, F., Hulme, P. and Iversen, M. (eds) (1991) *Uses of History: Marxism, Postmodernism and the Renaissance*, Manchester: Manchester University Press.

Belsey, C. (1991) 'Making Histories Then and Now: Shakespeare from *Richard II* to *Henry V*', in Barker, F., Hulme, P. and Iversen, M. (eds) *Uses of History: Marxism, Postmodernism and the Renaissance*, Manchester: Manchester University Press.

Bradbury, N. (ed.) (2002) 'Children in Literature', in *The Yearbook of English Studies*, 32, Leeds: Maney Publishing for Modern Humanities Research Association, 77–259.

Brantlinger, P. (1990) *Crusoe's Footprints: Cultural Studies in Britain and America*, New York: Routledge.

Buell, L. (1993) 'Literary History as a Hybrid Genre', in Cox, J. and Reynolds, L. J. (eds) *New Historical Literary Study: Essays on Reproducing Texts, Representing History*, Princeton, NJ: Princeton University Press.

Cannadine, D. (2002) *What is History Now?* Basingstoke: Palgrave Macmillan.

Carrington, B. (2001) 'Decentering the Centre: Cultural Studies in Britain and Its Legacy', in Miller, T. (ed.) *A Companion to Cultural Studies*, Oxford: Blackwell.

Cosgrove, D. (1984) *Social Formation and Symbolic Landscape*, London: Croom Helm.

Cox, J. N. and Reynolds, L. J. (eds) (1993) *New Historical Literary Study: Essays on Reproducing Texts, Representing History*, Princeton, NJ: Princeton University Press.

Daniels, S. and Cosgrove, D. (eds) (1988) *The Iconography of Landscape: Essays on the Symbolic Representation, Design, and Use of Past Environments*, Cambridge: Cambridge University Press.

Dollimore, J. and Sinfield, A. (eds) (1985) *Political Shakespeare: New Essays in Cultural Materialism*, Manchester: Manchester University Press.

Duncan, J. and Duncan, N. (1988) '(Re)Reading the Landscape', *Environment and Planning D: Society and Space* 6: 117–26.

Felperin, H. (1991) ' "Cultural Poetics" versus "Cultural Materialism": The Two New Historicisms in Renaissance Studies', in Barker, F., Hulme, P. and Iversen, M. (eds) *Uses of History: Marxism, Postmodernism and the Renaissance*, Manchester: Manchester University Press.

Fernández-Arnesto, F. (2002) 'What is History *Now?*', in Cannadine, D. (ed.) *What is History Now?* Basingstoke: Palgrave Macmillan.

Fiske, J. (1987) 'British Cultural Studies and Television', in Alien, R. C. (ed.) *Channels of Discourse: Television and Contemporary Criticism*, London: Routledge and Kegan Paul.

Gavin, A. E. (2003) 'The Past Reimagined: History and Literary Creation in British Children's Novels after World War Two', in Lawson-Lucas, A. (ed.) *The Presence of the Past in Children's Literature*, Westport, CT and London: Praeger.

Geertz, C. (1975) *The Interpretation of Cultures*, London: Hutchinson.

Gilroy, P. (1987) *There Ain't No Black in the Union Jack: The Cultural Politics of Race and Nation*, London: Routledge and Kegan Paul.

Giroux, H. (1998) 'Are Disney Movies Good for Your Kids?', in Steinberg, S. R. and Kincheloe, J. L. (eds) *Kinderculture: The Corporate Construction of Childhood*, Boulder, CO: Westview Press.

Grossberg, L., Nelson, C. and Treichler, P. (eds) (1992) *Cultural Studies*, New York: Routledge.

Hall, S. (1992) 'Cultural Studies and Its Theoretical Legacies', in Grossberg, L., Nelson, C. and Treichler, P. (eds) *Cultural Studies*, New York: Routledge.

——(1996) 'Cultural Studies and Its Theoretical Legacies', in Morley, D. and Chen, K. H. (eds) *Stuart Hall: Critical Dialogues in Cultural Studies*, London: Routledge.

Harvey, D. (1989) *The Condition of Postmodernity: An Enquiry into the Origins of Cultural Change*, Oxford: Blackwell.

——(2000) *Spaces of Hope*, Edinburgh: Edinburgh University Press.

Hunt, L. (ed.) (1989) *The New Cultural History*, Berkeley, CA: University of California Press.

Hunt, P. (1987) 'Landscapes and Journeys, Metaphors and Maps: The Distinctive Features of English Fantasy', *Children's Literature Association Quarterly* 12, 1: 11–14.

Inglis, F. (1975) *Ideology and the Imagination*, Cambridge: Cambridge University Press.

——(1981) *The Promise of Happiness: Value and Meaning in Children's Fiction*, Cambridge: Cambridge University Press.

——(1993) *Cultural Studies*, Oxford: Blackwell.

Jackson, P. (1989) *Maps of Meaning: An Introduction to Cultural Geography*, London: Unwin Hyman.

Jenkins, K. (1995) *'On What is History?' From Carr and Elton to Rorty and White*, London and New York: Routledge.

Jones, D. and Watkins, T. (eds) (2000) *A Necessary Fantasy? The Heroic Figure in Children's Popular Culture*, New York and London: Garland.

Kline, S. (1993) *Out of the Garden: Toys, TV and Children's Culture in the Age of Marketing*, London: Verso.

Knoepflmacher, U. C. (1977) 'Mutations of the Wordsworthian Child of Nature', in Knoepflmacher, U. C. and Tennyson, G. B. (eds) *Nature and the Victorian Imagination*, Berkeley, CA: University of California Press.

Krips, V. (2000) *The Presence of the Past: Memory, Heritage and Childhood in Postwar Britain*, New York: Garland.

Leavis, F. R. and Thompson, D. (1933) *Culture and Environment*, London: Chatto and Windus.

Lesnik-Oberstein, K. (1994) *Children's Literature: Criticism and the Fictional Child*, Oxford: Clarendon Press.

——(1998) *Children in Culture: Approaches to Childhood*, Basingstoke: Macmillan.

McGann, J. J. (1983) *The Romantic Ideology: A Critical Investigation*, Chicago, IL and London: University of Chicago Press.

Meek, M. (ed.) (2001) *Children's Literature and National Identity*, Stoke on Trent: Trentham Books.

Miller, T. (ed.) (2001) *A Companion to Cultural Studies*, Oxford: Blackwell.

Minogue, K. (1994) 'Philosophy', *Times Literary Supplement*, 25 November: 27–8.

Mitchell, D. (2000) *Cultural Geography: A Critical Introduction*, Oxford: Blackwell.

Montrose, L. A. (1989) 'Professing the Renaissance: The Poetics and Politics of Culture', in Veeser, H. A. (ed.) *The New Historicism*, London: Routledge.

Morey, A. (1997) 'Introduction' (Special issue, 'Beyond the Written Word: Children's Media of the Twentieth Century'), *Children's Literature Association Quarterly* 22, 1: 2–4.

Murdoch, G. (1995) 'Across the Great Divide: Cultural Analysis and the Condition of Democracy', *Critical Studies in Mass Communication* 12, 1: 89–95.

Myers, M. (1988) 'Missed Opportunities and Critical Malpractice: New Historicism and Children's Literature', *Children's Literature Association Quarterly* 13, 1: 41–3.

——(1989) 'Socializing Rosamond: Educational Ideology and Fictional Form', *Children's Literature Association Quarterly* 14, 2: 52–8.

——(1992) 'Sociologizing Juvenile Ephemera: Periodical Contradictions, Popular Literacy, Transhistorical Readers', *Children's Literature Association Quarterly* 17, 1: 41–5.

Perkins, D. (ed.) (1991) *Theoretical Issues in Literary History*, Cambridge and London: Harvard University Press.

Plotz, J. (1999) 'Introduction: The Child in the Marketplace', *Children's Literature Association Quarterly* 24, 3: 110–11.

Rahn, S. (2000) 'Snow White's Dark Ride: Narrative Strategies at Disneyland', *Bookbird* 38, 1: 19–24.

Richardson, A. (1992) 'Childhood and Romanticism', in Sadler, G. E. (ed.) *Teaching Children's Literature: Issues, Pedagogy, Resources*, New York: MLA.

Ricoeur, P. (1986) *Lectures on Ideology and Utopia*, New York: Columbia University Press.

Rose, G. (1993) *Feminism and Geography: The Limits of Geographical Knowledge*, Minneapolis: University of Minnesota Press.

Rose, J. (1984) *The Case of Peter Pan or The Impossibility of Children's Fiction*, London: Macmillan.

Seiter, E. (1993) *Sold Separately: Children and Parents in Consumer Culture*, New Brunswick, NJ: Rutgers University Press.

Smoodin, E. (1994) 'How to Read Walt Disney', in Smoodin, E. (ed.) *Disney Discourse: Producing the Magic Kingdom*, New York: Routledge.

Stephens, J. (1992) *Language and Ideology in Children's Fiction*, London: Longman.

Stevenson, D. (1996) 'The River Bank Redux? Kenneth Grahame's *The Wind in the Willows* and William Horwood's *The Willows in Winter*', *Children's Literature Association Quarterly* 21, 3: 126–32.

——(2003) 'Historical Friction: Shifting Ideas of Objective Reality in History and Fiction', in Lucas, A. L. (ed.) *The Presence of the Past in Children's Literature*, Westport, CT and London: Praeger, 23–30.

Thaler, D. (2003) 'Fiction Versus History: History's Ghosts', in Lucas, A. L. (ed.) *The Presence of the Past in Children's Literature*, Westport, CT and London: Praeger, 3–11.

Thompson, J. B. (1984) *Studies in the Theory of Ideology*, Cambridge: Polity Press.

Thum, M. (1992) 'Exploring "The Country of the Mind": Mental Dimensions of Landscape in Kenneth Grahame's *The Wind in the Willows*', *Children's Literature Association Quarterly* 17, 3: 27–32.

Townsend, J. R. (1990) *Written for Children: An Outline of English Language Children's Literature*, 5th edn, London: Bodley Head.

Veeser, H. A. (1994) *The New Historicism Reader*, London: Routledge.

Watkins, T. (1992) 'Cultural Studies, New Historicism and Children's Literature', in Hunt, P. (ed.) *Literature for Children: Contemporary Criticism*, London: Routledge.

——(1994) 'Homelands: Landscape and Identity in Children's Literature', in Parsons, W. and Goodwin, R. (eds) *Landscape and Identity: Perspectives from Australia*, Adelaide: Auslib Press.

White, H. (1973) *Metahistory: The Historical Imagination in Nineteenth-Century Europe*, Baltimore, MD: Johns Hopkins University Press.

——(1978) 'The Historical Text as Literary Artifact', in Canary, R. H. and Kozicki, H. (eds) *The Writing of History: Literary Form and Historical Understanding*, Madison, WI: The University of Wisconsin Press.

Williams, R. (1958) *Culture and Society 1780–1950*, London: Chatto and Windus.

——(1975) *The Country and the City*, St Albans: Paladin.

——(1976) *Keywords: A Vocabulary of Culture and Society*, London: Fontana.

——(1977) *Marxism and Literature*, Oxford: Oxford University Press.

——(1989) *The Politics of Modernism: Against the New Conformists*, London: Verso.

Wojcik-Andrews, I. (2002) 'Review of Valerie Krips, *The Presence of the Past: Memory, Heritage and Childhood in Postwar Britain*', *The Lion and the Unicorn* 26, 1: 123–6.

Zipes, J. (2001) *Sticks and Stones: The Troublesome Success of Children's Literature from Slovenly Peter to Harry Potter*, New York and London: Routledge.

Zitterkopf, D. (1984–5) 'Prairies and Privations: The Impact of Place in Great Plains Homestead Fiction for Children', *Children's Literature Association Quarterly* 9, 4: 171–3.

Further reading

Grossberg, L. (1997) *Bringing It All Back Home: Essays on Cultural Studies*, Durham, NC: Duke University Press.

Jenkins, H. (ed.) (1998) *The Children's Culture Reader*, New York: New York University Press.

Kinder, M. (1991) *Playing with Power in Movies, Television and Video Games: From Muppet Babies to Teenage Mutant Ninja Turtles*, Berkeley, CA: University of California Press.

——(ed.) (1999) *Kids' Media Culture*, Durham, NC and London: Duke University Press.

Pace, P. (1993) 'Subject to Power: The Postmodern Child Spectator', *The Lion and the Unicorn* 17: 226–9.

Warner, M. (1994) *From the Beast to the Blonde: On Fairy Tales and Their Tellers*, London: Chatto and Windus.

Watkins, T. (1995) 'Reconstructing the Homeland: Loss and Hope in the English Landscape', in Nikolajeva, M. (ed.) *Aspects and Issues in the History of Children's Literature*, Westport, CT: Greenwood Press.

5 Analysing texts
Linguistics and stylistics

John Stephens

Editor's Introduction

An understanding of how words can work on the page is fundamental to an understanding of how texts can be interpreted. This is particularly true of children's literature, in that authors adapt their language to the capacities of the child-reader(s) that they have constructed, and there is a long tradition of assumptions about what such readers can understand. This chapter uses the semiotic analysis developed in contemporary critical linguistics to explore fascinating aspects of fiction, including register, narrative voice, and focalisation.

P. H.

Because the contexts in which children's literature is produced and disseminated are usually dominated by a focus on content and theme, the language of children's literature receives little explicit attention. Yet the *way* things are represented, based on complex codes and conventions of language and presuppositions about language, is an important component of texts, and the study of it allows us access to some of the key processes which shape text production (Scholes 1985: 2–3). The assumption that what is said can be extricated from how it is said, and that language is therefore only a transparent medium, indicates at best a limited grasp of written genres or of the social processes and movements with which genres and styles interrelate.

The most pervasive concern of children's literature is the representation of SELF, a subjectivity which is the site of enunciation, whether as a poetic persona or, in fiction, as a narrator or a represented focalising character. The evocation of subjectivity as significance is a function of language and is effected by the manipulation of structural linguistic elements – stylistic expressivity – in a pragmatic context (that is, within the frameworks of situational implicature or macro-textual structure, for instance). Readers thus trace subjectivity in the text's configuration of more or less familiar stylistic and rhetorical strategies.

The language of fiction written for children readily appears to offer conventionalised discourses by means of which to 'encode' content (both story and message). The ubiquitous 'Once upon a time' of traditional story-telling, for example, not only serves as a formal story onset but also tends to imply that particular narrative forms, with a particular stock of lexical and syntactic forms, will ensue. But the contents and themes of that fiction are representations of social situations and values, and such social processes are inextricable from the linguistic processes which give them expression. In other words, the transactions between writers and readers take place within complex networks of social relations by means of language. Further, within the systems of a language it is possible for young readers to encounter in their reading an extensive range and variety of language uses.

Some textual varieties will seem familiar and immediately accessible, consisting of a lexicon and syntax which will seem identifiably everyday, but others will seem much less familiar, either because the lexicon contains forms or uses specific to a different speech community (as in, for example, English literatures written in variants of English in the UK, USA, Canada, Australia, South Africa, the Caribbean and elsewhere in the world), or because writers may choose to employ linguistic forms whose occurrence is largely or wholly restricted to narrative fiction, or because particular kinds of fiction evolve specific discourses. Books which may be said to have a common theme or topic will differ not just because that theme can be expressed in a different content but because it is expressed through differing linguistic resources. For example, a large number of children's books express the theme of 'self-awareness', but since that theme can be discerned in texts as diverse as Jefferies's *Bevis* and Dickinson's *A Bone from a Dry Sea*, it cannot in itself discriminate effectively between texts of different kinds.

Writers have many options to select from. Thus fiction offers a large range of generic options, such as the choice between fantasy and realism, with more specific differences within them, such as that between time-slip fantasy grounded in the knowable world or fantasy set in an imaginary universe. To make such a choice involves entering into a *discourse*, a complex of story types and structures, social forms and linguistic practices. That discourse can be said to take on a distinctive style in so far as it is distinguished from other actualisations by recurrent patterns or codes. These might include choices in lexis and grammar; use, types and frequency of figurative language; characteristic modes of cohesion; orientation of narrative voice towards the text's existents (that is, events, characters, settings). Aspects of such a style may be shared by several writers working in the same period and with a common genre, as, for example, contemporary realistic adolescent fiction, but it is usually more personal, as when we speak of the style of Kenneth Grahame or William Mayne or Zibby Oneal, and at times we may refer to the distinctive style of a particular text, such as Virginia Hamilton's *Arilla Sun Down* or M. T. Anderson's *Feed*. Because the patterns of a particular style are a selection from a larger linguistic code, however, and exist in a relationship of sameness and difference with a more generalised discourse, a writer remains to some degree subject to the discourse, and the discourse can be said to determine at least part of the meaning of the text. Moreover, a narrative discourse also encodes a reading position which readers will adopt to varying extents, depending on their previous experience of the particular discourse, their similarities to or differences from the writer's language community, their level of linguistic sophistication, and other individual differences. At a more obviously linguistic level, a writer's choices among such options as first/third person narration, single/multiple focalisation and direct/indirect speech representation further define the encoded reading position. Between them, the broader elements of genre and the more precise linguistic processes appear to restrict the possibility of wildly deviant readings, though what might be considered more probable readings depends on an acquired recognition of the particular discourse. If that recognition is not available to readers, the readings they produce may well seem aberrant.

The communication which informs the transactions between writers and readers is a specialised aspect of socio-linguistic communication in general. The forms and meanings of reality are constructed in language: by analysing how language works, we come nearer to knowing how our culture constructs itself, and where we fit into that construction. Language enables individuals to compare their experiences with the experiences of others, a process which has always been a fundamental purpose of children's fiction. The representation of experiences such as growing up, evolving a sense of self, falling in love or into conflict, and so on, occurs in language, and guarantees that the experiences represented are shared with human beings in general. Language can make present the felt experiences of people living in other places and at other times, thus enabling a reader to define his or her own subjectivity in terms of perceived potentialities and differences. Finally, the capacity of language to express things beyond everyday reality, such as abstract thought or possible transcendent experiences, is imparted to written texts with all its potentiality for extending the boundaries of intellectual and emotional experience.

The socio-linguistic contexts of text production and reception are important considerations for any account of reading processes. But beyond satisfying a basic human need for contact, reading can also give many kinds of pleasure, though the pleasures of reading are not discovered in a social or linguistic vacuum: as we first learn how to read we also start learning what is pleasurable and what not, and even what is good writing and what not. Our socio-linguistic group, and especially its formal educational structures, tends to precondition what constitutes a good story, a good argument, a good joke, and the better our command of socio-linguistic codes the greater is our appreciation. In other words, we learn to enjoy the process as well as the product. Writing and reading are also very individual acts, however, and the pleasure of reading includes some sense of the distinctive style of a writer or a text. One primary function of stylistic description is to contribute to the pleasure in the text by defining the individual qualities of what is vaguely referred to as the 'style' of a writer or text.

Stylistic description can be attempted by means of several methodologies. These range from an impressionistic 'literary stylistics', which is characteristic of most discussions of the language of children's literature, to complex systemic analyses. The latter can offer very precise and delicate descriptions, but have the limitation that non-specialists may find them impenetrable. This chapter works within the semiotic analysis developed in contemporary critical linguistics (Fairclough 1989; Stephens 1992).

> To discuss the textuality of children's fiction one has to begin by considering some assumptions about the nature of language on which it is grounded. Linguists recognise that language is a social semiotic, a culturally patterned system of signs used to communicate about things, ideas or concepts. As a system constructed within culture, it is not founded on any essential bond between a verbal sign and its referent.
>
> (Stephens 1992: 246–7)

This is an important point to grasp, because much children's fiction is written and mediated under the contrary, essentialist assumption, and this has major implications both for writing objectives and for the relationships between writers and readers. Fantasy writing in particular is apt to assert the inextricability of word and thing, but the assumption also underlies realistic writing which purports to minimise the distance between life and fiction, or which pivots on the evolution of a character's essential selfhood, and it often informs critical suspicion of texts which foreground the gap between signs and things.

The following passages throw some light on these contrary assumptions about language:

> The glade in the ring of trees was evidently a meeting-place of the wolves ... in the middle of the circle was a great grey wolf. He spoke to them in the dreadful language of the Wargs. Gandalf understood it. Bilbo did not, but it sounded terrible to him, and as if all their talk was about cruel and wicked things, as it was.
>
> (*The Hobbit*, Tolkien 1937/1987: 91)

Charlie did not know much about ice … The only piece he had known came from a refrigerated boat, and was left on the wharf, cloudy white, not clear, not even very clean. Charlie had waited until the boat went with its load of lamb carcasses, and then gone for it. By then it had melted. There was a puddle, a wisp of lambswool, and nothing more.

He did not even think this was the same stuff. He did not think this place was part of the world. He thought it was the mouth of some other existence coming up from the ground, being drilled through the rock. The pieces coming away were like the fragments from the bit of the carpentry brace Papa used for setting up shelves. An iron thing would come from the ground, Charlie thought, and another Papa would blow through the hole to make it clear. Last time all the dust had gone into Charlie's eye, because he was still looking through. Papa had thought him such a fool.

(*Low Tide*, Mayne 1992: 163–4)

The Tolkien and Mayne passages represent a principal character at a moment of incomprehension: Bilbo hears a foreign language and has no actual referents for the verbal signs; Charlie perceives a physical phenomenon (the point at which pieces of ice break from a glacier into a river, though *glacier* is not introduced for two more paragraphs) and struggles with the socio-linguistic resources at his disposal to find meaning in it. A significant difference between the two is the implication that the Wargs' language communicates meanings beyond sense. On a simple level, this is to say no more than that it is obvious what the sounds made by a nasty horde of wolves signify. But Tolkien directly raises the question of comprehension – 'Gandalf understood it' – and uses his overt, controlling narrative voice to confirm that Bilbo comprehends something which is a linguistic essential: the language is inherently 'dreadful' (presumably in the fuller sense of 'inspiring dread'); and the 'as it was' confirms the principle that 'the meaning is innate to its sound' suggested by the lexical set 'terrible, wicked and cruel'. Mayne focuses on the other side of the sign/thing relationship, in effect posing a question often posed in his novels: can a phenomenon be understood if it cannot be signified in language? Tolkien's shifts between narration and Bilbo's focalisation are clearly marked; Mayne slips much more ambiguously between these modes, a strategy which serves to emphasise the gap between phenomena and language. The first paragraph is a retrospective narration of Charlie's single relevant empirical experience, but because that ice then differed in colour and form ('cloudy white', 'a puddle') the past experience does not enable him to make sense of the present. Instead, in the second paragraph Charlie produces a fantastic (mis-) interpretation on the premise that what he sees is visually isomorphic with another previous experience. The upshot is that, once again, he seems 'such a fool', though that is only a temporary state induced by linguistic inadequacy and is set aside by the novel's congruence of story and theme. As a story, *Low Tide* is a treasure hunt gone wrong and then marvellously recuperated; a major thematic concern, articulated through the child characters' struggles to make sense of phenomena, language and the relationships between phenomena and language, is a child's struggle towards competence in his or her socio-linguistic context.

The texts thus demonstrate two very different approaches to the semiotic instability of language. A third, and very common, approach is to exploit that instability as a source of humour, and this partly explains why nonsense verse is considered to be almost entirely the province of childhood. A rich vein of narrative humour also runs from the same source. In Terry Pratchett's *Johnny and the Dead*, for example, humour is created by exploiting the arbitrary relationship between signs and things or actions, specifically the instabilities which can result when significations slip, multiply or change. In the following extract, a police station is fielding telephone calls reporting strange incidents. The macro-structural frame for the humour – that these incidents are caused by the dead from the local cemetery who have come out to explore the town in which they once lived – informs readers that both sides of the dialogue are grounded in misconception:

> The phone rang again as soon as he put it down, but this time one of the young constables answered it.
>
> 'It's someone from the university,' he said, putting his hand over the mouthpiece. 'He says a strange alien force has invaded the radio telescope. You know, that big satellite dish thing over towards Slate?'
>
> Sergeant Comely sighed. 'Can you get a description?' he said.
>
> 'I saw a film about this, Sarge,' said another policeman. 'These aliens landed and replaced everyone in the town with giant vegetables.'
>
> 'Really? Round here it'd be days before anyone noticed,' said the sergeant.
>
> The constable put the phone down.
>
> 'He just said it was like a strange alien force,' he said. 'Very cold, too.'
>
> 'Oh, a *cold* strange alien force,' said Sergeant Comely.
>
> 'And it was invisible, too.'
>
> 'Right. Would he recognize it if he didn't see it again?'
>
> The young policemen looked puzzled. I'm too good for this, the sergeant thought.
>
> 'All right,' he said. 'So we know the following. Strange invisible aliens have invaded Blackbury. They dropped in at The Dirty Duck, where they blew up the Space Invaders machine, which makes sense. And then they went to the pictures. Well, that makes sense too. It's probably *years* before new films get as far as Alfred Centuri ...'
>
> The phone rang again. The constable answered it.
>
> (Pratchett 1993: 122–3)

Signification in this extract pivots on the frameworks afforded by genres and the principles of situational implicature, particularly in the linguistic clash between the discourses (properly, 'registers') of police reporting, adhered to by the Sergeant, and of popular science fiction, which his gullible subordinates quickly adopt. The possibility that language does not communicate precisely is flagged by the constable's reformulation of 'radio telescope' as 'that big satellite dish thing'. The exasperated Sergeant then exploits the register clash to mock his subordinates, breaching the conversational principles of relation and clarity, as in his play on the meanings of 'vegetables' or his question, 'Would he recognize it if he didn't see it again?' The clashing of registers offers a succinct example of how context determines meaning. In such an example, 'correct use in context' extends beyond other nearby words and the grammar which combines them into intelligible form to include the situation of utterance and cultural context. The situation of utterance – the police station – clarifies the focus of reference, but at the same time foregrounds how the 'same' utterance can have a very different meaning in different contexts. The shifting of meaning begins to move towards excess in the Sergeant's mock summary interpretation of the information collected so far. It also moves, however, to a point of undecidability in the malapropism 'Alfred Centuri', since a reader cannot determine whether this is the Sergeant's error or a further example of mockery. In such ways, Pratchett's writings for younger readers are richly subversive, playing on meanings to such an extent as to suggest that, if allowed free play, language will tend to be uncontainable by situation. Such a view of language, however, tends to be uncommon in the domain of children's literature.

The issue of sign/referent relationship is of central interest here because it bears directly on linguistic function in children's fiction and the notion of desirable significances. The assumption that the relationship is direct and unproblematic has the initial effect of producing what might be termed closed meanings. The Tolkien example is especially instructive because it explicitly shows how language which is potentially open, enabling a variety of potential reader responses, is narrowed by paradigmatic recursiveness and essentialism. Writers will, of course, often aim for such specification, but what are the implications if virtually all meaning in a text is implicitly closed? The outcome points to an invisible linguistic control by writer over reader. As Hunt has argued, attempts to exercise such control are much less obvious when conveyed by stylistic features than by lexis or story existents (Hunt 1991: 109).

A related linguistic concept of major importance for the issue of language choice and writerly control is register, the principle which governs the choice among various possible linguistic realisations of the same thing. Register refers to types of language variation which collocate with particular social situations and written genres. Socially, for example, people choose different appropriate language variations for formal and informal occasions, for friendly disputes and angry arguments, and for specialised discourses: science, sport, computing, skipping rope games, role-play, and so on, all have particular registers made up of configurations of lexical and syntactical choices. Narrative fictions will seek to replicate such registers, but also, as with a wide range of writing genres, develop distinctive registers of their own. Genres familiar in children's fiction – such as folk and fairy stories, ghost and terror stories, school stories, teen romance, and a host of others – use some readily identifiable registers. Consider the use of register in the following passage from Anna Fienberg's *Ariel, Zed and the Secret of Life*. It describes three girls watching a horror movie, but one of them (Ariel) is giggling:

> When the girls looked back at the screen, the scene had changed. It was dusk, and shadows bled over the ground. A moaning wind had sprung up, and somewhere, amongst the trees, an owl hooted.
>
> 'Ooh, *look*,' hissed Lynn, her nails digging into her friend Mandy's arm. 'Is that him there, crouching behind that bush? Tell me what happens. I'm not looking any more.'
>
> 'The nurse is saying goodnight,' Mandy whispered, 'she's leaving. She'll have to go right past him.'
>
> *The Monster From Out of Town* was, indeed, breathing heavily behind a camellia bush. His clawed hands crushed flowers to a perfumed pulp, which made you think of what he would do to necks …
>
> Ariel grinned. The monster's mask was badly made and his costume looked much too tight.
>
> (Fienberg 1992: 9–10)

The scene from the movie is presented in the conventional register of the Gothic (dusk, shadows, bled, moaning wind, an owl hooted), though the unusual metaphor 'shadows bled' reconfigures the conventional elements with the effect of foregrounding the Gothic trait of overwording (or semantic overload). By then switching the retelling to the audience's perceptions and responses, Fienberg builds in a common Gothic narrative strategy, that of determining emotional response to scene or incident by building it in as a character's response. The switch also enables a version of the suspense so necessary to horror ('him … behind that bush'; 'the nurse … leaving'; 'his clawed hands'). These narrative strategies set up the deflation occurring with Ariel's response and the register shift which expresses it: detached and analytic, she epitomises the resistant reader who refuses the positioning implied by the genre. The deflation has the effect of retrospectively defining how far a genre can depend on its audience's unthinking acceptance of the emotional codes implied by its register.

Fienberg is making an important point about how fiction works (her novel is pervasively metafictive), and it is a point which is well applied to modes of fiction in which register is much less obtrusive. It is easy to assume that realistic fiction is based on a neutral register, though this is not really so, and a stylistic account can help disclose how its registers position readers even more thoroughly than do obvious registers such as that of Gothic. This is readily seen in the tradition of realism in adolescent fiction in the USA, which developed in the 1960s out of a psychology of adolescence based in the work of Erik Erikson re-routed through the textual influence of Salinger's *The Catcher in the Rye*. Thus a first-person adolescent narrator represents significant issues of adolescent development, such as 'experience of physical sexual maturity, experience of withdrawal from adult benevolent protection, consciousness of self in interaction, re-evaluation of values, [and] experimentation' (Russell 1988: 61). Cultural institutions, genre and style interact with a material effect, not just to code human behaviour but to shape it. A stylistic analysis offers one position from which we can begin to unravel that shaping process. Danziger's *Can You Sue Your Parents for Malpractice?* is thematically focused on the five concepts of adolescent development listed above; most are evident in the following passage:

> [Linda] says, 'How can you stop a buffalo from charging?'
> 'Take away his credit cards,' my mother answers.
> My father turns to her. 'You should know that one. Now that you're going back to work, I bet you're going to be spending like mad, living outside my salary.'
> 'Why don't you just accept it and not feel so threatened?' My mother raises her voice. She hardly ever does that.
> I can feel the knot in my stomach and I feel like I'm going to jump out of my skin.
> 'Who feels threatened?' he yells. 'That's ridiculous. Just because you won't have to depend on me, need me any more, why should I worry?'
> So that's why he's acting this way. He thinks it's the money that makes him important. Sometimes I just don't understand his brain.
> 'Why can't you ever celebrate anything?' she yells again.
> I throw my spoon on the table. That's it. I'm leaving. Linda follows me out. It's like a revolution. Nothing like this has ever happened before.
> (Danziger 1979/1987: 6)

An important part of the register here is the first person and – as often – present tense narration, particularly in so far as it constructs a precise orientation of narrative voice towards a conventional situation. The function of present tense narration is to convey an illusion of immediacy and instantaneity, suppressing any suggestion that the outcome is knowable in advance. Thus Lauren, the narrator, proceeds through specific moments of recognition and decision – 'I can feel ...'; 'So that's why ...'; 'That's it. I'm leaving'; 'It's like a revolution' – but each of these moments, as with the depiction of the quarrel itself, is expressed by means of a register which consists of the clichés which pertain to it. Linguistically, this has a double function. It is, now at the other end of the creative spectrum, another use of language which assumes an essential link between sign and referent; and in doing that through cliché it constitutes the text as a surface without depth, an effect reinforced by the way present tense narration severely restricts the possibility of any temporal movement outside the present moment. The outcome, both linguistically and thematically, is a complete closing of meaning: there is no interpretative task for a reader to perform, no inference undrawn. This closure even extends to the joke with which the passage begins.

Another way to describe this is to say that the metonymic mode of writing which characterises realistic fiction, and which enables particular textual moments to relate to a larger signifying structure (Stephens 1992: 148–249), has been directed towards a closing of meaning. Another aspect of the metonymic process is that a narrative may draw upon recognisable schemata repeatable from one text to another and which constitute a 'register' of metonyms of family life. This example could be categorised as: situation, the parental quarrel; pretext, money; actual focus, power and authority. With perhaps unintentional irony produced by the present tense verb, the repeatability of the scene is foregrounded by Lauren's remark that 'Nothing like this has ever happened before.' It happens all the time, especially in post-1960s realist adolescent fiction, and its function, paradoxically, is to confirm a model whereby the rational individual progresses to maturity under the ideal of liberal individuality, doing so through the assurance that the experience is metonymic of the experience of everybody in that age group.

The presence of a narrative voice which interprets the scene for the benefit of readers is a characteristic of another linguistic aspect of texts, the presentation of scene and incident through the representation of speech and thought and the strategy of focalisation. These are important aspects of point of view in narrative, the facet of narration through which a writer implicitly, but powerfully, controls how readers understand the text. Because readers are willing to surrender themselves to the flow of the discourse, especially by focusing attention on story or content, they are susceptible to the implicit power of point of view. Linguistically, point of view is established by focalisation strategies and by conversational pragmatics. Early children's fiction tended to favour narrator focalisation, and hence employed character focalisation only sporadically, so that it is only fleetingly present in, for instance, Richard Jefferies's *Bevis* (1882) or Ethel Turner's *Seven Little Australians* (1894), and, more recently, is generally absent from C. S. Lewis's children's books. Since around the middle of the twentieth century, however, sustained character focalisation has become the norm in third-person narration, and hence character subjectivity infiltrates the narrative, linguistically evident through lexis and idiom (expressions, phrases, habitual idioms, solecisms, malapropisms) and syntactic features. Hence a narrative has a potential to achieve a double-voiced effect whereby the sociolect, cultural preoccupations and ideological positionings attributed to a focalising character are visible within the language of narration. Most novels which are third-person narrations now include at least one focalising character, and this has important implications for the kind of language used, because in the vast majority of books written for children there is only one such focaliser, who is a child. Further, as with first-person narrators, readers will tend to align themselves with that focalising character's point of view.

Character focalisation is illustrated below, first in an example from *Bevis*, in which it is discernible as a mere trace, emerging from within narrator focalisation, and then in sequential passages from the end and beginning of the first two chapters of Dickinson's *A Bone from a Dry Sea*, which exemplify quite different ways in which incidents may be narrated as they impact on the mind of focalising characters.

> Bevis sat still and tried to think; and while he did so he looked out over the New Sea. The sun was now lower, and all the waves were touched with purple, as if the crests had been sprinkled with wine. The wind blew even harder, as the sun got near the horizon, and fine particles of sand were every now and then carried over his head from the edge of the precipice.
>
> What would Ulysses have done? He had a way of getting out of everything; but try how he would, Bevis could not think of any plan, especially as he feared to move much, lest the insecure platform under him should give way. He could see his reflection in the pool beneath, as if it were waiting for him to come in reality.
>
> (Jefferies 1882/1995: 143)

The shift from narrator to character focalisation is often signalled by verbs whose semantic node is 'perception', and that is so in this example. The text is shaped by the presence of represented thought and by direct or implied acts of seeing. The narrative representation of thought (marked here by the repeated verb 'think', and the slipping from direct thought to free indirect thought at the beginning of the second paragraph) and the references to acts of seeing ('looked' and 'could see') situate events within the character's mind but also maintain a separate narrating voice. This narration is evident here in aspects of register, as the lexical items 'fine particles' and 'insecure', and by the use of analogies and figurative language in the comparative and hypothetical *as if* clauses. There is no evident attempt at this moment to match linguistic level of narrative discourse to that of the character, though that does often happen. There is, nevertheless, an obvious contrast with the Danziger passage, which, depicting a main character of about the same age (fourteen), has access to a more limited range of registers. Figurative language is likewise less complex. Lauren's 'I can feel the knot in my stomach and I feel like I'm going to jump out of my skin' are cliché analogies, whereas in 'as if it were waiting for him to come in reality' the personifying attribution of a threatening purpose to the pool implies a greater fear than that actually named in the text and, opening out the space between sign and referent, gives readers an opportunity to draw inferences which are not fully determined by the text.

The two incidents presented in the Dickinson extract are placed in the same setting but four million years apart. In the first section, character focalisation again emerges from within narrator focalisation, but the second is predominantly character focalised. The focalisers are female children, the first an early hominid without a language to express her thoughts, and the second a sophisticated modern child:

> [A]s she ['Li'] lay among the crowded bodies in one of the caves ... she relived the adventure. She knew what she had done, and why. She understood that it had not been an accident. She realised, too, that the others would not understand.
>
> She had no words for this knowledge. Thought and understanding for her were a kind of seeing. She showed herself things in her mind, the rock-shelf, the shallow water, the need to lure the shark full-tilt onto the slope so that it would force itself out too far, and strand, and die; then her uncle triumphing and her mother scolding and herself cringing while she hugged her knowledge inside her.

Now she seemed to herself to be standing apart in the cave, seeing by the moon-light reflected from the bay one small body curled among the mass of sleepers. A thought which had neither words nor pictures made itself in her mind.
Different.
She's different. Yes, I'm different.

The truck wallowed along the gravelly road, if you could call it a road. Often there was nothing to mark it off from the rest of the brown, enormous plain, but Dad knew where he was because then there'd be tyre-ruts making the truck wallow worse than ever. Vinny clutched the handgrip on the dash to stop herself being thrown around. They'd done two hours from the airport, though it seemed longer, when Dad stopped by a flat-topped tree with a lot of grassy bundles hanging among the branches. Weaver-birds, Vinny guessed. She'd seen them on TV.

(Dickinson 1992: 12–13)

The opening chapter signals the emergence of subjectivity in an early hominid, and constitutes a creative challenge to the late twentieth-century contention that subjectivity does not exist outside of language. Rather, language is shown to derive from a perceiving subject. In contrast, Vinny's simple recording of scene as the narrative's focalising character at this point is implicitly posited on the assumption of her subjectivity as a 'deictic centre', a *here* and *now* which orients perception. Her status as focaliser is immediately established by suggestions of a particular sociolect and point of view ('if you could call it a road'; 'They'd done two hours'; the identification of her companion by the familiar 'Dad'), and presence of direct thought and then free indirect thought at the end of the paragraph. Unlike Li's 'kind of seeing', Vinny has the authority of information technology to enable her to attach names to things ('She'd seen them on TV'). The identification of the 'grassy bundles' with 'weaver-birds' implies a renaming which conveys the opposite effect from Pratchett's 'radio telescope', as the perception now moves from observation to identification.

What is always implicit in Vinny's subjectivity, a consciousness of identity and self-presence enabled by knowledge and reason, corresponds with the capacity for abstract thought which Li is groping towards as she struggles with proto-language. Thinking with 'neither words nor pictures' enables Li to enter symbolic language through a contrast between the deictics *she* and *I* in relation to notions of difference and alterity, and thereby she begins to access the position of observer of the self. The movement of the passage is thus from a narrator-inflected character focalisation to represented abstract thought.

The second linguistic construction of point of view is by means of represented conversation. Various modes are available to a writer (see Leech and Short 1981), and all appear in children's fiction. These modes range from reported speech acts, which are mainly an aspect of narrative, to direct speech dialogues, which readers must interpret in the light of their knowledge of the principles and conventions of conversation. Because the intermediate forms of indirect and free indirect speech representation allow both for subtle interplay between narratorial and character points of view and for narratorial control, they have tended to receive most attention in discussions of general fiction. With children's fiction, however, more attention needs to be paid to direct speech dialogue, both because it exists in a higher proportion and because of the general principle that the narrator in the text appears to have less control over point of view in dialogue. Leech and Short envisage a cline running between 'bound' and 'free' forms, where 'free' corresponds with closeness to direct speech (1981: 324). But point of view in such conversations is affected by two factors: the presence of narratorial framing, especially speech-reporting tags, that is, the devices for identifying speakers which may in themselves suggest attitudes; and the pragmatic principles which shape conversation. The following passage illustrates these factors.

> When they reached [the others] they slipped in behind Rebecca and Sue Stephens, and Juniper saw Ellie standing on the pavement buttoned up in her old red coat, Jake beside her. They waved and smiled.
>
> 'Your mum looks like ... a pop star,' said Sue. 'No, someone in a TV series,' said Rebecca.
>
> 'It must be strange to have a mother looking like that,' went on Sue, still staring behind her.
>
> 'How would I know? I've only had her, haven't I? I don't know any different mother, so I don't know if it's strange or not.'
>
> Sue kept on: 'Is that your dad? That one with the beard?'
>
> 'Shut up,' hissed Rebecca, then said very loudly and clearly, 'I liked your reading, Juniper. You were the best.'
>
> 'You sounded dead miserable but your arm didn't show. Nobody could tell. I expect Sir picked you because of being sorry for you. He's like that. What did you say?' asked Sue.
>
> 'I said Abbledy, Gabbledy Flook,' answered Juniper and then under her breath, Ere the sun begins to sink, May your nasty face all shrink, which came into her head out of nowhere, and wished herself away to a wide, pale beach with the sun shining down and a white horse galloping at the edge of the incoming tide, far, far away from the wind slicing down the pavement blowing up grit and rubbish as they made their way back to school.
>
> (Kemp 1986/1988: 78–9)

This exchange shows very clearly how meaning in conversations arises not from the simple sense of individual utterances but from the tenor of utterances in combination and as shaped by narratorial tagging. It also illustrates how a children's book makes use of the main principles which inform actual or represented conversations: the principle of cooperation, the principle of politeness, and the principle of irony. H. P. Grice (1975) argued that, in order to communicate in an orderly and productive way, speakers accept five conventions which organise what we say to one another: an utterance should be of an appropriate size; it should be correct or truthful; it should relate back to the previous speaker's utterance (a change of subject and a change of register may both be breaches of relation); it should be clear, organised and unambiguous; and each speaker should have a fair share of the conversation, that is, be able to take his or her turn in an orderly way and be able to complete what s/he wants to say (see Leech 1983). These conventions are very readily broken, and much of everyday conversation depends on simultaneously recognising and breaking one or more of them. In particular, many breaches are prompted by the operation of politeness in social exchange. Whenever conversational principles are breached, the product is apt to be humour, irony or conflict.

After a sequence of four utterances which more or less adhere to the principles of coherence and turn-taking but skirt the boundaries of politeness by drawing attention to Ellie's unusual appearance (shabby but beautiful, she doesn't conform to the girls' image of 'mother'), Kemp introduces a sequence built on crucial breaches of relation and politeness, beginning with Sue's 'Is that your dad?' This is flagged contextually because readers know that Juniper's father is missing, and textually because of the cline in the speech-reporting tags from the neutral 'said Sue' to the intrusively persistent 'Sue kept on', and the heavy tagging of Rebecca's interruption and shift of relation ('hissed Rebecca, then said very loudly and clearly'). Finally, of course, Juniper's escapist daydream cliché also serves as a narratorial comment on how painful she has found the exchange: indeed, the blowing 'grit and rubbish' becomes a metonym for the anguish at the heart of her being. Second, Sue's response to Rebecca's intervention is to apparently pursue relation but to breach politeness by turning attention to Juniper's missing arm. The upshot is Juniper's final spoken utterance – interrupting, impolite and nonsensical, it terminates the exchange and the discourse shifts into represented thought. Such an astute use of conversational principles is one of the most expressive linguistic tools available to a children's writer.

A stylistic examination of children's fiction can show us something very important, namely that a fiction with a high proportion of conversation and a moderately sophisticated use of focalisation has access to textual strategies with the potential to offset the limitations which may be implicit in a disinclination to employ the full range of lexical, syntactic and figurative possibilities of written discourse. But stylistic analysis is also never an end in itself, and is best carried out within a frame which considers the relationship of text to genre and to culture. Obviously enough, stylistics alone cannot determine the relative merits of Sue and Rebecca's preferences for 'a pop star' or 'someone in a TV series', and cannot determine whether a reader treats either category as prestigious or feels that both consign Ellie to a subject position without selfhood. The example illustrates two general principles in language analysis: that significance is influenced by the larger contexts of text and culture within which particular utterances are meaningful; and that particular language features or effects can have more than one function, simultaneously expressing both purposiveness and implicit, often unexamined, social assumptions.

Finally, attention to the language of children's fiction has an important implication for evaluation, adding another dimension to the practices of judging books according to their entertainment value as stories or according to their socio-political correctness. It can be an important tool in distinguishing between 'restrictive texts' which allow little scope for active reader judgements (Hunt 1991: 117) and texts which enable critical and thoughtful responses.

References

Danziger, P. (1979/1987) *Can You Sue Your Parents for Malpractice?*, London: Pan.
Dickinson, P. (1992) *A Bone from a Dry Sea*, London: Victor Gollancz.
Fairclough, N. (1989) *Language and Power*, London and New York: Longman.
Fienberg, A. (1992) *Ariel, Zed and the Secret of Life*, Sydney: Allen and Unwin.
Grice, H. P. (1975) 'Logic and Conversation', in Cole, P. and Morgan, J. L. (eds) *Syntax and Semantics Vol. 3, Speech Acts*, New York: Academic Press.
Hunt, P. (1991) *Criticism, Theory, and Children's Literature*, Oxford: Blackwell.
Jefferies, R. (1882/1995) *Bevis*, Ware: Wordsworth Classics.
Kemp, G. (1986/1988) *Juniper*, Harmondsworth: Puffin.
Leech, G. N. (1983) *Principles of Pragmatics*, London and New York: Longman.
Leech, G. N. and Short, M. H. (1981) *Style in Fiction*, London and New York: Longman.
Mayne, W. (1992) *Low Tide*, London: Jonathan Cape.
Pratchett, T. (1993) *Johnny and the Dead*, London: Doubleday.

Russell, D. A. (1988) 'The Common Experience of Adolescence: A Requisite for the Development of Young Adult Literature', *Journal of Youth Services in Libraries* 2: 58–63.

Scholes, R. (1985) *Textual Power: Literary Theory and the Teaching of English*, New Haven, CT and London: Yale University Press.

Stephens, J. (1992) *Language and Ideology in Children's Fiction*, London and New York: Longman.

Tolkien, J. R. R. (1937/1987) *The Hobbit*, London: Unwin Hyman.

Further reading

Fludernik, M. (1993) *The Fictions of Language and the Languages of Fiction*, London: Routledge.

Hunt, P. (1978) 'The Cliché Count: A Practical Aid for the Selection of Books for Children', *Children's Literature in Education* 9, 3: 143–50.

——(1988) 'Degrees of Control: Stylistics and the Discourse of Children's Literature', in Coupland, N. (ed.) *Styles of Discourse*, London: Croom Helm.

Knowles, M. and Malmkjær, K. (1996) *Language and Control in Children's Literature*, London: Routledge.

Kuskin, K. (1980) 'The Language of Children's Literature', in Michaels, L. and Ricks, C. (eds) *The State of the Language*, Berkeley: University of California Press.

Stephens, J. (1989) 'Language, Discourse, Picture Books', *Children's Literature Association Quarterly* 14: 106–10.

——(2002) 'Writing by Children, Writing for Children: Schema Theory, Narrative Discourse, and Ideology', in Bull, G. and Anstey, M. (eds) *Crossing the Boundaries*, French's Forest, NSW: Prentice Hall.

Thacker, D. (2001) 'Feminine Language and the Politics of Children's Literature', *The Lion and the Unicorn* 25, 1: 3–16.

Wyile, A. S. (2003) 'The Value of Singularity in First- and Restricted Third-Person Engaging Narration', *Children's Literature* 31: 116–41.

6   Readers, texts, contexts

Reader-response criticism

Michael Benton

Editor's Introduction

Much critical theory seems to be remote from actual books, actual readers, and individual reading events. Reader-response criticism – which approaches 'the Loch Ness Monster of literary studies' – in contrast, engages directly with the knotty problems of how readers understand texts, and how we can elicit and interpret individual response. It is thus particularly relevant to those who see the interaction of child and book as central to children's literature studies, and is important for all reading. Michael Benton's survey includes theories of how children see the process of reading fiction, how they develop as readers of literature, and how texts may be better understood from the point of view of the readers' response to them.

P. H.

The importance of reader-response criticism in the area of children's literature lies in what it tells us about two fundamental questions, one about the literature and the other about its young readers:

- Who is the implied child reader inscribed in the text?
- How do actual child readers respond during the process of reading?

The main advocates of reader-response criticism acknowledge the complementary importance of text and reader. They attend both to the form and language of poem or story, and to the putative reader constructed there, acknowledging, as Henry James put it, that the author makes 'his reader very much as he makes his characters ... When he makes him well, that is makes him interested, then the reader does quite half the labour' (quoted in Booth 1961: 302). Equally, they attend to the covert activity of the reading process, deducing the elements of response from what readers say or write, and/or developing theoretical models of aesthetic experience.

Whatever the particular orientation of the reader-response critic, one central issue recurs: the mystery of what readers actually do and experience. The subject of the reader's response is the Loch Ness Monster of literary studies: when we set out to capture it, we cannot even be sure that it is there at all; and, if we assume that it is, we have to admit that the most sensitive probing with the most sophisticated instruments has so far succeeded only in producing pictures of dubious authenticity. That the nature and dimensions of this phenomenon are so uncertain is perhaps the reason why the hunters are so many and their approaches so various. Accordingly, it is necessary to map the main historical development of reader-response criticism and, second, to outline the theoretical bases which its advocates share, before going on to consider how this perspective – whose concepts have been formulated largely in the area of adult literary experience – has been taken up by researchers interested in young readers and their books.

A shift of critical perspective

In the 1950s the criticism of literature was in a relatively stable state. In *The Mirror and the Lamp* (1953), M. H. Abrams was confidently able to describe 'the total situation' of the work of art as one with the text at the centre with the three elements of the author, the reader and the signified world ranged like satellites around it. What has happened since has destabilised this model. In particular, reader-response critics have argued that it is readers who make meaning by the activities they perform on texts; they see the reader in the centre and thus the privileged position of the work of art is undermined and individual 'readings' become the focus of attention. This is not to say that the emphasis upon reading and response which emerged in the 1960s was entirely new. It had been initiated famously by I. A. Richards forty years earlier; but Richards's (1924, 1929) seminal work, with its twin concerns of pedagogy and criticism, influenced subsequent developments in criticism in two contrary ways. For, in one sense, Richards privileged the text, and the American New Critics, particularly, seized upon the evidence of *Practical Criticism* to insist that close analysis of the words on the page was the principal job of critic and teacher. Yet, in another sense, Richards privileged the reader; and subsequently, modern reader-response criticism has developed to give the reader freedoms that infuriate text-oriented critics. Hence, Stanley Fish writes: 'Interpretation is not the art of construing but the art of constructing. Interpreters do not decode poems: they make them' (Fish 1980: 327). Or, even more provocatively: 'It is the structure of the reader's experience rather than any structures available on the page that should be the object of description' (152). As Laurence Lerner (1983: 6) has pointed out, perhaps the most important division in contemporary literary studies is between those who see literature as a more or less self-contained system, and those who see it as interacting with real, extra-literary experience (that of the author, or of the reader or the social reality of the author's or the reader's world). Reader-response critics clearly fall within this second category.

Reader-response criticism is difficult to map because of its diversity, especially in two respects: first, there are several important figures whose work stands outside the normal boundaries of the term; and second, there is overlap but not identity in the relationship between German 'reception theory' and Anglo-American reader-response criticism. On the first issue, two highly influential writers, D. W. Harding and Louise Rosenblatt, began publishing work in the 1930s which was ahead of its time (for example, Harding 1937; Rosenblatt 1938/1970) and their explorations of the psychological and affective aspects of literary experience only really began to have an impact upon educational thinking (and hence upon children's experiences of poems and stories in school) when the educational and literary theorists began to rehabilitate the reader in the 1960s and 1970s. Subsequently, Harding's paper on 'Psychological Approaches in the Reading of Fiction' (1962) and Rosenblatt's reissued *Literature as Exploration* (1938/1970) have been widely regarded as two of the basic texts in this area.

It is an indication of the diversity and loose relationships which characterise response-oriented approaches to literature that Harding and Rosenblatt are reduced to complimentary footnotes in the standard introductions to reader-response criticism (Tompkins 1980: xxvi; Suleiman and Crosman 1980: 45; Freund 1987: 158), and that writers in the German and Anglo-American traditions have, with the notable exception of Iser, little contact with or apparent influence upon one another. In a thorough account of German reception theory, Holub (1984) comments upon this divide and provides an excellent analysis of Iser's work to complement that of Freund (1987), whose book summarises the Anglo-American tradition.

The development of reader-response writings since the 1960s has steadily forged a new relationship between the act of reading and the act of teaching literature which, as is illustrated later, has significant consequences for the way the relationship between young readers and their books is conceptualised. Prior to this time, during the 1940s and 1950s, the reader was hidden from view as the critical landscape was dominated by the American New Criticism, whose adherents took a determinedly anti-reader stance to the extent that, despite a concern for 'close reading', the major statement of New Criticism views – Wellek and Warren's *Theory of Literature* (1949) – makes no mention of the reader and includes only two brief references to 'reading'. Subsequently, the development of reader-response studies has seen the momentum shift periodically from literary theory to educational enquiry and practice almost decade by decade.

The 1960s were dominated by education, with the most influential work published by the National Council of Teachers of English (Squire 1964; Purves and Rippere 1968), culminating in two surveys, one English and the other American (D'Arcy 1973; Purves and Beach 1972). The 1970s saw the full bloom of reader-response theorising by literary critics of whom Holland (1975), Culler (1975), Iser (1978) and Fish (1980) were perhaps the most notable figures, all of whom were well represented in the two compilations of papers that stand as a summary of work in this area at the end of the decade (Suleiman and Crosman 1980; Tompkins 1980). During the 1980s the emphasis moved back to education, where the main concern was to translate what had become known about response – both from literary theory and from classroom enquiry – into principles of good practice. Protherough (1983), Cooper (1985a), Benton and Fox (1985), Scholes (1985), Corcoran and Evans (1987), Benton *et al.* (1988), Dias and Hayhoe (1988), Hayhoe and Parker (1990), Benton (1992a), Many and Cox (1992) have all, in their different ways, considered the implications for practice of a philosophy of literature and learning based upon reader-response principles. In Britain, one of the more heartening results of this development was that the importance of the reader's response to literature was fully acknowledged in the new National Curriculum as embodied in the Cox Report (1989) and in the official documents that ensued. Such has been what one standard book on modern literary theory calls 'the vertiginous rise of reader-response criticism' (Jefferson and Robey 1986: 142) that its authors see it as threatening to engulf all other approaches.

What are the theoretical bases that such writers share? Reader-response criticism is a broad church, as a reading of the various overview books demonstrates (Tompkins 1980; Suleiman and Crosman 1980; Freund 1987). None the less, a number of principles can be said to characterise this critical stance. First is the rejection of the notorious 'affective fallacy'. In describing the 'fallacy' as 'a confusion of the poem and its results', and in dismissing as mere 'impressionism and relativism' any critical judgements based on the psychological effects of literature, Wimsatt and Beardsley (1954/1970) had left no space for the reader to inhabit. They ignored the act of reading. New Criticism, it could be said, invented 'the assumed reader'; by contrast, reader-response criticism deals with real and implied readers. Iser, Holland, Bleich and Fish operate from a philosophical basis that displaces the notion of an autonomous text to be examined in and on its own terms from the centre of critical discussion and substitutes the reader's recreation of that text. Reading is not the discovering of meaning (like some sort of archaeological 'dig') but the creation of it. The purpose of rehearsing this familiar history is its importance for children's reading. The central concerns of response-oriented approaches focus upon

1   what constitutes the source of literary meaning; and
2   the nature of the interpretative process that creates it.

Both issues are fundamental to how young readers read, both in and out of school.

The works of Iser on fiction and Rosenblatt on poetry, despite some criticism that Iser has attracted on theoretical grounds, have none the less had greater influence upon the actual teaching of literature and our understanding of children as readers than those of any other theoretical writers. No doubt this is because they avoid what Frank Kermode calls 'free-floating theory' and concentrate, in Iser's words, on 'an analysis of what actually happens when one is reading' (Iser 1978: 19). Iser's theory of aesthetic response (1978) and Rosenblatt's transactional theory of the literary work (1978, 1985) have helped change the culture of the classroom to one which operates on the principle that the text cannot be said to have a meaningful existence outside the relationship between itself and its reader(s). This transfer of power represents a sea-change in critical emphasis and in pedagogical practice from the assumptions most critics and teachers held even a genera-tion ago. Yet it is evolutionary change, not sudden revolution – a progressive rethinking of the way readers create literary experiences for themselves with poems and stories. In fact, reader-response is the evolutionary successor to Leavisite liberal humanism. It is perceived – within the area of literature teaching – as providing a framework of now familiar ideas which are widely accepted and to which other lines of critical activity often make refer-ence: the plurality of meanings within a literary work; the creative participation of the reader; the acknowledgement that the reader is not a *tabula rasa* but brings idiosyncratic knowledge and personal style to the act of reading; and the awareness that interpretation is socially, historically and culturally formed. All these ideas are ones that have had a sharp impact upon the study of texts and upon research into young readers' reading in the field of children's literature.

Young readers and their books

Reader-response approaches to children's literature which set out to answer the questions raised at the beginning of this chapter all have a direct relationship with pedagogy. Some are concerned with children's responses, mainly to fiction and poetry but latterly also to picture books, with the broad aim of improving our understanding of what constitutes good practice in literature teaching. Others employ reader-response methods in order to explore children's concepts and social attitudes. Others again are text-focused and use concepts and ideas from reader-response criticism of adult literature in order to examine children's books, with the aim of uncovering their implied audience and, thence, some-thing of the singularity of a specifically *children's* literature.

This diversity creates two problems: first, there is bound to be overlap. Many studies cover both textual qualities and children's responses as complementary aspects of a unitary experience which, as the foregoing discussion has argued, follows from the mainstream thinking of reader-response criticism. When considering a study under one or other of the headings below, therefore, its writer's principal orientation has been the guide. Second, there is bound to be anomaly. The nature and complexity of the studies varies greatly. In particular, there are two important collections of papers devoted to theoretical research and empirical enquiries in this area (Cooper 1985a; Many and Cox 1992). These are most conveniently considered between discussion of the first and second themes below to which most of their papers relate.

The discussion deals, in turn, with five themes: the process of responding; development in reading; types of reader behaviour; culturally oriented studies exploring children's attitudes; and text-oriented studies employing reader-response concepts.

The process of responding

The stances of those enquirers who have explored the response processes of young readers vary as much as those of the literary theorists, but the most common one is that of the teacher–researcher attempting to theorise classroom practice. The range and combinations of the variables in these studies are enormous: texts, contexts, readers and research methods are all divisible into subsets with seemingly infinite permutations. Among texts, short stories, poems, fairy tales and picture books are favoured, with a few studies focusing upon the novel and none on plays. Contexts, in the sense of physical surroundings, also influence response. The 'classroom' itself can mean a variety of things and clearly there are crucial differences between, say, monitoring the responses of thirty children within normal lesson time and four or five children who volunteer to work outside lessons. Most studies are small-scale enquiries run by individual researchers, perhaps with a collaborative element; hence, the focus is usually narrow when selecting the number, age-level, social background, gender and literacy level of the readers. Finally, reader-response monitoring procedures are generally devised in the knowledge that the medium is the message. The ways readers are asked to present their responses are fundamental influences upon those responses; they range from undirected invitations to free association or 'say what comes into your mind as you read', through various 'prompts' or guideline questions to consider, to the explicit questionnaire. Oral, written, or graphic responses and whether the readers are recording individually or in groups all provide further dimensions to the means of monitoring and collecting response data.

Guidance through this diversity is offered by two older books already mentioned (Purves and Beach 1972; D'Arcy 1973); and, more recently, by Galda (1983) in a special issue of the *Journal of Research and Development in Education* on 'Response to Literature: Empirical and Theoretical Studies', and by Squire's chapter 'Research on Reader Response and the National Literature Initiative' in Hayhoe and Parker (Squire 1990: 13–24). What follows does not attempt to be exhaustive but briefly to indicate the main lines that process studies have taken.

The process of responding became one of the main objects of enquiry during the 1980s. Studies of children's responses to poetry began to appear in articles or booklet form: Wade (1981) adapted Squire's (1964) work on short stories to compare how a supervised and an unsupervised group of middle-school children responded to a poem by Charles Tomlinson. Dixon and Brown (1984) studied the writings of seventeen-year-old students in order to identify what was being assessed in their responses; Atkinson (1985) built upon Purves and Rippere's (1968) categories and explored the process of response to poems by children of different ages. Several books also focused exclusively on young readers and poetry and, either wholly or in part, concerned themselves with the response process, notably Benton (1986), Dias and Hayhoe (1988) and Benton *et al.* (1988). The work of Barnes (1976), particularly, lies behind the enquiries of Benton (1986) into small group responses to poetry by thirteen- to fourteen-year-olds. What is characterised as 'lightly-structured, self-directed discussion' is seen as the means of optimising group talk about poems and as the most appropriate way for teacher–researchers to explore the process of response. Dias and Hayhoe (1988) build upon Dias's earlier work (1986) to develop responding-aloud proto-cols (RAPs) which, essentially, require individual pupils to think aloud as they attempt to make sense of a poem with the help, if needed, of a non-directive interviewer. Preparatory group discussions were used to build up confidence for the individual sessions. The RAP transcripts were then analysed to see how pupils negotiated meaning. Dias and Hayhoe claim that their study is 'designed to track the process of responding as it occurs' (1988: 51) and their methodology is a significant contribution to this end.

Similarly, the work of Benton and his co-authors (1988) focuses upon process. It shows three experienced teachers exploring how their students, aged fourteen and above, read and respond to poetry. Rosenblatt's transactional theory underpins the approach, espe-cially in Teasey's work, which gives the hard evidence for the reader's 'evocation' of a poem through meticulous, descriptive analyses of aesthetic reading. Bell's data shows the emphases of the response process from initial encounter through group discussion, to an eventual written account, in such a way that what in mathematics is called 'the working' can be observed – in this case, the slow evolution over time and in different contexts of how young readers make meaning. Hurst's focus is upon the whole class rather than indi-viduals. From studying the responses of pupils in a variety of classrooms and with different teachers and texts, he develops a model of three frames (story, poet, form), derived from Barnes and Todd's (1977) notion of the 'cycles of utterances' that characterise group talk, as a means of mapping the episodes of a group's engagement with a poem. The three enquiries are set against a critical appraisal of the main theorists in the field from Richards to Rosenblatt and all contribute to the development of a response-centred methodology.

The process of responding to fictional narrative was first examined by Squire (1964) and Purves and Rippere (1968), whose early studies provoked many adaptations of their work with students of different ages and backgrounds. These studies all tended to cate-gorise the elements of response, with Squire's list emerging as the most commonly quoted and replicated in studies of children's responses. Squire's study of adolescents responding to short stories described the six elements of response as literary judgements, interpreta-tional responses, narrational reactions, associational responses, self-involvement and prescriptive judgements (Squire 1964: 17–18). He showed that the greater the involve-ment of readers, the stronger was their tendency to make literary judgements; and that what he termed 'happiness-binding' (41) was a characteristic of adolescent readers' behaviour. Here, as in many studies of fiction reading, there is a noticeable move towards a broadly psychoanalytical explanation for the gratifications readers seek in fiction (compare Holland 1975). More recent studies include those of Fox (1979), whose phrase 'dark watchers' (32) is a memorable description of the imaginary, spectator role that young readers often adopt during reading; and Jackson (1980), who explored the initial responses of children to fiction which he later developed more fully throughout the secondary-school age range (Jackson 1983). Several books also focused wholly or in part upon young readers' response processes, notably Protherough (1983), Benton and Fox (1985) and Thomson (1986). Drawing upon enquiries he conducted in Hull, Protherough suggests that there are five major ways in which children see the process of reading fiction: projection into a character, projection into the situation, association between book and reader, the distanced viewer, and detached evaluation. There is a developmental dimension, and he argues that maturity in reading is connected with the ability to operate in an increasing number of modes.

Benton and Fox address the question of what happens when we read stories and consider that the process of responding involves the reader in creating a secondary world. This concept is elaborated with reference to children's accounts of their experiences with various stories. The reading experience is then characterised in two ways: first, as a four-phase process of feeling like reading, getting into the story, being lost in the book, and having an increasing sense of an ending; and second, as an activity consisting of four elements – picturing, anticipating and retrospecting, interacting and evaluating. This latter description has been taken up by others, notably Corcoran (Corcoran and Evans 1987: 45–51).

Thomson's work with teenage readers offers a further description of the elements of response to fiction and cross-hatches this with a developmental model. The requirements for satisfaction at all stages are enjoyment and elementary understanding. Assuming these are met, his six stages are described as: unreflective interest in action; empathising; analogising; reflecting on the significance of events and behaviour; reviewing the whole work as the author's creation; and the consciously considered relationship with the author. Thomson's is a sophisticated and detailed account, firmly rooted in young readers' fiction reading, and drawing effectively upon the theoretical literature summarised earlier in this chapter.

As can be seen from this summary, studies of the process of responding tend towards categorisation of the different psychological activities involved and towards descriptions of what constitutes maturation in reading. Two collections of papers which should contribute more than they do to our understanding of the process of responding are Cooper (1985a) and Many and Cox (1992), although in their defence it has to be said that the former has a focus upon the theories that should guide our study of readers and the research methodologies that derive from them, and the latter is primarily concerned with reader 'stance' (Rosenblatt 1978) as the discussion of types of reader below indicates. Brief comment upon these two collections is appropriate before moving on to consider reading development.

Only some of the seventeen papers in Cooper's compilation bear upon the subject of children and literature. The first of the three parts of the book is helpful in relating theoretical issues of response to practice, especially the chapters by Rosenblatt, Purves and Petrosky. In Part 2, Kintgen's piece stands out, not only because its focus is poetry (a comparative rarity in such company), but because it faces up to the problems of monitoring responses, and attempts to describe the mental activities and processes of the reader. Kintgen's subjects (as with many researchers) are graduate students, but the methodology here could readily transfer to younger readers. The four contributors to the final part of the book on classroom literature, whom one might expect to deal with children and their books, studiously avoid doing so, preferring instead to discuss theoretical and methodological issues such as the need to identify response research with literary pedagogy (Bleich), the use of school surveys (Squire 1985), and the evaluation of the outcomes of literary study (Cooper 1985b).

Many and Cox (1992) take their impetus from Cooper's book and their inspiration from Rosenblatt (1978). The first part gives theoretical perspectives on reader stance and response and includes specific consideration of readings of selected children's books (Benton 1992b) and of young readers' responses (Corcoran). The papers in Part 2 focus upon students' perspectives when reading and responding and tell us more about types of readers than about process; these are dealt with below. Part 3 deals with classroom interactions of teachers, students and literature. Hade explores 'stance' in both silent reading and reading aloud, arguing its transactional and triadic nature in the classroom. Zancella writes engagingly about the use of biography, in the sense of a reader's personal history, in responding to literature and how this influences the teacher's methods. Zarrillo and Cox build upon Rosenblatt's efferent/aesthetic distinction and urge more of the latter in classroom teaching in the light of their empirical findings that 'elementary teachers tend to direct children to adopt efferent stances towards literature' (245). Many and Wiseman take a similar line and report their enquiries into teaching particular books (for example, Mildred Taylor's *Roll of Thunder, Hear My Cry* (1976)) with efferent and aesthetic emphases to different, parallel classes. At various points, all these studies touch upon the issue of the process of responding; but, equally, they also relate to some of the other issues that are discussed in the remainder of this chapter.

Development in reading

Of these issues, the question of how children develop as readers of literature is one of the most frequently raised. This has been approached in four main ways: personal reminiscences of bookish childhoods (Sampson 1947; Inglis 1981); the growth of the child's sense of story in relation to the Piagetian stages of development (Applebee 1978; Tucker 1981); the development of literacy, with the idea of matching individual and age-group needs to appropriate books (Fisher 1964; Meek 1982); and deductions about development drawn from surveys of children's reading interests and habits (Jenkinson 1940; Whitehead *et al.* 1977). While none of these writers would see their work as necessarily falling strictly under the reader-response heading, all are in fact listening to what children as readers say about their experiences and, in more recent years, are conscious of interpreting their findings against a background of reader-response criticism. This awareness is evident, for example, in the work of Tucker (1980) who, in a paper entitled 'Can We Ever Know the Reader's Response?', argues that children's responses are different from adults' (in, say, the relative emphasis they give to the quality of the writing as opposed to the pace of the plot) before he goes on to relate their responses to intellectual and emotional development as psychologists describe it (the subject of his subsequent book (Tucker 1981)). In the highly influential work of Meek, too, from *The Cool Web* (Meek *et al.* 1977) onwards, reader-response criticism has been one of her perspectives – evident, for example, in her 'Prolegomena for a Study of Children's Literature' (1980: 35) and in her exploration of the relationship between literacy and literature in her account of the reading lessons to be found in picture books (Meek 1988). Or again, in the discussion of their findings of children's reading preferences at ten-plus, twelve-plus and fourteen-plus, Whitehead and his team speculate about the cognitive and affective factors involved in the interaction between children and their books. All are aware that response-oriented criticism should be able to tell us more about this interaction at different ages.

Developmental stages in literary reading are outlined by Jackson (1982), Protherough (1983) and Thomson (1986) on the basis of classroom enquiries with young readers as we have already seen; and there have been some small-scale studies of reading development focused upon responses to specific books. Hickman (1983) studied three classes, totalling ninety primary-school-aged children, and monitored their spontaneous responses, variations in solicited verbal responses, the implications of non-responses, and the role of the teacher in respect of two texts: Silverstein's *Where the Sidewalk Ends* (1974) and McPhail's *The Magical Drawings of Moony B. Finch* (1978). She was interested in the age-related patterns of responses and in the influences of the class teacher. Cullinan *et al.* (1983) discuss the relationship between pupils' comprehension and response to literature and report the results of a study, conducted with eighteen readers in grades 4, 6 and 8, which focused on readings of and taped responses to Paterson's *Bridge to Terabithia* (1977) and Le Guin's *A Wizard of Earthsea* (1968). Their data confirmed that there are clear developmental levels in children's comprehension and they claim that: 'Reader-response provides a way to look at the multidimensional nature of comprehension' (37). Galda (1992) has subsequently reported on a four-year longitudinal study of eight readers' readings of selected books representing realistic and fantasy fiction in order to explore any differences in responses to these two genres. The 'realistic' texts included Paterson's *Bridge to Terabithia* (1977) and S. E. Hinton's *The Outsiders* (1968); the 'fantasy' texts included L'Engle's *A Wind in the Door* (1973) and Cooper's *The Dark is Rising* (1981). She considers reading factors, such as developing analytical ability, and text factors, arguing that children find it easier to enter the world of realistic fiction than they do of fantasy stories; and concludes by advocating the 'spectator role' (Harding 1937; Britton 1970) as a stance that offers readers access to both genres.

Types of reader behaviour

The third theme concerns different sorts of readers or readings. It would be too much to claim that there is an established typology of readers; there have been few studies that venture beyond generalised discussions such as that between 'interrogative' and 'acquiescent' reading styles (Benton and Fox 1985: 16–17), itself a tentative extension of Holland's (1975) notion of personal style in reading behaviour. One study that does make some clear category decisions is that of Dias and Hayhoe (1988: 52–8) in respect of fourteen- and fifteen-year-old pupils reading and responding to poems. Their 'responding-aloud protocols' (RAPs), described earlier, revealed four patterns of reading: paraphrasing, thematising, allegorising and problem solving. They stress that these are patterns of reading not readers (57) but have difficulty throughout in maintaining this discrimination. None the less, theirs is the most sophisticated account to date of that phenomenon that most teachers and others concerned with children's books have noticed without being able to explain, namely that individual children reveal personal patterns of reading behaviour irrespective of the nature of the book being read. The study of these four reading patterns under the sub-headings of what the reader brings to the text, the reader's moves, closure, the reader's relationship with the text, and other elements is one that needs to be replicated and developed in relation to other types of text.

Fry (1985) explored the novel reading of six young readers (two eight-year-olds, two twelve-year-olds, two fifteen-year-olds) through tape-recorded conversations over a period of eight months. The six case studies give some vivid documentary evidence of individual responses (for example, on the ways readers see themselves in books (99)) and also raise general issues such as re-readings, the appeal of series writers like Blyton, the relation of text fiction and film fiction, and the developmental process. Many and Cox's (1992) collection of papers includes their own development of Rosenblatt's efferent/aesthetic distinction in respect of the stances adopted by a class of ten-year-olds in their responses to Byars's *The Summer of the Swans* (1970) and other stories. Encisco, in the same collection, builds upon Benton's (1983) model of the secondary world and gives an exhaustive case-study of one ten-year-old girl's reading of chapters from three stories in order to observe the strategies she uses to create her story world from these texts. Benton's development of the secondary world concept, after Tolkien (1938) and Auden (1968), is reappraised in Many and Cox (1992: 15–18 and 23–48) and has also been extended by the author to incorporate aspects of the visual arts, notably paintings and picture books (Benton 1992a). The concept as originally formulated appeared in the special issue of the *Journal of Research and Development of Education* (Agee and Galda 1983) along with several other articles that focus upon readers' behaviours. Beach (1983) looks at what the reader brings to the text and reports an enquiry aimed at determining the effects of differences in prior knowledge of literary conventions and attitudes on readers' responses through a comparison between high school and college English education students' responses to a short story by Updike. Pillar (1983) discusses aspects of moral judgement in response to fairy tales and presents the findings from a study of the responses of sixty elementary school children to three fables. The responses are discussed in terms of the principles of justice that distinguish them. This enquiry edges us towards the fourth theme, where reader-response methods are employed in culturally oriented studies.

Culturally oriented studies

Children's concepts and social attitudes have been the subject of reader-response enquiries in three complementary ways: multicultural and feminist studies, which explore how far literature can be helpful in teaching about issues of race or gender; whole-culture studies, which consider children's responses to literature in the context of the broad range of their interests; and cross-cultural studies, which compare the responses of young readers from different countries to the same texts to identify similarities and cultural differences. An article and a book about each group must suffice to indicate the emphases and the degree to which reader-response theory and practice have been influential.

Evans (1992) contains several studies with explicitly cultural concerns, among which is 'Feminist Approaches to Teaching: John Updike's "A & P"' by Bogdan *et al.*, which sets out to explore gender issues in the classroom via Updike's short story. They quote Kolodny (in Showalter 1985: 158) in support of the shift feminist studies makes from seeing reader-response in a purely experiential dimension to a more philosophical enquiry into how 'aesthetic response is … invested with epistemological, ethical, and moral concerns'. The feminist position is stated explicitly: 'Reading pleasure can no longer be its own end-point, but rather part of a larger dialectical process which strives for an "altered reading attentiveness" to gender in every reading act' (Evans 1992: 151). This dialectical response model is further elaborated and augmented by specific pedagogical suggestions to help young readers towards this new attentiveness.

Within the broadly, and somewhat uncomfortably, defined field of multicultural education, the most sophisticated use of reader-response criticism and practice is Beverley Naidoo's (1992) enquiry into the role of literature, especially fiction, in educating young people about race. Working with a teacher and his class of all-white thirteen- to fourteen-year-old pupils over a period of one academic year, Naidoo introduced a sequence of four novels to their work with increasingly explicit racial issues: *Buddy* (Hinton 1983), *Friedrich* (Richter 1978), *Roll of Thunder, Hear My Cry* (Taylor 1976) and *Waiting for the Rain* (Gordon 1987). Influenced by Hollindale's (1988) notion of 'the reader as ideologist', Rosenblatt's (1978, 1985) transactional theory and Benton's ethnographic approach to reader-response enquiries (Benton *et al.* 1988), Naidoo adopted an action-researcher role to develop 'ways of exploring these texts which encouraged empathy with the perspective of characters who were victims of racism but who resisted it' (22). Written and oral responses in journals and discussion were at the centre of the procedures. Many challenging and provocative issues are examined through this enquiry, including overt and institutionalised racism, whether teaching about race challenges or merely reinforces racism, the nature of empathy and the gender differences pupils exhibited. The cultural context, especially the subculture of the particular classroom, emerged as a dominant theme. The subtle interrelatedness of text, context, readers and writers is sensitively explored in a study that shows how reader-response methods can help to illuminate the values and attitudes that readers sometimes hide, even from themselves.

The second group of whole-culture studies tends to focus upon adolescent readers. Stories and poems, especially those encountered in school, are seen as but one aspect of the cultural context in which teenagers live and in which books are low on their agenda after television, computer games, rock music, comics and magazines. Beach and Freedman's (1992) paper, 'Responding as a Cultural Act: Adolescents' Responses to Magazine Ads and Short Stories', widens the perspective from the individual reader's 'personal' and 'unique' responses to accommodate the notion of response as a cultural practice. They discuss the cultural practices required in adolescent peer groups and note the ways in which these are derived from experiences with the mass media, with examples from adolescents' responses to magazine advertisements and short stories. Particular points of interest in the responses of these 115 eighth- and eleventh-grade pupils are the gender differences, the tendency to blur fiction and reality when talking about the advertising images, and the low incidence of critical responses.

Reader-response criticism also influences Sarland's (1991) study of young people's reading. He takes seriously both Chambers's (1977) account of the implied child reader (discussed below) and Meek's (1987) plea for an academic study of children's literature which situates it within the whole culture of young people. Building on Fry's (1985) work, he considers the popular literature that children read both in relation to a culture dominated by television and video and in relation to the 'official' literature read in school. By eliciting and analysing students' responses to such books as King's *Carrie* (1974) and Herbert's *The Fog* (1975), Sarland draws upon response-oriented theory and practice to discuss the importance of these texts to their readers and to begin to open up a subculture of which, at best, teachers are usually only hazily aware.

Cross-cultural studies are relatively uncommon for the obvious reason that they are more difficult to set up and sustain. Bunbury and Tabbert's article for *Children's Literature in Education* (1989, reprinted Hunt 1992) compared the responses of Australian and German children to an Australian bush-ranger story, Stow's *Midnite* (1967/1982). Using Jauss's notion of 'ironic identification', where the reader is drawn in and willingly submits to the fictional illusion only to have the author subvert this aesthetic experience, the enquiry considered a range of responses; while there are interesting insights into individual readings, it none the less ends inconclusively by stating: 'The best we can say is that the capacity to experience ironic identification extends along a spectrum of reading encounters which vary in intensity' (Hunt 1992: 124). The study is ambitious in tackling two difficult topics whose relationship is complex: children's sense of the tone of a text and the effect of translation upon the readers' responses. To begin to open up such issues is an achievement in itself.

Chapter 6 of Dias and Hayhoe's (1988) book makes explicit the international perspective on the teaching of poetry that permeates the whole of this Anglo-Canadian collaboration. Views from Australia, Britain, Canada and the USA on good practice in poetry teaching all share the same principle of developing pupils' responses. Clearly, cross-cultural influences grow more readily and are more easily monitored in English-speaking countries than elsewhere; yet there is sufficient evidence here of cultural diversity to encourage other researchers to explore the ways in which we can learn from each other about how children's responses to literature are mediated by the cultural contexts in which they occur.

Text-oriented studies

Studies of children's literature which directly parallel the work of, say, Iser (1974) or Fish (1980) in their close examination of particular texts are surprisingly rare. It is as if those who work in this field have been so concerned with pedagogy and children as readers that they have failed to exploit reader-response criticism as a means of understanding the nature of actual texts. Two concepts, however, which have received some attention are the 'implied reader' and the notion of 'intertextuality'. The first, developed by Iser (1974) after Booth (1961), for a time encouraged the search for the 'implied child reader' in children's books; the second followed from enquiries into how readers make meaning and the realisation of the complex relationships that exist between the readers, the text, other texts, other genres, and the cultural context of any 'reading'.

Although Chambers (1977) and Tabbert (1980) gave the lead, the implied child reader remains a neglected figure in children's book criticism. In 'The Reader in the Book' Chambers takes Iser's concept and advocates its central importance in children's book criticism. He illustrates Roald Dahl's assumptions about the implied adult reader of his story 'The Champion of the World' (1959) in contrast to those about the implied child reader of the rewritten version in the children's book *Danny: The Champion of the World* (1975), and argues that the narrative voice and textual features of the latter create a sense of an intimate, yet adult-controlled, relationship between the implied author and the implied child reader. He generalises from this example to claim that this voice and this relationship are common in children's books, and identifies both with the figure of the 'friendly adult storyteller who knows how to entertain children while at the same time keeping them in their place' (69). Much of the remainder of his article rests upon two further narrative features: 'the adoption of a child point of view' (72) to sustain this adult-author/child-reader relationship; and the deployment within the text of indeterminacy gaps which the reader must fill in order to generate meanings. These three characteristics – the literary relationship, the point of view, and the tell-tale gaps – are then exemplified in a critique of Boston's *The Children of Green Knowe* (1954).

Chambers's article is already regarded as a landmark in the development of criticism (Hunt 1990: 90), not least because it opened up one means of defining the singular character of a form of literature that is designated by its intended audience. That this lead has been followed so infrequently calls into question the seriousness of the whole critical enterprise in this field. Among the few who have exploited these concepts in relation to children's books is Tabbert (1980), who comments usefully on the notion of 'telling gaps' and 'the implied reader' in some classic children's texts and sees a fruitful way forward in psychologically oriented criticism, particularly in the methodology adopted by Holland. Benton (1992a) parallels the historically changing relationship between implied author and implied reader that is found in Iser's (1974) studies of Fielding, Thackeray and Joyce, with a corresponding critique of the openings of three novels by children's authors – Hughes's *Tom Brown's Schooldays* (1856), Day Lewis's *The Otterbury Incident* (1948) and Garner's *Red Shift* (1973). The emphases, however, here are upon the nature of the collaborative relationship and upon narrative technique rather than on the implied child reader. Shavit (1983: 60–7) extends Iser's concept to embrace the notion of childhood as well as the child as implied reader. After a historical perspective on the idea of childhood, the discussion focuses upon various versions of 'Little Red Riding Hood' in order to explore 'how far they were responsible for different implied readers' (61). In particular, she argues that prevailing notions of childhood helped determine the changing character of these texts over several centuries from Perrault's version to those of the present day.

By far the most rigorous account of the implied reader is that of Stephens (1992), given from a position that is sceptical about a mode of reading which locates the reader only within the text and ignores questions of ideology. He argues that in critical practice the being or meaning of the text is best characterised as 'a dialectic between textual discourse (including its construction of an implied reader and a range of potential subject positions) and a reader's disposition, familiarity with story conventions and experiential knowledge' (59). His account of ideology and the implied reader in two picture books (Cooper and Hutton, *The Selkie Girl*, 1986; Gerstein, *The Seal Mother*, 1986) develops this argument and leads him to take issue with Chambers's view of the implied reader on ideological grounds. He says of Chambers's account that: 'his own ideology of reading demands a reified "implicated" reader, led by textual strategies to discover a determinate meaning' (67). Stephens's conceptualisation of the implied reader is significant both of itself and in helping to explain the paucity of critical effort in this area following Chambers's article. For it tells us that criticism has moved on and, in particular, that such concepts can no longer be regarded as innocent aspects of narrative.

Stephens, too, offers the fullest account to date of intertextuality in the third chapter of his book, 'Not by Words Alone: Language, Intertextuality and Society' (1992: 84–119). He outlines seven kinds of relationship which may exist between a particular text and any other texts and goes on to discuss various manifestations of intertextuality in children's literature, notably in fairy tales. Agee (1983: 55–9) concentrates on the narrower focus of literary allusion and reader-response and begins to explore the intertextual patterning of such books as *Z for Zachariah* (O'Brien 1977), *Jacob I Have Loved* (Paterson 1981) and *Fahrenheit 451* (Bradbury 1967). Stephens and Agee both approach the topic exclusively through the study of texts.

Meek (1988) keeps young readers constantly in view when she draws upon the inter-text of oral and written literature, together with the Iserian concepts of the implied reader and indeterminacy gaps, in her brief but widely acclaimed paper *How Texts Teach What Readers Learn*. Her main texts are picture books: the telling gaps in *Rosie's Walk* (Hutchins 1969) and *Granpa* (Burningham 1984) and the play of intertexts in *The Jolly Postman* (Ahlberg 1986) and the short story 'William's Version' (Mark 1980) are explored with great subtlety, and display, above all, the quality that distinguishes the best sort of criticism of children's literature: the ability to listen to children's responses to a book and to 'read' these with the same effort of attention that is afforded to the text themselves. Reader-response criticism accommodates both the reader and the text; there is no area of literary activity where this is more necessary than in the literature that defines itself by reference to its young readership.

References

Abrams, M. H. (1953) *The Mirror and the Lamp: Romantic Theory and the Critical Tradition*, New York: Norton.

Agee, H. (1983) 'Literary Allusion and Reader Response: Possibilities for Research', in Agee, H. and Galda, L. (eds) 'Response to Literature: Empirical and Theoretical Studies', *Journal of Research and Development in Education* 16, 3: 55–9.

Agee, H. and Galda, L. (eds) (1983) 'Response to Literature: Empirical and Theoretical Studies', *Journal of Research and Development in Education* 16, 3: 8–75.

Applebee, A. N. (1978) *The Child's Concept of Story: Ages Two to Seventeen*, Chicago, IL and London: Chicago University Press.

Atkinson, J. (1985) 'How Children Read Poems at Different Ages', *English in Education* 19, 1: 24–34.

Auden, W. H. (1968) *Secondary Worlds*, London: Faber.

Barnes, D. (1976) *From Communication to Curriculum*, Harmondsworth: Penguin.

Barnes, D. and Todd, F. (1977) *Communication and Learning in Small Groups*, London: Routledge and Kegan Paul.

Beach, R. (1983) 'Attitudes, Social Conventions and Response to Literature', in Agee, H. and Galda, L. (eds) 'Response to Literature: Empirical and Theoretical Studies', *Journal of Research and Development in Education* 16, 3: 47–54.

Beach, R. and Freedman, K. (1992) 'Responding as a Cultural Act: Adolescents' Responses to Magazine Ads and Short Stories', in Many, J. and Cox, C. (eds) *Reader Stance and Literary Understanding: Exploring the Theories, Research and Practice*, Norwood, NJ: Ablex.

Benton, M. (1983) 'Secondary Worlds', in Agee, H. and Galda, L. (eds) 'Response to Literature: Empirical and Theoretical Studies', *Journal of Research and Development in Education* 16, 3: 68–75.

——(1992a) *Secondary Worlds: Literature Teaching and the Visual Arts*, Milton Keynes: Open University Press.

——(1992b) 'Possible Worlds and Narrative Voices', in Many, J. and Cox, C. (eds) *Reader Stance and Literary Understanding: Exploring the Theories, Research and Practice*, Norwood, NJ: Ablex.

Benton, M. and Fox, G. (1985) *Teaching Literature 9–14*, Oxford: Oxford University Press.

Benton, M., Teasey, J., Bell, R. and Hurst, K. (1988) *Young Readers Responding to Poems*, London: Routledge.

Benton, P. (1986) *Pupil, Teacher, Poem*, London: Hodder and Stoughton.

Bleich, D. (1985) 'The Identity of Pedagogy and Research in the Study of Response to Literature', in Cooper, C. R. (ed.) *Researching Response to Literature and the Teaching of Literature: Points of Departure*, Norwood, NJ: Ablex.

Bogdan, D., Millen, K. J. and Pitt, A. (1992) 'Feminist Approaches to Teaching: John Updike's "A & P"' in Evans, E. (ed.) *Young Readers, New Readings*, Hull: Hull University Press.

Booth, W. C. (1961) *The Rhetoric of Fiction*, Chicago, IL: University of Chicago Press.

Britton, J. N. (1970) *Language and Learning*, London: Allen Lane and The Penguin Press.

Bunbury, R. and Tabbert, R. (1989) 'A Bicultural Study of Identification: Readers' Responses to the Ironic Treatment of a National Hero', *Children's Literature in Education* 20, 1: 25–35.

Chambers, A. (1977) 'The Reader in the Book', *Signal* 23: 64–87.

Cooper, C. R. (ed.) (1985a) *Researching Response to Literature and the Teaching of Literature: Points of Departure*, Norwood, NJ: Ablex.

——(1985b) 'Evaluating the Results of Classroom Literary Study', in Cooper, C. R. (ed.) *Researching Response to Literature and the Teaching of Literature: Points of Departure*, Norwood, NJ: Ablex.

Corcoran, B. (1992) 'Reader Stance: From Willed Aesthetic to Discursive Construction', in Many, J. and Cox, C. (eds) *Reader Stance and Literary Understanding: Exploring the Theories, Research and Practice*, Norwood, NJ: Ablex.

Corcoran, B. and Evans, E. (eds) (1987) *Readers, Texts, Teachers*, Milton Keynes: Open University Press.

Cox, C. B. (1989) *English for Ages 5–16*, London: HMSO.

Culler, J. (1975) *Structuralist Poetics: Structuralism, Linguistics and the Study of Literature*, London: Routledge and Kegan Paul.

Cullinan, B. E., Harwood, K. T. and Galda, L. (1983) 'The Reader and the Story: Comprehension and Response', in Agee, H. and Galda, L. (eds) 'Response to Literature: Empirical and Theoretical Studies', *Journal of Research and Development in Education* 16, 3: 29–38.

D'Arcy, P. (1973) *Reading for Meaning*, vol. 2, London: Hutchinson.

Dias, P. (1986) 'Making Sense of Poetry', *English and Education*, Sheffield: NATE, 20(2).

Dias, P. and Hayhoe, M. (1988) *Developing Response to Poetry*, Milton Keynes: Open University Press.

Dixon, J. and Brown, J. (1984) *Responses to Literature: What is Being Assessed?*, London: Schools' Council Publications.

Encisco, P. (1992) 'Creating the Story World', in Many, J. and Cox, C. (eds) *Reader Stance and Literary Understanding: Exploring the Theories, Research and Practice*, Norwood, NJ: Ablex.

Evans, E. (ed.) (1992) *Young Readers, New Readings*, Hull: Hull University Press.

Fish, S. (1980) *Is There a Text in This Class?*, Cambridge, MA: Harvard University Press.

Fisher, M. (1964) *Intent upon Reading*, London: Brockhampton Press.

Fox, G. (1979) 'Dark Watchers: Young Readers and Their Fiction', *English in Education* 13, 1: 32–5.

Freund, E. (1987) *The Return of the Reader: Reader-Response Criticism*, London: Methuen.

Fry, D. (1985) *Children Talk about Books: Seeing Themselves as Readers*, Milton Keynes: Open University Press.

Galda, L. (1983) 'Research in Response to Literature', *Journal of Research and Development in Education* 16: 1–7.

——(1992) 'Evaluation as a Spectator: Changes across Time and Genre', in Many, J. and Cox, C. (eds) *Reader Stance and Literary Understanding: Exploring the Theories, Research and Practice*, Norwood, NJ: Ablex.

Hade, D. D. (1992) 'The Reader's Stance as Event: Transaction in the Classroom', in Many, J. and Cox, C. (eds) *Reader Stance and Literary Understanding: Exploring the Theories, Research and Practice*, Norwood, NJ: Ablex.

Harding, D. W. (1937) 'The Role of the Onlooker', *Scrutiny* 6: 247–58.

——(1962) 'Psychological Processes in the Reading of Fiction', *British Journal of Aesthetics* 2, 2: 113–47.

Hayhoe, M. and Parker, S. (eds) (1990) *Reading and Response*, Milton Keynes: Open University Press.

Hickman, J. (1983) 'Everything Considered: Response to Literature in an Elementary School Setting', in Agee, H. and Galda, L. (eds) 'Response to Literature: Empirical and Theoretical Studies', *Journal of Research and Development in Education* 16, 3: 8–13.

Hinton, N. (1983) *Buddy*, London: Heinemann Educational.

Hinton, S. E. (1968) *The Outsiders*, New York: Dell.

Holland, N. N. (1975) *Five Readers Reading*, New Haven, CT and London: Yale University Press.

Hollindale, P. (1988) 'Ideology and the Children's Book', *Signal* 55: 3–22.

Holub, R. C. (1984) *Reception Theory*, London: Methuen.

Hunt, P. (ed.) (1990) *Children's Literature: The Development of Criticism*, London: Routledge.

——(ed.) (1992) *Literature for Children: Contemporary Criticism*, London: Routledge.

Inglis, F. (1981) *The Promise of Happiness*, Cambridge: Cambridge University Press.

Iser, W. (1974) *The Implied Reader*, Baltimore, MD: Johns Hopkins University Press.

——(1978) *The Act of Reading: A Theory of Aesthetic Response*, Baltimore, MD: Johns Hopkins University Press.

Jackson, D. (1980) 'First Encounters: The Importance of Initial Responses to Literature', *Children's Literature in Education* 11, 4: 149–60.

——(1982) *Continuity in Secondary English*, London: Methuen.

——(1983) *Encounters with Books: Teaching Fiction 11–16*, London: Methuen.

Jefferson, A. and Robey, D. (1986) *Modern Literary Theory*, 2nd edn, London: Batsford.

Jenkinson, A. J. (1940) *What Do Boys and Girls Read?*, London: Methuen.

Kintgen, E. R. (1985) 'Studying the Perception of Poetry', in Cooper, C. R. (ed.) *Researching Response to Literature and the Teaching of Literature: Points of Departure*, Norwood, NJ: Ablex.

Lerner, L. (ed.) (1983) *Reconstructing Literature*, Oxford: Blackwell.

Many, J. and Cox, C. (eds) (1992) *Reader Stance and Literary Understanding: Exploring the Theories, Research and Practice*, Norwood, NJ: Ablex.

Many, J. and Wiseman, D. (1992) 'Analysing versus Experiencing: The Effects of Teaching Approaches on Students' Responses', in Many, J. and Cox, C. (eds) *Reader Stance and Literary Understanding: Exploring the Theories, Research and Practice*, Norwood, NJ: Ablex.

Meek, M. (1980) 'Prolegomena for a Study of Children's Literature', in Benton, M. (ed.) *Approaches to Research in Children's Literature*, Southampton: Department of Education, Southampton University.

——(1982) *Learning to Read*, London: Bodley Head.

——(1987) 'Symbolic Outlining: The Academic Study of Children's Literature', *Signal* 53: 97–115.

——(1988) *How Texts Teach What Readers Learn*, South Woodchester: Thimble Press.

Meek, M., Warlow, A. and Barton, G. (eds) (1977) *The Cool Web*, London: Bodley Head.

Naidoo, B. (1992) *Through Whose Eyes? Exploring Racism: Reader, Text and Context*, London: Trentham Books.

Petrosky, A. R. (1985) 'Response: A Way of Knowing', in Cooper, C. R. (ed.) *Researching Response to Literature and the Teaching of Literature: Points of Departure*, Norwood, NJ: Ablex.

Pillar, A. M. (1983) 'Aspects of Moral Judgement in Response to Fables', in Agee, H. and Galda, L. (eds) 'Response to Literature: Empirical and Theoretical Studies', *Journal of Research and Development in Education* 16, 3: 39–46.

Protherough, R. (1983) *Developing Response to Fiction*, Milton Keynes: Open University Press.

Purves, A. C. (1985) 'That Sunny Dome: Those Caves of Ice', in Cooper, C. R. (ed.) *Researching Response to Literature and the Teaching of Literature: Points of Departure*, Norwood, NJ: Ablex.

Purves, A. C. and Beach, R. (1972) *Literature and the Reader*, Urbana, IL: NCTE.

Purves, A. C. and Rippere, V. (1968) *Elements of Writing about a Literary Work*, Research Report No. 9, Champaign, IL: NCTE.

Richards, I. A. (1924) *Principles of Literary Criticism*, London: Routledge and Kegan Paul.

——(1929) *Practical Criticism*, London: Routledge and Kegan Paul.

Rosenblatt, L. (1938/1970) *Literature as Exploration*, London: Heinemann.

——(1978) *The Reader, the Text, the Poem: The Transactional Theory of the Literary Work*, Carbondale, IL: Southern Illinois University Press.

——(1985) 'The Transactional Theory of the Literary Work: Implications for Research', in Cooper, C. R. (ed.) *Researching Response to Literature and the Teaching of Literature: Points of Departure*, Norwood, NJ: Ablex.

Sampson, G. (1947) *Seven Essays*, Cambridge: Cambridge University Press.

Sarland, C. (1991) *Young People Reading: Culture and Response*, Milton Keynes: Open University Press.

Scholes, R. (1985) *Textual Power: Literary Theory and the Teaching of English*, New Haven, CT and London: Yale University Press.

Shavit, Z. (1983) 'The Notion of Childhood and the Child as Implied Reader', in Agee, H. and Galda, L. (eds) 'Response to Literature: Empirical and Theoretical Studies', *Journal of Research and Development in Education* 16, 3: 60–7.

Showalter, E. (ed.) (1985) *The New Feminist Criticism: Essays on Women, Literature and Theory*, New York: Pantheon.

Squire, J. R. (1964) *The Responses of Adolescents while Reading Four Short Stories*, Research Report No. 2, Champaign, IL: NCTE.

——(1985) 'Studying Response to Literature through School Surveys', in Cooper, C. R. (ed.) *Researching Response to Literature and the Teaching of Literature: Points of Departure*, Norwood, NJ: Ablex.

——(1990) 'Research on Reader Response and the National Literature Initiative', in Hayhoe, M. and Parker, S. (eds) *Reading and Response*, Milton Keynes: Open University Press.

Stephens, J. (1992) *Language and Ideology in Children's Fiction*, London: Longman.

Suleiman, S. R. and Crosman, I. (eds) (1980) *The Reader in the Text*, Princeton, NJ: Princeton University Press.

Tabbert, R. (1980) 'The Impact of Children's Books: Cases and Concepts', in Fox, G. and Hammond, G. (eds) *Responses to Children's Literature*, New York: K. G. Saur.

Thomson, J. (1986) *Understanding Teenagers Reading: Reading Processes and the Teaching of Literature*, Sydney: Methuen.

Tolkien, J. R. R. (1938) *Tree and Leaf*, London: Unwin Books.

Tompkins, J. P. (1980) *Reader-Response Criticism: From Formalism to Post-Structuralism*, Baltimore, MD: Johns Hopkins University Press.

Tucker, N. (1980) 'Can We Ever Know the Reader's Response?', in Benton, M. (ed.) *Approaches to Research in Children's Literature*, Southampton: Department of Education, Southampton University.

——(1981) *The Child and the Book*, Cambridge: Cambridge University Press.

Wade, B. (1981) 'Assessing Pupils' Contributions in Appreciating a Poem', *Journal of Education for Teaching* 7, 1: 40–9.

Wellek, R. and Warren, A. (1949) *Theory of Literature*, London: Cape.

Whitehead, F., Capey, A. C., Maddren, W. and Wellings, A. (1977) *Children and Their Books*, London: Macmillan.

Wimsatt, W. K. and Beardsley, M. (1954/1970) *The Verbal Icon: Studies in the Meaning of Poetry*, London: Methuen.

Zancella, D. (1992) 'Literary Lives: A Biographical Perspective on the Teaching of Literature', in Many, J. and Cox, C. (eds) *Reader Stance and Literary Understanding: Exploring the Theories, Research and Practice*, Norwood, NJ: Ablex.

Zarillo, J. and Cox, C. (1992) 'Efferent and Aesthetic Teaching', in Many, J. and Cox, C. (eds) *Reader Stance and Literary Understanding: Exploring the Theories, Research and Practice*, Norwood, NJ: Ablex.

Further reading

Beach, R. (1993) *A Teacher's Introduction to Reader-Response Theories*, Urbana, IL: National Council of Teachers of English.

Benton, M. (2000) *Studies in the Spectator Role: Literature, Painting and Pedagogy*, London: RoutledgeFalmer.

Britton, B. and Graesser, A. (eds) (1966) *Models of Understanding Text*, Mawah, NJ: Erlbaum.

Cranny-Francis, A. (1992) *Engendered Fiction: Analysing Gender in the Production and Perception of Texts*, Kensington, NSW: New South Wales University Press.

Davis, T. F. and Womak, K. (2001) *Formalist Criticism and Reader-Response Theory*, New York: Palgrave Macmillan.

Esrock, E. J. (1994) *The Reader's Eye: Visual Imaging as Reader Response*, Baltimore, MD: Johns Hopkins University Press.

Feagen, S. L. (1996) *Reading with Feeling: The Aesthetics of Appreciation*, Ithaca, NY: Cornell University Press.

Holland, N. N. (1968) *The Dynamics of Literary Response*, New York: Norton.

——(1973) *Poems in Persons*, New York: NortonKintsch, W. (1998) *Comprehension: A Paradigm for Cognition*, Cambridge: Cambridge University Press.

Nardocchio, E. (ed.) (1992) *Reader Response to Literature: The Empirical Dimension*, Berlin: de Gruyter.

Nell, V. (1988) *Lost in a Book: The Psychology of Reading for Pleasure*, New Haven, CT: Yale University Press.

7 Reading the unconscious
Psychoanalytical criticism

Hamida Bosmajian

Editor's Introduction

Much of what is written about children's literature is implicitly or explicitly concerned with the psychology of the readers, the authors, and the characters in the books. However, as Hamida Bosmajian points out, such criticism very often relies upon 'the informal developmental psychological knowledge of the interpreter without reference to any specific theory'. This chapter provides a clear guide to the key writers and thinkers in the field of psychology, from Freud and Jung to Lacan, and demonstrates how their work can be applied to the problems of elucidating children's literature.

P.H.

Because the child and childhood hold a privileged position in most psychoanalytical theories, the elective affinity between children's literature and psychological criticism seems even more natural than the affinity between psychology and literature in general. Psychoanalytic theory adds to the literary text a 'second dimension – unfolding what might be called the unconscious content of the work' (Holland 1970: 131), but the condensations and displacements at work in the author–text–reader relation are problematised in children's literature because of the double reader: adult/child.

Children's fiction might be impossible because it rests on the assumption that there is a child who can be addressed when, in actuality, 'children's fiction sets up the child as an outsider to its own process, and that aims, unashamedly, to take the child in' (Rose 1984: 2). The implied author, even in first-person narration by a child character, is a displacement of the contexts of personal and collective values and neuroses. Furthermore, while the analyst is supposedly the most reliable reader-interpreter of stories told in a psychoanalytic dialogue by the analysand-author, the reader of adult literature may or may not be a reliable interpreter of the text. In children's literature the implied reader is, moreover, highly unreliable and, therefore, most easily 'taken in'. Thus, the authorial self is in a sense liberated, in that the textual strategies and gaps that constitute the subtext of the work escape the implied reader, the child. The author can experience therapeutic release without anxieties over the scrutiny of an adult's psychoanalytical critique.

The nemesis for the projection of the naive implied reader is the adult reader as psychoanalytic critic of children's literature who exposes the gaps, substitutions and displacements of the author and appropriates the author's text as a symptom of individual or cultural neuroses that underlie and undermine values associated with growth and development. While psychoanalytic critics of adult literature amplify the reader's appreciation of the text, those same critics will, in the case of children's literature, conceal their interpretation from the child and, therewith, both censor and protect the author. The child may be imaged as myth of origin – as father of the man and mother of the woman – but in children's literature the adult is in control.

The correspondences between author–text–reader and analysand–psychoanalytic dialogue-analyst break down, for author–reader are not in a dialogical relation, no matter how intensely the reader *responds*, nor can the critic–interpreter make enquiries of a character in a narrative, as an analyst can in the psychoanalytic situation. While critics act as if one could ask about Alice's relation with her parents as she develops from pawn to queen in *Through the Looking Glass*, they forget that she is a linguistic construct, a trope for the unresolved problems of her author (Greenacre 1955). It is important that psychoanalytic critics are aware of the ambivalences inherent in their method and do not seize one aspect of a psychoanalytical theory as a tool for interpretation, thereby reducing the text to universals about human development (compare Hogan 1990; Knoepflmacher 1990; Phillips and Wojcik-Andrews 1990; Steig 1990; Zipes 1990).

The following discussion will focus on defining those psychoanalytic theories that have influenced the criticism of children's literature. Frequently such criticism relies on the informal developmental psychological knowledge of the interpreter without reference to any specific theory. This is especially true of realistic narratives for young adults. The strongest psychoanalytic tradition of criticism can be found in the interpretation of folk tales and *märchen* and, to a lesser extent, in fantasy literature. While Freud, Jung and their disciples have been important in interpretations of children's literature, the poststructuralist influence has not been as prevalent. Quite dominant, however, is the influence of psychological criticism that relates the development of the child character to the social context depicted in psychologically realistic narratives. Perhaps because of the deep issues involved in psychoanalytic criticism, critics of children's literature occasionally seem to screen discussions of psychoanalytical issues with analyses of social contexts, even where the topic is announced as being psychoanalytical (Smith and Kerrigan 1985).

Freudian criticism

Classical Freudian criticism interprets the work as an expression of psychopathography, as a symptom whose creation provided therapeutic release for the author. In 'The Relation of the Poet to Daydreaming' (1908), Freud saw the crucial relationship between child–play/poet–language:

> every child at play behaves like an imaginative writer, in that he creates a world of his own or, more truly, he arranges the things of this world and orders it in a new way that pleases him better ... Language has preserved this relationship between children's play and poetic creation.
>
> (1908/1963 9: 144)

Just as it does between dream and text.

Freud assumed that all psychoneurotic symptoms are generated by psychic conflicts between a person's sexual desires and the strictures of society. The conflict is expressed through substitutions and displacements, just as in literature a metaphor's tenor and vehicle condense two disparate ideas into one image that hides and reveals what is not articulated. Similarly, displacement substitutes socially acceptable modes for desires that are forbidden. Substitutions thus function as censors in dreams and daydreams, in play and in texts. Freud's first triad of unconscious, pre-conscious and conscious defines the unconscious as a non-verbal, instinctual and infantile given and as dominated by the pleasure principle. The desires and conflicts (oral, anal, oedipal) of childhood persist throughout the adult's life and can be made conscious only by being first raised to the level of the pre-conscious which facilitates the dynamic of consciousness and repression through condensation and displacement. Freud later modified his first triad with the paradigm of id, ego and superego, in part because he suspected a greater simultaneity in the dynamics of the psyche. The revised triad places the embattled ego between the deterministic forces of the id and the internalised strictures of society. It is here where we find the cause of the pessimism in Freudian psychoanalytic theory: the ego's inevitable discontent.

Crucial for Freudian critics of children's literature is the importance Freud gave to the child in the psychoanalytic process. Though the Oedipus complex has been accepted as part of child development, Freud's insistence on the polymorphous sexuality of the infant (1962/1975: 39–72) is somewhat more troubling for most critics of children's literature, for if such sexuality is displaced in the text but communicates itself sub-textually to the child-reader, then the author has transferred his infantile sexuality and communicates it to the child. Texts such as Dahl's *Charlie and the Chocolate Factory* (see Bosmajian 1985) and Sendak's *In the Night Kitchen* might fall into this category.

Freud's profound appreciation of the psychological importance of language was bound to lead him not only to interpretations of everyday language phenomena in the processes of repression and substitution, but also to interpretations of major authors of European literature. In 'The Occurrence in Dreams of Materials from Fairy Tales', Freud notes that fairy tales have such an impact on the mental life of the child that the adult will use them later as screen memories for the experiences of childhood (1913/1963: 59).

'The serious study of children's literature may be said to have begun with Freud', acknowledges Egan in his discussion of *Peter Pan* (1982: 37). Psychoanalysts have indeed been the precursors of the study of children's literature, which explains the powerful but dubious influence of Bruno Bettelheim's *The Uses of Enchantment* (1976), a discussion of familiar tales along infantile and adolescent psychosexual development. Bettelheim sees the child's libido as a threat to both a meaningful life and the social order; therefore, the child needs fairy tales to order his inner house by acquiring a moral education through the tales (5), for, as the stories unfold they 'give conscious credence and body to the id pressures and show ways to satisfy these that are in line with ego and superego' (6). Literary critics have strongly critiqued Bettelheim not only for his a-historicality and reductionism of Freud's theories (Zipes 1979), but also for his punitive pedagogy, for being 'oddly accusatory towards children' (Tatar 1992: xxii) and for displacing his 'own real life fantasies, particularly of the dutiful daughter who takes care of her father's needs' (xxv) into his interpretative work.

Jungian criticism

Jungian criticism discovers archetypes that are the basis for the images in a text. Pre-consciously, or consciously, the author connects with archetypal patterns of which the narrative becomes a variable whose content will somehow relate to the issue of the ego's integration with the self. Jung's concept of the therapeutic process begins with the recognition of the loss of an original wholeness, possessed by every infant, a wholeness lost through self-inflation and/or alienation of the ego. On a mythic level, the ego would experience a dark night of the soul followed by a breakthrough that establishes, not an integration with the self, but a connection with the transpersonal self. The end of Jungian analysis is not a complete individuation of the ego, but rather the analysand's recognition that growth is a life-long process, a quest, during which conscious and unconscious connect primarily through symbols and archetypes.

Jung assumed a personal unconscious consisting of memories and images gathered during a lifetime, for the archetypes, as experienced by the individual, are in and of the world. This personal unconscious is raised to consciousness when the analysand connects the personal with the collective unconscious. The collective unconscious is an *a priori* existence of 'organising factors', the archetypes understood as inborn modes of functioning, rather like a grammar that generates and structures the infinite variables of symbol formations whose recurrence is to be understood again as archetypal (Jung 1964: 67). Archetypes are 'without known origin; and they reproduce themselves in any time or any part of the world – even where transmission by direct descent or "cross-fertilisation" through migration must be ruled out' (69). Jung, too, believed that dreams are meaningful and can be understood (102) as their specific images connect with archetypes whose force can suddenly overwhelm the dreamer. Such an experience contrasts with the conscious use of representing archetypes through culturally defined images and motifs. Jung's own metaphoric use of archetypal images, such as shadow, anima or animus and self, blurred the distinction between archetype as a grammar and archetype as symbol.

Jung, whose theory has been criticised for demanding a vast amount of knowledge of myth, did not perceive the unconscious as an instinctual and libidinal battleground, although he posited a 'primitive psyche' in the child which functions in dreams and fantasies comparable to the physical evolution of mankind in the embryo (1964: 99). In Jung's 'Psychic Conflicts in a Child' (1946/1954: 8–46), the child-patient, obsessed with the origin of babies, fantasised that she would give birth if she swallowed an orange, similar to women in fairy tales whose eating of fruit leads to pregnancy. The child-patient was eventually enlightened by her father, but Jung concludes that, while false explanations are not advisable, no less inadvisable is the insistence on the right explanation, for that inhibits the freedom of the mind's development through concretistic explanations which reduce the spontaneity of image-making to a falsehood (34).

Because the essential nature of all art escapes our understanding, Jung did not perceive literature as psychopathography. We can interpret only 'that aspect of art which consists in the process of artistic creation' (1931/1966: 65). While he admits that literary works can result from the intentionality of the author, they are also those that 'force themselves on the author', reveal his inner nature, and overwhelm the conscious mind with a flood of thoughts and images he never intended to create: 'Here the artist is not identical with the process of creation; he is aware that he is subordinate to his work or stands outside it, as though he were a second person' (73). An author may, for a time, be out of fashion when, suddenly, readers rediscover his work, because they perceive in it archetypes that speak to them with renewed immediacy (77). We can, therefore, only discuss the psychological phenomenology in a work of literature.

It is evident how readily children's literature, especially when it has components of fantasy, connects with Jungian theories. Marie-Louise von Franz (1977, 1978) has written comprehensive studies of fairy tales which the Jungian critic tends to see as 'allegories of the inner life' that meet 'the deep-seated psychic and spiritual needs of the individual' (Cooper 1983: 154). The problem with such criticism is that it reduces images in fairy tales to fixed allegorical meanings without regard for historical and social contexts, as the Jungian critic basically explains metaphor with metaphor. Northrop Frye's discussion of archetypes in terms of convention and genre is an attempt to avoid such reductionism (1957). What makes the Jungian approach attractive to interpreters of children's literature is that the theory assumes an original wholeness that can be regained after alienation is overcome. This coincides with the comic resolution of so many narratives for children and young adults.

In Jungian literary criticism children's literature is often seen as privileged, just as the 'primitive psyche' of the child is in Jungian psychoanalysis. 'Children's literature initiates us into psychic reality, by telling about the creatures and perils of the soul and the heart's possibilities of blessing in images of universal intelligibility' (Hillman 1980: 5). At its best Jungian criticism is able to integrate the author's and the reader's needs as exemplified in Lynn Rosenthal's interpretation of Lucy Boston's *The Children of Green Knowe* (1980).

Ego psychology and object relations theories

The generation of psychoanalysts that was influenced by, reacted against and revised Freud, distinguishes itself by overcoming Freud's pessimism regarding the ego's inevitable discontent. While the new focus does not deny the existence of the unconscious, it emphasises the possibility of healthy growth and development in the ego's self-realisation in relation to its environment. Karen Horney and Abraham Maslow, Melanie Klein and Donald Winnicott describe possibilities for growth through constructive management of the id's pressures. Each insists that the developing psyche of the child responds to environmental conditions with a positive urge to self-actualisation that is thwarted only by hostile environments. From the perspective of ego psychology, author and reader participate in a shareable fantasy that constructively breaks down 'for a time the boundaries between self and other, inner and outer, past and future, and … may neutralise the primal aggressions bound up in those separations' (Holland 1968: 340). Psychoanalytic literary critics have, however, also been concerned that ego psychology tends to be in one direction only, 'namely from the ego as a publicly adjusted identity' (Wright 1984: 57).

Karen Horney and Abraham Maslow

According to Horney, the goal of psychoanalysis is the patient's discovery of the possibility of self-realisation and the recognition that good human relations are an essential part of this, along with the faculty for creative work and the acceptance of personal responsibility (1950: 334). Persistent denial of childhood conflicts and their screening with defensive self-delusions block self-realisation. Irrational expectations or 'neurotic claims' such as self-idealisation obscure not only self-hate, but also 'the unique alive forces' that each self possesses and that are distorted by the self-illusions. The therapeutic process weakens the obstructive forces so that the constructive forces of the real self can emerge (348). The constructive forces in ego psychology become known as the 'Third Force'.

Bernard Paris has applied 'Third Force' psychology to several canonical novels whose self-alienating characters fit Horney's descriptions of neurotic styles, while self-activating characters express their 'Third Force' as defined by Maslow (Paris 1974: 29). For Maslow, the 'Third Force' is our 'essentially biologically based inner nature', unique to the person but also species-wide, whose needs, emotions and capacities are 'either neutral, pre-moral or positively good' (1968: 3). Neuroses result when our hierarchically organised basic needs are not met (21). When one level of needs is satisfied, the needs of another level emerge as persons define themselves existentially. During that process the person has 'peak experiences', epiphanic moments that afford glimpses into the state of being fully actualised and can have the effect of removing symptoms, of changing a person's view of himself and the world, of releasing creativity and generally conveying the idea that life is worth living in spite of its difficulties (101). Maslow admits that not all peak experiences are moments of 'Being recognition' (100), but he insists that people are 'most their identities in peak experiences' (103) where they feel most self-integrated.

The development of the ego as self-reliant and socially accepted is perhaps most evident in the young adult novel whose comic resolution integrates the young person with socially acceptable norms. Frequently such narratives include the figure of the social worker or therapist who aids the process, or the young protagonist plans to become a therapist so as to 'help kids in trouble'. Such problem narratives are accessible to young readers through stories that occasionally seem like case studies. The young adult novel that projects the genuine misfit as a worthwhile subject is a rarity. The largely middle-class context of young adult novels generally furthers the optimism implied in ego psychology.

Melanie Klein and D. W. Winnicott

According to Klein, because the ego is not fully integrated at birth, it is subject to splitting and fragmentation as it projects states of feeling and unconscious wishes on objects or absorbs qualities of the object through introjection where they become defined as belonging to the ego.

Like Freud, Klein saw the 'exploration of the unconscious [as] the main task of psychoanalytic procedure, and that the analysis of transference [was] the means of achieving this' (1955/1975a: 123). Her analysands were primarily children whose inability to freely associate verbally led Klein to develop the psychoanalytic play technique already begun by Anna Freud (1925/1975b: 146).

The use of simple toys in a simply equipped room brought out 'a variety of symbolical meanings' bound up with the child's fantasies, wishes and experiences. By approaching the child's play in a manner similar to Freud's interpretation of dreams, but by always individualising the child's use of symbols, Klein felt she could gain access to the child's unconscious (1955/1975a: 137). She discovered that the primary origin of impulses, fantasies and anxieties could be traced back to the child's original object relation – the mother's breast – even when the child was not breastfed (138).

In commenting on the influence of Klein on literary theory, Elizabeth Wright regrets that Klein's demonstration of fantasy as a precondition of any engagement with reality has been neglected by literary critics who have instead focused on the aesthetic of ego psychology (1984: 83–4). It is through the structure of fantasy that the child acts out not only real or imagined damage, but also the desire for reparation. Klein saw the monsters and menacing figures of myths and fairy tales as parent displacements exerting unconscious influences on the child by making it feel threatened and persecuted, but such emotions 'can clear our feelings to some extent towards our parents of grievances, we can forgive them for the frustrations we had to bear, become at peace with ourselves' so that 'we are able to love others in the true sense of the word' (1925/1975b: 343).

In criticisms of children's literature, Klein's approach can reveal how the text enables the actualisation of the ego intentionally or how it falls short of it. For example, an interpretation of Bianco's *The Velveteen Rabbit* reveals it as a fantasy of unresolved ambivalence between the need to be loved and becoming independent, that is, real. Because 'the story never acknowledges the Rabbit's desire to grow away from the object of his attachment, and hence never acknowledges the basis for his entry into the depressive position, it cannot credit him with working through it' (Daniels 1990: 26). The Kleinian perspective also offers insight into the relation of fantasy to guilt and reparation as exemplified in White's *Charlotte's Web* (Rustin and Rustin 1987: 161).

While Klein focused on play as a means to the end of the therapeutic process, D. W. Winnicott saw play as intrinsically facilitating healthy development and group relationships. Even psychoanalysis is an elaborate playing 'in the service of communication with oneself and others' (1971: 41). In his studies of babies and children, Winnicott retained the psychoanalytic attention to inner reality along with an emphasis on the child's cultural and social context. Crucial in his discovery is the concept of the 'transitional object': 'one must recognise the central position of Winnie-the-Pooh' (xi). By transitional object and transitional space Winnicott designates the intermediate area of experience between the thumb and the teddy bear, between oral eroticism and true object relationships. Identifying the mother's breast as part of itself, the baby must develop the ability of the 'not me' through substitutions which are transitions between the illusion of identification and the acceptance of the 'not me'. The baby's relationship with the transitional object has special qualities: the infant assumes right but not omnipotence over the object which can be loved and changed, even mutilated, by the infant. Gradually, the infant will be able to detach itself from the object which becomes consigned to a limbo, rather than being introjected by the infant (1–5). The object is not a signifier for some hidden unconscious content, but a crucial partner in the game of intersubjectivity as the playing infant tests out the 'me'/'not me'.

Winnicott's concept of the transitional object not only lends itself to the interpretation of content images in narratives, but also to the text itself. Both author and reader can claim the text as transitional object. Small children do indeed appropriate a book as object – loving it, adding to it, mutilating it. An especially Winnicottian book would be Margaret Wise Brown's *Good Night Moon*, which has been cited as an example of the child's having just learned the distinction between animate and inanimate objects. 'Good night, bears' (toys) and 'good night, kittens' is acceptable, but saying good night to chairs and mittens provokes shrieks of laughter in the child (Applebee 1978: 41) who does not yet accept the object 'bear' as inanimate. *Good Night Moon* is, for a certain age, a transitional object containing many transitional objects that assuage bedtime anxieties as the child connects with all of them, thus assuring itself of the 'me' before the lights go out at bedtime.

Jacques Lacan: the return to Freud through language

For Freud the subconscious is the irreducible radical of the psyche, its universal, whose paradox it is that nothing raised from it remains unconscious: we can only be conscious *of something*. Thus the unconscious is replaced by the comprehensible mental acts of the ego, be they dreams, symbolisations or linguistic utterances. As Wright points out, for Jacques Lacan 'the dictum "the unconscious is structured like a language"' is borne out in that

> every word indicates the absence of what it stands for, a fact that intensifies the frustration of this child of language, the unconscious, since the absence of satisfaction has not to be accepted. Language imposes a chain of words along which the ego must move while the unconscious remains in search of the object it has lost.
>
> (Wright 1984: 111)

The unconscious as a language allows Lacan to revise Freud's self-sufficiency of the unconscious with social interaction. How this comes about through the development of the infant and how this relates to the perception of the text as psyche – a major shift away from the author's or reader's psyche – has special relevance to interpreters of children's literature.

Lacan distinguishes three stages in the infant's development: the imaginary, the symbolic and the real. In the imaginary or mirror stage, which can happen at the age of six months, the infant receives the *imago* of its own body (Lacan 1977: 3). Having seen itself only as fragmentary, the infant perceives in the mirror a symbolic 'mental permanence of the I', but this perception prefigures alienation, for the mirror stage is a spatial illusion of totality (4), an imaginary identification with reflection. The mirror stage, which is pre-verbal, conveys the illusion that the image will respond to the child's wishes, as did the mother–breast–infant identification. The symbolic stage is the stage of language, a stage that will form the subject henceforth only in and as dialogue. The implied assumption that language may have definitive authority is undermined or deconstructed by Lacan's argument that every utterance is permeated by the unconscious in the sense that wholeness, meaning and gratification of wishes are perpetually deferred. The real, not to be confused with 'external reality', describes what is lacking in the symbolic – 'it is the residue of articulation or the umbilical cord of the symbolic' (ix–x) (translator's note).

The literary text, then, is an image of the unconscious structured like a language. 'The lure of all texts,' comments Wright, 'lies in a revelation, of things veiled coming to be unveiled, of characters who face shock at this unveiling' (1984: 121). When this phenomenon is given utterance in the reader-interpreter's language, meaning is inevitably deferred. In contrast to Freudian interpretation, we have here no unearthing of authorial neuroses. The Lacanian consequence for reader and text is the realisation that

> the selves we see ourselves as being are as fictional [made up of language] as the stories of written fiction – limited images like those we see in mirrors when we first became conscious of our separateness – so fiction can be read in terms of the way it echoes our basic human activity of inventing ourselves and becoming conscious of the limitation of our invention. All we usually call reality is in fact fiction, and always less complete than the actual real world outside our consciousness.
>
> (Nodelman 1992: 93–4)

Perry Nodelman discusses how Cinderella becomes a fixed subject at the end of the story rather than the multifaceted one she was. As she completes her stage of becoming, she has actually lost wholeness in her state of being (94). An analysis of *Charlotte's Web* shows how Lacan's imaginary and symbolic stage work through the 'Miracle of the Web' in that Wilbur perceives himself and is perceived as transformed through the ability of words to reorient desire by demonstrating 'that things are desirable because they are signified and, therefore, significant' in and through language (Rushdy 1991: 56). Another Lacanian interpretation applies the concept of the subject being created by disjunction and discontinuity to Russell Hoban's *The Mouse and His Child* where the mouse child, submerged to the bottom of a pond, is jubilant when it sees itself reflected in the labelless Bonzo dog food can: 'He sees himself suddenly whole, apparently co-ordinated and in control' (Krips 1993: 95). The directive 'be happy' is in *The Mouse and His Child* as authoritative as Charlotte's five single-word texts in the web, in that it creates the illusion of desire fulfilled, even as desire is deferred.

Psychoanalytic theory and the feminist critique

The patrimony psychoanalytic criticism received from Freud has exerted a deep 'anxiety of influence' on the feminist critic (Gilbert and Gubar 1979: 45–92; Gallop 1982), primarily because of Freud's definition of female sexuality and his centring of the male myth of Oedipus, both of which reduce the female to an addendum. Revisionary readings of Freud, particularly those by French feminists influenced by Lacan, both appropriate and retain his powerful influence. Feminist readings of Jung underwent less radical revisions (Lauter and Rupprecht 1985). Even without specific reference to ego-relations and object psychology, the feminist critic, by delineating the struggle of the female in a patriarchially constructed world, finds in the concept of self-actualisation an ally in her attempt at social transformation.

While not denying the existence of the subconscious, feminist psychoanalytic criticism, including the feminist criticism of children's literature, privileges the concept of social construction in the development of the female. Nancy Chodorow's *The Reproduction of Mothering* has been especially influential in its synthesis of psychoanalysis and the sociology of gender where 'the reproduction of mothering occurs through social structurally induced psychological processes' and is 'neither a product of biology nor of intentional role training' (1978: 7). Here the critic of children's literature finds a female focus, especially for the mother–daughter relation (Barzilai 1990; Murphy 1990; Natov 1990). The focus on the body–self relations allows the feminist critic to explore unique female experiences that have been neglected in the study of literature. The focus on the social construction of female and male children, especially since the nineteenth-century middle-class self-definition of gender roles and the family, has guided feminists to valuable contextual insights into the history of children's literature and its readers.

A major issue in feminist criticism is the problematics of the female writer's precursors which has led Gilbert and Gubar to revise Bloom's 'anxiety of influence' (Bloom 1973) with 'anxiety of authorship' by which the female writer questions her claim to be a writer (Gilbert and Gubar 1979: 48–9). It remains to be seen whether the important role of female writers in children's literature and the status of children's literature as a field of study might be understood as defences against the pressures of the male-dominated literary and critical tradition.

Conclusion

The revisions and transformations by which psychoanalytical theories and criticisms continue to construct themselves have retained so far the concept of the unconscious and its powerful influence on the ego's development and struggle in the world. Children's literature, whose language signifies the substitutions and displacements necessitated in that struggle, intimates and makes acceptable the dream of desire. It is a great irony of our psychoanalytic age that the psychological self-help narratives for young readers abandon consideration of the powers of the id in favour of the social adjustment of the young ego and that they do so, usually, in the language of low mimetic accessibility where the mode of romance and poetry is gone. That phenomenon is itself worthy of psychoanalytical interpretations of authors, texts and readers.

References

Applebee, A. N. (1978) *The Child's Concept of Story*, Chicago, IL: University of Chicago Press.
Barzilai, S. (1990) 'Reading "Snow White": The Mother's Story', *Signs* 15, 3: 515–34.
Bettelheim, B. (1976) *The Uses of Enchantment*, New York: A. A. Knopf.

Bloom, H. (1973) *The Anxiety of Influence*, New York: Oxford University Press.

Bosmajian, H. (1985) '*Charlie and the Chocolate Factory* and Other Excremental Visions', *The Lion and the Unicorn* 9: 36–49.

Chodorow, N. (1978) *The Reproduction of Mothering. Psychoanalysis and the Sociology of Gender*, Berkeley, CA: University of California Press.

Cooper, J. C. (1983) *Fairy Tales: Allegories of the Inner Life*, Wellingborough: Aquarian Press.

Daniels, S. (1990) '*The Velveteen Rabbit*: A Kleinian Perspective', *Children's Literature* 18: 17–30.

Egan, M. (1982) 'The Neverland of Id: Barrie, *Peter Pan*, and Freud', *Children's Literature* 10: 37–55.

Franz, M.-L. von (1977) *Individuation in Fairy Tales*, Zurich: Spring.

——(1978) *An Introduction to the Psychology of Fairy Tales*, Irving, TX: Spring.

Freud, S. (1908/1963) 'The Relation of the Poet to Daydreaming', *Character and Culture*, trans. Strachey, J., New York: Macmillan.

——(1913/1963) 'The Occurrence in Dreams of Materials from Fairy Tales', *Character and Culture*, trans. Strachey, J., New York: Macmillan.

——(1962/1975) *Three Essays on the Theory of Sexuality*, trans. Strachey, J., New York: Harper-Collins.

Frye, N. (1957) *Anatomy of Criticism*, Princeton, NJ: Princeton University Press.

Gallop, J. (1982) *The Daughter's Seduction: Feminism and Psychoanalysis*, Ithaca, NY: Cornell University Press.

Gilbert, S. and Gubar, S. (1979) *The Madwoman in the Attic: The Woman Writer and the Nineteenth Century Literary Imagination*, New Haven, CT: Yale University Press.

Greenacre, P. (1955) *Swift and Carroll: A Psychoanalytic Study of Two Lives*, New York: International Universities Press.

Hillman, J. (1980) 'The Children, the Children!', *Children's Literature* 8: 3–6.

Hogan, P. (1990) 'What's Wrong with the Psychoanalysis of Literature?', *Children's Literature* 18: 135–40.

Holland, N. (1968) *The Dynamics of Literary Response*, New York: Oxford University Press.

——(1970) 'The "Unconscious" of Literature: The Psychoanalytic Approach', in Bradbury, N. and Palmer, D. (eds) *Contemporary Criticism*, Stratford-upon-Avon Series 12, New York: St Martin's.

Horney, K. (1950) *Neurosis and Human Growth: The Struggle toward Self-Realization*, New York: Norton.

Jung, C. G. (1931/1966) 'On the Relation of Analytical Psychology to Poetry', *The Spirit in Man, Art, and Literature. Collected Works* vol. 15, trans. Hull, R. F. C., New York: Random House.

——(1946/1954) 'Psychic Conflicts in a Child', *The Development of Personality. Collected Works* vol. 17, trans. Hull, R. F. C., New York: Random House.

——(1964) 'Approaching the Unconscious', *Man and His Symbols*, New York: Doubleday.

Klein, M. (1955/1975a) *Envy and Gratitude*, New York: Delacorte.

——(1925/1975b) *Love, Guilt and Reparation*, New York: Delacorte.

Knoepflmacher, U. C. (1990) 'The Doubtful Marriage: A Critical Fantasy', *Children's Literature* 18: 131–4.

Krips, V. (1993) 'Mistaken Identity: Russell Hoban's *Mouse and His Child*', *Children's Literature* 21: 92–100.

Lacan, J. (1977) *Ecrits*, trans. Sheridan, A., New York: W. W. Norton.

Lauter, E. and Rupprecht, C. S. (1985) *Feminist Archetypal Theory. Interdisciplinary Revisions of Jungian Thought*, Knoxville, TN: University of Tennessee Press.

Maslow, A. (1968) *Toward a Psychology of Being*, New York: D. Van Nostrand.

Murphy, A. (1990) 'The Borders of Ethical, Erotic, and Artistic Possibilities, *Little Women*', *Signs* 15, 3: 562–85.

Natov, R. (1990) 'Mothers and Daughters: Jamaica Kincaid's Pre-Oedipal Narrative', *Children's Literature* 18: 1–16.

Nodelman, P. (1992) *The Pleasures of Children's Literature*, New York: Longman.

Paris, B. J. (1974) *A Psychological Approach to Fiction*, Bloomington, IN: Indiana University Press.

Phillips, J. and Wojcik-Andrews, I. (1990) 'Notes toward a Marxist Critical Practice', *Children's Literature* 18: 127–30.

Rose, J. (1984) *The Case of Peter Pan or The Impossibility of Children's Fiction*, London: Macmillan.

Rosenthal, L. (1980) 'The Development of Consciousness in Lucy Boston's *The Children of Green Knowe*', *Children's Literature* 8: 53–67.

Rushdy, A. H. A. (1991) ' "The Miracle of the Web": Community, Desire and Narrativity in *Charlotte's Web*', *The Lion and the Unicorn* 15, 2: 35–60.

Rustin, M. and Rustin, M. (1987) *Narratives of Love and Loss: Studies in Modern Children's Fiction*, New York: Verso.

Segel, E. (1986) ' "As the Twig Is Bent ...": Gender and Childhood Reading', in Flynn, E. A. and Schweikart, P. (eds) *Gender and Reading*, Baltimore, MD: Johns Hopkins University Press.

Smith, J. and Kerrigan, W. (1985) *Opening Texts: Psychoanalysis and the Culture of the Child*, Baltimore, MD: Johns Hopkins University Press.

Steig, M. (1990) 'Why Bettelheim? A Comment on the Use of Psychological Theories in Criticism', *Children's Literature* 18: 125–6.

Tatar, M. (1992) *Off with Their Heads! Fairy Tales and the Culture of Childhood*, Princeton, NJ: Princeton University Press.

Winnicott, D. W. (1971) *Playing and Reality*, New York: Tavistock/Routledge and Kegan Paul.

Wright, E. (1984) *Psychoanalytic Criticism*, New York: Methuen.

Zipes, J. (1979) *Breaking the Magic Spell: Radical Theories of Folk and Fairy Tales*, Austin, TX: University of Texas Press.

——(1990) 'Negating History and Male Fantasies through Psychoanalytic Criticism', *Children's Literature* 18: 141–3.

Further reading

Bloch, D. (1978) *'So the Witch Won't Eat Me': Fantasy and the Child's Fear of Infanticide*, New York: Grove Press.

Jung, C. G. (1964) *Man and His Symbols*, New York: Doubleday.

Rollin, L. (1990) 'The Reproduction of Mothering in *Charlotte's Web*', *Children's Literature* 18: 42–52.

Tucker, N. (1981) *The Child and the Book: A Psychological and Literary Exploration*, New York: Cambridge University Press.

8 Feminism revisited

Lissa Paul

Editor's Introduction

Fifteen years ago, Lissa Paul wrote that 'there is good reason for appropriating feminist theory to children's literature. Both women's literature and children's literature are devalued and regarded as marginal or peripheral by the literary and educational communities.' This chapter takes the position that many of feminism's battles are over, and is concerned with re-interpreting texts, reclaiming devalued texts, and redirecting feminist theory to provide a 'welcoming climate for texts by people marginalised by patriarchal colonial societies'.

P. H.

At the end of the original version of this essay on feminism and children's literature, in the first edition of this book, I wondered what feminist theory would look like in the new millennium. Now I know. It's over. It's not that criticism of children's books influenced by feminism is no longer being written. There is a lot of very good feminist-inspired criticism about – and it has changed the landscape of children's literature studies. What's over is the feminist movement that supported the development of feminist criticism in the 1970s and 1980s. Feminism is over in the same way that Romanticism is over, and rationalism is over and existentialism is over and Marxism is over. We've been changed by those critical movements and they all continue to influence our readings of texts. But the movements themselves have been relegated to their particular historical periods. Although feminism as a critical movement is over, its influence is alive and well and exerting itself on what we read, and on how we interpret and value what we read.

The end of feminism in the late 1990s seems to have been precipitated by women (white, middle-class women) who felt that the feminist campaign promises of the early 1970s hadn't quite been kept: that gender equity still wasn't possible, that there was still a glass ceiling preventing them from reaching the tops of their professions, and that it was still all but impossible to have, simultaneously, a successful career, a good marriage, a happy family – and perfect beauty. Several books by jaded feminists told this story – but two turned out to be most influential: *The Beauty Myth: How Images of Beauty Are Used against Women* (1991) by Naomi Wolf, and *Backlash: The Undeclared War against American Women* (1992) by Susan Faludi. 'Backlash', in fact, became the word to describe the end of feminism – and the rise of various kinds of men's movements and concerns about the failure of boys to do as well as girls on standardised tests. Despite the end of feminism, the basic tenets of feminist theory I outlined in the earlier essay are still very much with us (and available in a wonderful collection of essays, *Feminisms*, edited by Robyn Warhol and Diane Herndl) including attention to: distinctive patterns of women's writing (écriture feminine); to the 'resisting' feminine reader who recognises that 'good' literature had been implicitly defined as masculine; to the historical reclamation of a feminine literary tradition; and to the inclusion of voices other than white male ones. These critical ways of seeing continue to influence the ways in which literature, including children's literature, is written, read and understood. Portions of the original essay that traced the history of feminist scholarship in children's literature have been left intact. This new essay is not so much rewritten as overwritten – to reflect the ways in which feminist criticism has become an integral part of the landscape of children's book criticism in the twenty-first century.

In the original essay, I named 'the destabilisation of hierarchical orders' as one of the mobilising features of feminist theory – and then pointed out, ironically, that people working as children's literature scholars still set up an implicit hierarchical system that put literary critics at the top and put librarians, teachers – and children – lower down. The heartening news is that the boundaries have been breached. In 2002, for example, *The Journal of Children's Literature*, a refereed journal published by the National Council of Teachers of English (so primarily a journal for people working in education faculties rather than literature faculties), published a special issue, 'Feminist Approaches to Children's Literature'. Essays by literary scholars Lynne Vallone and Wolfgang Iser appear in the same issue as education scholars Ruth McKoy Lowery and Patricia Austin. There is a shared critical ground, visible in the works cited in both kinds of essays: literary scholars attending to the work of education scholars – and vice versa. That's encouraging in the twenty-first century, especially as the future of children's literature studies will probably demand more interdisciplinary co-operation and attention. But not all the updated news is so good.

Issues of gender equity remain unresolved, despite the body of work pointing towards ways of addressing discriminatory practices. In 'Sexism and Children's Literature: A Perspective for Librarians' (1981), Christine Nicholls recognises that 'sexism is a type of colonialism', but she then goes on to suggest that solutions to the problem include the use of 'white out' and the abandonment of books no longer in accord with contemporary definitions of gender equity. Hugh Crago (a psychotherapist and a fine children's literature critic) offers a sensitively worked-out corrective. In 'Sexism, Literature and Reader-Response: A Reply to Christine Nicholls', he reminds Nicholls (and the rest of us) that responses to texts are subject to large fluctuations, especially in fluid forms like fairy tales where versions, translations and illustrations all contribute to shaping the interpretative possibilities of texts. He also foregrounds the idea that there is really no such thing as 'the one-way cause and effect relationship' (Crago 1981: 161) between reader and text – something implicit in the Nicholls article and in a great many like it.

There are two points worth highlighting here. One is that the emphasis on sex-role stereotyping and sexism, still found most often in education and library science journals, is connected with an honest front-line attempt to create a more female-friendly climate, especially in schools. That's good. The other point worth keeping in mind is that post-structuralist discussions, especially those on semiotics, deconstruction, ideology and subjectivity, make it possible to develop language and strategies that speak – to borrow a phrase from Carol Gilligan – 'in a different voice'. For an academic feminist children's literature critic, feminist admonitions to remember our histories and value members of our communities continue to sound.

Children's literature offers to children the promise of inclusion in a literate community (something regarded as culturally valuable, at least nominally). The critical apparatus surrounding children's books offers an intellectual understanding of what inclusion means and how it might be achieved. What feminist theory has done for children's literature studies – and for all fields of literary study – is to insist on the right to be included, not just as honorary white men. Beverly Lyon Clark, in 'Fairy Godmothers or Wicked Stepmothers?', makes the issue explicit when she encourages children's literature scholars to talk back and 'recognise whom we are stepping on, whom we are putting down, and why' (1993: 174). Clark's questioning of the relations between children's literature critics and feminist critics continued to resonate through the 1990s.

In the original essay I cited two special feminist issues of two children's literature journals. The *Children's Literature Association Quarterly* ran a special section, edited by Anita Moss, in the Winter 1982 edition: 'Feminist Criticism and the Study of Children's Literature'. In that early collection of essays there were several reviews of books of feminist literary criticism, each sketching possible critical lines children's literature critics might find worth exploring. Virginia Wolf, for instance, writes about alternatives to the heroic quest in science fiction; and Lois Kuznets about texts that value communities rather than kingdoms. In December 1991, *The Lion and the Unicorn* published an issue called 'Beyond Sexism: Gender Issues in Children's Literature'. By that time the lessons of feminist theory had been internalised, and critics were actively constructing a feminist tradition in children's literature. There was a switch from 'feminist criticism' to 'gender' studies, marking the subtle inclusion of gay and lesbian studies into the fray. 'Gender', even in the early 1990s, was being used as a code to prevent feminist studies from becoming a pink-collar ghetto. The broadening of the items on an initially feminist agenda progressed apace through the 1990s. In 1993, the *Children's Literature Association Quarterly* published a special section, 'Mothers and Daughters in Children's Literature', edited by Mitzi Myers. And in September 1999, Kenneth Kidd was the guest editor for an issue of *The Lion and the Unicorn* (24, 3) on sexuality and children's literature.

In keeping with emphasis in this essay on tracking the historical record of feminist influence on children's literature studies – and taking to heart critic Jane Gallop's cryptic caution to remember that 'history is like a mother' (1992: 206–39) – I'm going to focus on three broad areas of academic children's literature criticism influenced (unanxiously) by feminist theory: the rereading of texts for previously unrevealed interpretations; the reclaiming of texts that had been devalued or dismissed; and the redirection of feminist theory into providing a welcoming climate for texts by people marginalised by patriarchal colonial societies. The titles in each of my three sections in this essay, 'Rereading', 'Reclaiming' and 'Redirection', take their cue from Adrienne Rich's ideas that feminist poetics are about 'revision' (Rich 1976).

Rereading

The desire for feminist rereading comes from an understanding of the ways ideological assumptions about the constitution of good literature (or criticism for that matter) work. By the early 1970s, feminist critics like Kate Millett (1977) had made it common knowledge that assumptions about good literature had been predicated on the belief that the adult white male was normal, while virtually everyone else was deviant or marginal. And so was born a critical desire to see if a feminine literary tradition, and feminine culture, could be made visible. By using techniques from deconstruction (derived largely from Derrida) and from contemporary discussions of ideology (from Althusser and Pierre Bourdieu) and subjectivity (largely derived from Lacan), feminist critics began to look at the ways ideological assumptions are played out in the text. They searched for a feminine tradition of 'other' stories: mother, daughter, sister stories (Chodorow (1978), Hirsch (1989)); a preference for survival tactics over honour (Gilligan (1982)); a search for a 'both/and' feminine plot rather than an 'either/or' oedipal plot (Hirsch); a preference for multi-plicity, plurality, jouissance and a valuing of pro-creations, re-creations and new beginnings (Cixous (1991), Gallop, Rich); a questioning of rigid male/female gender distinctions (Butler); and an insistence women not white or Anglophone have a voice too (hooks (1992), Spivak). Feminist children's literature critics also participate in this recovery of a female literary tradition (Clark, Kidd (2000), Myers (1986, 1987, 1991), Pace, Paul (1987/1990, 1998), Trites, Vallone (1990, 1991) and Zipes among others). The following small sketches of reinterpretation, rehabilitation and re-creation demonstrate the range of ways in which that tradition is being revealed.

Reinterpretation

Feminist reinterpretations of familiar classics like *The Secret Garden* and *Little Women* turn stories we thought were about struggles to conform to the social order into stories about women's healing and successful communities of women (Bixler (1991), Nelson, Auerbach). *Little Women* – as read by Edward Salmon (a nineteenth-century authority on children's literature) in his 1888 obituary of Alcott in *Atalanta* – is a story about instructing girls to be 'the proper guardians of their brothers' and to be 'all-powerful for good in their relations with men' (449). But for Nina Auerbach, in *Communities of Women* (1978), it is the story of 'the formation of a reigning feminist sisterhood whose exemplary unity will heal a fractured society' (37). The critical rereading turns it from a story about women learning how to serve men into a story of women supporting each other.

The turn to the new millennium raised Louisa Alcott's status in the literary canon of children's books – in much the same way that Virginia Woolf's status as a modernist was raised by feminist scholarship. As Rita Felski argues in *Literature after Feminism* (2003), Woolf wasn't considered in the same league as Joyce or Eliot until feminist critics argued for her aesthetic as well as her political contributions. Alcott, too, had always been popular, but it wasn't until considerations of her literary merit became a feminist project that the status of *Little Women* as an American classic came to be understood in the same way as *The Adventures of Tom Sawyer* by Mark Twain is understood as an American classic. The brilliance of Alcott's most famous book is made visible in an enlightening collection of twenty essays, assembled by editors Janice M. Alberghene and Beverly Lyon Clark, *'Little Women' and the Feminist Imagination: Criticism, Controversy, Personal Essays* (1999). What is immediately clear in the collection is the way in which feminist theory has widened out to include discussions beyond the obvious mother/daughter or father/daughter relations. Victoria Roberts offers a comic strip *Little Women*, Roberta Seelinger Trites considers lesbian politics in the story, and Jan Susina writes about (resisting) male readers. Susan Laird writes about teaching, Susan Gannon about film versions of the book, and Aiko Moro-oka provides a bibliography that offers a glimpse of the way Alcott's work is received in Japan. Those are just a few of the essays in the collection – but the range speaks eloquently to what feminist theory has become in the twenty-first century. Gender relations, gender politics, reception, translations (into other languages and other media) all seem perfectly at home under the collective umbrella of the 'feminist imagination'.

Rehabilitation

The rehabilitation of works by Mary Wollstonecraft, Maria Edgeworth and other 'lady moralists' of the Georgian and Romantic periods is one of the major success stories of academic feminist children's literature criticism. Although I am going to focus on criticism by Mitzi Myers, credit also goes to Anita Moss (1988, 1993–4) and Lynne Vallone.

As Mitzi Myers pointedly states, texts by Georgian 'lady' moralists, as rendered in standard overviews of children's literature, suffer from 'something like the critical equivalent of urban blight' (Myers 1986: 31). John Rowe Townsend dismisses these women as ranging 'from the mildly pious to the sternly moralistic' (1974: 39). Harvey Darton refers to 'the truculent dogmatic leanings of Mrs Sherwood and Mrs Trimmer' and the 'completely dogmatic' Mary Godwin (1982: 156, 196).

Myers offers different readings. She participates in what feminist critic Elaine Showalter calls 'gynocriticism', that is, criticism that attends to 'the woman as producer of textual meaning, with the history, themes, genres, and structures of literature by women' (Showalter 1985: 128). What Myers asks is how those Georgian women found autonomy and influence in a world where those freedoms were denied. Her answers transform lady moralists scorned for their conformity into the founding mothers of a feminist pedagogical tradition.

These and other late eighteenth- and early nineteenth-century women, including Dorothy and Mary Ann Kilner and Eliza Fenwick, for example, all knew how to convey the sounds of real children fighting and playing and learning. *Opening the Nursery Door: Reading, Writing and Childhood 1600–1900* (Hilton *et al.* 1997) is a collection of essays about women as teachers, inspired by Jane Johnson (1706–59), wife of a Buckinghamshire vicar, and a mother. Her homemade domestic teaching materials – poems, stories and alphabet mobiles – survive in the archive in the Lilly Library of Indiana University. Her story provided the impetus for other stories in the collection about maternal pedagogies.

In Georgian England, where there were few roles for (upper-class) women except as wives, mothers and governesses, Mary Wollstonecraft, Maria Edgeworth and other women like Mrs Trimmer and Mrs Sherwood transformed their roles. They constructed 'an almost unrecognised literary tradition', one that 'accepts and emphasizes the instructive and intellectual potential of narrative' (Myers 1986: 33). Maria Edgeworth, for example, creates female protagonists as 'desiring' subjects, not just objects of desire. And Mary Wollstonecraft, in her *Mrs Mason* stories, redefines power in unpatriarchal terms 'as pedagogic and philanthropic power' (43). For a full-length portrait of the relationship between maternal pedagogy and power, *Becoming Victoria* (2001) by Lynne Vallone offers a brilliant analysis of the educational influences that shaped the young Princess Victoria into a queen.

Re-creation

Although I've focused so far on the way academic critics construct feminist traditions in children's literature, I'm mindful of the ways authors who published while under the influence of late twentieth-century feminism changed the way we read. Author Ursula Le Guin has chronicled the change most dramatically. In *Earthsea Revisioned* (1993), the published version of a lecture she gave in Oxford in 1992, Le Guin records the influence of gender politics on her *Earthsea* quartet. The first three *Earthsea* novels, published between 1968 and 1972, are in the genre of the traditional heroic fantasy, something Le Guin defines as 'a male preserve: a sort of great game-park where Beowulf feasts with Teddy Roosevelt, and Robin Hood goes hunting with Mowgli, and the cowboy rides off into the sunset alone' (Le Guin 1993: 5).

Le Guin does not apologise for the male-order, hierarchical world in the first three novels. But twenty years after their publication she recognises things about that world that she didn't understand when she made it. With the insights of contemporary feminist theory, she understands that, at the time, she was 'writing partly by the rules, as an artificial man, and partly against the rules, as an inadvertent revolutionary' (7). In her revolutionary mode, in a partly conscious attempt to create a hero from a visible minority, Le Guin made Ged and all the good guys in the *Earthsea* books black, and the bad guys white. Nevertheless, the good guys were standard male-order heroes anyway. They lived lives of 'continence; abstinence; denial of relationship' (16). And they worked in a world predicated on 'power as domination over others, unassailable strength, and the generosity of the rich' (14).

But in *Tehanu*, the fourth and final *Earthsea* book, published seventeen years after the third, Le Guin scraps male-order heroism. She creates Tenar, a feminist pro-creative, re-creative hero: 'All her former selves are alive in her: the child Tenar, the girl priestess Arha ... and Goha, the farmwife, mother of two children. Tenar is whole but not single. She is not pure' (Le Guin 1993: 18). The traditional male hero, the dragonslayer and dragonlord, marked by his capacity to defeat evil, to win, and to receive public adoration and power, is nowhere in sight. In the new mythology Le Guin creates, the dragon is transformed into a familiar, a guide for a new female hero: 'The child who is our care, the child we have betrayed, is our guide. She leads us to the dragon. She is the dragon.' Le Guin moves out of the hierarchical ordering of the heroic world, and into a new world where the search is for wildness, a 'new order of freedom' (26).

At the turn of the millennium, Le Guin's fantasy novels seem touchingly well behaved in the context of the fantasy novels produced by younger women who never experienced a pre-feminist world. The fantasies of Francesca Lia Block belong here: urban, closer to wish-fulfilment dream than medieval romance, her stories, particularly those in the *Girl Goddess #9: Nine Stories* (1996) collection, open out into a more overtly sexual world than the world of Earthsea.

Reclaiming

One of the most significant feminist projects of the feminist movement was the reissuing of long out-of-print books by women authors. Many had been gathering dust on library shelves for dozens, sometimes hundreds, of years. Most had long since ceased to make any money for anyone. But the feminist press Virago, particularly, put many of these authors into circulation, including Vera Brittain, Miles Franklin and Charlotte Perkins Gilman. Now easily available in good-quality paperback editions, they are read for pleasure, not just among scholars, though scholars were often the first to create the demand for these books by finding them, writing about them and bringing them to university course lists and to public attention.

Though there is no exactly comparable resurrection of authored fiction in children's literature (Angela Brazil is as unlikely to be reissued as Talbot Baines Reed), there is interest in rethinking the genre of the school story, as Beverly Lyon Clark demonstrates in *Regendering the School Story: Sassy Sissies and Tattling Tomboys* (1996).

There is, however, one class of texts enjoying a new lease on life as a direct result of the second wave of feminism: fairy tales. In fact, the shift in fairy-tale fashions provides a virtual paradigm for shifts in feminist poetics. In the 1970s, with the rise of the second wave of feminist theory, there was increasing discomfort with the gender dynamics in popular Grimm, Andersen and Perrault fairy tales (though Simone de Beauvoir had already drawn attention to passive Grimm heroines twenty years earlier in *The Second Sex*

(1953)). Girls and women play dead or doormats (as in 'Snow White', 'Cinderella', and 'Sleeping Beauty') or are severely mutilated (as in 'The Little Mermaid'). The move was on for female heroes (I'll use the term in preference to 'heroines' – who tend to wait around a lot). Unfortunately, the female heroes of the early 1970s tended not to be of a different order, as is Tenar in Le Guin's *Tehanu*. They tended to be more like men tricked out in drag. The stories were the same as those with male heroes in them. But instead of the stories being about boys seeking adventure, profit and someone to rescue, girls were in the starring roles. They rescued instead of being rescued. Like television situation comedies that colour middle-class families black, most of those tales died natural deaths. *The Paper Bag Princess* by Robert Munsch is a dubious exception. It is still in print, and the princess uses the feminist tactic of deceit to defeat the dragon and rescue the prince. But as the prince suffers from the traditionally feminine vice of vanity, s/he is essentially rejected for a lack of machismo.

When revisionist tales virtually disappeared in the late 1970s, reclaimed tales looked like a more viable alternative. But in the first collections of reclaimed tales, the preference for male characteristics in female heroes was still much in evidence. In the introduction to *Tatterhood and Other Tales*, for example, Ethel Johnston Phelps states a preference for stories with 'active and courageous girls and women in the leading roles', ones who are 'distinguished by extraordinary courage and achievements' (1978: xv). In other words, she prefers the same old male type, who, as Valerie Walkerdine suggests, is 'gender-neutral, self-disciplined, and active' (1990: 120). That is, the preferred hero is still a man. The post-feminist age seems to have produced a thriving genre of fairy-tale fantasies. Revisionist tales in this tradition include *Deerskin* (1993) by Robin McKinley and *White as Snow* (2000) by Tanith Lee – both of whom are very prolific and successful. And critics such as Roberta Seelinger Trites, in *Waking Sleeping Beauty: Feminist Voices in Children's Novels* (1997) and Jack Zipes in *Happily Ever After: Fairy Tales, Children and the Culture Industry* (1997) track the quickly shifting contours of feminist readings.

Two collections of reclaimed fairy tales for Virago by Angela Carter (1991, 1992) speak in a different voice, enabling modern readers to hear the voices of women from other times and other cultures. They are so good they are difficult to put down. She doesn't just present tales about the unrelieved glory of women – a male-order project anyway. Instead, she tries 'to demonstrate the extraordinary richness and diversity of responses to the same common predicament – being alive – and the richness and diversity with which femininity, in practice is represented in "unofficial" culture: its strategies, its plots, its hard work' (Carter 1991: xiv). One of her favourite stories from this collection was apparently 'Tongue Meat', a Swahili story that tells of a languishing queen who only revives when fed 'tongue meat', something that turns out to be a metaphor for stories. The tales of girls and women that Angela Carter revives are exactly that kind of 'tongue meat'. They establish an alternative feminist tradition – one that hadn't been visible before. Angela Carter's death in 1992 at the age of just fifty-two was deeply felt in literary circles. She had been a gifted story-teller and a visionary interpreter of fairy-tale and fantasy traditions. British novelist and scholar Marina Warner (who wrote the introduction to Carter's second volume of tales) has taken up Carter's legacy. In fact Warner defines herself as a 'mythographer'. Her feminist study of fairy tales, *From the Beast to the Blonde: On Fairytales and Their Tellers* (1994), moves sinuously, making connections between scholarly study and contemporary culture. *No Go the Bogeyman: Scaring, Lulling and Making Mock* (Warner 1998) about threatening lullabies and comic ogres, constitutes a revisionist companion volume.

While it is true that fairy tales seem to have enjoyed the most dramatic revival as a result of twinned interests in women's studies and children's literature studies, other reclamation projects are also taking place. The texts being rediscovered by feminist critics are important because they provide a historical context for our own ideological assumptions about gender, about what constitutes good literature, and about what is worth remembering, circulating and retaining for study. The boundaries between male and female, child and adult, increasingly blurred as the twentieth century drew to a close. Critic Judith Butler, especially in *Gender Trouble* (1990), put forward the idea that gender was a kind of disguise anyway, that it was a kind of performance. Her work opened up the world of trans-gendered possibilities. For children's literature authors and critics, it became possible to breach child/adult boundaries too. The most visible examples are in books that crossed over into films. *Freaky Friday* (1972), by Mary Rodgers, about a mother and daughter who change bodies, has twice been made into films (suggesting the resonance of the idea). Steven Spielberg's *Hook* (1991) played with cross-age boundaries as Pan, the boy who never grows up, does, then – within the bounds of the film – has a second chance at childhood. There is an excellent discussion of this cross-age phenomenon by Patricia Pace in 'Robert Bly Does Peter Pan' (1996).

Although my discussion of the reclamation projects undertaken by feminist critics focuses on prose fiction and fairy tales, the reclamation of women poets is probably more dramatic. One of the most compelling studies of women's texts lost and found is 'Lost from the Nursery: Women Writing Poetry for Children 1800–1850', by Morag Styles (1990). Styles came to write the article because she casually noticed how few women were represented in poetry anthologies for children, especially poets who published before 1900. As she began to explore, she discovered consistent patterns working to obliterate women poets from the record.

In early anthologies, Styles found that poems which had quickly become popular in their own time, like 'Twinkle Twinkle Little Star' or 'Mary Had a Little Lamb', rapidly became separated from their authors as they entered anthologies. They were usually attributed to the anonymous authors of oral tradition. So while generations of children learned to say 'Twinkle Twinkle Little Star', few knew it was by Jane Taylor, or that Sarah Hale wrote 'Mary Had a Little Lamb', or that 'The Months of the Year' was by Sara Coleridge.

The systematic exclusion of these women from the children's literature canon accords precisely with the ideological reasons for their exclusion from the literary canon – and from positions of power and influence. Styles explains that 'the colloquial domestic writing of some women whose concern in literature for children (and often for adults) is with relationships, affection, friendship, family life often located in the small-scale site of the home' (Styles 1990: 203) was devalued, lost and forgotten in a world where large-scale adventures and public rhetoric were valued. So the voices of Jane and Anne Taylor 'talking lovingly and naturally' in their poetry collections were lost. And Dorothy Wordsworth, with her 'private, colloquial and domestic' poetry (202), was relegated to a footnote in her brother's life.

By bringing the domestic cadences of women 'lost from the nursery' to our eyes and ears again, Styles provides a climate that warms to the domestic scene and to the softer, more direct colloquial cadences of the female voice. She teaches us to listen with different ears to the different voice of women's poetry for children. In a broader literary context, there has also been a re-evaluation of Christina Rossetti's poetry. Where once she was relegated to the 'B' list of nineteenth-century poets, she seems to have moved up as critics listen more carefully to her poetry and recognise how finely tuned her ear was to poetic cadences. Poet Tom Paulin writes a wonderful tribute to Rossetti's 'subtly stringent ear' in a *Times Literary Supplement* review (18 January 2002) of a collection of her poems edited by Betty Flowers.

I don't want to leave this section without mentioning other ways in which children's literature critics are gradually recovering a female literary tradition. By revealing the constructions of gendered patterns of childhood reading, academic feminist critics are beginning to locate the origins of ideological constructions of gender. Two studies of nineteenth-century girls' books and boys' books were published within a year of one another: *Girls Only? Gender and Popular Children's Fiction in Britain, 1880–1910*, by Kimberley Reynolds in 1990, and *Boys Will Be Girls: The Feminist Ethic and British Children's Fiction, 1857–1917*, by Claudia Nelson in 1991. The sudden focus on that late nineteenth- and early twentieth-century time period is more than coincidental. It marks a critical recognition of that period as the time when colonial and patriarchal values were being actively inscribed in the culture. In widely circulating periodicals like the *Girl's Own Paper* (published initially by the Religious Tract Society) girls were encouraged to accept simultaneously characteristics gendered feminine – 'purity, obedience, dependence, self-sacrifice and service' – and an 'image of feminine womanhood ... expanded to incorporate intelligence, self-respect, and ... the potential to become financially dependent'. The result was a set of 'contradictory tendencies characteristic of femininity: reason and desire, autonomy and dependent activity, psychic and social identity' (Nelson 1991: 141). Those contradictions still haunt women today.

Other critics participate in the recovery of more recent histories of the relations between gender and reading. A collection of essays, *Girls, Boys, Books and Toys: Gender in Children's Literature and Culture* (1999), edited by Beverly Lyon Clark and Margaret Higonnet, demonstrates the range of topics that seem to have been prompted by feminism but then engage a joyous, large critical grasp. There is a postcolonial essay by Claudia Marquis, an essay on contemporary Indian stories by Rajeswari Sunder Rajan, an essay on dolls' houses by Lois R. Kuznets and an essay by Lynne Vallone on '*Riot Grrr*' zines (magazines linked to a punk-inspired movement of fourteen- to twenty-five-year-olds, called 'Riot Grrrls').

Relations between public success and childhood reading were recounted in several reading memoirs published in the late 1980s and early 1990s. The women writing them at the height of, or late in, their professional careers seem to be offering clues that might be of use to librarians and teachers interested in creating a more supportive academic environment for girls. In '*My Book House as Bildung*', Nancy Huse reconstructs her childhood reading of Olive Miller's *My Book House* as a way of establishing a maternal pedagogical line that influenced her choice of an academic career. And in the children's literature journal *Signal*, Nancy Chambers has published several reading memoirs by well-known women who are active in a range of children's literature fields. Among them are ones by children's book editor Margaret Clark (1991); author Jane Gardam (1991); and Susan Viguers (1988) writing about her children's-literature-expert mother. In *The Child That Books Built: A Life in Reading* (2002), Francis Spufford (a man) eloquently explains how the books of his childhood in the late 1960s and 1970s formed his literary and ideological tastes. All reveal how childhood reading enabled them to enter public worlds of letters on bridges built from private, domestic literate environments.

The tunes – to borrow a phrase from Margaret Meek (1992) – of women's texts are different from the ones established in the canon as being of value. What feminist theory has revealed, especially in reconstructions of a female literary tradition, is that the disproportionate emphasis placed on adventure, power, honour and public success squeezed out feminine valuing of maternal, domestic voices, ideas of sisterhood and stories about the lives of women. While only the feminist fairy tales may have found popular readership, scholarship teaches us to value domestic scenes and colloquial voices, and to remember our histories. It enables us to make familiar the new texts that come our way. The scholarship enables us to appreciate their difference.

Redirection

The second wave of feminism began in the late 1960s when a whole generation of white, well-educated 'baby-boomer' women found that they were still relegated to making the coffee and stuffing envelopes. They were still excluded from the dominant discourses. The consciousness-raising groups of the 1970s began as a means of mobilising collective voices in order to gain inclusion. The right to be included: that became a basic tenet of feminist theory. So feminist theory changed to become increasingly inclusive: the feminist studies of the 1970s grew into gender studies in the 1980s. In the 1990s another change happened as feminist criticism evolved into gender studies – and ultimately become aligned with post-colonial and cultural studies. Feminist critics relocated into the emerging disciplines. Critics such as Gayatri Spivak (1987), Trinh T. Minh-ha (1989), and bell hooks (1992), recognising the similarities between political power plays and gender power plays, have helped feminist criticism shed its Eurocentric, middle-class look. English critics are also tentatively moving outside their own linguistic and cultural borders, listening to other critics and scholars. For Anglophone scholars, access to the work being done in non-English-speaking countries is still limited. But there are signs that attempts are being made to gain access to both other literatures and other critics – and their views on the influence of feminism. In Germany, the International Youth Library in Munich is significant. It was founded after the Second World War by Jella Lepman – who was also responsible for the International Board on Books for Young People (IBBY). There are essays on feminist theory and children's literature in *Jugendkultur im Adoleszenzroman*, edited by Hans-Heino Ewers (1994). And there are publications (of various cross-cultural stripes) coming out of children's literature research institutes in several countries, including the Centre for Children's Literature in Denmark and the International Charles Perrault Research Institute in Paris. The International Research Society in Children's Literature brings scholars from all over the world together. Scandinavian scholars, such as Maria Nikolajeva, Mia Österlund and Riita Oittinen, teach and write in Anglophone contexts. And Emer O'Sullivan, originally from Ireland, works and writes in both English and German. Essay collections, published particularly in Europe, are beginning to reflect a much more global, multi-lingual perspective. For access to some of these critics see, for example, *Children's Literature as Communication* (2002), edited by Roger Sell, *Female/Male: Gender in Children's Literature* (1999), a collection published by the Baltic Centre for Writers and Translators, and *Children's Literature and National Identity* (2001), edited by Margaret Meek.

For children's literature critics in the twenty-first century, there is an increased awareness of the way primitives and children are frequently (t)roped together. In keeping with feminist agendas, this new theoretical line is changing both the readings and the text. It is true that there is nothing in children's literature or children's literature criticism as yet that is as dramatic as the acknowledgement in Marina Warner's novel *Indigo* that it was a work of postcolonial theory, *Colonial Encounters* by Peter Hulme, that spurred her to write the novel. But there are changes, as children's literature increasingly includes the images and voices of people of colour. I'm thinking especially of writers for children like John Agard, Grace Nichols, James Berry, Valerie Bloom and Joy Kogawa, who probe at the ways patriarchal powers have screwed up, how they've ruined the environment in favour of profit, and how they locked up people designated as 'other' on the grounds that if they were foreign they were dangerous.

The unpicking of the child/primitive trope is also the subject of academic study. Stephen Slemon and Jo-Ann Wallace, professors at the University of Alberta in Canada, taught a graduate course together called, 'Literatures of the Child and the Colonial Subject: 1850–1914'. In an article they wrote together about their experience, 'Into the Heart of Darkness? Teaching Children's Literature as a Problem in Theory' (1991), they discuss their struggle with the construction of the child in pedagogical and institutional terms. They write about the child who, like the 'primitive', is treated 'as a subject-in-formation, an individual who often does not have full legal status and who therefore acts or who is acted against in ways that are not perceived to be fully consequential' (20). Postcolonial discourse illuminates ways in which authority over the 'other' is achieved in the name of protecting innocence. The ideological assumption is that primitives and children are too naive (or stupid) to look after themselves, so need protecting – like rainforests.

The critical lessons in feminist/postcolonial theory increasingly have to do with ideology and with constructions of the subject. That's quite different from what used to be the common feature of children's literature and children's literature criticism – the notion of the identity quest, with its attendant assumption that there was such a thing as a stable identity. Instead, contemporary critical emphasis is on the ways we are constructed by the socialising forces pressuring us in all aspects of our lives: relationships with parents and families, class, gender and cultural patterns and expectations.

The implications for the unpicking of the child/primitive trope are part of something provoking a new crisis of definition in children's literature and children's literature criticism and teaching. While children's literature is predicated on the notion that children are essentially blank or naive and in need of protection and instruction, then issues of suitability or unsuitability are important. But as children become differently constructed in the light of feminist and postcolonial theory, so does children's literature. Distinctions between them and us no longer become categorising features and suitability recedes as an issue.

The effects of this ideological shift begin to become apparent in criticism and in texts. Critics who work in feminist theory, postcolonial studies and children's literature all find themselves interested in common grounds: in the dynamics of power, in ideology, in the construction of the subject. And authors produce texts in which child/adult categories are no longer the significant ones. Jane Gardam's books, for example, appear in Abacus editions that don't make adult/child distinctions. And Angela Carter's Virago fairy tales are catalogued in the library not with children's literature or women's literature – but as anthropology.

The second wave of feminist theory has profoundly changed what we read and how we read. New texts and reclaimed texts have changed the canon so that more people are included and the 'dead white male' is less dominant. There is an increased awareness and valuing of maternal pedagogies and traditions of women's writing. Tastes have developed for colloquial, domestic voices pitched in higher registers and speaking in other cadences. Even when I came to the end of this essay the first time, I predicted that the second wave of feminist theory was coming to an end. But I didn't know how many of the innovations that had been put in place would become normalised. I didn't know that there would be political moves towards more liberal attitudes: that lesbians, gays and people with a range of religious and cultural beliefs might be encouraged, at least nominally, to live openly. The end of feminism has not meant a plunge into the dark ages. It has opened up a kind of criticism that, in its best forms, is informed by the insights of feminist theory – and the joy.

References

Alberghene, J. M. and Clark, B. L. (eds) (1999) *'Little Women' and the Feminist Imagination: Criticism, Controversy, Personal Essays*, New York: Garland.

Auerbach, N. (1978) *Communities of Women: An Idea in Fiction*, Cambridge, MA: Harvard University Press.

Beauvoir, S. de (1953) *The Second Sex*, New York: Random House.

'Beyond Sexism: Gender Issues in Children's Literature' (1991), *The Lion and the Unicorn* 15, 2 (special issue).

Bixler, P. (1991) 'Gardens, Houses, and Nurturant Power in *The Secret Garden*', in McGavran, J. (ed.) *Romanticism and Children's Literature in Nineteenth Century England*, Athens, GA: University of Georgia Press.

Block, F. L. (1996) *Girl Goddess #9: Nine Stories*, New York: HarperCollins.

Butler, J. (1990) *Gender Trouble: Feminism and the Subversion of Identity*, London: Routledge.

Carter, A. (ed.) (1991) *The Virago Book of Fairy Tales*, London: Virago.

——(1992) *The Second Virago Book of Fairy Tales*, London: Virago.

Chodorow, N. (1978) *The Reproduction of Mothering: Psychoanalysis and the Sociology of Gender*, Berkeley, CA: University of California Press.

Cixous, H. (1991) *Coming to Writing and Other Essays*, Cambridge, MA: Harvard University Press.

Clark, B. L. (1993) 'Fairy Godmothers or Wicked Stepmothers? The Uneasy Relationship of Feminist Theory and Children's Literature Criticism', *Children's Literature Association Quarterly* 18: 171–6.

——(1996) *Regendering the School Story: Sassy Sissies and Tattling Tomboys*, New York: Garland.

Clark, B. L. and Higonnet, M. (eds) (1999) *Girls, Boys, Books, Toys: Gender in Children's Literature and Culture*, Baltimore, MD: Johns Hopkins University Press.

Clark, M. (1991) 'Early to Read', *Signal* 65: 112–19.

Crago, H. (1981) 'Sexism, Literature and Reader-Response: A Reply to Christine Nicholls', *Orana* 17, 4: 159–62.

Darton, F. J. H. (1982) *Children's Books in England: Five Centuries of Social Life*, 3rd edn, rev. Alderson, B., Cambridge: Cambridge University Press.

Ewers, H.-H. (ed.) (1994) *Jugendkultur im Adoleszenzroman. Jugendliteratur der 80er und 90er Jahre zwischen Moderne und Posmoderne*, Munich: Weinheim.

Faludi, S. (1992) *Backlash: The Undeclared War against American Women*, New York: Anchor Books.

Felski, R. (2003) *Literature after Feminism*, Chicago, IL: University of Chicago Press.

Female/Male: Gender in Children's Literature (1999) Papers from International Symposium, Gotland: Baltic Centre for Writers and Translators.

'Feminist Approaches to Children's Literature' (2002) *Journal of Children's Literature* 28, 2 (Fall) (special issue).

'Feminist Criticism and the Study of Children's Literature' (1982) *Children's Literature Association Quarterly* 7, 4 (special section).

Gallop, J. (1992) *Around 1981: Academic Feminist Literary Theory*, New York: Routledge.

Gardam, J. (1991) 'A Writer's Life and Landscape', *Signal* 66: 179–94.

Gilligan, C. (1982) *In a Different Voice: Psychological Theory and Women's Development*, Cambridge, MA: Harvard University Press.

Hilton, M., Styles, M. and Watson, V. (eds) (1997) *Opening the Nursery Door: Reading, Writing and Childhood 1600–1900*, London: Routledge.

Hirsch, M. (1989) *The Mother/Daughter Plot: Narrative, Psychoanalysis, Feminism*, Bloomington, IN: Indiana University Press.

hooks, b. (1992) 'Representing Whiteness in the Black Imagination', in Grossman, L., Nelson, C. and Treichler, P. (eds) *Cultural Studies*, New York: Routledge.

Hulme, P. (1986) *Colonial Encounters: Europe and the Native Caribbean, 1492–1797*, New York: Methuen.

Huse, N. (1988) '*My Book House* as *Bildung*', *Children's Literature Association Quarterly* 13, 3: 115–21.

Kidd, K. (ed.) (1999) 'Sexuality and Children's Literature', *The Lion and the Unicorn* 24, 3 (special issue).

——(2000) 'Boyology in the Twentieth Century', *Children's Literature* 28: 44–72.

Kuznets, L. (1982) 'Defining Full Human Potential: Communities of Women, an Idea in Fiction, and toward a Recognition of Androgyny', *Children's Literature Association Quarterly* 7, 4: 10.

Le Guin, U. K. (1993) *Earthsea Revisioned*, Cambridge: Children's Literature New England in association with Green Bay Publications.

Lee, Tanith (2000) *White as Snow*, New York: Tor.

McKinley, R. (1993) *Deerskin*, New York: Ace Books.

Meek, M. (1992) 'Transitions: The Notion of Change in Writing for Children', *Signal* 67: 13–32.

——(ed.) (2001) *Children's Literature and National Identity*, Stoke on Trent: Trentham Books.

Millett, K. (1977) *Sexual Politics*, London: Virago.

Minh-ha, Trinh T. (1989) *Woman, Native, Other*, Bloomington, IN: Indiana University Press.

Moss, A. (1988) 'Mothers, Monsters, and Morals in Victorian Fairy Tales', *The Lion and the Unicorn* 12, 2: 47–59.

——(ed.) (1993–4) 'Mothers and Daughters in Children's Literature', *Children's Literature Association Quarterly* 18, 4 (special section).

Munsch, R. (1980) *The Paper Bag Princess*, Toronto: Annick Press.

Myers, M. (1986) 'Impeccable Governesses, Rational Dames, and Moral Mothers: Mary Wollstonecraft and the Female Tradition in Georgian Children's Books', *Children's Literature* 14: 31–59.

——(1987) ' "A Taste for Truth and Realities": Early Advice to Mothers on Books for Girls', *Children's Literature Association Quarterly* 12, 3: 118–23.

——(1991) 'Romancing the Moral Tale: Maria Edgeworth and the Problematics of Pedagogy', in McGavran, J. (ed.) *Romanticism and Children's Literature in Nineteenth-Century England*, Athens, GA: University of Georgia Press.

Nelson, C. (1991) *Boys Will Be Girls: The Feminist Ethic and British Children's Fiction, 1857–1917*, New Brunswick, NJ: Rutgers University Press.

Nicholls, C. (1981) 'Sexism and Children's Literature: A Perspective for Librarians', *Orana* 17, 3: 105–11.

Pace, P. (1996) 'Robert Bly Does Peter Pan: The Inner Child as Father to the Man in Steven Spielberg's *Hook*', *The Lion and the Unicorn* 20, 1: 113–20.

Paul, L. (1987/1990) 'Enigma Variations: What Feminist Theory Knows about Children's Literature', in Hunt, P. (ed.) *Children's Literature: The Development of Criticism*, London: Routledge.

——(1998) *Reading Otherways*, Stroud: The Thimble Press.

——(2002) 'The Cadence in the Song', *Times Literary Supplement*, review of Christina Rossetti: *The Complete Poems*, 18 January: 3–4.

Phelps, E. J. (1978) *Tatterhood and Other Tales*, New York: The Feminist Press.

Reynolds, K. (1990) *Girls Only? Gender and Popular Children's Fiction in Britain, 1880–1910*, New York: Harvester Wheatsheaf.

Rich, A. (1976) 'When We Dead Awaken: Writing as Re-Vision', in Rich, A., *On Lies, Secrets, and Silence: Selected Prose 1966–1978*, New York: Norton.

Rodgers, M. (1972) *Freaky Friday*, New York: Harper and Row.

Salmon, E. (1888) 'Miss L. M. Alcott', *Atalanta* 1, 8: 447–9.

Sell, R. (ed.) (2002) *Children's Literature as Communication*, Amsterdam: John Benjamins Publishing.

Showalter, E. (1985) 'Toward a Feminist Poetic', in Showalter, E. (ed.) *The New Feminist Criticism: Essays on Women, Literature, and Theory*, New York: Pantheon.

Slemon, S. and Wallace, J. (1991) 'Into the Heart of Darkness? Teaching Children's Literature as a Problem in Theory', *Canadian Children's Literature* 63: 6–23.

Spivak, G. (1987) *In Other Worlds: Essays in Cultural Politics*, New York: Methuen.

Spufford, F. (2002) *The Child That Books Built: A Life in Reading*, London: Faber and Faber.

Styles, M. (1990) 'Lost from the Nursery: Women Writing Poetry for Children 1800–1850', *Signal* 63: 177–205.

Townsend, J. R. (1974) *Written for Children: An Outline of English-language Children's Literature*, Harmondsworth: Penguin.

Trites, R. S. (1997) *Waking Sleeping Beauty: Feminist Voices in Children's Novels*, Iowa City, IA: University of Iowa Press.

Vallone, L. (1990) 'Laughing with the Boys and Learning with the Girls: Humor in Nineteenth-Century American Juvenile Fiction', *Children's Literature Association Quarterly* 15, 3: 127–30.

——(1991) '"A Humble Spirit under Correction": Tracts, Hymns, and the Ideology of Evangelical Fiction for Children, 1780–1820', *The Lion and the Unicorn* 15, 2: 72–95.

——(2001) *Becoming Victoria*, New Haven, CT: Yale University Press.

Viguers, S. T. (1988) 'My Mother, My Children, and Books', *Signal* 55: 23–32.

Walkerdine, V. (1990) *Schoolgirl Fictions*, London: Verso.

Warhol, R. R. and Herndl, D. P. (1997) *Feminisms: An Anthology of Literary Theory and Criticism*, New Brunswick, NJ: Rutgers University Press.

Warner, M. (1992) *Indigo: or Mapping the Waters*, London: Chatto and Windus.

——(1994) *From the Beast to the Blonde: On Fairytales and Their Tellers*, London: Chatto and Windus.

——(1998) *No Go the Bogeyman: Scaring, Lulling and Making Mock*, London: Chatto and Windus.

Wolf, N. (1991) *The Beauty Myth: How Images of Beauty Are Used against Women*, New York: Morrow.

Wolf, V. (1982) 'Feminist Criticism and Science Fiction for Children', *Children's Literature Association Quarterly* 7, 4: 13–16.

Wollstonecraft, M. (1791/2001) *Original Stories from Real Life*, Washington, DC: Woodstock.

Zipes, J. (1997) *Happily Ever After: Fairy Tales, Children and the Culture Industry*, London: Routledge.

Further reading

Auerbach, N. and Knoepflmacher, U. C. (1992) *Forbidden Journeys: Fairy Tales and Fantasies by Victorian Women Writers*, Chicago, IL: University of Chicago Press.

Barrs, M. and Pidgeon, S. (1993) *Reading the Difference: Gender and Reading in Primary School*, London: Centre for Language in Primary Education.

John, J. G. (1990) 'Searching for Great-Great Grandmother: Powerful Women in George MacDonald's Fantasies', *The Lion and the Unicorn* 15, 2: 27–34.

Kuznets, L. (1991) 'Two Newbery Medal Winners and the Feminine Mystique: Hitty, Her First Hundred Years and Miss Hickory', *The Lion and the Unicorn* 15, 2: 1–14.

Miller, J. (1990) *Seduction: Studies in Reading and Culture*, London: Virago.

Nikola-Lisa, W. (1991) 'The Cult of Peter Rabbit: A Barthesian Analysis', *The Lion and the Unicorn* 15, 2: 61–6.

Paul, L. (1990) 'Escape Claws: Cover Stories on *Lolly Willowes* and *Crusoe's Daughter*', *Signal* 63: 206–20.

Warner, M. (1994) *Managing Monsters: Six Myths of Our Time*, The Reith Lectures, London: Vintage

9 Decoding the images

How picture books work

Perry Nodelman

Editor's Introduction

Picture books are commonly assumed to be the province of the very young, or pre-literate child – a simple form that is beneath serious critical notice. However, they can be seen as children's literature's one genuinely original contribution to literature in general; they are a polyphonic form that embodies many codes, styles, textual devices and intertextual references, and which frequently pushes at the boundaries of convention. If you take the first view, it may seem unlikely that anyone could write a 6,000-word chapter on a single picture book, let alone a single picture. But Perry Nodelman's analysis of the first picture from John Burningham's *Mr Gumpy's Outing* demonstrates not only how much there is to say about a picture, but also how much there is to learn about the process of reading pictures.

P. H.

I open a book. I see a picture of a man, standing on a path in front of a house. Under the picture, printed words appear: 'This,' they tell me, 'is Mr Gumpy.'

What could be more straightforward, more easily understood? And for good reason: the book, John Burningham's *Mr Gumpy's Outing* (1970), is intended for the least experienced of audiences – young children; and therefore it is a 'picture book', a combination of verbal texts and visual images. We provide children with books like this on the assumption that pictures communicate more naturally and more directly than words, and thus help young readers make sense of the texts they accompany.

But are pictures so readily understood? And are picture books really so straightforward? If I try for a moment to look at the picture of Mr Gumpy without engaging my usual assumptions, I realise that I'm taking much about it for granted.

Burningham's image does in some way actually resemble a man, as the words 'man' or 'Mr Gumpy' do not; it is what linguists identify as an 'iconic' representation, whereas the words are 'symbolic', arbitrary sounds or written marks which stand for something they do not resemble. Nevertheless, if I didn't know that what I'm actually looking at – marks on a page – represented something else, I would see nothing in the picture but meaningless patches of colour. I need some general understanding of what pictures are before I can read these patches as a person, apparently named Mr Gumpy, living in a real or fictional world which exists somewhere else, outside the picture.

Even so, my previous knowledge of pictures leads me to assume that this man is different from his image. He is not four inches tall. He is not flat and two-dimensional. His eyes are not small black dots, his mouth not a thin black crescent. His skin is not paper-white, nor scored with thin orange lines. I translate these qualities of the image into

This is Mr Gumpy.

Figure 1 From *Mr Gumpy's Outing* by John Burningham. Copyright © 1971 John Burningham. Reprinted by permission of Jonathan Cape and Henry Holt and Co. Inc.

the objects they represent, and assume that the four-inch figure 'is' a man of normal height, the orange lines on white merely normal skin.

But before I can translate the lines into skin, I must know what skin is, and what it looks like. I must have a pre-existing knowledge of actual objects to understand which qualities of representations, like the orange colour here, do resemble those of the represented objects, and which, like the lines here, are merely features of the medium or style of representation, and therefore to be ignored.

For the same reason, I must assume that the sky I see above the man does not end a few inches above his head – that this is a border, an edge to the depiction, but not a representation of an edge in the world depicted. And I must realise that the house is not smaller than the man and attached to his arm, but merely at some distance behind him in the imaginary space the picture implies.

But now, perhaps I'm exaggerating the degree to which the picture requires my previous knowledge of pictorial conventions? After all, more distant real objects do appear to us to be smaller than closer ones. But while that's true, it's also true that artists have been interested in trying to record that fact – what we call perspective – only since the Renaissance, and then mostly in Europe and European-influenced cultures. Not all pictures try to represent perspective, and it takes a culture-bound prejudice to look at visual images expecting to find perspective and, therefore, knowing how to interpret it.

Children must learn these prejudices before they can make sense of this picture. Those who can accurately interpret the relative size of Mr Gumpy and the house do so on the expectation that the picture represents the way things do actually appear to a viewer. Applying that expectation might lead a viewer to be confused by Burningham's depiction of Mr Gumpy's eyes. These small black dots evoke a different style of representation, caricature, which conveys visual information by means of simplified exaggeration rather than resemblance. In order to make sense of this apparently straightforward picture, then, I must have knowledge of differing styles and their differing purposes, and perform the complex operation of interpreting different parts of the pictures in different ways.

So far I've dealt with my understanding of this image, and ignored the fact that I enjoy looking at it. I do; and my pleasure seems to be emotional rather than intellectual – a sensuous engagement with the colours, shapes and textures that leads me to agree with Brian Alderson (1990: 114), when he names *Mr Gumpy's Outing* as one of 'those picture books which have no ambitions beyond conveying simple delight'. But Alderson forgets the extent to which experiencing that simple delight depends on still further complex and highly sophisticated assumptions about what pictures do and how viewers should respond to them.

These particular assumptions are especially relevant in considering art intended for children. Ruskin famously suggested in 1857 that taking sensuous pleasure in pictures requires adults to regain an 'innocence of the eye' he described as 'childish' (quoted in Herbert 1964: 2). The implication is that children themselves, not having yet learned the supposedly counterproductive sophistication that leads adults to view pictures only in terms of their potential to convey information, are automatically in possession of innocent eyes, automatically capable of taking spontaneous delight in the colours and textures of pictures.

But according to W. J. T. Mitchell (1986: 118),

> This sort of 'pure' visual perception, freed from concerns with function, use, and labels, is perhaps the most highly sophisticated sort of seeing that we do; it is not the 'natural' thing that the eye does (whatever that would be). The 'innocent eye' is a metaphor for a highly experienced and cultivated sort of vision.

Indeed, I suspect my own pleasure in the way Burningham captures effects of light falling on grass and bricks relates strongly to the impressionist tradition the picture evokes for me – a tradition that built a whole morality upon the pleasure viewers could and should take in just such effects.

Could I have the pleasure innocently, without the knowledge of impressionism? I suspect not; as Arthur Danto asserts (1992: 431), 'To see something as art requires something the eye cannot descry – an atmosphere of artistic theory, a knowledge of the history of art: an artworld.' The 'simple delight' sophisticated adults like Brian Alderson and me take in this picture is not likely to be shared by children unaware of the ethical value of an 'innocent eye', untutored in the 'artworld'.

Nor is the picture the only thing I've read in the context of previous assumptions. There are also the words. 'This is Mr Gumpy,' they say. But *what* is, exactly? The paper page I'm looking at? The entire image I see on it? Of course not – but I must know conventions of picture captioning to realise that these words are pointing me towards a perusal of the contents of the image, in order to find somewhere within it a depiction of the specific object named.

And besides, just *who* is telling me that this is Mr Gumpy? It's possible, even logical, that the speaker is the person in the picture – as it is, for instance, when we watch TV news broadcasts; and then perhaps he's telling us that Mr Gumpy is the name of the watering can he's holding? It's my prior knowledge of the narrative conventions of picture books that leads me to assume that the speaker is not the figure depicted but someone else, a narrator rather than a character in the story, and that the human being depicted is the important object in the picture, and therefore the most likely candidate to be 'Mr Gumpy'.

As does in fact turn out to be the case – but only for those who know the most elementary conventions of reading books: that the front of the book is the cover with the bound edge on the left, and that the pages must be looked at in a certain order, across each double-page spread from left to right and then a turn to the page on the other side of the right-hand sheet. And, of course, these conventions do not operate for books printed in Israel or Japan, even if those books contain only pictures, and no Hebrew or Japanese words.

In other words: picture books like *Mr Gumpy's Outing* convey 'simple delight' by surprisingly complex means, and communicate only within a network of conventions and assumptions, about visual and verbal representations and about the real objects they represent. Picture books in general, and all their various components, are what semioticians call 'signs' – in Umberto Eco's words (1985: 176), 'something [which] stands to somebody for something else in some respect or capacity'.

The most significant fact about such representations is the degree to which we take them for granted. Both adults and children do see books like *Mr Gumpy* as simple, even obvious, and, as I discovered myself in the exercise I report above, it takes effort to become aware of the arbitrary conventions and distinctions we unconsciously take for granted, to see the degree to which that which seems simply natural is complex and artificial.

It's for that reason that such exercises are so important, and that thinking of picture books in semiotic terms is our most valuable tool in coming to understand them. According to Marshall Blonsky, 'The semiotic "head", or eye, sees the world as an immense message, replete with signs that can and do deceive us and lie about the world's condition' (1985: vii). Because we assume that pictures, as iconic signs, do in some significant way actually resemble what they depict, they invite us to see objects *as* the pictures depict them – to see the actual in terms of the fictional visualisation of it.

Indeed, this dynamic is the essence of picture books. The pictures 'illustrate' the texts – that is, they purport to show us what is meant by the words, so that we come to understand the objects and actions the words refer to in terms of the qualities of the images that accompany them – the world outside the book in terms of the images within it. And the world as they show it is not necessarily the world all viewers would agree to seeing. Speaking of what he identifies as 'visual culture', Nicholas Mirzoeff sets all visual information firmly in the context of the specific culture that produces and receives it, and describes it as 'a constantly challenging place of social interaction and definition in terms of class, gender, sexual and racial identities' (1999: 4). Picture books, with their intended purpose of showing viewers what the world implied by the words looks like, and thus means, are particularly powerful milieus for these sorts of interactions.

Furthermore, the intended audience of picture books is by definition inexperienced – in need of learning how to think about their world, how to see and understand themselves and others. Consequently, picture books are a significant means by which we integrate young children into the ideology of our culture.

As John Stephens suggests, 'Ideologies … are not necessarily undesirable, and in the sense of a system of beliefs by which we make sense of the world, social life would be impossible without them' (1992: 8). But that does not mean that all aspects of social life are equally desirable, nor that all the ideology conveyed by picture books is equally acceptable. Picture books can and do often encourage children to take for granted views of reality that many adults find objectionable. It is for this reason above all that we need to make ourselves aware of the complex significations of the apparently simple and obvious words and pictures of a book like *Mr Gumpy's Outing*. As Gillian Rose says, 'Looking carefully at images ... entails, among other things, thinking about how they offer very particular visions of social categories such as class, gender, race, sexuality, able-bodiedness, and so on' (2001: 11).

What, then, do John Burningham's picture and text mean? What have I been led to assume is 'natural' in agreeing that this *is*, in fact, Mr Gumpy?

Most obviously, I've accepted that what matters most about the picture is the human being in it: it encourages a not particularly surprising species-centricity. But it does so by establishing a hierarchic relationship among the objects depicted: only one of them is important enough to be named by the text, and so require more attention from the viewer. Intriguingly, young children tend to scan a picture with equal attention to all parts; the ability to pick out and focus on the human at the centre is therefore a learned activity, and one that reinforces important cultural assumptions, not just about the relative value of particular objects but also about the general assumption that objects do indeed have different values and do therefore require different degrees of attention.

Not surprisingly, both the text and the picture place the human depicted within a social context. He is *Mr* Gumpy, male and adult, his authority signalled by the fact that he is known only by his title and last name and that he wears the sort of jacket which represents business-like adult behaviour. The jacket disappears in the central portions of the book, as visual evidence that Mr Gumpy's boat trip is a vacation from business as usual, during which the normal conventions are relaxed. Then, at the end, Mr Gumpy wears an even fancier jacket as host at a tea party which, like the meals provided to children by adults at the end of children's stories from 'Little Red Riding Hood' through Potter's *Peter Rabbit* (1902) and Sendak's *Where the Wild Things Are* (1963), confirms the benefits for children of an adult's authority.

But despite the absence of this visual sign of his authority in many of the pictures, Mr Gumpy always remains *Mr* Gumpy in the text – and he is always undeniably in charge of the children and animals who ask to accompany him on his ride, always entitled to make the rules for them. Apparently, then, his authority transcends the symbolism of the jacket, which might be donned by anybody and therefore represents the status resident in a position rather than the power attached to an individual person. Mr Gumpy's authority must then emerge from the only other things we know about him: that he is male and adult, and that, as the text makes a point of telling us, he 'owned' the boat.

Apparently it is more important for us to know this than anything about Mr Gumpy's marital status or past history or occupation – about all of which the text is silent. Both by making ownership significant and by taking it for granted that adult male owners have the right to make rules for children and animals, who don't and presumably can't own boats, the book clearly implies a social hierarchy.

Nor is this the only way in which it supports conventional values. A later picture shows us that one of the children, the one with long hair, wears a pink dress, while the other has short hair and wears shorts and a top. In terms of the behaviour of actual children, both might be girls; but a repertoire of conventional visual codes would lead most viewers to assume that the child in shorts is male – just as we assume that trouser-wearing figures on signs signal men's washrooms, skirt-wearing figures women's washrooms. But whether male or not, the wearer of shorts behaves differently from the wearer of the dress. A later picture of the aftermath of a boating accident shows the one wet child in shorts sensibly topless, the other equally wet child still modestly sodden in her dress. This picture takes for granted and so confirms that traditionally female attire requires traditionally constraining feminine behaviour.

I suggested earlier that the text is silent about Mr Gumpy's marital status. That silence might itself speak loudly, for it mirrors and might be seen to represent the silences created by the closeting of homosexuality in the world outside the book – the need of many people *not* to speak about it. I might then follow Melynda Huskey's advice, view the book as might queer theorists (those interested in becoming aware of the attitudes to homosexuality lurking in literary texts), and try to 'make visible the ways in which queerness inheres in a variety of picture books' (2002: 69). If I do that, I find myself focusing on the fact that Mr Gumpy seems to be living on his own, surrounded by a traditionally feminine aura of domesticity and with no apparent female connections – the kind of bachelor often assumed to be secretly gay. I have, in other words, presumed to 'out' Mr Gumpy. Mr Gumpy's outing might reveal the degree to which picture books, indeed children's books generally, replicate counter-productive cultural prejudices about sexual diversity by their forms of silence about it.

More obviously, the story of *Mr Gumpy's Outing* revolves around Mr Gumpy eliciting promises that the children not squabble, the cat not chase the rabbit, and so on, before he allows them on to his boat; the creatures break their promises, and the boat tips. My knowledge of the didactic impulse behind most picture-book stories leads me to expect that an ethical judgement is about to be made: either Mr Gumpy was wrong to demand these promises, or the children and animals were wrong to make them.

Curiously, however, the book implies no such judgement. The pictures, which show Mr Gumpy as a soft, round man with a pleasant, bland face, suggest that he is anything but the sort of unreasonable disciplinarian we ought to despise; and even though the breaking of promises leads to a spill, nothing is said or shown to insist that we should make a negative judgement of the children and animals. After all, exactly such outbreaks of anarchy are the main source of pleasure in most stories for young children, and therefore to be enjoyed at least as much as condemned. Mr Gumpy himself is so little bothered that he rewards the miscreants with a meal, and even an invitation to come for another ride.

Not accidentally, furthermore, the promises all relate to behaviour so stereotypical as to seem inevitable: in the world as we most often represent it to children in books, on TV and elsewhere, cats always chase rabbits – and children always squabble. In centring on their inability to act differently, and the fun of the confusion that ensues when they don't, this story reinforces both the validity of the stereotypes and the more general (and again, conservative) conviction that variation from type is unlikely.

But why, then, would Mr Gumpy elicit promises which, it seems, could not be kept? This too the text is silent on; but the silence allows us to become aware that his asking the children and animals to do what they are not sensible enough to do reinforces the story's unspoken but firm insistence on his right to have authority over them. If they ever did mature enough to keep their word, then we couldn't so blindly assume they were unwise enough to need his leadership. Someone else might be wearing that jacket at the final tea party.

Mr Gumpy's Outing thus reinforces for its implied young readers a not uncommon set of ideas about the similarity of children to animals, the inevitability of child-like irresponsibility in both, and the resultant need for adult authority. In accepting all this as natural, readers of *Mr Gumpy's Outing* and many other apparently 'simple' picture books gain complex knowledge, not just of the world they live in but also of the place they occupy as individual beings within it – their sense of who they are.

This latter is important enough to deserve further exploration. Like most narrative, picture-book stories most forcefully guide readers into culturally acceptable ideas about who they are through the privileging of the point of view from which they report on the events they describe. Knowing only what can be known from that perspective, we readers tend to assume it ourselves – to see and understand events and people as the narrative invites us to see them. Ideological theorists call such narrative perspectives 'subject positions': in occupying them, readers are provided with ways of understanding their own subjectivity – their selfhood or individuality. But, as John Stephens suggests, 'in taking up a position from which the text is most readily intelligible, [readers] are apt to be situated within the frame of the text's ideology; that is, they are subjected to and by that ideology' (1992: 67).

All stories imply subject positions for readers to occupy. Because picture books do so with pictures as well as words, their subject positions have much in common with what Christian Metz (1982) outlines as the one films offer their viewers. The pictures in both offer viewers a position of power. They exist only so that we can look at them: they invite us to observe – and to observe what, in its very nature as a representation, cannot observe us back.

In *Mr Gumpy's Outing*, Burningham makes the authority of our viewing position clear in the same way most picture-book artists do: by almost always depicting all the characters with their faces turned towards us, even when that makes little sense in terms of the activities depicted. Indeed, the picture in which Mr Gumpy stands with his back to his house while smiling out at us makes sense only in terms of the conventions of photography or portrait painting; as in family snapshots, he is arranged so as to be most meaningfully observable by a (to him) unseen viewer who will be looking at the picture some time after it was made. In confirmation of the relationship between this image and such snapshots, the caption tells us, 'This *is* Mr Gumpy', in the same present tense we use to describe photographic images of events past (for example, 'This *is* me when I *was* a child'). The story that follows switches to the more conventional past tense of narratives.

In making their faces available to an unseen observer, the characters in *Mr Gumpy's Outing* imply not just the observer's right to gaze, but also their somewhat veiled consciousness of an observer – and therefore their own passive willingness, even desire, to be gazed at. Like the actors in a play or movie, and like characters in most picture books, they share in a somewhat less aggressive form the invitation to voyeurism that John Berger (1972) discovers in both pin-up photographs and traditional European paintings of nudes. Their implied viewer is a Peeping Tom with the right to peep, to linger over details, to enjoy and interpret and make judgements.

But meanwhile, of course, the power such pictures offer is illusory. In allowing us to observe and to interpret, they encourage us to absorb all the codes and conventions, the signs that make them meaningful; they give us the freedom of uninvolved, egocentric observation only in order to enmesh us in a net of cultural constraints that work to control egocentricity. For that reason, they encourage a form of subjectivity that is inherently paradoxical. They demand that their implied viewers see themselves as both free and with their freedom constrained, and both enjoy their illusory egocentric separation from others and yet, in the process, learn to feel guilty about it.

Interestingly, *Mr Gumpy* confirms the central importance of such paradoxes by expressing them, not just in the position of its implied viewer, but also in the ambivalence of its story's resolution. Are we asked to admire or to condemn the children and animals for being triumphantly themselves and not giving in to Mr Gumpy's attempts to constrain them? In either case, does their triumphantly being themselves represent a celebration of individuality, or an anti-individualist conviction that all cats always act alike? And if all cats must always act in a cat-like way, what are we to make of the final scene, in which the animals all sit on chairs like humans and eat and drink out of the kinds of containers humans eat and drink from? Does this last image of animals and children successfully behaving according to adult human standards contradict the apparent message about their inability to do so earlier, or merely reinforce the unquestionable authority of the adult society Mr Gumpy represents throughout?

These unanswerable questions arise from the fact that the story deals with animals who both talk like humans and yet cannot resist bleating like sheep – who act sometimes like humans, sometimes like animals. While such creatures do not exist in reality, they appear frequently in picture books, and the stories about them almost always raise questions like the ones *Mr Gumpy* does. In the conventional world of children's picture books, the state of animals who talk like humans is a metaphor for the state of human childhood, in which children must learn to negotiate between the animal-like urges of their bodily desires and the demands of adults that they repress desire and behave in socially acceptable ways – that is, as adult humans do. The strange world in which those who bleat as sheep naturally do, or squabble as children naturally do, must also sit on chairs and drink from teacups, is merely a version of the confusing world children actually live in. *Mr Gumpy* makes that obvious by treating the children as exactly equivalent to the other animals who go on the outing.

The attitude a picture book implies about whether children should act like the animals they naturally are or the civilised social beings adults want them to be is a key marker in identifying it either as a didactic book intended to teach children or as a pleasurable one intended to please them. Stories we identify as didactic encourage children towards acceptable adult behaviour, whereas pleasurable ones encourage their indulgence in what we see as natural behaviour. But, of course, both types are didactic.

The first is more obviously so because it invites children to stop being 'child-like'. In the same way as much traditional adult literature assumes that normal behaviour is that typical of white middle-class males like those who authored it, this sort of children's story defines essentially human values and acceptably human behaviour as that of adults like those who produce it.

But books in the second category teach children *how* to be child-like, through what commentators like Jacqueline Rose (1984) and myself (1992) have identified as a process of colonisation: adults write books for children to persuade them of conceptions of themselves as children that suit adult needs and purposes. One such image is the intractable, anti-social self-indulgence that Mr Gumpy so assertively forbids and so passively accepts from his passengers. It affirms the inevitability and desirability of a sort of animal-likeness – and child-likeness – that both allows adults to indulge in nostalgia for the not-yet-civilised and keeps children other than, less sensible than, and therefore deserving of less power than, adults.

That picture books like *Mr Gumpy* play a part in the educative processes I've outlined here is merely inevitable. Like all human productions, they are enmeshed in the ideology of the culture that produced them, and the childlikeness they teach is merely what our culture views as natural in children. But as a form of representation which conveys information by means of both words and pictures, picture books evoke (and teach) a complex set of intersecting sign systems. For that reason, understanding of them can be enriched by knowledge from a variety of intellectual disciplines.

Psychological research into picture perception can help us understand the ways in which human beings – and particularly children – see and make sense of pictures; Evelyn Goldsmith (1984) provides a fine summary of much of the relevant research in this area. The *gestalt* psychologist Rudolph Arnheim (1974: 11) provides a particularly useful outline of ways in which the composition of pictures influences our understanding of what they depict, especially in terms of what he calls 'the interplay of directed tensions' among the objects depicted. Arnheim argues (11) that 'these tensions are as inherent in any precept as size, shape, location, or colour', but it can be argued that they might just as logically be viewed as signs – culturally engendered codes rather than forces inherent in nature.

In either case, the relationships among the objects in a picture create variations in 'visual weight': weightier objects attract our attention more than others. In the picture of Mr Gumpy in front of his house, for instance, the figure of Mr Gumpy has great weight because of its position in the middle of the picture, its relatively large size, and its mostly white colour, which makes it stand out from the darker surfaces surrounding it. If we think of the picture in terms of the three-dimensional space it implies, the figure of Mr Gumpy gains more weight through its frontal position, which causes it to overlap less important objects like the house, and because it stands over the focal point of the perspective. Meanwhile, however, the bright red colour of the house, and the arrow shape created by the path leading towards it, focus some attention on the house; and there is an interplay of tensions among the similarly blue sky, blue flowers and blue trousers, the similarly arched doorway and round-shouldered Mr Gumpy. Analysis of such compositional features can reveal much about how pictures cause us to interpret the relationships among the objects they represent.

Visual objects can have other kinds of meanings also: for a knowledgeable viewer, for instance, an object shaped like a cross can evoke Christian sentiments. Because picture books have the purpose of conveying complex information by visual means, they tend to refer to a wide range of visual symbolisms, and can sometimes be illuminated by knowledge of everything from the iconography of classical art to the semiotics of contemporary advertising. Consider, for instance, how the specific house Burningham provides Mr Gumpy conveys, to those familiar with the implications of architectural style, both an atmosphere of rural peacefulness and a sense of middle-class respectability.

Furthermore, anyone familiar with Freudian or Jungian psychoanalytical theory and their focus on the unconscious meanings of visual images will find ample material for analysis in picture books. There may be Freudian implications of phallic power in Mr Gumpy's punt pole, carefully placed in the first picture of him on his boat so that it almost appears to emerge from his crotch; in the later picture of the aftermath of the disastrous accident, there is nothing in front of Mr Gumpy's crotch but a length of limp rope. Meanwhile, Jungians might focus on the archetypal resonances of the watering can Mr Gumpy holds in the first few pictures, its spout positioned at the same angle as the punt pole in the picture that follows, and the teapot he holds in the last picture, its spout also at the same angle. The fact that this story of a voyage over and into water begins and ends with Mr Gumpy holding objects that carry liquid, and thus takes him from providing sustenance for plants to providing sustenance for other humans and animals, might well suggest a complex tale of psychic and/or social integration.

Nor is it only the individual objects in pictures that have meaning: pictures as a whole can also express moods and meanings, through their use of already existing visual styles which convey information to viewers who know art history. Styles identified with specific individuals, or with whole periods or cultures, can evoke not just what they might have meant for their original viewers, but also what those individuals or periods or cultures have come to mean to us. Thus, Burningham's pictures of Mr Gumpy suggest both the style of impressionism and the bucolic peacefulness that it now tends to signify.

In addition to disciplines which focus on pictures, there has been an extensive theoretical discussion of the relationships between pictures and words which is especially important in the study of picture books. Most studies in this area still focus on the differences Lessing (1766/1969) pointed out centuries ago in *Laocoön*: visual representations are better suited to depicting the appearance of objects in spaces, words to depicting the action of objects in time. In a picture book like *Mr Gumpy*, therefore, the text sensibly says nothing about the appearance of Mr Gumpy or his boat, and the pictures are incapable of actually moving as a boat or an animal does.

But pictures can and do provide information about sequential activity. In carefully choosing the best moment of stopped time to depict, and the most communicative compositional tensions among the objects depicted, Burningham can clearly convey the action of a boat tipping, what actions led the characters to take the fixed positions they are shown to occupy, and what further actions will result. Furthermore, the sequential pictures of a picture book imply all the actions that would take the character from the fixed position depicted in one picture to the fixed position in the next – from not quite having fallen into the water in one picture to already drying on the bank in the next. Indeed, it is this ability to imply unseen actions and the passage of time that allows the pictures in picture books to play the important part they do in the telling of stories.

Nevertheless, the actions implied by pictures are never the same as those named in words. The bland statement of Burningham's text, 'and into the water they fell', hardly begins to cover the rich array of actions and responses the picture of the boat tipping lays out for us. W. J. T. Mitchell (1986: 44) concludes that the relationship between pictures and accompanying texts is 'a complex one of mutual translation, interpretation, illustration, and enlightenment'. Once more, *Mr Gumpy's Outing* reveals just how complex.

Burningham's text on its own without these pictures would describe actions by characters with no character: it takes the pictures and a knowledge of visual codes to read meaning into these simple actions. Without a text, meanwhile, the pictures of animals that make up most of the book would seem only a set of portraits, perhaps illustrations for an informational guide to animals. Only the text reveals that the animals can talk, and that it is their desire to get on the boat. Indeed, the exact same pictures could easily support a different text, one about Mr Gumpy choosing to bring speechless animals on board until the boat sinks from their weight and he learns a lesson about greed. So the pictures provide information about the actions described in the words; and at the same time, the words provide information about the appearances shown in the pictures.

If we look carefully, in fact, the words in picture books always tell us that things are not merely as they appear in the pictures, and the pictures always show us that events are not exactly as the words describe them. Picture books are inherently ironic, therefore: a key pleasure they offer is a perception of the differences in the information offered by pictures and texts.

Such differences both make the information richer and cast doubt on the truthfulness of each of the means which convey it. The latter is particularly significant: in their very nature, picture books work to make their audiences aware of the limitations and distortions in their representations of the world. Close attention to picture books automatically turns readers into semioticians. For young children as well as for adult theorists, realising that, and learning to become more aware of the distortions in picture-book representations, can have two important results.

The first is that it encourages consciousness and appreciation of the cleverness and subtlety of both visual and verbal artists. The more readers and viewers of any age know about the codes of representation, the more they can enjoy the ways in which writers and illustrators use those codes in interesting and involving ways. They might, for instance, notice a variety of visual puns in *Mr Gumpy's Outing*: how the flowers in Burningham's picture of the rabbit are made up of repetitions of the same shapes as the rabbit's eyes, eyelashes and ears, or how his pig's snout is echoed by the snout-shaped tree branch behind it.

The second result of an awareness of signs is even more important: the more both adults and children realise the degree to which all representations misrepresent the world, the less likely they will be to confuse any particular representation with reality, or to be unconsciously influenced by ideologies they have not considered. Making ourselves and our children more conscious of the semiotics of the picture books through which we show them their world and themselves will allow us to give them the power to negotiate their own subjectivities – surely a more desirable goal than repressing them into conformity to our own views.

References

Alderson, B. (1990) 'Picture Book Anatomy', *The Lion and the Unicorn* 14, 2: 108–14.

Arnheim, R. (1974) *Art and Visual Perception: A Psychology of the Creative Eye*, Berkeley, CA: University of California Press.

Berger, J. (1972) *Ways of Seeing*, London: BBC and Penguin.

Blonsky, M. (ed.) (1985) *On Signs*, Baltimore, MD: Johns Hopkins University Press.

Burningham, J. (1970) *Mr Gumpy's Outing*, London: Cape.

Danto, A. (1992) 'The Artworld', in Alperson, P. (ed.) *The Philosophy of the Visual Arts*, New York and Oxford: Oxford University Press, 426–33.

Eco, U. (1985) 'Producing Signs', in Blonsky, M. (ed.) *On Signs*, Baltimore, MD: Johns Hopkins University Press.

Goldsmith, E. (1984) *Research into Illustration: An Approach and a Review*, Cambridge: Cambridge University Press.

Herbert, R. L. (ed.) (1964) *The Art Criticism of John Ruskin*, Garden City, NY: Doubleday Anchor.

Huskey, M. (2002) 'Queering the Picture Book', *The Lion and the Unicorn* 26, 1: 66–77.

Lessing, G. E. (1766/1969) *Laocoön: An Essay upon the Limits of Poetry and Painting*, trans. Frothingham, E., New York: Farrar, Straus and Giroux.

Metz, C. (1982) *The Imaginary Signifier: Psychoanalysis and the Cinema*, Bloomington, IN: Indiana University Press.

Mirzoeff, N. (1999) *An Introduction to Visual Culture*, London and New York: Routledge.

Mitchell, W. J. T. (1986) *Iconology: Image, Text, Ideology*, Chicago, IL: University of Chicago Press.

Nodelman, P. (1992) 'The Other: Orientalism, Colonialism, and Children's Literature', *Children's Literature Association Quarterly* 17, 1: 29–35.

Potter, B. (1902) *The Tale of Peter Rabbit*, London: Frederick Warne.

Rose, G. (2001) *Visual Methodologies*, London: Sage.

Rose, J. (1984) *The Case of Peter Pan or The Impossibility of Children's Fiction*, London: Macmillan.

Sendak, M. (1963) *Where the Wild Things Are*, New York: Harper and Row.

Stephens, J. (1992) *Language and Ideology in Children's Fiction*, London and New York: Longman.

Further reading

Anstey, M. and Bull, G. (2000) *Reading the Visual: Written and Illustrated Children's Literature*, Sydney: Harcourt.

Children's Literature 19 (1991) New Haven, CT: Yale University Press (an issue of this journal devoted to discussions of picture books).

Doonan, J. (1993) *Looking at Pictures in Picture Books*, South Woodchester: Thimble Press.

Gombrich, E. H. (1972) 'Visual Image', *Scientific American* 227: 82–94.

Kiefer, B. Z. (1995) *The Potential of Picture Books: From Visual Literacy to Aesthetic Understanding*, Englewood Cliffs, NJ and Columbus, OH: Merrill.

Lewis, D. (2001) *Reading Contemporary Picturebooks: Picturing Text*, London and New York: RoutledgeFalmer.

Mirzoeff, N. (ed.) (2002) *The Visual Culture Reader*, 2nd edn, London and New York: Routledge.

Mitchell, W. J. T. (1994) *Picture Theory*, Chicago, IL and London: University of Chicago Press.

Moebius, W. (1986) 'Introduction to Picturebook Codes', *Word and Image* 2, 2: 63–6.

Nikolajeva, M. and Scott, C. (2001) *How Picturebooks Work*, New York and London: Garland.

Nodelman, P. (1988) *Words about Pictures: The Narrative Art of Children's Picture Books*, Athens, GA: University of Georgia Press.

——(1992) *The Pleasures of Children's Literature*, White Plains, NY: Longman.

Schwarcz, J. H. (1982) *Ways of the Illustrator: Visual Communication in Children's Literature*, Chicago, IL: American Library Association.

Schwarcz, J. H. and Schwarcz, C. (1991) *The Picture Book Comes of Age*, Chicago, IL and London: American Library Association.

10 Bibliography

The resources of children's literature

Matthew Grenby

Editor's Introduction

The study of children's literature is not only about the interpretation and uses of texts, but includes a consideration of the texts as objects. Bibliographical studies can provide invaluable historical information, and provide interpreters with accurate, and contextualised, texts. There are many hundreds of large and distinguished historical collections of children's books across the world, and the opportunities for bibliographical research are huge. Matthew Grenby explores these large and largely untapped resources, describes the work that has been done, and suggests future directions.

P. H.

Bibliography can mean many things. Simple enumerative bibliography lists precisely what was published in a given period or genre, or by a particular author. Analytical bibliography can go much further, exploring the often complicated progress from author's manuscript to published book, the processes of book manufacture and marketing, and the nature of readers' and other writers' responses (an admirable précis, 'Descriptive Bibliography', is provided by Terry Belanger in *Book Collecting: A Modern Guide*: Peters 1977: 97–101). Few would doubt that good bibliographical work of any of these varieties can be hugely useful in understanding the origins and development of children's literature. Most would also agree that the bibliographical groundwork has yet to be adequately laid for the study of children's books. Brian Alderson, for instance, is sure that it has not. In 1975 he told the Bibliographical Society that 'there is much elementary bibliographical work still to be done' in the field of children's literature (Alderson 1977: 206). Twenty years later, his opinion was unchanged, and he added the charge that the energy that might usefully have been spent undertaking this work had been wasted on solipsistic critical analyses of the same old texts: 'Oh dear,' he wrote, 'so much bibliographical groundwork to be done, and all we get is floss' (Alderson 1995a: 17). It is from a statement like this that we can begin to see why children's literature bibliography – ostensibly such an uncomplicated part of scholarship – has recently become the subject of some contention.

What Alderson was suggesting was that a deep division exists between bibliography and literary criticism, and especially any criticism based on literary theory: what he called 'floss'. For Alderson, it was imperative that good bibliographical work should form the basis for all scholarly enquiry into children's literature, and any time spent on critical exegesis was wasted while there was still so much basic scholarship to be done. Peter Hunt, among other children's literature scholars, rose to the bait. 'Critical' and 'theoretical' approaches were every bit as valuable as bibliography, Hunt wrote in a response to

Alderson, and their practitioners should not be inhibited by any lack of bibliographical work, however regrettable that lack might be (Hunt 1995). Both had valid points. Hunt's contention that it was unwarranted to attack critics who neglected to check publication dates, or dared not expound the conflicting evidence of different editions, impressions, issues and corrected and uncorrected states (to say nothing of colophons and watermarks), was surely only reasonable. For his part, Alderson was correct to point out that children's books, far more than books for adults, were created in the publishing process, by publishers, illustrators, marketers, teachers and so on, rather than only by authors whose texts transferred smoothly from manuscript to printed page to readers' minds. It is a convincing argument that this long process, with its various mediating factors, is best analysed by descriptive and textual bibliography (Alderson 1995a and 1995b).

Alderson was also surely correct to argue that children's literature does still lack a firm bibliographical base. The history of children's literature in some periods and some places has simply not been written in any detail. Hardly anything is known about which books children read in medieval or early modern Europe, for instance. Likewise (though Alderson was less concerned about this), bibliographies of the children's literature of Asia, Africa, the Middle East and Latin America, when they exist at all, seldom stretch back much beyond the middle of the twentieth century. Partly this is because there are so many different competing approaches to children's books which draw scholars away from bibliographic research. Scholars come at children's literature as historians of education, as library scientists, as cultural historians, as well as from literary backgrounds, and there is consequently less insistence on the virtues of bibliography. Partly, the lack of bibliography is also due to the relatively recent arrival of children's literature as a recognised field of academic enquiry. Having been taken seriously only for decades rather than for centuries, children's literature studies have simply not accumulated the scholarly infrastructure, including bibliography, which has accreted around other more established areas of literary research. That recent scholars have leapfrogged the description-based 'bibliographic stage', and that analytical literary criticism has now become the dominant mode of academic enquiry into children's literature, is difficult to deny. A glance at Irving P. Leif's *Children's Literature: An Historical and Contemporary Bibliography*, published in 1977, confirms this, with articles like 'Wittgenstein, Nonsense and Lewis Carroll' (Pitcher 1965) beginning to oust the likes of 'Carroll's withdrawal of the 1865 *Alice*' (Ayres 1934) from the 1960s onwards. That Leif's remains one of the only two full-scale print-format bibliographies of children's literature studies is also testament to the decline of this approach (the other is Haviland 1966 *et seq.*).

Does this mean that children's literature bibliography is dying? The answer, surely, is no. The dichotomy exposed by the brief spat between Alderson and Hunt was rather artificial. Critics and bibliographers are actually not always at each others' throats. (Can it have been coincidence that the issue of the *Children's Books History Society Newsletter* which contained the Alderson–Hunt exchange bore on its front cover John Tenniel's image of Tweedledum and Tweedledee preparing to fight?) They have, it must be admitted, tended to congregate in different locales. The bibliographers have usually been self-funded individuals, often book collectors or dealers. The critics have tended to thrive in the relatively well-resourced and perhaps rather artificial environment of university literature departments. But there was actually much more common ground between these two groups than at first meets the eye. Hunt did nothing to dispute the importance of bibliography as *one* approach to children's books. Similarly, Alderson argued against any attempt at 'driving a wedge' between those who are interested in the 'physical and historical aspects of documents' and 'those who care about what the documents say'. There should be no separation between these two approaches, 'but a continuum of critical activity' (Alderson 1995b: 23). Both Hunt and Alderson tacitly accepted, then, that bibliography and literary criticism could work in tandem. This is precisely what happens in practice. The very lack of bibliographical work has necessitated the incorporation of historical, and for that matter enumerative, bibliography into even the most theoretical of children's literature studies. Thus, to take one example, if we wish to know about the history of Norwegian children's books, we can turn to Kari Skjønsberg's 'Nationalism as an Aspect of the History of Norwegian Children's Literature, 1814–1905' (Nikolajeva 1995: 105–14). Although it appears in a volume remarkable for its rigorously theoretical approach to children's books, the essay provides an instructive survey of Norwegian children's books alongside its exploration of the role of children's literature in nation-building in the nineteenth century. Likewise, books like *The Black American in Books for Children: Readings in Racism* (MacCann and Woodard 1985), or Jack Zipes's *The Brothers Grimm. From Enchanted Forests to the Modern World* (Zipes 1988: especially 183–4), perform bibliographic as well as analytical and ideological tasks.

The crossover between these two supposedly inimical approaches is also evident in the most orthodox bibliographical works. Bibliography, after all, is never neutral. Alongside their checklists of titles and editions, even the most dependable and putatively 'objective' bibliographies almost always include literary analysis, artistic and ideological judgements, and attempts to arrange texts according to certain predetermined criteria. F. J. Harvey Darton's path-breaking bibliographical survey of *Children's Books in England* (Darton, revised Alderson 1932/1982), for example, set an astonishingly durable ideological agenda. Darton divided British children's literature into categories which were broadly chronological but which also demarcated children's books according to whether they were godly or imaginative, fairy tales or moral tales, based on strict pedagogic principles or aiming to inspire levity. Those histories of British children's literature which have followed have almost always stuck to these categories, even if the particular titles they have included have been slightly different from those chosen by Darton as milestones to modernity (Muir 1954; Townsend 1965/1995; Thwaite 1963/1972; and Quayle 1971 and 1983). Indeed, the most recent attempts to survey the history of British children's books have tended to schematise the story even further. For Geoffrey Summerfield, children's books can most usefully be understood as either didactic or entertaining, and the tension between these two tendencies was what has powered the development of the genre (Summerfield 1984). Straying further from Darton's paradigm, Mary Jackson attempted to situate her history of early children's books in the context of contemporary politics and economics (Jackson 1989). From the point of view of bibliography, though, her book is more useful for its willingness to draw on a larger corpus of cheap and popular texts than Darton, and for her inclusion of research on authors and publishers which had been published since Alderson last revised Darton's book in 1982. Also important as supplements to Darton, who only really got into his stride in the mid-eighteenth century, are the attempts to chart the murky origins of British children's literature. In this field, William Sloane's *Children's Books in England and America in the Seventeenth Century* (Sloane 1955) and Ruth K. MacDonald's *Literature for Children in England and America from 1646 to 1774* (MacDonald 1982) will soon be joined by a bibliography of all books published for children in Britain before 1800 by Ruth B. Bottigheimer (Bottigheimer, forthcoming; for a summary of the key texts of British children's 'incunabula' see Alderson 1999).

All these books deal almost exclusively with English literature, into which the Scottish,

Irish and Welsh traditions have generally been silently subsumed. Little effort has so far been made to reclaim them. Although a substantial amount of critical analysis has now been carried out into particular Scottish children's books, for instance, no full-scale bibliography of books for children published in Scotland, or about Scottish subjects, exists. The most useful source remains a short essay on *The Scottish Contribution to Children's Literature* published in the mid-1960s (Douglas 1966) and whatever can be gleaned from Colin Manlove's admirable critical survey of Scottish fantasy literature (Manlove 1996). There is a similar paucity of bibliographic work on the children's literature of Ireland (Madden 1955 remains useful). In fact, it is only the history of Welsh children's literature which has received any sustained attention, and there is still much work to be done (S. Jones 1990; M. and G. Jones 1983, in Welsh).

Even if the bibliography of British children's literature is itself in need of revision (and Darton's final chapter is entitled 'The Eighties and Today', meaning the 1880s, not the 1980s!), it is far further forward than that in most other parts of the world. The major exception to this is Germany. The *Handbuch zur Kinder- und Jugendliteratur*, with (to date) four huge volumes dealing with discrete chronological periods from the very first children's books to 1850, is now probably the most authoritative bibliography of children's literature in existence (Brüggermann and Ewers 1982; Brüggermann and Brunken 1987, 1991; and Brunken *et al.* 1998; all in German). With astonishingly thorough entries on individual children's books, arranged chronologically within broad generic categories, it functions both as an immensely detailed encyclopedia and an in-depth narrative history of children's literature in German. Members of the same team which produced the *Handbuch* have also produced a shorter history of Austrian children's literature (Ewers and Seibert 1997, in German) and a bibliography of German-Jewish children's literature from the eighteenth century to 1945 (Shavit and Ewers 1994, in German). The only comparably thorough listing of a nation's children's books is probably Marcie Muir and Kerry White's survey of Australian books for children (Muir 1992; White 1992). Muir's volume, covering the period 1774 to 1972, contains over 8,000 children's books either published in or dealing with Australia, and a further 700 items dealing with the southwest Pacific area. The second volume, by White, takes the bibliography up to 1988.

When we consider the achievement of the *Handbuch zur Kinder- und Jugendliteratur* in particular, and the lack of any comparable volumes for other regions, complaints about the scantiness of existing bibliographical work seem more justified. The only substantial general survey of western European children's books remains Brian Alderson's translation of Bettina Hürlimann's *Three Centuries of Children's Books in Europe* (Hürlimann 1967), an absorbing if rather miscellaneous overview. For more detail, almost all western European nations have their own 'Darton' – that is to say, a mid-twentieth century surveyor of the nation's children's literature (mostly available only in the language of that nation, but sometimes in English). For a cursory survey of French children's literature, for instance, one might turn to J. G. Deschamps's *The History of French Children's Books*, in English, or François Caradec's *Histoire de la littérature enfantine en France*, in French (Deschamps 1934; Caradec 1977). For Italy there is the work of Louise Hawkes and Vincenzina Battistelli; for the Netherlands there is Leonard de Vries; for Denmark there is Helgo Mollerup; for the Czech and Slovak republics there is Helga Mach; for Portugal there is Henrique Marques; and for Spain there is Carolina Toral y Peñaranda and, perhaps best of all, Carmen Bravo-Villasante, who has mapped Spanish children's literature from the twelfth to the twentieth centuries (Hawkes 1933; Battistelli 1962; de Vries 1964; Mollerup 1951; Mach, 'Czech and Slovak Children's Literature' in Haviland 1973:

365–73; Marques 1928; Toral y Peñaranda 1958; Bravo-Villasante 1963). This is just a sample of the now somewhat ageing national histories available. Others can be found in the 'Further Reading' sections in the nation-by-nation chapters at the end of this Encyclopedia (and others still by consulting Leif 1977, and the excellent Pellowski 1968). One or two national traditions have received more recent treatments, such as the survey of eighteenth-century Dutch children's literature by Piet Buijnsters with Leontine Buijnsters-Smets, and of pre-twentieth-century Swiss children's books by Claudia Weilenmann (Buijnsters and Buijnsters-Smets 1997; Weilenmann 1993). One will search in vain, however, for satisfactory bibliographies of certain nations. To date, for example, there is no substantial survey of Russian or Soviet children's literature. Once again, though, research which is not primarily bibliographic in nature can be of great use. Evgeny Steiner's *Stories for Little Comrades*, though concentrating mostly on the illustration of children's books in the 1920s and 1930s, provides useful information on what was published for children in the early years of the Soviet Union (Steiner 1999; see also McGill University 1999). Similarly, recent explorations of the interactions between different national traditions of writing for children, though they may be grounded in intertextual theory, have been valuable in reminding us that good bibliographical work, even if it purports to survey only the literature of one country, must always acknowledge the trans-national context. Mariella Colin's 'Children's Literature in France and Italy in the Nineteenth Century: Influences and Exchanges' makes this point well (Nikolajeva 1995: 77–87).

Beyond Europe, the availability of good bibliographies of children's books becomes even more patchy. As one might expect, American children's literature has been relatively well surveyed, the best assessments having been provided by d'Alte Welch's massive *A Bibliography of American Children's Books Printed Prior to 1821* and Gillian Avery's *Behold the Child* (Welch 1972, which originally appeared in the *Proceedings of the American Antiquarian Society*, 1963–67; Avery 1994. The rather more venerable Blanck 1956 is also still useful). A good example of the way in which well-focused critical bibliography can make excellent analytical cultural history is Sarah Kennerly's exploration of the children's books published by the Confederacy during the American Civil War (Kennerly 1957). Canadian children's literature in English is well served by Sheila Egoff and Judith Saltman's *The New Republic of Childhood* (Egoff and Saltman 1990), though its generic rather than chronological organisation makes it difficult to handle as a bibliography. The scholarly journal *Canadian Children's Literature* has carried a number of useful bibliographic articles, such as those on Canadian children's poetry (Stanbridge 1986) and on British Columbian children's literature (Kealy 1994). For its part, the Mexican tradition has been traced by Beatriz Donet and Guillermo Murria Prisant's *Palabra de juguete*, a two-volume bibliography and anthology which seeks to place Mexican children's literature from the pre-Hispanic and colonial periods to the twentieth century in its international contexts (Donet and Prisant 1999, in Spanish). The children's literature of each Central and South American nation is thoroughly described in the separate sections of Manuel Peña Muñoz's recent *Había una vez – en América. Literatura Infantil de America Latina* (Muñoz 1997, in Spanish). A number of other checklists cover children's books *about* Hispanic culture. Although they were originally intended to aid parents and teachers to locate appropriate books for young Hispanic-American readers, they have now become useful bibliographic tools for those carrying out research into the children's books of the second half of the twentieth century (see for example Schon 1980). The same might be said of several American-published bibliographies of children's books about, rather than from, the Soviet Union (Povsic 1991), Eastern Europe (Povsic 1986), the Indian subcontinent (Khorana 1991) and Africa (Schmidt 1975–9; Khorana 1994). Designed to make 'books about other countries available to American youth' so as to deepen their 'understanding of the international community', these contain only books published in English, since 1900, most of which were published in the USA (Povsic 1991: xi). They may not actually represent the children's literature of these different regions, but they do open up new fields of enquiry to the researcher.

Bibliographies of books for children actually published in Africa, the Middle East and Asia are rare. Useful information on the former can be found in the recent *The Companion to African Literatures* (Killam and Rowe 2000: 63–7) and J. O. U. Odiase's *African Books for Children and Young Adults*, a basic checklist of books for children published in Africa from the 1960s to the 1980s (Odiase 1986). Naturally, no bibliography on a continental scale exists for Asia, and only one or two bibliographies exist on the national scale (for the Philippines, for example, see Seriña and Yap 1980). An excellent review of the way in which Confucian primers gave way to more ideologically invested and Western-influenced children's books in China is to be found in Mary Ann Farquhar's *Children's Literature in China*. Even if the book is not a bibliography as such, its analysis of the artistic and political content of inter-war, Revolutionary and Maoist children's books rests upon a solid survey of twentieth-century Chinese books for children (Farquhar 1999; see also Cohn 2000). No such work exists as yet for other regions of Asia, although there is much to be gleaned from those works cited in the relevant sections in this Encyclopedia. Even Japan lacks a national children's literature bibliography (but Kitano 1967, Shimi 1987 and Herring 2000 are useful). Bibliographic and historical work has been undertaken on Indian children's literature, although, because of the ethnic diversity of the country, these have been faced with the almost impossible task of summarising the history of fourteen separate traditions, one for each main linguistic grouping. From Provash Ronjan Dey's *Children's Literature of India*, for instance, we learn that Urdu and Telegu children's literature began in the mid-nineteenth century, while the first children's books written in Tamil or Punjabi, say, did not appear until the 1930s (Dey 1977; see also Manorama Jafa's 'Children's Literature in India' in Dasgupta 1995: 33–42).

In fact, children's literature can often be most profitably surveyed and investigated on the basis of language rather than nation. The more than 300 children's books published in Hebrew listed in Uriel Ofek's *Hebrew Children's Literature*, for instance, extend over the period 1506 to 1905, but, perhaps more strikingly, they also span several continents (Ofek 1979, in Hebrew). Bibliography, which can follow the flight of texts across political boundaries, has a significant role to play in illuminating the full extent and complexity of the web of influences which have lain behind the development of children's literature. In a sense, national bibliographies, though the reasons for constructing them have been extremely cogent, have prevented us from seeing this web of connections. Most national bibliographers worth their salt know full well that one cannot map the history of children's literature in one country without reference to others. The story of British and French children's literature in the eighteenth and nineteenth centuries, for instance, is, in miniature, the history of political and social ideas and their transmission, of the French Enlightenment and the commercial revolution in Britain, of the French Revolution and the pious and loyal conservative reaction to it in Britain. A comparative approach, exploring the points of contact and of discrepancy between these two literary traditions, rather than concentrating just on one nation or the other, would be a fascinating task. A bibliographical survey tracing the congruities and disruptions in the interchange of ideas on children's books across the English Channel would be the necessary starting point. So far no such work has been undertaken.

Regrettably, even the bibliography of particular genres of children's books, which could be the perfect vehicle for tracing international connections, seldom manages to overcome national borders. Children's fantasy stories, for example, were widely traded between countries. Yet in recent bibliographies of the genre as it developed in the Anglo-American tradition, very few references are made to translations or alterations of the texts once exported, nor to the foreign books which either inspired the Anglo-American texts or were themselves inspired by them (on fantasy literature see Pflieger 1984; Lynn 1995; Manlove 1996; and Barron 1999). The same is true of the one, otherwise excellent, bibliography of boys' stories by Eric Quayle, which only gives the merest hint that children's literature was developing along similar trajectories in nations besides Britain and America (Quayle 1973; on a similar theme see James and Smith 1998). The lack of comparative work is particularly striking when Quayle discusses the militaristic narratives which flourished in Britain in the first three decades of the twentieth century. Were such stories also being written and read in Germany or France or Russia, one cannot help wondering? Likewise, recent encyclopedias of girls' and boys' school stories provide valuable guides to the genres, arranged alphabetically by author with many entries including a diligently researched bibliography, but they do not attempt to leap over political borders. The *Encyclopaedia of Girls' School Stories* refers only to books from Britain, Australia and New Zealand, along with a few works by North American authors 'who consciously wrote in the British tradition' (Sims and Clare 2000: 38). The *Encyclopaedia of Boys' School Stories*, though it expands the chronological range of books covered, includes only British books (Kirkpatrick 2000; see also Kirkpatrick 2001). Other regions of the world produced a different kind of school story, we are told, but the connections and discrepancies, though they are surely one of the most interesting aspects of this kind of project, are not investigated.

The reason for this is clear: bibliographical work requires a huge amount of toil, which must somehow be circumscribed. The *Encyclopaedia of Girls' School Stories* has six pages of bibliographic detail on the books of Elinor M. Brent-Dyer's Chalet School series alone, for instance, while Robert Kirkpatrick devotes five closely packed pages to the books of Charles Hamilton (alias Frank Richards) – original, re-written, re-printed, serialised and pseudonymous (Sims and Clare 2000: 75–81; Kirkpatrick 2000: 153–8). When an international approach is undertaken, however, the rewards are obvious. Ruth B. Bottigheimer's survey of children's Bibles covers five centuries but also several countries, most especially the German and the Anglo-American traditions (Bottigheimer 1996). Both Bottigheimer's analysis of the texts and the bibliographical work upon which her study is founded enable the reader to assess not only change over time, but also, by comparisons across geographical boundaries, the specific characteristics of each nation's understanding of the way the scriptures should be presented to children. (For a survey of post-war religious writing for children, almost entirely American, see Pearl 1988.) Similarly, the best of the several bibliographies of the writing of Mark Twain stands out because it traces the dissemination of his writing around the world. Bibliography is at its most provocative when it tells us, for instance, that a new edition of *Huckleberry Finn* and *Tom Sawyer* has been put out in Argentina almost every year since the 1930s, that *Extracts from the Diary of Adam and Eve*, first published by Twain in 1906, had appeared in Yiddish in Warsaw by 1913, or that a Marathi *Prince and the Pauper* was the first of Twain's works to be published in India, in 1908 (Rodney 1982: 220–4, 190, 240. For a more standard Twain bibliography see Johnson 1935).

Other generically based bibliographies have examined an eclectic range of subjects: movable and toy books (Haining 1979), pop-up books (Montanaro 2000), British ABCs (Garrett 1994), American etiquette books (Bobbitt 1947), 'Cries of London' books (Shesgreen and Bywaters 1998), children's miniature libraries (Alderson 1983), plays published for toy theatres (Speaight 1999), fairy tales (Opie and Opie 1974), historical fiction for children (Moffat 2000) and British children's periodicals (Drotner 1988, and see also Grey 1970 on the very first *The Lilliputian Magazine*). Recent generic bibliographies designed to enable teachers and parents to find books to educate their children according to specific agendas may be of little help to historians of children's literature today, but in time they will provide a valuable resource for scholars researching the culture of childhood in the late twentieth and early twenty-first centuries. Bibliographies are now available, to take one or two examples, of children's books with gay and lesbian themes (Day 2000), of children's books about war and peace (Eiss 1989), and of books dealing with World War II (Holsinger 1995). The more bibliographers concentrate on these narrow areas, however, the more the existence of wide tracts of uncharted territory becomes manifest. We have, say, a sturdy bibliography of children's books dealing with Ancient Greece and Rome, from 1834 to 1994 (Brazouski and Klatt 1994), but we have no catalogues of some of the major, long-standing genres such as animal stories, or the legends of the Seven Champions of Christendom, or Sinbad. There are also few bibliographies of those under-appreciated books which kept the children's book trade alive: religious works and textbooks. So long as these fields go unsurveyed, we will not be able to understand how children's publishing established itself as a sustainable commercial enterprise, nor what was the whole reading experience of the average child. With regard to textbooks, at least, the situation is starting to improve. Numerous articles exploring neglected aspects of textbook history have been published in *Paradigm*, the journal of the new Textbook Colloquium (see http://w4.ed.uiuc.edu/faculty/westbury/Paradigm/index.htm) and one or two print and on-line bibliographies have begun to appear (Price 1992 for textbooks used in New Zealand before 1960; Woodward *et al.* 1988, which lists mostly post-1975 textbooks; Palmer 2002 for science textbooks).

The contrast between the excellent bibliographical work which *has* been undertaken, and the huge areas of children's literature which have not been explored, is also obvious when we consider how bibliographers have treated individual authors. A favoured few have been the subject of exhaustive bibliographic work. Lewis Carroll's output, for instance, had been thoroughly catalogued by the 1920s ('the age of bibliographies', as Carroll's bibliographer put it: Williams 1924: vii). By the 1980s, a checklist of works about Carroll's writing could fill a substantial volume on its own (Guiliano 1981). With little left to catalogue, the minutiae of Carroll's letters to the press have now become the subject of their own annotated bibliography (Lovett 1999). The works of Beatrix Potter and Lucy Maud Montgomery have also been exhaustively explored (Linder 1971, and Hobbes and Whalley 1985 on Potter; Russell *et al.* 1986, and Garner and Hawker 1989 on Montgomery's books, Izawa 2002 on her Japanese editions – there have been 123 Japanese editions of *Anne of Green Gables* in the last fifty years – and Elizabeth Rollings Epperly on her manuscripts, in Rubio 1994: 74–83). Also well served, to varying extents, have been J. M. Barrie (Cutler 1931; Markgraf 1989), A. A. Milne (Haring-Smith 1982), Robert Louis Stevenson (Slater 1914; Prideaux 1917), Louisa May Alcott (Ullom 1969), Arthur Ransome (Hammond 2000; Wardale 1995), Richmal Crompton (Schutte 1993; and see also Cadogan with Schutte 1990) and Maurice Sendak (Hanrahan 2001). In recent years, other children's writers, mostly British, have begun to have their work explored in detail, and not only squarely canonical authors either. Mary Martha Sherwood (Cutt 1974), George MacDonald (Shaberman 1990) and Barbara Hofland (Butts 1992) have become the subjects of full-length studies, for example.

Many other eminent children's authors have not been so fortunate. Can it really be, one wonders, that the only bibliography of C. S. Lewis's work is a privately printed pamphlet by Aidan Mackey (Mackey 1991)? In one or two cases authors who have not so far been honoured with a single volume-length bibliography have had their output logged by periodical articles. Maria Edgeworth's very confusing publishing history, for example, has occupied many pages of that august bibliographic journal, *The Book Collector* (Colvin and Morgenstern 1977; Pollard 1971; Renier 1972; Schiller 1974a. For a summary see the essay on Edgeworth at the Hockliffe Project website: Grenby 2001). Other authors have benefited from having a dedicated admirer research their work and publish the results wherever the opportunity has been offered. The newsletter of the Children's Books History Society has made many such offers, and almost every issue includes an intriguing bibliography of a minor children's author. Morna Daniels has lovingly listed and discussed the Josephine books by Mrs H. C. Cradock, for instance, while Mary Shakeshaft and Betty Gilderdale have done the same for two prolific late nineteenth-century authors, Charlotte Yonge and Lady Barker (Daniels 2002; Shakeshaft 2001; Gilderdale 2001). From time to time – and especially in the heyday of the early 1970s – the more prestigious bibliographical periodicals have also carried articles about children's authors or individual children's books. Usually these concern only well-known authors and titles. Thus, for instance, the work of A. A. Milne has been mapped in *Studies in Bibliography* (Payne 1970), and *Little Black Sambo* in *The Book Collector* (Schiller 1974b). A few key texts have been privileged by having specialist work conducted into detailed aspects of their history. The fate of Hans Christian Andersen's *Eventyr* in Britain has been delineated by Brian Alderson, for example, and Nina Demourova has provided a summary of the career of Peter Pan in Russia (Alderson 1982; Routh and Demourova 1995: 19–27). Some of the important foundational texts of British children's literature have also been the subject of minute investigation, such as Thomas Boreman's *Gigantick Histories* (Stone 1933) and John Newbery's *Goody Two-Shoes* (Roberts 1965). Overall, though, only a small fraction of British children's authors have been charted, let alone those from other parts of the world.

The single bibliography which perhaps best illuminates when and how children's literature became established as a proliferating and profitable genre is not a catalogue of the works of an individual author, but of a single work: Daniel Defoe's *Robinson Crusoe* (Lovett 1991). In the 1750s, we find, a new edition of this (admittedly exceptional) children's book appeared every year or two. By 1800, the British and American markets could bear four or five editions annually. By the end of the nineteenth century there were likely to be at least eight or nine British and American printings each year (see also Stach 1991 for a bibliography of German-language Robinsonnades). No similarly complete bibliography has been completed for Jonathan Swift's *Gulliver's Travels* (although see Teerink and Scouten 1963), but a number of other single works have been honoured with their own bibliographies, notably *Struwwelpeter*, whose complete publishing history has been traced several times (most recently by Chester 1987, and Rühle in 1999, in German). It is also worth noting that bibliographies of authors who wrote mostly for adults can be useful to those studying children's reading. Sir Walter Scott, for example, wrote only one work specifically for children (*Tales of a Grandfather*), but as well as listing the many editions of this, a recent bibliography of Scott's work suggests that many chapbook and dramatic versions of his works quickly appeared, probably directed largely at the children's market (Todd and Bowden 1998).

As has already been mentioned, one of the factors inhibiting bibliographic work on children's books has been the fact that, for so much of its history, particularly in Britain, the production and character of children's literature have been governed by the operations of publishers rather than the talent of writers (Alderson 1977: 206). This being the case, there are limits to what bibliographies of individual authors can achieve, especially when dealing with the books of the eighteenth and early nineteenth centuries. Consequently, bibliographers have adapted, and some of the best surveys of children's literature to appear recently have examined the output of individual publishing houses. The first of these ground-breaking works was Sydney Roscoe's bibliography of the production of John Newbery and his successors (Roscoe 1973; see also Townsend 1994). Peter Opie, the doyen of children's book collection, thought Roscoe's work enabled the study and collection of children's books to 'come of age' (Opie 1975: 259). Even before Roscoe, M. J. P. Weedon had already examined the business dealings of John Marshall, one of the generation of booksellers to follow John Newbery (Weedon 1949). It has been the annotated checklists compiled by Marjorie Moon which have done most to open up the study of early nineteenth-century British children's books. Her bibliographies of the children's books published by Benjamin Tabart and by John Harris have set new standards (Moon 1990, 1992). Even more so than Roscoe, Moon produced not merely lists of books, but succeeded in focusing interest on particular approaches to children's books adopted in the early 1800s, the extent and importance of which had previously been neither explored nor explained. This kind of work continues with Lawrence Darton's checklist of the children's books, games and educational aids published by his ancestors' famous Quaker publishing house (Darton 2003; see also David 1992).

Alongside the major publishing houses like Harris and Darton, many much smaller operations were also producing children's books in the late eighteenth and early nineteenth centuries. These are beginning to be investigated, the firm run by the Godwins receiving particular attention – perhaps because of the notoriety of William Godwin, its co-proprietor and leading author, as much as for its contribution to children's literature (Kinnell 1988; Alderson 1998; William St Clair, 'William Godwin as Children's Bookseller' in Avery and Briggs 1989: 165–79). The publishing activities of Joseph Cundall (McLean 1976), James Burns (Alderson 1994), Thomas Tegg (Barnes and Barnes 2000), the Religious Tract Society (Alderson and Garrett 1999) and, somewhat later, Blackie and Son (Daniels 1999) have also begun to receive attention. Much of the activity in the British children's book trade in the period was located in the provinces rather than London. Much of what was produced there is now generally considered under the heading of 'chapbooks', that is to say, fairy tales, fables and popular stories and verses, generally only eight or sixteen pages long. Few copies of these delicate books have survived, which has made the bibliographers' task difficult. A few studies have been attempted, however. The output of Lumsden of Glasgow, Kendrew of York and Davison of Alnwick has been catalogued as far as has been possible (Roscoe and Brimmell 1981; Davis 1988; Isaac 1968 and 1996). Other books celebrating the chapbook literature of various local enterprises are less scholarly but still give a flavour of what was produced by small, provincial presses, Edward Pearson's compendium of woodcuts from the firm of Rusher of Banbury for instance (Pearson 1890). A number of websites, often showing images of the holdings of research libraries and with searchable catalogues, are also useful in pinning down the history of this ephemeral literature (Lilly Library: Elizabeth W. Ball Collection).

Often chapbooks lack even a publisher's imprint, so that would-be bibliographers are denied such basic tools of their trade as a publisher's name and location, let alone a date of publication. When this happens it has sometimes proved possible to trace the use and re-use of the wood-blocks from which the illustrations were printed, and thereby to deduce roughly from when a particular edition dates. In fact, the development of children's book illustration has raised its own bibliography. Several outlines have been produced, notably Whalley and Chester's *A History of Children's Book Illustration* (1988; see also Muir 1971/1985; Whalley 1974; Gottlieb 1975; Ray 1976; Martin 1989), while *The Dictionary of 20th Century British Book Illustrators* (Horne 1994) remains a standard reference work. There are useful volumes on American (Mahoney *et al.* 1947 *et seq.*) and Australian art (Muir 1982). More specialised studies have been produced of individual illustrators, including, among others, C. E. and H. M. Brock (Kelly 1975), Heath Robinson (Lewis 1973), William Nicholson (Campbell 1992) and Thomas Bewick, whose output has been exhaustively catalogued by Sydney Roscoe (Roscoe 1953). Remarkably, Roscoe's work on Thomas Bewick has now been eclipsed by Nigel Tattersfield's outstanding biography and bibliography of the younger and less celebrated of the Bewick brothers, John (Tattersfield 2001). Because John Bewick specialised in illustrating chil-dren's books, and because Tattersfield's study draws upon Bewick's own ledger of commissions, this is a bibliography which provides a unique insight into the mechanics of children's book publishing at the turn of the nineteenth century. Another bibliographic approach sometimes adopted has been to review the changing illustrations to a single text. Ségolène Le Men, for example, has surveyed the history of illustrations for the Mother Goose stories from their first publication in 1697 to the editions interpreted by Gustave Doré in the later nineteenth century (Le Men 1992). Chris Routh has given an account of the illustrated editions of *Peter Pan* (Routh and Demourova 1995: 2–19).

It is clear, then, that there is a long way to go before bibliographical foundations are fully laid. The children's literatures of many parts of the world have not been charted in any detail and there has been little attempt to survey children's literature across national boundaries. Indeed, it is still the case that many important library holdings of children's books have not been catalogued (for a list of special collections see Jones 1995). Even some of the most notable collections in the UK and North America have been only partially indexed. The catalogues for the Renier Collection at the National Art Library in London (the largest in Britain), the Opie Collection in Oxford University's Bodleian Library and the Cotsen Collection at Princeton University (the largest American holding) are all only now under construction, the former two on-line, the latter in print form (Cotsen Collection 2000). When completed, they will join the on-line catalogue of the Lilly Library at Indiana University (for a description see Johnson 1987) and what remains the best available printed catalogue, that of the Osborne Collection in Toronto (St John 1975; still only partly on-line), as tremendously useful bibliographic resources, especially for Anglo-American material. The libraries of private collectors generally remain a much more firmly closed book (but see Alderson and Moon 1994, and Clive Hurst's examina-tion of Peter Opie's accession diaries in Avery and Briggs 1989: 19–44).

On the other hand, it must also be obvious that reports of the death of children's litera-ture bibliography have been exaggerated. This essay, though it has listed almost 200 books, articles and websites, does not pretend to be an exhaustive list of the bibliographical sources currently available, and – hopefully – it will soon be out of date. Bibliographical works are still appearing. Progress is being made in cataloguing public collections. Both catalogues and bibliographies can now reach unprecedentedly large audiences, can be updated far more easily, and can be produced far more cheaply, because of the advent of the internet. Literary criticism has not killed off bibliography. Those who say that arrival of children's books in university literature departments, and the consequent ascendancy of literary criticism, is undermining bibliography might do well to remember that, in its own time, even Sydney Roscoe's magisterial bibliography of the Newberys' children's books, and other such 'new tools being provided for the study of children's literature', caused some 'disquiet' to Peter Opie, the doyen of early children's book collecting (Opie 1975: 263–4). Opie feared that Roscoe's too-useful study would deny collectors like himself the pleasure of making their own discoveries and perhaps open up the field to new, less personally erudite, and less amateur, buyers. In fact, Roscoe's work was in itself a great contribution to children's book scholarship, and inspired many more. So too will the university-led study of children's books – in its turn a new 'professionalisation' of the field – enable us to understand more about children's literature. Critical, theoretical and historical approaches to children's books, as well as pedagogical and library-orientated studies, have all contributed to what we know about which books were published for children and when – the goals of bibliography. They have also made good bibliographic work more necessary than ever. If the study of children's literature is to continue and mature, it will surely be necessary for all these approaches to children's literature to advance together.

References

Alderson, B. (1977) 'Bibliography and Children's Books: The Present Position', *The Library*, 5th series, 32: 203–13.

——(1982) *Hans Christian Andersen and His 'Eventyr' in England*, Wormley: Five Owls Press for International Board on Books for Young People, British Section.

——(1983) 'Miniature Libraries for the Young', *The Private Library*, 3rd series, 6: 3–38.

——(1994) 'Some Notes on James Burns as a Publisher of Children's Books', *Bulletin of the John Rylands University Library of Manchester* 76: 103–26.

——(1995a) 'A Widish, Widish World', *Children's Books History Society Newsletter* 51: 14–17.

——(1995b) 'Brian Alderson Replies', *Children's Books History Society Newsletter* 52: 22–6.

——(1998) ' "Mister Gobwin" and His "Interesting little Books, Adorned with Copper Plates" ', *Princeton University Library Chronicle* 59: 159–89.

——(1999) 'New Playthings and Gigantick Histories. The Nonage of English Children's Books', *Princeton University Library Chronicle* 60: 178–95.

Alderson, B. and Garrett, P. (1999) *The Religious Tract Society as a Publisher of Children's Books*, Hoddesdon: The Children's Books History Society.

Alderson, B. and Moon, M. (1994) *Childhood Re-Collected: Early Children's Books from the Library of Marjorie Moon*, Royston: Provincial Book Fairs Association.

Avery, G. (1994) *Behold the Child: American Children and Their Books 1621–1922*, London: Bodley Head.

Avery, G. and Briggs, J. (1989) *Children and Their Books. A Celebration of the Work of Iona and Peter Opie*, Oxford: Clarendon Press.

Ayres, H. M. (1934) 'Carroll's Withdrawal of the 1865 *Alice*', *The Huntington Library Bulletin* 6: 153–63.

Barnes, J. J. and Barnes, P. P. (2000) 'Reassessing the Reputation of Thomas Tegg, London Publisher, 1776–1846', *Book History* 3: 45–60.

Barron, N. (1999) *Fantasy and Horror. A Critical and Historical Guide to Literature, Illustration, Film, TV, Radio, and the Internet*, Lanham, MD and London: Scarecrow Press.

Battistelli, V. (1962) *Il libro del fanciullo. La letteratura per l'infanzia*, 2nd edn, Florence: La Nuova Italia.

Blanck, J. (1956) *Peter Parley to Penrod. A Bibliographical Description of the Best-Loved American Juvenile Books*, New York: R. R. Bowker.

Bobbitt, M. R. (1947) *A Bibliography of Etiquette Books Published in America before 1900*, New York: New York Public Library.

Bottigheimer, Ruth B. (1996) *The Bible for Children. From the Age of Gutenberg to the Present*, New Haven, CT and London: Yale University Press.

——(forthcoming) *Origins to 1800: A Working Bibliography of Children's Books in Britain* [provisional title].

Bravo-Villasante, C. (1963) *Historia de la Literatura Infantil Española*, 3rd edn, Madrid: Doncel.

Brazouski, A. and Klatt, M. (1994) *Children's Books on Ancient Greek and Roman Mythology. An Annotated Bibliography*, New York, Westport, CT and London: Greenwood Press.

Brüggermann, T. and Brunken, O. (1987) *Handbuch zur Kinder- und Jugendliteratur. Vom Beginn des Buchdrucks bis 1570*, Stuttgart: J. B. Metzler.

——(1991) *Handbuch zur Kinder- und Jugendliteratur. Von 1570 bis 1750*, Stuttgart and Weimar: J. B. Metzler.

Brüggermann, T. and Ewers, H.-H. (1982) *Handbuch zur Kinder- und Jugendliteratur. Von 1750 bis 1800*, Stuttgart: J. B. Metzler.

Brunken, O., Hurrelmann, B. and Pech, K.-U. (1998) *Handbuch zur Kinder- und Jugendliteratur, von 1800 bis 1850*, Stuttgart: J. B. Metzlersche Verlagsbuchhandlung.

Buijnsters, P. J. and Buijnsters-Smets, L. (1997) *Bibliografie van Nederland se school- en kinderboeken 1700–1800*, Zwolle: Waanders Uitgev.

Butts, D. (1992) *Mistress of Our Tears: A Literary and Bibliographical Study of Barbara Hofland*, Aldershot: Scolar Press.

Cadogan, M. with Schutte, D. (1990) *The William Companion*, London: Macmillan.

Campbell, C. (1992) *William Nicholson: The Graphic Work*, London: Barrie and Jenkins.

Caradec, F. (1977) *Histoire de la littérature enfantine en France*, Paris: Albin Michel.

Chester, T. R. (1987) *Occasional List No. 1: Struwwelpeter*, London: The Renier Collection of Historic and Contemporary Children's Books, Bethnal Green Museum of Childhood.

Cohn, D. J. (2000) *Virtue by Design. Illustrated Chinese Children's Books from the Cotsen Children's Library*, Los Angeles, CA: Cotsen Occasional Papers.

Colvin, C. E. and Morgenstern, C. (1977) 'The Edgeworths. Some Early Educational Books', *The Book Collector* 26: 39–43.

Cotsen Collection (2000) *A Catalogue of the Cotsen Children's Library. 1: The Twentieth Century, A–L*. Princeton, NJ: Princeton University Library.

Cutler, B. D. (1931) *Sir James M. Barrie. A Bibliography, with Full Collations of the American Unauthorized Editions*, New York: Greenberg.

Cutt, M. N. (1974) *Mrs Sherwood and Her Books*, London: Oxford University Press.

Daniels, M. (1999) *The Firm of Blackie and Son and Some of Their Children's Books*, Hoddesdon: Children's Books History Society, Occasional Paper V.

——(2002) 'Mrs Craddock', *Children's Books History Society Newsletter* 72: 15–19.

Darton, F. J. H. (1932/1982) *Children's Books in England: Five Centuries of Social Life*, 3rd edn, rev. Alderson, B., Cambridge: Cambridge University Press.

Darton, L. (2003) *The Dartons. An Annotated Check-List of Children's Books, Games and Education Aids Issued by Two Publishing Houses 1787–1870*, London: British Library.

Dasgupta, A. (ed.) (1995) *Telling Tales in India*, New Delhi: Indian Council for Cultural Relations, New Age International Publishers.

David, L. (1992) *Children's Books Published by William Darton and His Sons*, Bloomington, IN: The Lilly Library.

Davis, R. (1988) *Kendrew of York and His Chapbooks for Children with a Checklist*, London: The Elmete Press.

Day, F. A. (2000) *Lesbian and Gay Voices: An Annotated Bibliography and Guide to Literature for Children and Young Adults*, New York, Westport, CT and London: Greenwood Press.

de Vries, L. (1964) *A Short History of Children's Books in the Netherlands*, The Hague: Ministry of Foreign Affairs.

Deschamps, J.-G. (1934) *The History of French Children's Books 1750–1900. From the Collection of J.-G. Deschamps*, Boston, MA: Bookshop for Boys and Girls.

Dey, P. R. (1977) *Children's Literature of India*, Calcutta: Academy for Documentation and Research on Children's Literature.

Donet, B. and Prisant, G. M. (1999) *Palabra de juguete; una historia y una antología de la literatura infantil y juvenil en México*, Mexico City: Lectorum.

Douglas, A. (1966) *The Scottish Contribution to Children's Literature*, Glasgow: W. and R. Holmes (reprinted from *Library Review* for 1965–6, 20: 241–6 and 301–7).

Drotner, K. (1988) *English Children and Their Magazines*, New Haven, CT and London: Yale University Press.

Egoff, S. and Saltman, J. (1990) *The New Republic of Childhood. A Critical Guide to Canadian Children's Literature in English*, Toronto: Oxford University Press.

Eiss, H. (1989) *Literature for Young People on War and Peace: An Annotated Bibliography*, New York, Westport, CT and London: Greenwood Press.

Ewers, H.-H. and Seibert, E. (1997) *Geschichte der österreichischen Kinder- und Jugenliteratur. Vom 18. Jahrhundert bis zur Gegenwart*, Vienna: Buchkultur.

Farquhar, M. A. (1999) *Children's Literature in China. From Lu Xun to Mao Zedong*, Armonk, NY and London: M. E. Sharpe.

Garner, B. C. and Hawker, M. (1989) '*Anne of Green Gables*: An Annotated Bibliography', *Canadian Children's Literature* 55: 18–41.

Garrett, P. (1994) 'After Henry', Hoddesdon: Children's Books History Society, Occasional Paper I.

Gilderdale, B. (2001) 'A Forgotten Lady Author: Lady Barker, 1831–1911', *Children's Books History Society Newsletter* 70: 24–8.

Gottlieb, G. (1975) *Early Children's Books and Their Illustrators*, New York: Pierpont Morgan Library.

Grenby, M. (2001) 'Maria Edgeworth', the Hockliffe Project website: http://www.cta.dmu.ac.uk/projects/Hockliffe.

Grey, J. E. (1970) '*The Lilliputian Magazine*: A Pioneering Periodical', *Journal of Librarianship* 2: 107–15.

Guiliano, E. (1981) *Lewis Carroll. An Annotated International Bibliography 1960–77*, Brighton: Harvester Press.

Haining, P. (1979) *Moveable Books. An Illustrated History. Pages and Pictures of Folding, Revolving, Dissolving, Mechanical, Scenic, Panoramic, Dimensional, Changing, Pop-up and Other Novelty Books from the Collection of David and Brian Philips*, London: New English Library.

Hammond, W. G. (2000) *Arthur Ransome: A Bibliography*, Winchester: St Paul's Bibliographies; New Castle, DE: Oak Knoll Press.

Hanrahan, J. Y. (2001) *Works of Maurice Sendak, Revised and Expanded to 2001: A Collection with Comments*, Saco, ME: published for the author.

Haring-Smith, T. (1982) *A. A. Milne. A Critical Bibliography*, New York and London: Garland.

Haviland, B. (1973) *Children and Literature: Views and Reviews*, Glenview, IL: Scott, Foresman.

Haviland, V. (1966) *Children's Literature. A Guide to Reference Sources*, Washington, DC: Library of Congress. First supplement 1972, second supplement 1977, both with M. N. Coughlan.

Hawkes, L. R. (1933) *Before and after Pinocchio: A Study of Italian Children's Books*, Paris: The Puppet Press.

Herring, A. (2000) *The Dawn of Wisdom. Selections from the Japanese Collection of the Cotsen Children's Library*, Los Angeles, CA: Cotsen Occasional Papers.

Hobbes, A. S. and Whalley, J. I. (1985) *Beatrix Potter. The V & A Collection: The Leslie Linder Bequest of Beatrix Potter Material*, London: The Victoria and Albert Museum and Frederick Warne.

Holsinger, M. P. (1995) *The Ways of War. The Era of World War II in Children's and Young Adult Fiction. An Annotated Bibliography*, Metuchen, NJ and London: Scarecrow Press.

Horne, A. (1994) *The Dictionary of 20th Century British Book Illustrators*, Woodbridge: Antique Collectors' Club.

Hunt, P. (1995) 'Scholars, Critics and Standards: Reflections on a Sentence by Brian Alderson', *Children's Books History Society Newsletter* 52: 18–22.

Hürlimann, B. (1967) *Three Centuries of Children's Books in Europe*, trans. Alderson, B., London: Oxford University Press.

Isaac, P. (1968) *William Davison of Alnwick, Pharmacist and Printer 1781–1858*, Oxford: Oxford University Press.

——(1996) 'William Davison of Alnwick and Provincial Publishing in His Time', *Publishing History* 40: 5–32.

Izawa, Y. (2002) 'A Bibliography of the Works of L. M. Montgomery in Japan', *Annals of the Institute for Research in Humanities and Social Sciences* 11: 37–62.

Jackson, M. V. (1989) *Engines of Instruction, Mischief and Magic: Children's Literature in England from Its Beginning to 1839*, Aldershot: Scolar Press.

James, E. and Smith, H. R. (1998) *Penny Dreadfuls and Boys' Adventures: The Barry Ono Collection of Victorian Popular Fiction in the British Library*, London: British Library.

Johnson, E. L. (1987) *For Your Amusement and Instruction: The Elizabeth Ball Collection of Historical Children's Materials*, Bloomington, IN: The Lilly Library.

Johnson, M. (1935) *A Bibliography of the Works of Mark Twain. Samuel Langhorne Clemens. A List of First Editions in Book Form and of First Printings in Periodicals and Occasional Publications of His Varied Literary Activities. Revised and Enlarged*, New York and London: Harper and Brothers.

Jones, D. B. (1995) *Special Collections in Children's Literature. An International Directory*, 3rd edn, Chicago, IL: American Library Association.

Jones, M. and Jones, G. (1983) *Dewiniaid Difyr. Llenorion Plant Cymru Hyd Tua 1950*, Llandysul: Gwasg Gomer.

Jones, S. (1990) 'New from the Land of Youth. Anglo-Welsh Children's Literature – a Tradition in the Making', *The New Welsh Review* 2: 6–10.

Kealy, J. K. (1994) 'Bibliography of British Columbian Children's Literature', *Canadian Children's Literature* 74: 39–62.

Kelly, C. M. (1975) *The Brocks: A Family of Cambridge Artists and Illustrators*, London: Skilton.

Kennerly, S. L. (1957) 'Confederate Juvenile Imprints: Children's Books and Periodicals Published in the Confederate States of America, 1861–1865', unpublished PhD dissertation, University of Michigan.

Khorana, M. (1991) *The Indian Subcontinent in Literature for Children and Young Adults. An Annotated Bibliography of English-Language Books*, New York, Westport, CT and London: Greenwood Press.

——(1994) *Africa in Literature for Children and Young Adults: An Annotated Bibliography of English-Language Books*, Westport, CT: Greenwood Press.

Killam, D. and Rowe, R. (2000) *The Companion to African Literatures*, Oxford: James Currey; Bloomington: Indiana University Press.

Kinnell, M. (1988) 'Childhood and Children's Literature: The Case of M. J. Godwin and Co., 1805–25', *Publishing History* 24: 77–99.

Kirkpatrick, R. J. (2000) *The Encyclopaedia of Boys' School Stories*, Aldershot and Burlington, VT: Ashgate.

——(2001) *Bullies, Beaks and Flannelled Fools: An Annotated Bibliography of Boys' School Fiction 1742–2000*, 2nd edn, London: privately published for the author.

Kitano, N. (1967) 'The Development of Children's Literature in Japan', unpublished Master's thesis, University of Chicago.

Le Men, S. (1992) 'Mother Goose Illustrated: From Perrault to Doré', *Poetics Today* 13: 17–39.

Leif, I. P. (1977) *Children's Literature: An Historical and Contemporary Bibliography*, Troy, NY: Whitson.

Lewis, J. (1973) *Heath Robinson, Artist and Comic Genius*, London: Constable.

Lilly Library The Elizabeth W. Ball Collection, http://www.indiana.edu/~liblilly/overview/lit_child.shtml.

Linder, L. (1971) *A History of the Writings of Beatrix Potter*, London and New York: Frederick Warne.

Lovett, C. (1999) *Lewis Carroll and the Press. An Annotated Bibliography of Charles Dodgson's Contributions to Periodicals*, New Castle, DE and London: Oak Knoll Press and The British Library.

Lovett, R. W. with Lovett, C. (1991) *Robinson Crusoe. A Bibliographical Checklist of English Language Editions (1719–1979)*, New York, Westport, CT and London: Greenwood Press.

Lynn, R. N. (1995) *Fantasy Literature for Children and Young Adults: An Annotated Bibliography*, New York: Bowker.

MacCann, D. and Woodard, G. (1985) *The Black American in Books for Children: Readings in Racism*, Metuchen, NJ: Scarecrow Press.

MacDonald, R. K. (1982) *Literature for Children in England and America from 1646 to 1774*, Troy, NY: Whitson.

McGill University Library, Department of Special Collections, Digital Collections Program (1999) *Children's Books of the Early Soviet Era*, an exhibition on-line at http://digital.library.mcgill.ca/russian/intro.htm.

Mackey, A. (1991) *C. S. Lewis. A Bibliography*, Bedford: A. Mackey.

McLean, R. (1976) *Joseph Cundall: A Victorian Publisher*, Pinner: Private Libraries Association.

Madden, P. J. (1955) 'Children's Books in Ireland', *An leabharlann* 13: 33–44.

Mahoney, B. E. *et al.* (1947/1958/1968/1978) *Illustrators of Children's Books 1744–1945* (and supplements to 1978), Boston, MA: The Horn Book.

Manlove, C. N. (1996) *Scottish Fantasy Literature. A Critical Survey*, Edinburgh: Canongate Academic.

Markgraf, C. (1989) *J. M. Barrie, an Annotated Secondary Bibliography*, Greensboro, NC: ELT.

Marques, H. Jnr (1928) *Algumas achegas para uma bibliografia infantile*, Lisbon: Oficinas Gráficas da Biblioteca Nacional.

Martin, D. (1989) *The Telling Line: Essays on Fifteen Contemporary Book Illustrators*, London: MacRae.

Moffat, M. S. (2000) *Historical Fiction for Children. A Bibliography*, Darlington: Castle of Dreams Books. See also the associated and updated website at http://www.marysmoffat.co.uk.

Mollerup, H. (1951) 'Danish Children's Books before 1900', *The Junior Bookshelf* 15: 50–6.

Montanaro, A. R. (2000) *Pop-up and Moveable Books. A Bibliography – Supplement I: 1991–1997*, Lanham, MD and London: Scarecrow Press.

Moon, M. (1990) *Benjamin Tabart's Juvenile Library: A Bibliography of Books for Children Published, Written and Sold by Mr Tabart 1801–1920*, Winchester: St Paul's Bibliographies.

——(1992) *John Harris's Books for Youth 1801–1843*, rev. edn, Folkestone: Dawson.

Muir, M. (1982) *A History of Australian Children's Book Illustration*, Melbourne: Oxford University Press.

——(1992) *Australian Children's Books. A Bibliography. Volume 1: 1774–1972*, Melbourne: Melbourne University Press.

Muir, P. (1954) *English Children's Books, 1600–1900*, London: Batsford.

——(1971/1985) *Victorian Illustrated Books*, London: Batsford.

Muñoz, M. P. (1997) *Había una vez – en América. Literatura Infantil de America Latina*, Santiago: Dolmen Estudio.

Nikolajeva, M. (1995) *Aspects and Issues in the History of Children's Literature*, Westport, CT: Greenwood Press, Contributions to the Study of World Literature No. 60.

Odiase, J. O. U. (1986) *African Books for Children and Young Adults*, Benin City, Nigeria: Nation-wide Publication Bureau in collaboration with Unique Bookshop.

Ofek, U. (1979) *Hebrew Children's Literature: The Beginnings*, Tel Aviv: Porter Institute for Poetics and Semiotics.

Opie, P. (1975) 'John Newbery and His Successors', *The Book Collector* 24: 259–69.

Opie, P. and Opie, I. (1974) *The Classic Fairy Tales*, Oxford: Oxford University Press.

Palmer, B. (2002) *Science Textbooks and Historical Science Online*, on-line at http://www.ntu.edu.ac/faculties/education/online.htm.

Payne, R. (1970) 'Four Children's Books by A. A. Milne', *Studies in Bibliography. Papers of the Bibliographical Society of the University of Virginia* 23: 127–39.

Pearl, P. (1988) *Children's Religious Books. An Annotated Bibliography*, New York and London: Garland.

Pearson, E. (1890) *Banbury Chap Books and Nursery Toy Book Literature*, London: A. Reader.

Pellowski, Anne (1968) *The World of Children's Literature*, New York and London: R. R. Bowker.

Peters, J. (ed.) (1977) *Book Collecting: A Modern Guide*, New York and London: R. R. Bowker. Belanger's essay 'Descriptive Bibliography' is also available at http://www.bibsocamer.org/bibdef.htm.

Pflieger, P. (1984) *A Reference Guide to Modern Fantasy for Children*, New York, Westport, CT and London: Greenwood Press.

Pitcher, G. (1965) 'Wittgenstein, Nonsense, and Lewis Carroll', *Massachusetts Review* 6: 591–611.

Pollard, M. (1971) 'Maria Edgeworth's *The Parent's Assistant*. The First Edition', *The Book Collector* 20: 347–51.

Povsic, F. (1986) *Eastern Europe in Children's Literature. An Annotated Bibliography of English-Language Books*, New York, Westport, CT and London: Greenwood Press.

——(1991) *The Soviet Union in Literature for Children and Young Adults. An Annotated Bibliography of English-Language Books*, New York, Westport, CT and London: Greenwood Press.

Price, H. (1992) *School Textbooks Published in New Zealand to 1960*, Palmerston North, NZ: Dunmore Press/Gondwanaland Press.

Prideaux, W. F. with Livingston, L. S. (1917) *A Bibliography of the Works of Robert Louis Stevenson. A New and Revised Edition*, London: Frank Hollings.

Quayle, E. (1971) *The Collector's Book of Children's Books*, London: Studio Vista.

——(1973) *The Collector's Book of Boys' Stories*, London: Studio Vista.

——(1983) *Early Children's Books. A Collector's Guide*, London: David and Charles.

Ray, G. N. (1976) *The Illustrator and the Book in England from 1790 to 1914*, New York: Pierpont Morgan Library.

Renier, A. (1972) 'Maria Edgeworth's *The Parent's Assistant* 1796, First Edition: An Unrecorded Copy of Part II, Vol. II', *The Book Collector* 21: 127–8.

Roberts, J. (1965) 'The 1765 Edition of *Goody Two-Shoes*', *The British Museum Quarterly* 29: 67–70.

Rodney, R. M. (1982) *Mark Twain International. A Bibliography and Interpretation of His World-wide Popularity*, Westport, CT and London: Greenwood Press.

Roscoe, S. (1953) *Thomas Bewick: A Catalogue Raisonné*, Oxford: Oxford University Press.

——(1973) *John Newbery and His Successors, 1740–1814: A Bibliography*, Wormley: Five Owls Press.

Roscoe, S. and Brimmell, R. A. (1981) *James Lumsden and Son of Glasgow, Their Juvenile Books and Chapbooks*, Pinner: Private Libraries Association.

Routh, C. and Demourova, N. (1995) *The Neverland. Two Flights Over the Territory*, Hoddesdon: Children's Books History Society, Occasional Paper II.

Rubio, M. H. (1994) *Harvesting Thistles: The Textual Garden of L. M. Montgomery: Essays on Her Novels and Journals*, Guelph, ON: Canadian Children's Press.

Rühle, R. (1999) '*Böse Kinder'; kommertierte Bibliographie von Stuwwelpeter und Max-und-Moritzi-aden mit biographischen Daten zu Verfassern und Illustratoren*, Osnabrück: H. Th. Wenner.

Russell, R. W., Russell, D. W. and Wilmshurst, R. (1986) *Lucy Maud Montgomery: A Preliminary Bibliography*, Waterloo, ON: University of Waterloo.

St John, J. (1975) *The Osborne Collection of Early Children's Books, 1476–1910*, Toronto: Toronto Public Library.

Schiller, J. G. (1974a) 'Maria Edgeworth's *The Parent's Assistant* 1796, First Edition: Part I', *The Book Collector* 23: 258.

——(1974b) '*The Story of Little Black Sambo*', *The Book Collector* 23: 381–6.

Schmidt, N. J. (1975) *Children's Books on Africa and Their Authors: An Annotated Bibliography*, New York: Africana Publishing. With a supplement (1979).

Schon, I. (1980) *A Hispanic Heritage. A Guide to Juvenile Books about Hispanic People and Cultures*, Metuchen, NJ and London: Scarecrow Press.

Schutte, D. (1993) *William: The Immortal: An Illustrated Bibliography*, privately published.

Seriña, L. M. and Yap, F. A. (1980) *Children's Literature in the Philippines. An Annotated Bibliography of Filipino and English Works 1901–1979*, Manila, Philippines: National Book Store.

Shaberman, R. (1990) *George MacDonald: A Bibliographical Study*, Winchester: St Paul's Bibliographies.

Shakeshaft, M. (2001) 'Charlotte Mary Yonge: Reflecting Her Century', *Children's Books History Society Newsletter* 71: 7–14.

Shavit, Z. and Ewers, H.-H. *et al.* (1994) *Deutsch-jüdische Kinder- und Jugendliteratur von der Haskala bis 1945. Die deutsch- und hebräischsprachigen Schriften des deutschsprachigen Raums. Ein bibliographisches Handbuch*, Stuttgart and Weimar: J. B. Metzler.

Shesgreen, S. and Bywaters, D. (1998) 'The First London Cries for Children', *Princeton University Library Chronicle* 59: 223–50.

Shimi, T. (1987) *Japanese Children's Books at the Library of Congress: A Bibliography of Books from the Postwar Years, 1946–1985*, Washington, DC: Library of Congress.

Sims, S. and Clare, H. (2000) *The Encyclopaedia of Girls' School Stories*, Aldershot and Burlington, VT: Ashgate.

Slater, J. H. (1914) *Robert Louis Stevenson. A Bibliography of His Complete Works*, London: G. Bell and Sons.

Sloane, W. (1955) *Children's Books in England and America in the Seventeenth Century. A History and Checklist, Together with* The Young Christian's Library, *the First Printed Catalogue of Books for Children*, New York: Columbia University and Kings Crown Press.

Speaight, G. (1999) *The Juvenile Drama: A Union Catalogue Comprising the Holdings of Five Libraries or Museums in England and Three in America*, London: The Society for Theatre Research.

Stach, R. with Schmidt, J. (1991) *Robinson und Robinsonaden in der deutschsprachigen Literatur: Eine Bibliographie*, Würzburg: Königshausen and Neumann.

Stanbridge, J. (1986) 'An Annotated Bibliography of Canadian Poetry Books Written in English for Children', *Canadian Children's Literature* 42: 51–61.

Steiner, E. (1999) *Stories for Little Comrades. Revolutionary Artists and the Making of Early Soviet Children's Books*, trans. Miller, J. A., Seattle and London: University of Washington Press.

Stone, W. M. (1933) *The Gigantick Histories of Thomas Boreman*, Portland, ME: Southworth Press.

Summerfield, G. (1984) *Fantasy and Reason. Children's Literature in the Eighteenth Century*, London: Methuen.

Tattersfield, N. (2001) *John Bewick (1760–95). Engraver on Wood*, New Castle, DE and London: Oak Knoll Press and the British Library.

Teerink, H. and Scouten, A. H. (1963) *A Bibliography of the Writings of Jonathan Swift. Second Edition, Revised and Corrected*, Philadelphia: University of Pennsylvania Press.

Thwaite, M. F. (1963/1972) *From Primer to Pleasure in Reading*, 2nd edn, London: Library Association.

Todd, W. B. and Bowden, A. (1998) *Sir Walter Scott. A Bibliographical History 1796–1832*, New Castle, DE: Oak Knoll Press.

Toral y Peñaranda, C. (1958) *Literatura Infantil Española*, Madrid: Editorial Coculsa.

Townsend, J. R. (1965/1995) *Written for Children. An Outline of English-Language Children's Literature*, London: The Bodley Head.

——(1994) *Trade & Plumb-Cake for Ever, Huzza! The Life and Work of John Newbery 1713–1767*, Cambridge: Colt Books.

Ullom, J. C. (1969) *Louisa May Alcott. An Annotated, Selected Bibliography*, Washington, DC: Library of Congress.

Wardale, R. (1995) *Ransome at Sea: Notes from the Chart Table*, Kendal: Amazon Publications.

Weedon, M. J. P. (1949) 'Richard Johnson and the Successors to John Newbery', *The Library. A Quarterly Review of Bibliography*, 5th series, 4: 25–63.

Weilenmann, C. with Cetlin, J. (1993) *Annotierte Bibliographie der Schweizer Kinder- und Jugendliteratur von 1750 bis 1900*, Schweizerischen Jugendbuch-Institut, Stuttgart: Metzler.

Welch, d'A. (1972) *A Bibliography of American Children's Books Printed Prior to 1821*, Worcester, MA: American Antiquarian Society/Barre Publishers.

Whalley, J. I. (1974) *Cobwebs to Catch Flies: Illustrated Books for the Nursery and Schoolroom, 1700–1900*, London: Elek.

Whalley, J. I. and Chester, T. R. (1988) *A History of Children's Book Illustration*, London: John Murray with the Victoria and Albert Museum.

White, K. (1992) *Australian Children's Books. A Bibliography. Volume 2: 1973–1988*, Melbourne: Melbourne University Press.

Williams, S. H. (1924) *A Bibliography of the Writings of Lewis Carroll*, London: Office of *The Bookman's Journal*.

Woodward, A., Elliott, D. L. and Nagel, C. (1988) *Textbooks in School and Society: An Annotated Bibliography and Guide to Research*, New York: Garland.

Zipes, J. (1988) *The Brothers Grimm. From Enchanted Forests to the Modern World*, New York and London: Routledge and Kegan Paul.

11 Understanding reading and literacy

Sally Yates

Editor's Introduction

The development of literacy may seem to be the most obvious application of children's litera-ture. However, there have been recurrent debates on the most effective techniques for achieving literacy, and especially on the relative merits of using 'children's literature' and of using specially developed 'reading schemes'. Even the definition of literacy is far from stable. Sally Yates considers technical and cultural aspects of this topic.

P. H.

> The reading process has always to be described in terms of texts and contexts as well as in terms of what we think readers actually do.
>
> (Meek 1988: 6)

Defining literacy

In defining literacy, it is now common to go beyond simply describing the decoding of written text and to include reference to creation of meaning from print, as decoding without making sense has no purpose. UNESCO, for example, which has a mission to achieve a 50 per cent improvement in levels of adult literacy by 2015, and has declared 2003–12 the United Nations literacy decade (UNESCO 2003), defines literacy broadly as referring to 'the skills used in everyday life or those that allow one to function competently in society'. That is, a recognition of the purposes for fostering literacy is essential. What counts as literacy, then, is dependent on the literacy demands of a particular society, and can be seen to be dynamic, reflecting changing expectations of society. It makes a distinction between literacy in time and place, and recognises cultural and social influences on literacy. In her biography of Samuel Pepys, for example, Claire Tomalin describes the literacy learning of his grammar-school education as being the translation of texts from English into Latin and back again to English, a literacy curriculum well suited to prepare him for his future role as a civil servant in seventeenth-century England (Tomalin 2003). This would not, of course, be a literacy that would prepare someone for literate life in the twenty-first century, and it would not have been a useful form of literacy for many others in the seventeenth century.

In a rapidly changing world, definitions of literacy need to reflect the multiple literacies that might be encountered in engaging with the literate world. UNESCO goes further, though, recognising that a mere functional literacy is inadequate and that access to complex literary texts is also essential if equality of knowledge and experience is to be achieved. It encourages books and reading through a call for national book policies.

Books are one of the most interactive means of communication and are still a haven for recent and distant memory, a source of recreation for the present and a richer platform from which to envisage the future.

(UNESCO 2003)

Fischer claims that 'transformations' are occurring in every realm of literacy, occupational, informational, recreational, and devotional and ritualistic reading, 'as societies everywhere exploit the written word for commercial gain' (Fischer 2003: 311). He goes on to say:

Of course, only those societies will best succeed that encourage and support a legitimate 'culture of reading', in particular the respect and love of books. In the past these have been especially East Asians (Chinese, Koreans, Japanese), Indians and Jews (also Moslems in the Middle Ages), followed by Europeans and, later, North Americans.

(Fischer 2003: 311)

So the place of literature in defining and developing literacy remains paramount despite developing technologies and literacy practices, and the growth of interest in children's literature for supporting literacy is evident in the work of the IBBY (International Board on Books for Young People) World Congresses which showcase both texts and issues.

Even partial illiteracy will cause people to be excluded and perhaps alienated from a good deal of their own culture. Although there has been a steady fall in the number of adult illiterates, 20.3 per cent of the world's population was illiterate in 2000; this figure is expected to drop to 16.5 per cent by 2010. This average, though, includes figures of 45 per cent illiterate in Ethiopia in 2000, 55.4 per cent in Iraq, 77 per cent in Niger, and includes a high proportion of female illiterates in some societies. A disturbing number of children globally are either not receiving education or failing to achieve literacy by the end of their schooling, and there are clear links between poverty and illiteracy or low standards of literacy even in countries with good literacy rates.

Throughout history, cultures of childhood and access to printed material have been fundamental to expectations for literacy and access to education for learning to read and write. In a society where few had access to books, universal literacy was not required and education was restricted to those needing to use literacy in their work, and with access to the written text. In this there were class and gender inequalities, some still mirrored in access to education and literacy. The extension of schooling in Europe in the sixteenth century to 'the lower classes' for religious education (Cunningham 1995) was an impetus continued in England during later centuries through Sunday Schools, which allowed for working children access to literacy. Cunningham makes a distinction, though, between the motives of society in promoting education, and those of the individual, where

a basic level of literacy was valued for two reasons. First, it enabled people to make some sense of the demands made on them by the printed rules and ordinances which flowed in copious abundance from the state. And secondly, it gave them access to the popular literature of ballads, chapbooks and almanacks which flourished in this period.

(Cunningham 1995: 102)

Thus the desire for functional literacy and for reading for pleasure has proven to be a strong motivator. Literacy was also valued as an aid to 'social advancement'. Interestingly, once education was made compulsory in Europe, there was greater opposition to schooling.

Although the move to universal literacy in Europe and the USA was linked to the need for the population to read the Bible for religious purposes, of course, once literate, the empowered masses could choose what they read, and thus two major issues at the heart of literacy arise. First, a consideration of the means by which we can most effectively create universal literacy, and second, control of what the literate population read. This second issue has always been, and continues to be, a focus for debate in relation to children's reading matter, as the recent debates on the content and suitability of the Harry Potter books has illustrated. J. K. Rowling's books have been the most banned books of recent years, heading the list of the American Library Association's Office for Intellectual Freedom's 'most challenged books' for three years running, with the primary claims against them being that they were 'ungodly'.

One of the contributory factors to low literacy levels in some parts of the world is the language of literacy instruction. As we saw, Samuel Pepys's grammar-school education was in Latin, lack of access to which was a barrier to education beyond elementary level for the lower classes in England until the early twentieth century. Calls to educate children in the 'vernacular' were instrumental in broadening access to education to a wider constituency. In Botswana there has been a call for Yoruba rather than English to be used as the medium for learning for the first six years of schooling, and Zambia and Malaysia too are calling for teaching in the 'national language' or 'mother-tongue'.

The National Curriculum in England has been criticised for failing to recognise children's linguistic and literacy experience in languages other than English, with the result that children could be excluded from the 'literacy club'. This is despite evidence that children operating in more than one language have increased levels of meta-cognitive and meta-linguistic aware-ness. The social and cultural variations in literacy practices in the home and community are further evidence of the diversity identified in the seminal ethnographic study by Shirley Brice Heath, who has also raised awareness of these issues (Heath 1983). In studying the literacy practices of three contrasting communities in the USA, one middle class, one black working class and one white working class, she found profound divergence in the text-types read and the behaviours engaged in while reading them. Concepts of childhood and the roles of adults in supporting children's literacy were fundamentally different in terms of expectations and social contexts for reading. The implications of the study for education and literacy teaching in schools are that the approaches to literacy in school advantaged the white middle-class chil-dren, but failed to recognise the different knowledge, experience and concepts of literacy in either the white or black working-class communities. Heath used her findings to inform her work with teachers in 'bridging language and cultural differences and discovering how to recognise and use language as power' (Heath 1983: 266).

There is strong evidence that, while books can extend and challenge children's knowl-edge and experience, children learn literacy better from texts with some cultural familiarity, with traditional tales and folk tales being particularly useful. The dominance of books written in English being translated into other languages leads to situations where, for example, children in Mexico are often reading books depicting life in the USA or Europe.

Fischer suggests that the possibility of a future 'global monoculture', with English-language 'supersellers' dominating the publishing world, means that 'Chilean children grow up knowing more about the US's Wild West than their own Atacama Desert; Indian children identify more with Harry Potter than the Vedas; and Mickey Mouse is more familiar to Chinese children than Chairman Mao' (Fischer 2003: 316).

Also, cultural assumptions in texts available internationally have an influence on comprehension and may reinforce feelings of exclusion.

Literacy teaching

Common practice in countries with an alphabetically based writing system is to start with learning the relationship between sound and symbol through recognising and naming the letters of the alphabet and, through use of a syllabary, combining the sounds into word segments. This has been a method common in the UK and USA for centuries, with children learning from the seventeenth century by means of a hornbook or its successor, the battledore, containing the alphabet and lists of syllables for learning, such as *ab, eb, ib, ob, ub*, preparatory to reading. But in addition, these early 'books' included some whole text to be read and learned alongside the letters. Extracts from the Bible, the catechism, short moral rules and verse were designed to improve the mind, but functioned also to contextualise the word parts. They introduced a literary form of written language and encouraged the learning of text through repetition, which could then support the learner in applying the phonic knowledge gained in the drill and exercise. This combination of use of grapho-phonic knowledge combined to make words used alongside whole texts is still the foundation of literacy teaching in much of the world.

Our knowledge of the ways in which children may have been supported into literacy in the home in the early eighteenth century has been enhanced by the discovery of sets of cards and home-made books produced by Jane Johnson, the wife of a Lincolnshire vicar in England. These were designed to teach her four children to read and include alphabet cards and verses, moral statements and 'A Very Pretty Story'. It is clear that the intention here was to structure literacy learning within a moral climate, using phonic methods and appreciation of whole literary texts (Hilton *et al.* 1997). This marriage of structured learning and pleasure in reading, use of whole texts and word parts, has been a continuing feature of developments in literacy.

Mary Hilton is critical of the concept of the 'young literacy learner' from the late nineteenth century in England. She claims that the child was treated as 'empty vessel' with no previous knowledge, and offered 'graded, decontextualised exercises in reading and writing skills, which gradually increase in difficulty and complexity, under conditions of surveillance and control' (Hilton 1996: 3). This education failed to take account of the child's interests and experience or to 'make literate sense of their experience', which raises wider questions about how children learn to read at home and at school, what approaches are used in schools and what texts are read in the learning process.

Languages vary in their sound–symbol correspondence, with English orthography about 75 per cent regular (Brookes 2003). Brookes claims that this degree of regularity means that phonics is the obvious first approach for teaching reading, but in comparison with many other alphabetic languages, the orthography of English can pose many problems for the reader. The introduction of whole-word recognition approaches to the learning process 'look and say' has been seen by some as a challenge to the traditional phonic approach. There are many irregular words in children's early vocabularies, though, which can only be learnt by sight recognition, and most children will develop a sight vocabulary of words alongside their phonics learning. Ferreiro and Teberosky, researching the reading of children in Buenos Aires, claimed that 'No collection of words, no matter how vast, in itself constitutes a language; without precise rules for combining those elements to produce acceptable phrases, there is no language' (Ferreiro and Teberosky 1979: 7).

Children have already become proficient language users orally by the time they start schooling, and a number of studies have demonstrated how children's spoken-language errors, such as the application of rules to irregular past tenses or plurals (for example, 'runned' instead of 'ran', 'eated' instead of 'ate', or 'sheeps' instead of the plural 'sheep') demonstrate an understanding of the rules of grammar within their language. If they are to transfer this knowledge into the very particular written genres of literature, children must tell and have stories told or read to them from an early stage. Certainly, linguistic knowledge and understanding of morphemes is perhaps a more helpful strategy than simple syllabaries in breaking down words (for example: un/help/ful/ness).

Oral competence is one aspect of the knowledge children bring with them to school: but children in the developed world may also be drawing on years of interactive engagement with a literate and print-rich world by the time they enter school, and whatever their diversity of social and cultural experience, this is knowledge on which teachers should draw in their early teaching of literacy. Evidence from the work of Harste *et al.* (1984) in Canada, Ferreiro and Teberosky in South America and Clay (1979) in New Zealand has demonstrated the concepts of print which children bring to school. Children's experience of books may be variable, and Clay's methods of observing children's behaviour with picture books provides a wealth of evidence for the teacher in understanding the scope of that familiarity (Clay 1979). But children watch television, they accompany their carers to the shops, to the post office and bank, to clinics. They see print on packages and hoardings, titles of films and television programmes, greetings cards and junk mail. The children in Ferreiro and Teberosky's study 'knew', even when they could not actually read, that, to be 'readable', print had to have at least three letters, and they could not all be the same (Ferreiro and Teberosky 1979: 28). They understood that printed marks conveyed meaning, even before they could distinguish between numbers and letters. Some letters could be named, with Z for Zorro being easily recognisable owing to the high interest engendered by the popular character at the time, and they could, when asked, explain that text and pictures were needed to read their picture books. Ferreiro and Teberosky challenge the expectation that children should learn mechanistically in the early stages: 'Not yet knowing how to read does not prevent children from having precise ideas about the characteristics a written text must have for reading to take place' (1979: 27). Children know that the print on the cartons and tins in shops conveys some message about what is inside (Harste *et al.* 1984: 24), and global marketing ensures that many children can recognise the Coca-Cola sign (so good for alliterative phonics), and the large yellow M of McDonald's.

Even with new technologies allowing us to monitor eye- and brain-activity during the reading process, we cannot know exactly what goes on in the mind of the reader. But the work of psycholinguists such as Ken Goodman has made apparent the complexity of learning to read: that is, to read and understand and not simply to decode print (Goodman 1982). Goodman claims that effective, experienced readers bring everything they know to the reading process: graphic and phonic knowledge, semantic and syntactic knowledge, knowledge and understanding of books and story, and knowledge and experience of the world. Good readers make use of all this knowledge when reading. They predict, check by looking at the grapho-phonic cues, read on, read back, and draw on knowledge of story conventions 'Once upon a time …', 'A long, long time ago …', 'Meanwhile …', to create a meaningful reading experience. The search for meaning and full comprehension of written texts requires the reader's critical engagement with the text and consideration of the author's style and purpose in creating the text (Bearne 1996: 311). Bearne stresses too the need for teachers to be critical readers and to be knowledgeable and analytical in approaching texts.

Literature for literacy

The selection of texts for developing literacy has long been a site for controversy. Since the early use of the hornbook and primers produced for teaching reading, texts have been developed with the aim of supporting children's paths to literacy. The debate about style and content continues at both emotive and academic levels. What needs to be considered here is the balance between texts with supportive language which will, in Vygotskyan terms, 'scaffold' the child's learning, and texts which will motivate and encourage reading. Criticisms levelled at some basal readers include the banal and restricted language and the encouragement of unnatural reading behaviours. Children will read Blue Book Two because they have read Blue Book One, without developing their ability to choose by preference of author or content. The need for good books to read so that children could be 'cozened into a knowledge of their books' was expressed by John Locke in the seventeenth century (Townsend 1990: 12). Margaret Meek has written persuasively on the nature of texts that teach children how to read through their patterned language and layers of meaning. 'Children who encounter such books learn many lessons that are hidden for ever from those who move directly from the reading scheme to the worksheet' (Meek 1988: 19).

The pedagogic world tends to divide into those who believe children need structured texts, Barthes's 'lisible' or readerly texts for the passive reader, and those who believe that, to be fully literate, we need also to engage with 'scriptible' or 'writerly' texts, that demand the reader's active engagement in the search for meaning. Indeed, such texts may not have one interpretation, but will be open to discussion. The ability to fill in the 'gaps' in the text, to draw on the semiotic codes provided in texts and pictures in books, is an essential skill (Iser 1978).

The National Literacy Strategy in England and the First Steps approach in Australia encourage use of good literary texts for developing reading. In Nigeria, development of daily story-reading and -telling, despite a shortage of resources, ensures literacy learning is contextualised in narrative storying and that children are motivated to learn. However, the skill of the teacher in selecting and analysing appropriate texts as preparation for effective learning is variable. Lack of training for teachers has been a major setback in acquiring literacy in some parts of the world. Even in the USA and the UK, lack of knowledge by teachers can prevent adequate engagement with texts and fully developed literacy. The analysis of test results and inspection reports on the teaching of literacy in the UK several years into the National Literacy Strategy in England, for example, has revealed some concerns at lack of measured progress in some aspects of literacy (Brookes 2003). The early training for the introduction of the strategy was on processes of organisation and particular practices with the support of prepared plans. What was not offered to many teachers was the systematic study of the way texts are constructed, and the linguistic and literary knowledge necessary to analyse and work creatively with children was an assumed, rather than an actual, reality. As a result, some children are still learning to read on structured basal readers accompanied by decontextualised exercises. There are, however, articles by enlightened and well-informed teachers, published in teachers' journals at national and international level, revealing some outstanding practice in challenging children and extending reading, developing sophisticated responses to texts while valuing the contexts in which children are learning.

In considering the debate about reading schemes or basal readers as a foundation for literacy teaching rather than a range of good 'real books', Hunt points out that reading children's literature is not always seen as 'work', and this dichotomy between learning as work and reading for pleasure as 'play' is perhaps at the heart of much of the affective response to this debate (Hunt 1994: 175).

One other aspect of text choice is the encouragement of children's own reading patterns and preferences in order for them to take ownership of reading for themselves and to fit in with the social groups in which they operate, for example by taking a particular comic regularly, or collecting series books which may not be of intrinsic literary merit. Peter Dickinson has defended this reading behaviour in his article 'A Defence of Rubbish' (Dickinson 1976): few adults would not admit to reading some texts which are of dubious literary worth, and Dickinson's point is that, as long as the overall reading diet is varied, reading some less worthy texts can be beneficial to developing as a reader.

Multiliteracies

The definition of literacy at the start of this chapter reflected the broad literacy contexts which children have now to manage if they are to succeed. This requires an ability to read for a range of purposes from a wide range of texts. Computer literacy requires a range of behaviours developed from the linear reading of books and other printed texts, but new vocabularies are developing to reflect the different reading behaviours expected. The use of mobile phones and text-messaging has developed a language of its own, which children are both decoding and inventing with zest.

The understanding of semiotic codes used to create meaning in picture books (see Moebius 1992) applies equally to reading other texts which mix graphics and writing, and multi-modal texts make even further demands, as moving image and sound are incorporated. The quality of the texts emerging is varied. Some of those writing so enthusiastically about the need to embrace the new literacies demonstrate a blindness to one of the most crucial factors. As Eve Bearne says:

> The sudden and proliferated range of texts and 'representations of the world' mean that it is even more critical for children to be able to exert discrimination and choice over the literacies and literacy practices which they encounter daily … it becomes imperative to be able to read and write with the eyes of a critic.
>
> (Bearne 1996: 318)

The work of Jackie Marsh and Elaine Millard (2000) has highlighted the importance of addressing popular culture in bridging the gap between home and school. They recognise the rich experience many children have at home of watching television and video and playing computer games, and have developed literacy practices in school which recognise, value and build on the out-of-school experience (Marsh and Millard 2000: 95). In defending their focus on popular culture from accusations of debasing the curriculum, Marsh and Millard argue that 'if schools focus on increasingly outmoded forms of literacy, then children's motivation toward the literacy diet offered in the classroom will be affected further' (2000: 186). They also argue that the critical literacies developed through studying popular culture are transferable skills, able to be applied to 'a wide range of texts, for popular culture does not hold the monopoly on manipulation' (188).

As it is increasingly likely that children will be familiar with many of the works of literature on the shelf through having watched the video in advance, it is senseless to work against the flow, and there is every incentive to explore new ways of working that can exploit such knowledge. For older generations, the analogy may be made with *The Wizard of Oz*. For many of us, the film starring Judy Garland is the 'definitive text', yet it was made only owing to the immense popularity of the books by L. Frank Baum: it was the *Harry Potter* of its day. Reading the text following an extensive acquaintance with the film provides a glimpse of what coming to many books is like for the child of the twenty-first century. Evidence from book sales of film and television tie-ins is evidence that, far from multi-media experience killing book reading, the two can co-exist. Studies of children's reading choices also demonstrate that a range of fiction is being read (Collins *et al.* 1997; Millard 1997; Hall and Coles 1999), with one in seven of the most popular titles in Hall and Coles's study linked to media productions. The range and diversity of what children read increases with age, and there is evidence of reading from popular culture as well as classics such as *The Secret Garden*. It is clear that children are still tuned into and turned on by books and able to justify their choices and rejections.

We have reached the position, as Unsworth suggests, that

> in the twenty-first century the notion of literacy needs to be reconceived as a plurality of literacies and *being* literate must be seen as anachronistic. As emerging literacies continue to impact on the social construction of these multiple literacies, *becoming* literate is the more apposite description.
>
> (Unsworth 2001: 8)

References

Bearne, E. (1996) 'Mind the Gap: Critical Literacy as a Dangerous Underground Movement', in Styles, M., Bearne, E. and Watson, V. (eds) *Voices Off: Texts, Contexts and Readers*, London: Cassell.

Brookes, G. (2003) *Sound Sense: The Phonics Element of the National Literacy Strategy: A Report to the Department for Education and Skills, July 2003*, www.standards.dfes.gov.uk (accessed 12 November 2003).

Clay, M. (1979) *The Early Detection of Reading Difficulties*, London: Heinemann.

Collins, F. M., Hunt, P. and Nunn, J. (1997) *Reading Voices: Young People Discuss Their Reading Choices*, Plymouth: Northcote House.

Cunningham, H. (1995) *Children and Childhood in Western Society since 1500*, London: Longman.

Dickinson, P. (1976) 'A Defence of Rubbish', in Fox, G., Hammond, G. and Jones, T. (eds) (1976) *Writers, Critics and Children*, London: Heinemann.

Ferreiro, E. and Teberosky, A. (1979) *Literacy before Schooling*, London: Heinemann.

Fischer, S. (2003) *A History of Reading*, London: Reaktion.

Goodman, K. (1982) 'The Reading Process', in Gollasch, F. (ed.) *Language and Literacy: The Selected Writings of Kenneth S. Goodman*, vol. 1, Boston, MA: Routledge and Kegan Paul.

Hall, C. and Coles, M. (1999) *Children's Reading Choices*, London: Routledge.

Harste, J., Woodward, V. and Burke, C. (1984) *Language Stories and Literacy Lesson*, Portsmouth, NH: Heinemann.

Heath, S. B. (1983) *Ways with Words: Language, Life, and Work in Communities and Classrooms*, Cambridge: Cambridge University Press.

Hilton, M. (ed.) (1996) *Potent Fictions: Children's Literacy and the Challenge of Popular Culture*, London: Routledge.

Hilton, M., Styles, M. and Watson, V. (eds) (1997) *Opening the Nursery Door: Reading, Writing and Childhood 1600–1900*, London: Routledge.

Hunt, P. (1994) *An Introduction to Children's Literature*, Oxford: Oxford University Press.

Iser, W. (1978) *The Art of Reading: A Theory of Aesthetic Response*, London: Routledge and Kegan Paul.

Marsh, J. and Millard, E. (2000) *Literacy and Popular Culture: Using Children's Culture in the Classroom*, London: Paul Chapman.

Meek, M. (1988) *How Texts Teach What Readers Learn*, South Woodchester: Thimble Press.

Millard, E. (1997) *Differently Literate: Boys, Girls and the Schooling of Literacy*, London: Routledge-Falmer.

Moebius, W. (1992) 'Introduction to Picture Book Codes', in Hunt, P. (ed.) *Children's Literature: The Development of Criticism*, London: Routledge.

Tomalin, C. (2003) *Samuel Pepys: The Unequalled Self*, London: Viking.

Townsend, J. R. (1990) *Written for Children*, London: The Bodley Head.

UNESCO (2003) http://portal.unesco.org/education/ev.php (accessed 19 December 2003).

Unsworth, L. (2001) *Teaching Multiliteracies across the Curriculum: Changing Contexts of Text and Image in Classroom Practice*, Buckingham: Open University Press.

12 Intertextuality and the child reader

Christine Wilkie-Stibbs

Editor's Introduction

Part of the meaning that readers make from texts depends on their ability to recognise the texture of allusion, reference and quotation that exists within almost all texts. Christine Wilkie-Stibbs explores the inevitable complexity of texts for children, and how subtle the interactions can be between readers and intertextual references.

P. H.

The term 'intertextuality' is now common in literary discourse. It is used most often and most simply to refer to literary allusions and to direct quotation from literary and non-literary texts. But this is only one small part of the theory, which has its origins in the work of Julia Kristeva (1969) and Mikhail Bakhtin (1973). Since poststructuralist thinking has extended the idea of the text beyond the boundaries of its being merely a written discourse, the possibilities for theories and theorisations of intertextuality are now legion. Intertextuality embraces discourse *per se*, in its uttered, illustrated, written, mimed or gestured manifestations; it includes images and moving images, the social and cultural context, subjectivities – which are the reading/seeing/speaking/writing/painting/thinking subjects – and, indeed, language itself. Theorists and teachers of literature alike are recognising the place of intertextual understandings in literary studies for readers' reception and production of texts, as an adjunct to reader-response theory. Teachers are engaging with the concept of intertextuality in their use of literature with young children as a means by which to build up 'interpretive communities' (Fish 1980) among young readers, to give a window on the processes of meaning-making during a reading, and for engaging in text creation and production (see, for example, Bloome and Egan-Robertson 1993; Bromley 1996; Cairney 1990, 1992; Lemke 1992; Many and Anderson 1992; Short 1992; Sipe 2000). Intertextual considerations and understandings are also important in the translation of texts where a source text from one language and culture is translated for a culturally and linguistically different target audience (see Desmet 2001; O'Sullivan 1998).

Kristeva (1969: 146) coined the term 'intertextuality', recognising that texts can only have meaning because they depend on other texts, both written and spoken, and on what she calls the 'intersubjective' knowledge of their interlocutors, by which she meant their total knowledge – from other books, from language-in-use, and the context and conditions of the signifying practices which make meanings possible in groups and communities (Kristeva 1974/1984: 59–60). The literary text, then, is just one of the many sites where several different discourses converge, are absorbed, are transformed and assume a meaning because they are situated in this circular network of interdependence which is called the intertextual space.

Kristeva was keen to point out that intertextuality is not simply a process of recognising sources and influences. She built on the work of Bakhtin, who had identified the word as the smallest textual unit, situated in relation to three coordinates: of the writer, the text and exterior texts. For the first time in literary history, the literary text (the word) took on a spatial dimension when Bakhtin made it a fluid function between the writer/text (on the horizontal axis) and the text/context (on the vertical axis). This idea replaced the previous, Formalist notion that the literary text was a fixed point with a fixed meaning. Bakhtin described this process as a dialogue between several writings, and as the intersection of textual surfaces: 'any text is a mosaic of quotations; any text is the absorption and transformation of another' (in Kristeva 1980/1981: 66).

The theory of intertextuality was refined and extended by Jonathan Culler (1981), and by Roland Barthes (1970/1975), who included the reader as a constituent component of intertextuality. Culler described intertextuality as the general discursive space in which meaning is made intelligible and possible (1981: 103), and Barthes invented the term 'infinite intertextuality' to refer to the intertextual codes by which readers make sense of a literary work, which he calls a 'mirage of citations'. They dwell equally in readers and in texts but the conventions and presuppositions cannot be traced to an original source or sources. 'The "I" which approaches the text is already a plurality of other texts, of infinite, or more precisely, lost codes (whose origins are lost)' (Barthes 1975/1976: 16).

The idea that texts are produced and readers/viewers make sense of them only in relation to the already embedded codes which dwell in texts and readers (and in authors too, since they are readers of texts before they are authors) has ramifications which challenge any claim to textual originality or discrete readings. In this sense, then, all texts and all readings are intertextual. This brings us close to Genette's use of the term 'transtextuality' (1979: 85–90), by which he is referring to *everything* that influences a text either explicitly or implicitly.

This dynamic and spatial model of intertextuality has peculiar implications for an intertextuality of children's literature because the writer/reader axis is uniquely positioned in an imbalanced power relationship. Adults write for each other, but it is not usual for children to write literature for each other. This phenomenon would effectively make children the powerless recipients of what adults choose to write for them and children's literature an intertextual sub-genre of adult literature. But we now know through the empirical studies involving young children in the 'game of intertextuality' that the intertextual processes through which children take ownership of a particular text preclude the imperialism of the text and the author. Inevitably, the phenomenon of intertextuality sets up a curious kind of hegemony in children's books, in which adults who write for children (who by definition are no longer themselves children) consciously or unconsciously operate in and are influenced by the intertextual space which is the literature they read as children. That books read in childhood and childhood experiences have a profound bearing on adult perceptions is borne out by the numerous adults, many of whom are themselves writers of children's books, who refer to the influences on them of their childhood reading matter. Examples can be found in Francis Spufford's *The Child That Books Built: A Memoir of Childhood and Reading* (2002); in the short author biographies in Eccleshare's *Beatrix Potter to Harry Potter: Portraits of Children's Writers* (2002) of Malorie Blackman (122), Anne Fine (112), Shirley Hughes (114), Dick King-Smith (108), J. K. Rowling (101–3), Philip Pullman (124) and Jacqueline Wilson (120); and the sections in James Carter's *Talking Books* (1999), 'How the Reader Became a Writer', relating to the numerous author/illustrator interviews. Nevertheless, and despite children's demonstrable ability to take textual ownership through their own intertextual references, the writer/reader relationship is asymmetric because children's intersubjective knowledge cannot be assured. A theory of intertextuality of children's literature is, therefore, unusually preoccupied with questions about what a piece of writing (for children) presupposes. What does it assume, what *must* it assume to take on significance? (See Culler 1981: 101–2.)

For these reasons the interrelationship between the components of intertextuality, of writer/text/reader–text/reader/context, are quite special when we are addressing a theory of intertextuality of children's literature. For example, we might legitimately ask what sense and meanings young readers make in their readings of Philip Pullman's award-winning *His Dark Materials* trilogy which, as Millicent Lenz points out, draws overtly and implicitly on intertextual references to particle physics and quantum mechanics, on deeply existential questions on the nature of sin and Fall, and is influenced by Milton's *Paradise Lost*, the poetry of William Blake and the complex theory of natural grace in Henrich von Kleist's essay, 'On the Marionette Theatre' (Hunt and Lenz 2001: 42–82).

By now it should be clear that the theory of intertextuality is dynamic and dialogic, located in theories of writing, reader-response theory, the social production of meaning, and inter-subjectivity (the 'I' who is reading is a network of citations). It is also a theory of language because the reading subject, the text and the world are not only situated in language, they are also constructed by it. So, not only do we have a notion of all texts being intertextual, they become so because they are dialectically related to, and are themselves the products of, linguistic, cultural and literary codes and practices; and so too are readers, writers, illustrators and viewers.

In the process of making meaning with a particular text, we know that children (and adults, see Hartman 1995) have recourse to a battery of intertextual phenomena, calling upon, for example, their knowledge of previously read fictions, visual texts – film, illustration and TV programmes, texts of popular culture – cartoon, video, comic books, advertisements and songs (see Many and Anderson 1992; Bloome and Egan-Robertson 1993; Sipe 2000), and that they do so at many levels of textual engagement such as plot structures, character and character motivation, language and language patterns, themes and illustrations.

Culler (1975: 139) described the urge towards integrating one discourse with another, or several others, as a process of *vraisemblance*. It is the basis of intertextuality. Through this process of *vraisemblance* readers are able to identify, for example, the set of literary norms and the salient features of a work by which to locate genre, and also to anticipate what they might expect to find in fictional worlds. Through *vraisemblance* the child reader has unconsciously to learn that the fictional worlds in literature are representations and constructions which refer to other texts that have been normalised: that is, those texts that have been absorbed into the culture and are now regarded as 'natural'.

At the level of literary texts (the intertext), it is possible to identify three main categories of intertextuality: (1) texts of quotation which quote or allude to other literary or non-literary works; (2) texts of imitation which seek to parody, pastiche, paraphrase, 'translate' or supplant the original, which seek to liberate their readers from an over-invested admiration in great writers of the past, and which often function as the pre-text of the original for later readers (Worton and Still 1990: 7); and (3) genre texts where identifiable shared clusters of codes and literary conventions are grouped together in recognisable patterns which allow readers to expect and locate them, and to cause them to seek out similar texts. At the level of literary response, young readers' intertextual responses might usefully be classified in terms of the links they make overtly with other texts, their personal experiences which bear upon their relationship with the focus text, and their inclination to manipulate the focus text in the pull towards reinvention, recreation, rewriting.

Texts of quotation are probably the simplest level at which child readers can recognise intertextuality. Examples are Janet and Allan Ahlberg's The Jolly Postman series (1986/1997), John Prater's *Once Upon a Time* (1993), Jon Scieszka's *The Stinky Cheese Man* (1992) and his *The True Story of the 3 Little Pigs* (1989), Roald Dahl's *Revolting Rhymes* (1987). All these fictions quote from or allude to a variety of fairy tales. They make explicit assumptions about their readers' knowledge of previously read fairy tales: 'Everyone knows the story of the Three Little Pigs. Or at least they think they do' (Scieszka 1989: first opening), and 'I guess you think you know this story/You don't, the real one's much more gory' (Dahl 1987: 5). So, as well as assuming familiarity with an 'already read' inter-text, the 'focused texts' are at the same time foregrounding their own authenticity; that is, they purport to be more authoritative than the texts they are quoting and are thereby undermining the 'truth' of their pre-texts. They cleverly destabilise the security of their readers by positioning them ambivalently in relation to (1) what they think they know already about the fairy tales and (2) the story they are now reading. At the discursive level, then, these particular examples of texts of quotation are doing much more than simply alluding to other texts; they are supplanting the pre-texts and challenging their readers' 'already read' notions of the reliable narrator by an act of referring back which tells the reader that what they knew previously about these tales was all lies. And The Jolly Postman series is, at the very least, breaking readers' 'already read' boundary of fictionality by presenting them with a clutch of touchable, usable, readable written artefacts – letters, postcards, cards, invitations, board games, posters, etc. – from, to and about characters in fiction, which are facsimile versions of their real-life counterparts.

Every text of quotation which relocates the so-called primary text in a new cultural and linguistic context must be by definition a parody and a distortion. All the examples I have given parody the telling of traditional tales: *Once Upon a Time* (Prater 1993), 'Once upon a time' (Scieszka 1992: passim), and 'Once upon a bicycle' (Ahlberg 1986/1997: first opening). But the challenge to authority and problems of authenticity for these quotation texts of fairy tales lies in the fact that the tales themselves are a collage of quotations, each of which has assumed a spurious 'first version' authenticity but for which the ur-text does not exist, or at least cannot be located. The situation of fairy tales in contemporary culture is analogous to Barthes's notion of 'lost codes'. The tales are intelligible because they build on already embedded discourses which happened elsewhere and at another time; they are part of the sedimented folk memory of discourse and they function now by the simple fact that other tales like them have already existed. Children's intertextual experience is peculiarly achronological, so the question about what sense children make of a given text when the intertextual experience cannot be assumed, is important.

What happens, though, in readings where such intertextual knowledge cannot be assumed or assured, such as in cases of cultural transfer or readerly inexperience, where the intertextual references are unknown and unavailable to the target audience? What sense do children make, can children make, of a textual encounter in these circumstances? A student teacher explains how her class of four- and five-year-olds, who were only just beginning to build a foundation knowledge of books, failed to understand *The Jolly Postman*

> because it has quite a difficult formula with the original story and additional texts as an additional layer to the story in the form of letters, cards, advertisements, etc. As well as attempting to make sense of the story, they also needed knowledge of these other genres, familiarity with other fairy stories and nursery rhymes and perhaps even an understanding of puns, jokes and play on words.

She goes on to describe how one child attempts to take control of the text in his retelling of the story of 'The Three Little Pigs':

> When the child reached the part of the tale where the wolf falls into the pot of boiling water, he explained that the wolf 'splashed and bashed and kicked his legs'. This was not in the original text that we had read, but the child had played with what he knew, had immersed himself in the text and had come up with a playful comment that expressed an understanding of the story. The children compare and contrast the stories they are reading with those they already have knowledge of to make up a schema for a particular genre. It is therefore obvious that the more stories the children know the more they can understand/interpret richly any given story.
>
> (Stapleton 2002)

The question of readers' meaning-making is raised also in the process of translating a source text into another language where it is a matter of cultural and linguistic specificity. Desmet relates how the Ahlbergs' Jolly Postman series has been translated into Dutch by the use of such translation strategies as: '*literal translation* of shared intertexts, *substitution* for intertexts likely to be unknown to the intended target audience, and *addition* or *compensation*' (Desmet 2001: 31, my italics). The end result of the text which has been the subject of translation may be, as Desmet suggests, 'a new differently intertextual text' (31). Translation between languages (and indeed between different media) is a catalyst for questions about the authority of one text over another and about the possible loss of some of the source text's cultural authority in the process of translation; it also returns us to the question already raised of the role and authority of the reader in the intertextual space as the *producer* rather than the *decoder* of embedded textual meanings. In instances where a source text is written in English, but requires the transfer of a different cultural knowledge to its target readership, the narrative itself often attempts to compensate for any assumed shortfall in knowledge between it and its intended young readership by filling in any potential gaps with embedded explanations.

Adeline Yen Mah's *Chinese Cinderella: The Secret Story of an Unwanted Daughter* (1999) is a very good example. It apparently alludes overtly to the Westernised version of the Cinderella folk tale in its title, but in fact it alludes to the story of 'Ye Xian, the original Chinese Cinderella'. The autobiographical narrative is set against a background of Chinese history spanning the period 1937–52, and focuses on the cruelties inflicted on Adeline as an unwanted girl-child in one of China's elite families in the shadow of first the Japanese and then the Communist takeovers of mainland China. She describes her struggle for an education and her family's attempts to avoid the impact on their wealth and lifestyle of the invasions, by their continuous and restless moving between Tianjin and Shanghai and, eventually, to Hong Kong. A knowledge of cultural and historical facts, and of her family's pre-revolutionary status, are important to the reader's understanding of her family's motivations and behaviour; consequently, explanations of the historical background are slipped into the narrative between accounts of the everyday cruelties her family inflict on Adeline's family- and school-life. For example, in letting her young reader know the significant status of her family home in the 'French Concession' of Tianjin, she explains:

> China had lost a war (known as the Opium War) against England and France. As a result, many coastal cities in China (such as Tianjin and Shanghai) came to be occupied by foreign soldiers. The conquerors parceled out the best areas of these treaty

ports for themselves, claiming them as their own 'territories' or 'concessions'. Tianjin's French Concession was like a little piece of Paris transplanted into the centre of this big Chinese city ... We were ruled by French citizens under French law.

(1999: 5–6, 231)

A knowledge of Chinese custom and language is also integrally important for Western readers' understanding of this narrative; so they are given a lesson in the protocol of naming in Chinese families in the two-page 'Author's Note' at the start of the book; chapter headings are written bilingually in English and Chinese with Chinese characters, and Chinese characters with their phonetic transliterations are repeated throughout to name names. Especially enlightening for the reader's understanding of the richness and beauty of the Chinese language and significance of the characters, is a three-page explanation posed as a dialogue between Adeline and her grandfather ('Ye Ye'), focusing on just one character in the Chinese script: ('bei') (172–4).

Mirjam Pressler's *Shylock's Daughter* (1999, 2000) has been translated into English from the original German by Brian Murdoch. The story is set within the framework of Shakespeare's *The Merchant of Venice*, in the Ghetto of sixteenth-century Venice. Clearly the reader's previous knowledge of the original play as an intertext enhances the reading of this text, but the absence of it does not close it down altogether. More importantly for the reader's understanding is a knowledge, which cannot be assumed, of Jewish sects and culture, customs and Law, to explain and enlighten the mores and behaviours of the key characters – Shylock, his daughter Jessica and her Christian lover, Antonio. Similarly to the Adeline Yen Mah's book, the narrative takes care of the 'gaps' through a battery of discreet, *en passant* explanations: for example:

'You know he doesn't like it when you spend all your time with the Sephardim – with those Spanish Jews!'

(2000: 15)

These Jews were mostly Marranos – that is, they had been forced to accept baptism.

(25)

Levi Meshullam was a Sephardic Jew, and the laws that applied to him were different from those for Ashkenazi Jews like her father.

(52)

The lords had simply cancelled the *condotta*, the settlement treaty for Jews.

(26)

The regulations, which the *cattaveri*, the controllers, enforced with such strict attention.

(68)

What a splendid *zimara* he had been wearing this evening, that full well-cut coat with the broad sleeves.

(52)

'Acts of Charity like that, *mitzvoth*, are supposed to be done secretly and not in public.'

(65)

However, the book alludes to the original play in a number of subtle ways that are not explained, for which first-hand knowledge of the play would provoke a richer kind of reading. Some of the dialogue, especially Shylock's, is quoted directly from *The Merchant of Venice*; the book adopts the much-used Shakespearean device of having girls disguised as boys and women as men (as with Jessica and Portia). There is an allusion to a wider intertext of Shakespeare, with an emphasis in the book on the idea of characters play-acting, of their playing a part in their own lives, and the book uses the Shakespearean device of 'plays within plays'.

These examples of texts which allude overtly to previous intertexts again raise the wider questions of the status of the so-called 'ur-text', and the effect of the intertexts on the reader's knowledge, perception and reception of any one, or all, of them. Children's exposure to other media such as film, television animations, and video, means increasingly that they are likely to encounter the media adaptations of a children's fiction before they encounter the written text and to come to regard it as the 'original' from which to approach and on which to base and 'make sense' of their (later) reading of the written version. This raises further questions about whether the nature of the later reading is qualitatively and experientially different if the ur-text (source text) happens to have been a Disney cartoon version of, say, 'Snow White'.

Disney adaptations of fairy tales are particularly interesting to an intertextuality of children's literature because, as touchstones of popular culture, they reflect the way in which each generation's retellings have assumed and foregrounded the dominant socio-linguistic and cultural codes and values at a particular moment in history: for example, Disney's foregrounding Snow White's good looks alongside qualities of moral rectitude and goodness claimed for her by earlier, written versions.

But it is not only the stories which change in the repeated intertextual quotations – the intertextual context of the reading and their reception also changes. For example, contemporary feminist post-Freudian readings of Carroll's *Alice's Adventures in Wonderland* (1865), or Burnett's *The Secret Garden* (1911), make them different kinds of texts from what was previously possible. Similarly, a contemporary child reader's readings of, say, a modern reprint of the original tales of Beatrix Potter will be quite different from those of the readers for whom they were originally intended. In their reading of *Jemima Puddle-Duck* (1908), for example, today's child readers are less likely than child readers from the earlier part of the century to recognise the ingredients of duck stuffing for what they are. This is not because, like Jemima, they are simpletons, but because their stuffing today is more likely to be from a packet. Their probable inability to recognise the ingredients of duck stuffing removes an opportunity to anticipate Jemima's fate well in advance of narration. And not only do contemporary child-readers have an intertextual familiarity with Beatrix Potter's character, Jemima Puddle-Duck, and her Potter co-star, Peter Rabbit, from a proliferation of non-literary artefacts, including video adaptations: they can also now read about them in series adaptations in Ladybird books (1992 on). Ladybird has developed a very powerful position in Britain as a publisher of low-priced hardback formula books – especially retellings of traditional tales – with simplified language and sentence constructions. They are a good example of the texts of imitation I described earlier. For some children in Britain they will be the only written version of traditional tales they have encountered. Comparison between the Ladybird and original versions of *Jemima Puddle-Duck* reveals linguistic and syntactic differences that make assumptions about their respective implied readers; and there are other syntactic, micro-discursive and linguistic differences which encode different socio-linguistic climates and – by extension – imply

different language-in-use on the parts of their respective readerships. What we see in operation in these two texts is the tension and interplay between two idiolects and two
sociolects: the uses of language in each text and their situation in, and reception by, their
respective socio-historic contexts and readers. Each is operating as a textual and intertextual
paradigm of its time, but the first-version text can only be 'read' through a network of late
twentieth-century intertexts.

Susan Cooper's *The Dark Is Rising* series (1965–77) and Alan Garner's *The Owl Service*
(1984) rely for their fullest reading on the young reader's knowledge of Arthurian and
Celtic myth, especially of the *Mabinogion*. Together these texts are examples of the type of
two-world fantasy genre where child readers can come to recognise, and to expect, such
generic conventions as character archetype, stereotype and the archetypal plot structures
of quest and journeys. The novels allude only obliquely to their mythical sources, even
though myth is integral to their stories. Thus, even in readings that do not rely on knowledge of the myth, readers might intuit the echoes of myth as they read and absorb the
novels' more subtle messages and connections.

Similarly, Robert Cormier's *After the First Death* (1979) and Jill Paton Walsh's novels
Goldengrove (1972) and *Unleaving* (1976) allude, respectively, to lines from Dylan
Thomas's poem 'A Refusal to Mourn the Death, by Fire, of a Child in London' ('After
the first death, there is no other') and Gerard Manley Hopkins's 'Spring and Fall'
('Márgarét, áre you grieving/Over Goldengrove unleaving?'). In each case, a perfectly
coherent reading of the text is possible without the reader's knowledge of the intertextual
poetic allusions; but the potential for a metaphoric reading is enhanced by the reader's
previous knowledge of them. In the case of Paton Walsh's *Goldengrove*, for example, the
metaphor for metaphysical transience first mooted by Hopkins in his 'Spring and Fall'
image of the Goldengrove unleaving, is employed again by Paton Walsh as the name of
the fictional house, 'Goldengrove', from which the book takes its title. This is the place of
symbolic and literal change where the two teenage characters spend their (significantly)
late-summer vacation of maturation and realisation. The image is extended in numerous
other references: changing body-shapes, changed sleeping arrangements, changed attitudes to each other, and not least, in repeated references to the falling leaves of late
summer. It also invokes and parodies the style and content of Virginia Woolf's *To The
Lighthouse* (1927), with a polyphony which moves effortlessly between several viewpoints,
and positions its readers accordingly. This polyphonic, multilayered structure, which is also
a feature of the Cormier novel, is particularly interesting to an intertextuality of children's
literature because it breaks the intertextual discursive codes and conventions of the single
viewpoint and linear narrative that are typical of the form.

Young readers who come to these novels by Cooper, Garner, Cormier and Paton Walsh
with an explicit knowledge of their intertexts will have a markedly different experience of
reading. They will experience what Barthes has described as the 'circular memory of
reading' (Barthes 1975/76: 36). This describes a reading process where the need
consciously to recall and to refer back to specific obligatory intertexts, now being quoted
as metaphor and/or metonymy in the focused texts, restricts the reader's opportunity for
free intertextual interplay at the point of reading. The reading experience in such cases
moves away from a textually focused reading that is a more usual kind of narrative engagement to one that is simultaneously centrifugal and centripetal as the reader seeks to refer
to the 'borrowing' and at the same time to integrate it into a new context. It is the
essence of this kind of reading to deny readers an opportunity for linear reading as they
move in and out of the text to make connections between it and the intertext(s).

Jamila Gavin's award-winning *Coram Boy* (2000) draws on the historical fact of Thomas Coram's establishing in 1741 the first children's hospital 'For the Maintenance and Education of Exposed and Deserted Children', children who were otherwise brutalised, and eventually died, in the charity orphanages of the period. In her Foreword to the book, Gavin describes how the Coram Foundation still exists today, and that it continues to work on behalf of children; that the performance of Handel's *Messiah*, which is a key event in the book, actually took place at the Hospital. The 'Coram man' is pivotal to the events of the story. He collects abandoned children, ostensibly to deliver them up to the Hospital for safe keeping, but disposes of them instead before they could ever have reached it. Such a man, Gavin explains, never actually existed. The 'Coram boys' were real enough as inmates of the eighteenth-century Hospital, but the characters and events of the story are otherwise all imaginary. As in *The Chinese Cinderella* and *Shylock's Daughter*, the Foreword situates the historical events but, unlike those books, there are no explanatory pauses in the narrative itself to 'educate' the reader's lack of factual knowledge en route. *Coram Boy* weaves a path through actual and imaginary events which assume equal status in the mind of the reader, who is then unable to differentiate between fact or fiction in what *de facto* has become a linear rather than centripetal experience of reading. Another Paton Walsh novel, *A Parcel of Patterns* (1983), is also a fictionalised historical account, of the bubonic plague's destruction of the inhabitants of the Derbyshire village of Eyam. It uses many secondary signals to ground the events in their historic context and to ensure that readers locate the events in these pre-textual happenings by, for example, the use of paratextual devices such as the words of the publisher's introduction: 'Eyam (pronounced Eem) is a real village in Derbyshire and many of the events in this evocative novel are based on what actually happened there in the year of the Plague' (Paton Walsh 1983).

Another example is the use of direct quotation from historic artefacts, not least from the inscription of the great bell of Eyam 'SWEET JESU BE MY SPEDE' (54). The book reinforces the historic authenticity of its subject matter by a consistent capitalisation throughout of the word Plague, and by use of an invented dialect which pastiches what we know about the dialect of seventeenth-century Derbyshire.

In contrast, Robert Westall's novel *Gulf* (1992) is embedded in the events of the 1991 so-called 'Gulf War' in the wake of the Iraqi invasion of Kuwait. *Gulf*, unlike *A Parcel of Patterns*, could have assumed a shared, contemporary readership. Equally, it clearly assumes that its readership has a shared intertextual experience, and this makes recovery of the pre-text more likely and therefore calls for little explanation and contextualisation. But the novel's foregrounded meaning centres on the need for its readers to see the connection between the out-of-body experiences of the narrator's younger brother, Figgis, and the experiences of a young Iraqi boy soldier whose life he shares. The detail of the geography and history of Iraq is an intertextual experience that cannot be assumed, at least not for its target Western readership; consequently, as in so many of the narratives already mentioned, they are dealt with by way of explanation: 'I looked up Tikrit in our atlas; it was north of Baghdad. Then I read in the paper it was where Saddam Hussein himself came from' (Westall 1992: 47). This is another example of the way in which texts written for children sometimes have a felt need to be overreferential; the need to fill intertextual gaps to mobilise a positive reading experience in their young readers which, incidentally, may be one of the single distinguishing characteristics of children's literature *per se*.

Literature for children has to tread a careful path between a need to be sufficiently overreferential in its intertextual gap-filling so as not to lose its readers, and the need to leave enough intertextual space and to be sufficiently stylistically challenging to allow readers free intertextual interplay. It is on the one hand formally conservative, yet it is charged with the awesome responsibility of initiating young readers into the dominant literary, linguistic and cultural codes of the home culture. On the other hand, it has seen the emergence of what we now confidently call the 'new picture books' and the 'new young adult novel', some of which have featured in this essay. Picture-book writers and illustrators are challenging conventional literary forms of children's literature and breaking the codes. In so doing they amass a wide-ranging repertoire of generic possibilities which effectively extends the horizons of young people's literary competences and encourages them to ever-increasingly participate in Barthes's 'circular memory of reading'.

A theory of intertextuality of children's literature challenges readers and writers of children's literature to acknowledge the lost codes and practices and underlying discursive conventions by which it functions and has been defined historically. It shows why theoretical practice is so important to reading practice. It urges a different poetics of literary engagement in which the young reader's part in the process of meaning-making is legitimised by the theory itself because it endorses and valorises their propensity for intertextual interplay. The texts mentioned here act only as illustrative paradigms of the theory of intertextuality of children's literature in a cornucopia of other possible texts. Some of these texts, like so many others in the field, have a metafictional dimension which causes readers to pay attention to their fabric, to the devices of artifice in literature and to the textuality, as well as the actuality, of the world to which they allude. The theory of intertextuality of children's literature is a rich field in which to engage young people's awareness of the importance of the activity of making intertextual links in the interpretive process. It brings them to a gradual understanding of how they are being (and have been) textually constructed in and by this intertextual playground. The texts of children's literature are exciting sites on which to mobilise a child-reader subjectivity that is intertextually aware and literarily competent.

References

Ahlberg, J. and Ahlberg, A. (1986/1997) *The Jolly Postman or Other People's Letters*, London: Heinemann.

Bakhtin, M. (1973) *Problems of Dostoevsky's Poetics*, trans. R. W. Rostel, Ann Arbor, MI: Ardis.

Barthes, R. (1970/1975) *S/Z*, trans. R. Miller, London: Cape.

——(1975/1976) *The Pleasure of the Text*, trans. R. Miller, London: Cape.

Bloome, D. and Egan-Robertson, A. (1993) 'The Social Construction of Intertextuality in Classroom Reading and Writing Lessons', *Reading Research Quarterly* 28: 305–23.

Bromley, H. (1996) 'Spying on Picture Books: Exploring Intertextuality with Young Children', in Watson, V. and Styles, M. (eds) *Talking Pictures. Pictorial Texts and Young Readers*, London: Hodder and Stoughton, 101–11.

Cairney, T. (1990) 'Intertextuality: Infectious Echoes from the Past', *The Reading Teacher* 44: 478–84.

——(1992) 'Fostering and Building Students: Intertextual Histories', *Language Arts* 69: 502–7.

Carter, J. (1999) *Talking Books: Children's Authors Talk about the Craft, Creativity and Process of Writing*, London: Routledge.

Culler, J. (1975) *Structuralist Poetics: Structuralism, Linguistics and the Study of Literature*, London: Routledge and Kegan Paul.

——(1981) *The Pursuit of Signs: Semiotics, Literature, Deconstruction*, London: Routledge and Kegan Paul.

Dahl, R. (1987) *Revolting Rhymes*, London: Jonathan Cape.

Desmet, M. K. T. (2001) 'Intertextuality/Intervisuality in Translation: *The Jolly Postman*'s Intercultural Journey from Britain to the Netherlands', *Children's Literature in Education* 32, 1: 31–43.

Eccleshare, J. (2002) *Beatrix Potter to Harry Potter: Portraits of Children's Writers*, London: National Portrait Gallery.

Fish, S. (1980) *Is There a Text in This Class? The Authority of Interpretive Communities*, Cambridge, MA: Harvard University Press.

Genette, G. (1979) *The Architext: An Introduction*, trans. J. E. Lewin, Berkeley and Los Angeles: University of California Press.

Hartman, D. K. (1995) 'Eight Readers Reading: The Intertextual Links of Proficient Readers Reading Multiple Passages', *Reading Research Quarterly* 30: 520–61.

Hunt, P. and Lenz, M. (2001) *Alternative Worlds in Fantasy Fiction*, London and New York: Continuum.

Kristeva, J. (1969) *Semiotiké*, Paris: Éditions du Seuil.

——(1974/1984) *Revolution in Poetic Language*, trans. M. Waller, New York: Columbia University Press.

——(1980/1981) *Desire in Language: A Semiotic Approach to Literature and Art*, trans. T. Gora, A. Jardine and L. Roudiez, Oxford: Blackwell.

Lemke, J. L. ((1992) 'Intertextuality and Educational Research', *Linguistics and Education* 4: 575–86.

Many, J. E. and Anderson, D. D. (1992) 'The Effect of Grade and Stance on Readers' Intertextual and Autobiographical Responses to Literature', *Reading Research and Instruction* 31: 60–9.

O'Sullivan, E. (1998) 'Losses and Gains in Translation: Some Remarks on the Translation of Humour in the Books of Aidan Chambers', trans. A. Bell, in *Children's Literature* 26: 185–204, New Haven, CT: Yale University Press.

Paton Walsh, J. (1983) *A Parcel of Patterns*, Harmondsworth: Viking Kestrel.

Prater, J. (1993) *Once Upon a Time*, London: Walker.

Pressler, M. (1999, 2000) *Shylock's Daughter*, trans. Brian Murdoch, Frankfurt am Main: Alibaba Verlag GmbH; London: Macmillan Children's Books.

Scieszka, J. (1989) *The True Story of the 3 Little Pigs*, New York: Viking.

——(1992) *The Stinky Cheese Man*, New York: Viking.

Short, K. G. (1992) 'Researching Intertextuality within Collaborative Classroom Learning Environments', *Linguistics and Education* 4: 313–33.

Sipe, L. R. (2000) ' "Those Two Gingerbread Boys could be Brothers": How Children Use Intertextual Connections during Storybook Readalouds', *Children's Literature in Education* 31, 2: 73–90.

Spufford, F. (2002) *The Child That Books Built: A Memoir of Childhood and Reading*, London: Faber and Faber.

Stapleton, L. (2002) 'How Does the Theory of Intertextuality Inform and Affect Children's Reading?', undergraduate assignment, Institute of Education, University of Warwick.

Westall, R. (1992) *Gulf*, London: Methuen.

Worton, M. and Still, J. (eds) (1990) *Intertextuality*, Manchester: Manchester University Press.

Yen Mah, A. (1999) *The Chinese Cinderella: The Secret Story of an Unwanted Daughter*, London: Penguin Books.

Further reading

Bloom, H. (1973) *The Anxiety of Influence*, New York: Oxford University Press.

——(1975) *A Map of Misreading*, New York: Oxford University Press.

Genette, G. (1982) *Palimpsestes*, Paris: Éditions du Seuil.

Hunt, P. (1988) 'What Do We Lose when We Lose Allusion? Experience and Understanding Stories', *Signal* 57: 212–22.

Nikolajeva, M. (1996) *Children's Literature Comes of Age: Toward a New Aesthetic*, New York and London: Garland.

Riffaterre, M. (1984) 'Intertextual Representation: On Mimesis as Interpretive Discourse', *Critical Inquiry* 11, 1: 141–62.

Stephens, J. (1990) 'Intertextuality and the Wedding Ghost', *Children's Literature in Education* 21, 1: 23–36.

——(1992) *Language and Ideology in Children's Fiction*, London: Longman.

Valdes, M. J. (ed.) (1985) *Identity and the Literary Text*, Toronto: University of Toronto Press.

13 Healing texts

Bibliotherapy and psychology

Hugh Crago

Editor's Introduction

The question of how texts influence their readers has always been of particular interest for those in the field of children's books. From earliest times, children's books have been partly or entirely didactic in intent – but how far can intent be related to actual influence?

Hugh Crago's discussion of how books can be used as a mode of psychotherapy relates to reader-response theory, psychology, and literacy, as well as the function of literature in general.

P.H.

Bibliotherapy is one of an enormous range of methods for helping human beings in emotional distress. The word itself suggests a specific therapeutic modality (as in 'art therapy', 'occupational therapy' or 'dance therapy' – all of which were developed specifically to meet the needs of patients perceived to be wholly or partly beyond the reach of mainstream psychotherapeutic methods). In fact, bibliotherapy has not remotely established its claim to such status, and may never do so, but it still has a direct, though peripheral, relationship to the whole field of *psychotherapy*.

However, because the printed text (*biblio-*) is the medium through which the helping/healing is considered to occur (whereas the concept should really cover non-printed 'texts' such as oral story-telling and the viewing of visual narratives like films and picture books), bibliotherapy must also be considered in relation to the study of literature as received by its audience, a field now categorised as reception theory (Tabbert 1979) and reader response. With these bibliotherapy once again enjoys a presently tenuous but potentially significant connection.

Indeed, we may as well say clearly at the outset that both the theory and the practice of bibliotherapy have suffered from a failure to explore fully (or even in many cases to recognise) these connections. Few advocates of bibliotherapy have had much knowledge of reader-response theory – much of which postdates the pioneering work in bibliotherapy. Even fewer have had much personal acquaintance with the wider fields of psychology and psychotherapy. For their part, most psychologists have simply avoided dealing with a subject as complex and difficult to quantify as the potential effects of narrative on human lives. Much of what purports to be received wisdom on the subject of bibliotherapy is thus of dubious value, and perhaps it is not surprising that bibliotherapy has not been taken seriously by many people.

In so far as bibliotherapy has been seen as particularly relevant to children and adolescents, its proponents have been influenced by misleading assumptions about the nature of childhood, in particular the Rousseau-derived belief that children are especially susceptible to suggestion through print in comparison with adults, and ignorance of the real similarities and differences between child readers and adult readers (outlined briefly in Crago 1979). In fact, as we shall see, there is little difference between children and adults at the level of reading where lasting emotional impact is most likely to occur.

What psychotherapy is

Psychotherapy comprises a body of knowledge about what may go wrong with human beings, along with a set of practices designed to improve happiness and competence in the face of life's inevitable stresses. Lay people commonly assume that such work is in the province of psychologists, but the academic discipline of psychology has no compelling claim on the practice of psychotherapy, and many 'scientific' psychologists eschew psychotherapy except in extremely restricted forms. Psychiatry, because of its association with mental illness, is the other profession most associated with psychotherapy, but once again psychiatrists need not necessarily practise it.

Psychotherapy, which Freud called 'the talking cure', is best understood as something which may be practised by social workers, family therapists, doctors, marriage counsellors, even nurses and occupational therapists, as well as by psychiatrists and psychologists. In non-Western cultures, shamans and other traditional healers operate out of a very different conceptual framework from that employed by European psychotherapists, but at a fundamental level satisfy the same needs in their troubled clientele – needs for reassurance, meaning and healing confrontation. This makes it clear that there is no universally 'true' system of psychotherapeutic theory, and that no single professional guild in our own, or any other, culture 'owns' psychotherapeutic practice.

The co-evolution of story and consciousness

In pre-literate cultures, narrative has always functioned in multiple ways, preserving accumulated knowledge, articulating meaning, offering cathartic release and pleasure, and promoting 'healing' in the broad sense of reassurance as to each listener's place in the scheme of things. A single myth or ceremony may embody all of these functions simultaneously. We can reasonably assume that the prehistoric antecedents of our own culture were similar. The earliest written versions of oral narratives that we possess appear to have operated in much the same way as prime-time television does today: offering their audiences culturally central messages that confirmed listeners in their existing understandings of what was right and wrong, acceptable and unacceptable, heroic and ignoble.

In the European Middle Ages, where story-telling occurred – whether in church, or around the hearth at night – it would probably have been experienced in the same shared way, and with the same multiple dimensions, as myth and bardic epic. One reason why it has been possible for scholars in our own century (for example, Bettelheim 1976) to 'discover' the therapeutic potential of traditional folk tales is precisely because it has always been there. Those tales formed part of a collective, oral culture which spoke to a collective psyche, not individual psyches, and which inevitably embodied messages of broad relevance to the community in general (Crago 2003).

The coming of print to Western Europe, followed a few centuries later by the spread of mass literacy, formed part of a process of gradual individualisation of consciousness. Jaynes (1976) and Wilber (1986) have independently constructed speculative overviews of the evolution of consciousness, which differ in details but agree on a shift from a collective consciousness in which individuals were embedded in a 'group mind' – brilliantly simulated in William Golding's *The Inheritors* (1955) – to the form of consciousness we know today, where people experience themselves as 'separate', and in which the 'private space inside the head' is experienced as under the control of the individual, and inaccessible to others except under certain conditions. John Fowles's extraordinary novel *A Maggot* (1985) presents one of the best descriptions of this shift from pre-modern to modern consciousness.

There are some grounds for believing that the concept of 'private thoughts' was actually assisted by the development of diary-writing among the Protestant middle class in the seventeenth century (Stone 1977). Private writing enhanced the individual's sense of awareness of his or her own uniqueness, just as the private documentation of the development of one's own children, which seems to have commenced during the nineteenth century (Steedman 1982), enhanced parental consciousness of those children's individuality. Simultaneously, an increasing life span and a better standard of living (including the possibility of a 'room of one's own') for a larger proportion of the population in the centuries following the industrial revolution supported the movement to value the lives of individual human beings even when they were not famous and powerful.

The Romantic movement, coinciding as it did with the first phase of industrialisation, was a powerful cultural stimulus to the emergence of the individual sensibility, setting the tone for two centuries in which the individual mind, personality and emotions would become the central subject for poets, novelists, dramatists and (ultimately) film makers. As human beings increasingly experienced themselves as separate and even isolated ('I am a rock, I am an island,' sang Paul Simon in the 1960s, explicitly contradicting Donne's seventeenth-century 'No Manne is an Islande'), it became doubly important for literature to offer validation for that individuality by opening windows into the private worlds of other individuals, and by increasingly portraying a whole range of highly specialised subjects, which would of necessity appeal only to particular audiences who could identify with them. 'Bardic' literature (which in its broadest sense included oral folk tales) had by contrast offered only matter that appealed to the common denominator, and had spoken only to the values which all its listeners possessed in common. Thus highly individualised fictions support and extend the development of highly individualised consciousness.

The emergence of individual psychotherapy, as practised by Freud, and as elaborated vastly throughout the twentieth century, can also be seen as part of the development of an individualised consciousness, setting up a relationship similar to that of the confessional, but extending its scope to deal with the entire realm of emotional, existential and behavioural distress, now conceived in more secular than spiritual terms. Psychotherapy at its inception and still predominantly today deals explicitly with the inner world of the individual. It is commonly assumed that a highly individualised relationship must be established between client and therapist in order for any intervention strategy to work. The client or patient must first feel understood, valued and empowered before he or she is likely to accept challenge to existing habits of thought and feeling.

The encounter between a modern reader and a printed text is similar in many ways to the therapeutic encounter we have just examined. Like a confession, and like a therapy session, what happens between reader and printed text is a mystery – unless the reader chooses to tell us about it, and even then, there will be much that has occurred in the reading process that will have been below the level of consciousness. Once again, it is a question of a very 'private' transaction, in which an exquisite degree of 'matching' is required between the external agent (book) and the individual if any self-insight or change on the reader's part is to be elicited. The whole notion of bibliotherapy rests on the possibility of such matching.

The growing popularity of psychotherapy has in turn influenced narrative fiction, which has become increasingly confessional (dealing explicitly with aspects of inner life hitherto considered entirely private), and increasingly concerned with abnormal mental and emotional states. This has been true equally in adult and in young people's fiction, where 'problem novels' for adolescents have been a burgeoning area in publishing over the past thirty years. The existence of such novels, dealing with potentially life-threatening, highly individualised problems (such as anorexia nervosa, see Pantanizopoulos 1989), appears to be the most recent fictional manifestation of the individualisation of consciousness.

Bibliotherapy: a twentieth-century notion

In its broadest historical context, the concept of 'bibliotherapy' belongs to the ancient *dulcis et utile* debate, in which some scholars advocated a role for literature as 'useful' or 'instructive' in some moral sense, while others maintained that stories existed primarily or even purely to give pleasure. Since Greek and Roman times, one side or the other has prevailed for periods of a century or more, but the weight of evidence has always suggested that people continued to listen and read regardless of what the 'experts' thought. Within the field of children's literature, the debate has focused in particular on the ambiguous category of fairy tales, originally oral narratives which, having been appropriated by 'child culture' from the nineteenth century, have been at varying times attacked as morally dangerous or politically incorrect, defended as 'pure escapism', and re-conceptualised as 'morally instructive' or psychologically growthful.

In fact, there are few examples of successful and popular literature which do not offer both delight and 'instruction' in some form or other. The debate seems rather to reflect a continuing moral uneasiness, in which the intensity with which we humans have always immersed ourselves in story has prompted us to seek justification for an involvement so seemingly unrelated to the hard business of daily life.

Simsova (1968), Hatt (1976) and Nell (1988) all draw attention to the extraordinary work of Nicholas Rubakin in the USSR in the 1920s, work which anticipates by nearly half a century the claim of reader-response theory that readers experience texts in their own images (Holland 1975). Rubakin also argued for something akin to Piagetian 'schemas' as facilitating comprehension, and recognised the possibility of 'scientifically' matching types of reader with types of books (the typology of reader personalities being broadly based on Jung's system). Such an enterprise of social engineering was likely enough to appeal to a revolutionary government, but Rubakin's ideas were never fully operationalised even in the USSR, and in the West (like his fellow Russians Vladimir Propp and Kornei Chukovsky) Rubakin achieved no recognition until many years after the first appearance of his work.

Rubakin's pioneering efforts were not strictly directed towards 'therapy'. The idea of bibliotherapy as such seems to have originated in Germany and the USA in the early years of the century, but in Britain the term 'reading therapy' has been preferred until relatively recently. Jean M. Clarke (in Clarke and Postle 1988) summarises the development of this practice in Britain from the initial stage in which the provision of libraries for patients in mental hospitals was vaguely seen as 'a good thing' and reading as vaguely 'curative' without any apparent grasp of the dynamics involved (or the manifest potential difficulties). Much later in the century, librarians working in hospitals were joined by a handful of social workers who had independently concluded that reading might be a source of insight and care.

In the idealistic and therapeutically oriented culture of the USA, the idea of biblio-therapy has enjoyed a somewhat wider constituency (Pardeck and Pardeck 1984). Fader and McNeil's *Hooked in Books* (1969) directed attention to a single client group (alienated and anti-print teenagers) and their enthusiastic anecdotal evidence of triumphant success in transforming teenagers into bookaholics inspired a generation of teachers. The idea that reading was in itself a 'wonder drug' with the power to 'transform lives' was not new, but it led to a number of attempts to use books to alleviate individual and social ills; thus Manning and Casbergue (1988) outline 'Bibliotherapy for Children in Stepfamilies'. In Pittsburgh, Elizabeth Segel and Joan Friedman set up a modestly conceived but eventually nationally influential programme to bring quality picture books into the homes of the city's poor, in order to encourage early literacy and to promote cultural enrichment (Segel 1989). More strictly 'therapeutic' was Butler's work in New Zealand. *Cushla and Her Books* (Butler 1979) argues that picture books were instrumental in the rehabilitation of a child with multiple handicaps.

The basic idea of bibliotherapy, as established by (predominantly) librarians, runs approximately as follows. A child or adult has a problem. A skilled librarian, teacher or (Clarke would prefer) 'reading therapist' suggests a story which in some way bears on that problem. If the intervention is successful, the reader recognises that the book has some-thing personally significant to say to him/her, perhaps becomes conscious of the dimensions of his/her problem, and sometimes perceives potential solutions to it. The reader then returns the book to the professional, perhaps wishing to discuss it (and through it, his or her own problems), perhaps asking for more books 'like that one', which the professional then sensitively provides on the basis of feedback as to the reader's reception of the first.

The practical obstacles to the widespread employment of such a process, as opposed to the broader concept of 'reading as enrichment', are considerable. With the possible excep-tion of staff in small private mental institutions or private boarding schools, few librarians are likely ever to know their constituents well enough, or have time enough, to play such a role, which requires both intimate knowledge of the individual and wide knowledge of literature. Moreover, bibliotherapy is open to ethical objections if it is foisted upon mental patients or older children without their having requested it, and (more pragmatically) will in such cases almost certainly be resisted openly or covertly. Worse still, existing bibliother-apeutic theory seems inadequately informed as to how narratives actually interact with human lives.

How stories affect individuals

Pre-literate children in our own and other cultures spontaneously compose songs, chants, monologues and other forms of 'phatic' expression, often to the accompaniment of motor play, and apparently in rough imitation of adult talk, song and story. Children who grow up with television emulate its manner and matter in their compositions (Sutton-Smith 1981); those brought up on oral stories are influenced by that mode, and print-soaked children imitate the mode of print (Crago and Crago 1983). There are, however, distinc-tive structural principles in children's compositions which mark them off from adult models, and which suggest some innate paradigm that modifies direct imitation.

Later in life, such spontaneous story-making 'goes underground', taking the form of the 'inner newsreel' discussed by Becker (1972) and Klinger (1971). Adults do not normally chant out aloud as they make beds, tee off on the golf course or type at their computer station, but their minds do run an endless stream of loosely arranged images, thoughts and inner dialogues – a waking version of dreaming.

All of this evidence suggests that story-telling, or at least arranging the raw material of experience into some sort of pattern, is a process almost as fundamental to human life as breathing. In these ur-narratives, we are both 'creators' and 'audiences', both 'partici-pants' and 'spectators': the roles are not substantially distinguished.

'Absorbed' or 'ludic reading', as investigated by Victor Nell (1988), is virtually a trance state, where readers willingly become oblivious to the world around them. Normal consciousness is put on hold and the print seems to elicit the production of highly person-alised images – some based on memories, some 'constructed'. Thus the reader 'merges' with the characters and events of the work. Nell, one of the few mainstream psychologists to offer anything useful on the affective dimension of reading, points out that, where ludic reading is in question, there is no point in distinguishing fiction from non-fiction or popular fiction from 'good literature': the process occurs regardless of category. However, it is unlikely that ludic reading would normally occur unless in response to narrative material. It is as if there is something intrinsically consciousness-altering about the narrative form itself. Ludic readers are skilled in seeking out texts which will offer them the experience they desire and can often successfully select on the basis of only small samples of writing (a process akin to that by which we 'instinctively' assess strangers after a few minutes' acquaintance). Radway (1993), describing women readers choosing romance novels, verifies this finding.

If deep absorption in narrative has nothing to do with literary quality, then adult ludic readers are probably functionally identical with child readers/listeners, for whom aesthetic sophistication has little to do with enjoyment. Schlager (1977) found that children's pref-erences among award-winning children's books had more to do with 'matching' between the themes of the books and the developmentally appropriate themes of middle childhood than with literary sophistication or level of textual difficulty.

Together, these findings suggest that the optimal conditions for 'bibliotherapy' would be when a reader (child or adult) already capable of ludic reading (many readers do not read in this deeply absorbed manner) encounters a text (fiction or non-fiction, pot-boiler or classic) which matches his or her developmental stage and recurrent inner themes.

But whereas the bibliotherapists have proposed a fairly crude model, in which the reading therapist seeks for a literal correspondence between the content of the text and the reader's own 'problem' or life situation, it is far more likely that the 'merging' of reader and text will occur when the correspondence is partly or wholly metaphorical.

Human addiction to story is an aspect of our symbol-making nature: our very language is strongly metaphorical and our dreaming uses the language of symbol and analogy. When we read a story that is obviously very similar in its characters and events to our own life experience, we may read it with enjoyment and appreciation, consciously appreciating the parallels; but if our life experience is painful, then we may reject such a story alto-gether: it will take us back to something we might prefer to forget.

Thus, when offered a short text (Wild's *Beast* (1993)) featuring a protagonist with obsessive-compulsive symptoms, three early adolescent boys with similar symptoms read only a few pages, or failed to read the novel at all, although their reading skills were more than adequate for the task, because, as they said, the protagonists were 'too much like themselves'. Daniels (1992), on the other hand, describes an orphaned Vietnamese adolescent living in Britain who was deeply affected by a novel about a porpoise who becomes separated from its mother and is cruelly treated by its human captors.

The emergence of ur-narrative very early in human life strongly suggests that story is indeed a 'natural' mode of self-expression and self-healing. But for a print text to 'plug into' the inner newsreel of an individual and temporarily replace it as an ongoing source of images, feelings and self-talk, exquisitely fine unconscious matching must occur, so that the reader 'recognises' something of high personal significance, while simultaneously failing to pin down its precise meaning. I maintain (Crago 1993) that such matching is akin to 'falling in love'. In both cases, an instinctive, largely unconscious recognition of similarity occurs, while consciously, the individuals concerned are aware only of a powerful emotional 'pull' and a sense of 'rightness' or 'fitness' in being with the other person (or text). Texts that are self-selected on such a basis are likely to be read and re-read with total absorption.

In this 'systemic' model of reader–text interaction, readers initially 'influence' books, rather than the other way around (Holland 1975). But when preferred texts are read again and again, or are brooded over in memory, they become, in turn, potent shaping influences over the reader's future self-concept and life path. Key texts may then become 'potentiating devices', eliciting from individuals the full development of what is already latent within them, but which might never flower otherwise. Needless to say, such potentiation can be negative as well as positive. *Der Ring des Niebelungen* and *Also Sprache Zarathustra* may have 'potentiated' Hitler's grandiose and paranoid fantasies; Wagner and Nietzsche are not therefore responsible for the Holocaust or the Second World War.

Here the theory of literacy response begins to converge with recent developments within the field of psychotherapy itself where, quite independently of the bibliotherapy movements, the 1980s brought a new consciousness of the power of 'story-telling' as an intervention device. Probably originating in Jay Haley's (1973) lively account of the therapeutic 'wizardry' of Milton Erickson, the concept of therapeutic story-telling has been picked up and popularised. Cameron-Bandler (1978), Gordon (1978) and Mills and Crowley (1986) all emphasise the power of metaphor to 'slip past' the defences of the conscious mind.

Such practitioners have little acquaintance with literary history – otherwise they would surely have recognised that their 'therapeutic metaphor' amounts to little more than a re-labelling of the time-honoured genres of allegory and fable. What is new is their highly individualised focus. Therapeutic stories, they maintain, must be constructed specifically to suit the emotional dynamics of individuals. Also worth noting is their insistence that 'the unconscious does not recognise negatives' ('whatever you do, please don't smoke' becomes 'smoke!'); thus stories attempting to be 'curative' through the language of symbol and metaphor must be positive in intent and in the specific propositions they employ. A different approach, corresponding more closely with the principles outlined above, is taken by Androutsopoulou (2001), whose practice includes paying close attention to texts that clients report having found intensely meaningful, and 'reading' such texts as metaphoric statements of the clients' own inner themes and narratives. Such an approach is in essence similar to the psychodynamic interpretation of readers' responses to fictions proposed by Norman Holland (1975).

Not to be confused with 'therapeutic metaphor' is the development of so-called 'Narrative Therapy' (Epston and McNeil 1989). Originating as a variant of strategic family therapy, but employing Foucauldian notions about power, language and meaning, Narrative Therapy invites clients to become aware of how they have been participants in the construction of a 'dominant story' of their own life (for example, 'my life is a total failure') and instead to consider alternative ways in which they might have constructed their personal narratives. This encourages the noticing and valuing of instances when the person subverted or resisted the 'dominant story' – and the construction (for example) of an alternative self-narrative of success and 'heroic resistance' to perceived problematic influences. An example of the use of literary texts as an adjunct to such approaches can be found in Ridley (1999).

Whither bibliotherapy?

The sobering truth about bibliotherapy is that such a form of healing is more likely to occur through the reader's own unconscious selection of texts that will 'speak' to her or him than through the planned recommendations of a professional mediator. This is not to say that bibliotherapy in its existing form cannot offer modest contributions. First, the reading of narratives that literally or symbolically parallel one's own condition can provide a language in which a child or adult may begin to talk about what has previously been inchoate. Thus the intense interest shown by many adolescent girls in accounts of eating disorders, drug addiction and sexual abuse, even when they themselves do not have such problems, suggests that these stories provide a way of articulating their own sense of alienation, aggression or low self-esteem.

Second, the reading of books can provide the comfort of knowing that one is not alone, and thus function as a 'safer', more private version of a psychotherapy or self-help group. Third, reading can provide vicarious insight into one's problems, and even a measure of integration of previously disowned feelings. In the sense that it is entirely private, reading is thus far safer than seeking an interview with a therapist or counsellor; but, on the other hand, it is far easier to put a book down than to walk out of a therapist's office at the mention of an uncomfortable truth. Fourth, reading can, at a metaphorical level, and sometimes even at a literal one, provide suggestions, akin to hypnotic suggestions, of ways to resolve the reader's problems – suggestions which may bypass conscious resistance on the sufferer's part.

Recognition of such potential usefulness led Australian family therapists in the late 1980s to set up the Family Award, a prize given for a children's book which would address real difficulties faced by children as members of families, and offer solutions which were credible and achievable. The Family Award is now fifteen years old, and includes a separate award for a picture-book text for younger readers. The annual listing of 'books which may be useful in therapy' cautions that texts should always be read critically before being recommended to young clients, and that recommendations should be made, not as 'stand alone' interventions, but as part of the ongoing therapeutic relationship (Award Committee 2003).

On the other hand, reading by itself, like any form of 'therapeutic' activity, from painting to gardening or sport, is not likely to embody the element of caring confrontation that seems fundamental to much successful psychotherapy. If the theory of emotional 'matching' is correct, then readers will nearly always reject a text that contains too painful a self-confrontation; and they will be drawn again and again to those narratives which will encourage them to construct their lives much as before, albeit, perhaps, in a more vivid, enriched way.

This leaves a heavy onus on the bibliotherapist to provide what the text itself cannot, and, while a sensitive librarian may do as well as a professional therapist with a relatively 'easy' client, it is likely that clients (child or adult) with more deeply rooted dysfunctions will prove far beyond even a well-trained teacher or librarian's ability to help.

If bibliotherapy is to fulfil its promise, its practitioners must learn to diagnose their clients' patterns of preferred reading through careful observation and questioning over time. Personally significant texts, which are read again and again, are the most efficient indicators of those patterns. The professional could then recommend further texts which embody the same patterns, or seek to engage the client in discussion of one of his or her existing 'special books'. If bibliotherapy is understood as a way of affirming and extending an individual personality rather than as a way of 'curing' or 'changing' a person, then its chances of being useful will be far greater. In her Earthsea quartet, Ursula Le Guin's Mages can call up a magical wind to fill their sails if required; but they cannot magically compel an existing wind to blow in the opposite direction.

References

Androutsopoulou, A. (2001) 'Fiction as an Aid to Therapy: A Narrative and Family Rationale for Practice', *Journal of Family Therapy* 23, 3: 278–95.

Award Committee (2003) 'Announcement of the Fifteenth Annual Award (for Books Published in 2001)', *Australian and New Zealand Journal of Family Therapy* 23, 1: 47–8.

Becker, E. (1972) *The Birth and Death of Meaning*, 2nd edn, Harmondsworth: Penguin.

Bettelheim, B. (1976) *The Uses of Enchantment: The Meaning and Importance of Fairy Tales*, New York: Knopf.

Butler, D. (1979) *Cushla and Her Books*, London: Hodder and Stoughton.

Cameron-Bandler, L. (1978) *They Lived Happily Ever After: A Book about Achieving Happy Endings in Coupling*, Cupertino, CA: Meta Publications.

Clarke, J. and Postle, E. (eds) (1988) *Reading Therapy*, London: Clive Bingley.

Crago, H. (1979) 'Cultural Categories and the Criticism of Children's Literature', *Signal* 30: 140–50.

—— (1993) 'Why Readers Read What Writers Write', *Children's Literature in Education* 24, 4: 277–90.

—— (2003) 'What Is a Fairy Tale?', *Signal* 100, 8–26.

Crago, M. and Crago, H. (1983) *Prelude to Literacy: A Preschool Child's Encounter with Picture and Story*, Carbondale: Southern Illinois University Press.

Daniels, J. (1992) 'Stories We Tell Ourselves: Stories We Tell Others', in Styles, M., Bearne, E. and Watson, V. (eds) *Exploring Children's Literature*, London: Cassell.

Epston, D. and McNeil, E. (1989) *Literate Means to Therapeutic Ends*, Adelaide: Dulwich Centre Publications.

Fader, D. and McNeil, E. (1969) *Hooked on Books*, London: Pergamon.

Gordon, T. (1978) *Therapeutic Metaphors: Helping Others through the Looking Glass*, Cupertino, CA: Meta Publications.

Haley, J. (1973) *Uncommon Therapy: The Psychiatric Techniques of Milton H. Erikson, MD*, New York: Norton.

Hatt, F. (1976) *The Reading Process: A Framework for Analysis and Description*, London: Bingley.

Holland, N. (1975) *Five Readers Reading*, New Haven, CT: Yale University Press.

Jaynes, J. (1976) *The Origin of Consciousness in the Breakdown of the Bicameral Mind*, Boston, MA: Houghton Mifflin.

Klinger, E. (1971) *The Structure and Function of Fantasy*, New York: Wiley-Interscience.

McLeod, J. (1997) *Narrative and Psychotherapy*, London: Sage.

Manning, D. and Casbergue, R. (1988) 'Bibliotherapy for Children in Stepfamilies', *Clearing House* 62, 3: 124–7.

Mills, J. and Crowley, R. in collaboration with Ryan, M. (1986) *Therapeutic Metaphors for Children and the Child within*, New York: Brunner-Mazel.

Nell, V. (1988) *Lost in a Book: The Psychology of Reading for Pleasure*, New Haven, CT: Yale University Press.

Pantanizopoulos, J. (1989) ' "I'll Be Happy when I'm Thin Enough": The Treatment of Anorexia Nervosa in Adolescent Fiction', *ALAN* 17, 1: 9–10.

Pardeck, J. and Pardeck, J. (1984) *Young People with Problems: A Guide to Bibliotherapy*, New York: Greenwood Press.

Radway, J. (1993) *Reading the Romance: Women, Patriarchy and Popular Literature*, Chapel Hill: University of North Carolina Press.

Ridley, C. (1999) 'Anorexia Told off by the Arabian Nights', in Bowen, B. and Robinson, G. (eds) *Therapeutic Stories: A Collection of Stories and Narrative Ideas*, Canterbury: AFT Publishing, 37–43.

Schlager, N. (1977) 'Predicting Children's Choices in Literature: A Developmental Approach', *Children's Literature in Education* 9, 3: 136–42.

Segel, E. (1989) 'Collaborations: Putting Children's Literature to Work for Children at Risk', in Gannon, S. R. and Thompson, R. A. (eds) *When Rivers Meet: Selected Papers from the 1989 International Conference of the Children's Literature Association*, Pleasantville, NY: Pace University, 27–31.

Simsova, S. (ed.) (1968) *Nicholas Rubakin and Bibliopsychology*, Hamden, CT: Archon/London: Bingley.

Steedman, C. (1982) *The Tidy House: Little Girls Writing*, London: Virago.

Stone, L. (1977) *The Family, Sex and Marriage in England, 1500–1800*, London: Weidenfeld and Nicolson.

Sutton-Smith, B. (1981) *The Folkstories of Children*, Philadelphia: University of Pennsylvania Press.

Tabbert, R. (1979) 'The Impact of Children's Books: Cases and Concepts', *Children's Literature in Education* 10, 2: 92–102.

Wilber, K. (1986) *Up from Eden: A Transpersonal View of Human Evolution*, Boston, MA: Shambhala.

Further reading

Appleyard, J. (1990) *Becoming a Reader: The Experience of Fiction from Childhood to Adulthood*, Cambridge: Cambridge University Press.

Crago, H. (1985) 'The Place of Story in Affective Development: Implications for Educators and Clinicians', in Curry, N. (ed.) *The Feeling Child*, New York: Haworth.

Lesnik-Oberstein, K. (1994) *Children's Literature: Criticism and the Fictional Child*, Oxford: Clarendon Press.

14 What the authors tell us

Peter Hunt

[A good book] leads to the unknown, the unknown of one's soul, for example.
(Martin Auer, in Metcalf 2002: 57)

'A lot of discussion about children's literature,' the author Nina Bawden observed, 'suffers from pompous inflation' (Bawden 1987: 68), but on the whole children's authors display a down-to-earth concern with the complex situation in which they find themselves. They are commonly reluctant to theorise: Lucy Boston expressed the extreme view: 'I'm against all theoreticians. No original writing could result from a theory, could it?' (Wintle and Fisher 1974: 284). Joan Aiken is a little more tolerant:

> I suppose one ought to have theories about writing for children, but with me the theories seem to come second to the writing. However ... what I believe is that children's books should never minimise the fact that life is tough; virtue ought to triumph in the end, because even the best-regulated children's lives are so insecure that they need reassurance, but there's no point in pretending that wickedness and hardship don't exist. And one should never, never write down to a hypothetical children's level or reduce one's vocabulary ... But I'm sure, really, that the main thing is just to shove all theories aside and enjoy the writing; that's the only way to produce good work.
>
> (Townsend 1971: 25)

Nonetheless, children's authors have continually to confront questions of quite who their audiences are and how they can entertain and influence them; they have to make decisions in terms of language and content, and this in the context of pressure from publishers, parents, the educational establishment and would-be censors. This chapter brings together comments from over fifty authors, throwing light on many such issues.

It is common, for example, to find that people have a low opinion of children's authorship as a profession – as K. M. Peyton said, 'My mother asks me, "When are you going to write a proper book?"' ('On Not Writing a Proper Book', in Blishen 1975: 123). Ivan Southall has questioned the suggestion that writing for children is a 'lesser' activity:

> The viewpoint mystifies me – that works for children must necessarily be minor works by minor writers, that deliberately they are generated and projected at reduced voltage, that they evade truth, that they avert passion and sensuality and the subtleties of life and are unworthy of the attention of the serious artist or craftsman ... Adult scaling-down of the intensity of the child state is a crashing injustice, an outrageous distortion of what childhood is about.
>
> ('Sources and Responses', in Haviland 1980: 85)

They might, of course, be consoled by C. S. Lewis's robust defence in 'On Three Ways of Writing for Children':

> Critics who treat *adult* as a term of approval, instead of merely a descriptive term, cannot be adult themselves. To be concerned about being grown up, to admire the grown up because it is grown up, to blush at the suspicion of being childish; these are the marks of childhood and adolescence ... The modern view seems to me to involve a false conception of growth ... surely arrested development consists not in refusing to lose old things but in failing to add new things?
>
> (Lewis 1966: 25)

A preliminary question is, who do children's authors write for? A specific child or an abstract child or a specific age-group – or for themselves? One school of thought can be traced at least to Robert Louis Stevenson. In writing about *Treasure Island* to W. E. Henley, he said: 'It's awful fun, boys' stories. You just indulge the pleasure of your heart, that's all; no trouble, no strain' (Colvin 1911: 49). Arthur Ransome famously quoted these lines, in a letter to H. J. B. Woodfield, editor of *The Junior Bookshelf*, in 1937:

> That, it seems to me, is the secret. You just indulge the pleasure of your heart. You write not *for* children but for yourself, and if, by good fortune, children enjoy what you enjoy, why then you are a writer of children's books ... No special credit to you, but simply thumping good luck. Every writer wants to have readers, and than children there are no better readers in the world.
>
> (Crouch and Ellis 1977: 6)

Ransome then went on to a much-imitated dictum:

> I do not know how to write books for children and have the gravest doubts as to whether anybody should try to do any such thing. To write *for* children seems to me to be a sure way of writing what is called a 'juvenile', a horrid, artificial thing, a patronising thing, a thing that betrays in every line that author and intended victims are millions of miles apart, and that the author is enjoying not the stuff of his book but a looking-glass picture of himself or herself 'being so good with children'.
>
> (Crouch and Ellis 1977: 6)

This view can be refined, as by Lucy Boston: 'If you write for the child that was, in your own mind there's no division between that child and yourself now, so that it should be valid for both' (Wintle and Fisher 1974: 283). Philippa Pearce concurs: 'Writing about and for children, one should have a view almost from the inside, to re-create – not what childhood looks like now, but what it felt like then' (Nodelman 1996: 164). Equally, writers feel that when they are absorbed in the act of writing, audience ceases to be a problem; Susan Cooper's first book was started as a competition entry, but rapidly became something else:

> Now I was no longer writing for a deadline or for money; I was writing for me, or perhaps for the child I once was and in part still am. I dismissed all thought of the ... prize and I sat there with my back against the sofa and my head in a private world.
>
> (Cooper 1990: 20)

There are dissenting voices, however. Betsy Byars:

> Now I know that there's a theory today that we must never write for children and, after all, we're all just big kids, but I don't believe that. It's partly because I refuse to think of myself as a large wrinkled child, but also because, through my children, I have come to see that childhood is a special time, that children are special, that they do not think like adults or talk like adults. And even though we adults sometimes feel that we are exactly the same as when we were ten, I think that's because we can no longer conceive of what ten was really like, and because what we have lost, we have lost so gradually that we no longer miss it.
>
> (Byars 1982: 6)

Meindert DeJong develops this:

> You may try to go back [to childhood] by way of memory, but that memory is an adult memory, an adult conception of childhood for adults – and not for children … When you write for children from adult memory, you satisfy only the other adults who have also forgotten their inner childhood, and have substituted for it an adult conception of what the child needs and wants in books.
>
> (Townsend 1971: 75)

Certainly, there seems to be common agreement that writing with a particular aim or an age group in mind is a route to disaster. Sheena Porter observed that 'it is definitely wrong to write any book with the conscious aim of making it suitable for a particular type of child. The good book must make itself' (Crouch and Ellis 1977: 132). Rumer Godden concurs:

> I think children's books should be either information, straight, or else they should be for entertainment. I think you find this worst of all in pony books – they teach a child how to look after a pony through a story. And I always think that's pretty horrid … As soon as anyone tries to write a novel with a target, he's bound to fail.
>
> (Wintle and Fisher 1974: 293)

Similarly, John Rowe Townsend:

> I think insofar as one has any of the instincts of the artist … or craftsman … one must write first for oneself with the aim of making something. I think that the book comes first and the audience comes afterwards … You are both a craftsman and communicator, and you must carry out each function with proper respect for the other. But as soon as you start thinking in terms of *catering* – a word I particularly detest – for a special readership, then I think you are heading for disaster.
>
> (Wintle and Fisher 1974: 239–40)

Therefore, although there is a very distinctive market, authors are generally cautious about writing directly 'for' it. Ivan Southall, in a striking diatribe, castigated bad writers who 'do not judge themselves by the best; they shut their souls to that; they read the worst and say "I can do better than that"' (Haviland 1980: 87). He distinguishes between the 'honest' second-rate and the 'blatantly commercial second-rate'. 'We are giving them what they want is the alleged doctrine of these people. I believe they do not want it for a moment and would never miss it if it were not there' (90). C. S. Lewis was equally scathing about 'manufacturing' a book: if your story sprang from telling a story to an individual child,

> There is no question of 'children' conceived as a strange species whose habits you have 'made up' like an anthropologist or a commercial traveller. Nor, I suspect, would it be possible, thus face to face, to regale the child with things calculated to please it but regarded by yourself with indifference or contempt.
>
> (Lewis 1966: 23)

And he goes on to observe that the only way that he can write stories 'consists in writing a children's story because a children's story is the best art-form for something you have to say' (23).

Thus you must write *for* children, not covertly for two different audiences. As Roald Dahl observed:

> What narks me tremendously is people who pretend they're writing for young children and they're really writing to get laughs from adults. There are too many of those about. I refuse to believe that Carroll wrote *Alice* for that little girl. It's much too complex for that.
>
> (Wintle and Fisher 1974: 110)

He is not alone. The artist John Burningham said: 'I think there's a horrendous movement of people who think there's a formula: "let's draw everybody in party hats", but really they're appealing to adults while the children are actually bored' (Heaton 1988: 2).

Of course, not everyone agrees. W. E. Johns, who wrote over a hundred books about his flying hero, Biggles, was clear about his aims:

> I give boys what they want, not what their elders and betters think they ought to read. I teach at the same time, under a camouflage. Juveniles are keen to learn, but the educational aspect must not be too obvious or they become suspicious of its intention.
>
> (Trease 1964: 80)

All writers for children must, naturally, find themselves in a position of teaching, and our perception of what constitutes authorial intention changes. For example, William Makepeace Thackeray wrote in 1846 in *Fraser's Magazine*:

> One cannot help looking with secret envy on the children of the present day, for whose use and entertainment a thousand ingenious and beautiful things are provided which were quite unknown some few scores of years since, when the present writer and reader were very possibly in the nursery state. Abominable attempts were made in those days to make useful books for children, and cram science down their throats as calomel used to be administered under the pretence of a spoonful of currant-jelly.
>
> ('On Some Illustrated Books for Children', Salway 1976: 286–7)

If the majority of writers do not see their role as specific to a child or to education or manipulation, why do they write for children? Some, like Alan Garner, follow Ransome: 'Simply, children make the best audience. Connect with a child and you really connect. Adolescence is the same only more so' (quoted in Philip 1981: 154). Other writers take an even more noble position: Paula Fox ('Some Thoughts on Imagination in Children's Literature'):

> When you read to a child, when you put a book in a child's hands, you are bringing that child news of the infinitely varied nature of life. You are an awakener.
>
> (Hearne and Kaye 1981: 24)

Some, like Paul Zindel and Ralph Steadman, have a high sense of mission. Zindel:

> You realise the enormity of the responsibility that you've brought children into the world, and if you don't like life and what you've given them is something you don't like, then it's a terrible thing. So I think there is a big responsibility that you pass on to the children a sense of faith, that life is good, that it's an adventure and that it's something to be chosen over oblivion.
>
> (Clark 1989: 15)

Steadman:

> Each child has a unique view of our world. Our world, that is, for now.
>   In the meantime, we have a duty, a clear duty to help sustain the openness of a child's pure vision and its wholesome acceptance of what it sees and feels in the world around it and within its own private world ...
>   In a child we're presented with the raw material, the clean slate, the possessor of potent senses, the ready absorber of the slightest whim. We must realise that every confrontation, every spark of human intention and every touch is registered by this miracle, and the life force within it will use whatever it can grasp to further the motives of a tender captive mind.
>   The best of children's books are secret doors [which you can only enter if you believe what is on the other side] ... They are readily available with a child to help you and yet inaccessible if you spurn the child's natural delight in the possibility of everything impossible.
>
> (Steadman 1990: 25)

Others have a more specific intention, notably Roald Dahl, here quoted from two interviews with Mark West:

> The person who is what I call a fit reader has a terrific advantage over people who are not readers. Life becomes richer if you have the whole world of books around you, and I'll go to practically any length to bring this world to children.
>
> (West 1988: 74)

> When I'm writing for adults, I'm just trying to entertain them. But a good children's book does more than entertain. It teaches children the use of words, the joy of playing with language. Above all it teaches children not to be frightened of books ... If they are going to amount to anything in life, they need to be able to handle books.

> If my books can help children become readers, then I feel I have accomplished something important.
>
> (West 1990: 65–6)

Consequently, it is a task to be taken seriously, especially in the light of Joan Aiken's dictum that 'A children's book should be written ... remembering how few books children have time to read in the course of a childhood and that the impact of each one is probably equivalent to a dozen, or twenty, encountered at a later age' ('Between Family and Fantasy', in Haviland 1980: 63).

As to the more profound motivations, Gillian Rubenstein has a theory 'that most people who end up writing for children [had] some kind of trauma which makes them feel that age emotionally for the rest of their lives because that's where they experienced their strongest emotions' (Nieuwenhuizen 1991: 232). Equally, there is a certain scepticism about anyone who claims an easy relationship with childhood, as expressed by E. L. Konigsburg: 'It seems to me that people who profess to love *children* really love *childhood* and, what's more ... they really love only one childhood – their own – and only one aspect of it, called *innocence*' ('Ruthie Britten and Because I Can', in Hearne and Kaye 1981: 68). Lloyd Alexander also comments on this:

> With all the best intentions in the world many adults have a very peculiar view of childhood. It's strange, because we were all children at some point, though we've forgotten that. We sentimentalise childhood. We look upon it very often as a happy golden age. There are a great many writers for children, and splendid writers for children, who are perhaps more interested in recapturing their own childhood; whereas I am trying to come to terms with my adulthood ... I speak to the child as a growing person.
>
> (Wintle and Fisher 1974: 212, 213)

The next question that authors confront is: what changes do you make for a child audience? A large majority of authors do not feel inclined to make changes, even under pressure from publishers. To journey-person writers, some of these stances may seem idealistic or privileged. Richard Adams:

> From de la Mare I derived early the idea that one must at all costs tell the truth to children, not so much about mere physical pain and fear, but about the really unanswerable things – what Thomas Hardy called 'the essential grimness of the human situation'.
>
> (Adams 1974: 92)

David Martin:

> People in the children's book world ask ... 'Is it suitable?' 'Is it the right age level?' 'Is it about a contemporary problem?' These are important questions, but *not* of primary importance. The primary question should be '*Is this a good book?*', or '*Is this a good writer, writing a good book?*'
>
> (Nieuwenhuizen 1991: 173)

Yet you can be optimistic, as is John Rowe Townsend:

I don't think one ought to worry too much about corrupting children, so long as one's books are honest. It has always seemed to me (and this may sound unduly inspirational) that what is honestly intended, and done as truthfully as the author is able to do it, cannot intrinsically be regarded as harmful. On the whole I am inclined to think that children will pass unharmed over what they do not understand. The objection to the heavy sex novel is not that it is going to corrupt them, but that it is going to bore them stiff – by elaborating on experiences that are beyond meaning for them.

(Wintle and Fisher 1974: 245)

But reality does bite. C. S. Lewis made what he saw as limitations into advantages:

Writing 'juveniles' certainly modified my habits of composition. Thus it (a) imposed a strict limit on vocabulary (b) excluded erotic love (c) cut down reflective and analytical passages (d) led me to produce chapters of nearly equal length, for convenience in reading aloud. All these restrictions did me great good – like writing in strict metre.

(Meek *et al.* 1977: 158)

Out in a less cloistered atmosphere, Jean Ure, an accomplished and committed writer of teenage novels, gives the example of using 'four-letter-words' in her book *One Green Leaf*, and its fate in the USA:

I finally made a stand ... I gave the good and defensible reasons, heard no more, and thought with smug satisfaction that here was *one* author who couldn't be bullied into submission.

Poor innocent fool! On receiving my advance copies from the States, what did I find? In the face of my bold authorial intransigence, the whole speech had been wiped out entirely.

I could, of course, have got back to the publishers and made tremendous waves ... but equally of course I didn't. I bowed in the end to the inevitable economic pressures.

(Ure 1989: 19)

This whole question of what adults allow writers to give children opens up many curious questions about adults' approach to childhood. As Penelope Lively points out, childhood itself is a gross oversimplification:

One of the oddest things we do to children is to confront them with someone else who is also eight, or ten, or seven, and insist that they be friends ... What concerns me is the misconception that people are fossilised at any particular point in a lifetime. We are none of us 'the young' or 'the middle-aged' or 'the old'. We are all of these things. To allow children to think otherwise is to encourage a disability – a disability both of awareness and communication.

('Children and Memory', in Heins 1977: 229–30)

Consequently, it is a mistake ever to underestimate the child reader: Ann Fine:

I don't underestimate children, especially those who read a lot. They will have come across many ideas through books and through talking with intelligent people. They are more sophisticated and advanced in their thinking even though they may not be able to articulate these ideas. Just because they can't reproduce ideas at an adult level is no reason to think they can't take them on board.

(Bierman 1991: 16)

Shirley Hughes, in a Woodfield Lecture in 1983, 'Word and Image', linked this idea to the role of the illustrator:

With a child audience you can never *assume* any level of literacy. But it is a great mistake to think that an unlettered audience is necessarily an unperceptive one, or that their visual reactions are crude or undeveloped. I suspect that children are at their most perceptive in this way before they start to read, and that after they have acquired this thrilling and prestigious skill their visual awareness tends to drop a little … Our job as illustrators probably starts from that wonderful moment when a baby gets hold of a book and suddenly realises that the image on one page *connects* with the one overleaf … What we are after is to build on this excitement.

(Fearne 1985: 74)

For all this faith in the reader, questions like 'Should books be frightening?' constantly arise. Catherine Storr, in an article, 'Things That Go Bump in the Night' in the *Sunday Times Magazine* (March 1971), wrote:

I believe that children should be allowed to feel fear … Walter de la Mare … believed that children were impoverished if they were protected from everything that might frighten them … Once one has answered this basic question … the second problem arises of how it is to be presented. This is really a technical problem which has to be faced by every writer for children.

(Meek *et al.* 1977: 123)

What is *fear*, in this context? Jan Mark:

It is debatable whether or not fear of the unknown is greater than fear of the known, but in childhood so much is unknown that a child, in order to make sense of fear, must isolate and identify it; only the known can be dealt with.

(Mark 1986: 9)

Or, as Lloyd Alexander put it, 'Children … have the same emotions … They may be not as complex … but as primary colours, fear is fear, happiness is happiness, and love is the same sense for a child as it is for any other' (Wintle and Fisher 1974: 212). His answer is that 'the child … can experience and come to terms with unsettling emotions within the safety of a work of art' (Alexander 1982: 67). In some senses, as Bernard Ashley notes, the problem has to be resolved through technique:

We will want to share things with older children, argue a case, show what evil is before it's conquered by good … Walter de la Mare … said that a child who has not experienced fear will never be a poet. It isn't what we include, I suggest, it's how we include it.

(Ashley 1986: 27–8)

Much of this argument becomes bound up with our concepts of 'rubbish'. Mollie Hunter is characteristic of those who take their position of responsibility seriously:

> There is a need for heroes in children's literature ... There is no particular harm in children's reading rubbish as long as they also have plenty of good stuff available for comparison. But it has to be recognised that the [Superman-type] presentation of the concept of hero could also be pernicious rubbish in that its equation of might with right elevates the use of force to a prime ethos.
>
> (Hunter 1983: 146)

But perhaps the most important and suggestive comment was Peter Dickinson's, in his 'A Defence of Rubbish'. His sixth defence of children's 'unrespectable' reading-matter was:

> it may not be rubbish after all. The adult eye is not necessarily a perfect instrument for discerning certain sorts of values. Elements – and this particularly applies to science fiction – may be so obviously rubbishy that one is tempted to dismiss the whole product as rubbish. But among those elements there may be something new and strange to which one is not accustomed, and which one may not be able to assimilate oneself, as an adult, because of the sheer awfulness of the rest of the stuff; but the innocence – I suppose there is no other word – of the child's eye can take or leave in a way that I feel an adult cannot, and can acquire valuable stimuli from things which appear otherwise overgrown with a mass of weeds and nonsense.
>
> (Dickinson 1970/1976: 76)

After all, this is the same argument as that used by Lewis Carroll, who wrote of *The Hunting of the Snark*:

> As to the meaning of the *Snark* I'm very much afraid I didn't mean anything but nonsense! Still, you know, words mean more than we mean to express when we use them: so a whole book ought to mean a great deal more than the writer meant.
>
> (Carroll 1973: 22)

What, then, should be changed? Of form and content, the simplification of language might seem to be the less problematic, but here again, authors express great faith in their audience, and a reluctance to bow to simplistic arguments. Eleanor Cameron takes a firm view of this: 'A writer ... should feel himself [*sic*] no more under the necessity to restrict the complexity of his plotting because of differences in child understanding ... than he feels the necessity of restricting his vocabulary' (Cameron 1969: 87), and E. B. White, himself an expert on style, links this with 'writing down':

> Anyone who writes down to children is simply wasting his time ... Some writers deliberately avoid using words they think the child doesn't know. This emasculates the prose, and, I suspect, bores the reader. Children are game for anything. They love words that give them a hard time, provided they are in a context that absorbs their attention.
>
> (Haviland 1974: 87)

That context is a matter of craft and skill, as Jill Paton Walsh points out:

The children's book presents a technically more difficult, technically more interesting problem – that of making a fully serious adult statement, as a good novel of any kind does, and making it utterly simple and transparent … The need for comprehensibility imposes an emotional obliqueness, an indirection of approach, which like elision and partial statement in poetry is often a source of aesthetic power.

('The Rainbow Surface', in Meek *et al.* 1977: 192–3)

Consequently, we may assume that many writers will continue to tackle such problems; as Chris Powling, author, and ex-editor of the British children's book magazine, *Books for Keeps*, put it: 'We could be in for some real advances in children's writing. The most significant writing for children always takes risks!' (Mills 1992: 17).

Can such risks be taken with 'content items', where censorious adults are inclined to intervene? The historical novelist Ronald Welch, once a teacher: 'I know from my own experience that children detest people who talk or write down to them; they are eager to accept the challenge of a more adult approach' (Crouch and Ellis 1977: 77). And yet the position of the adult can be untenable, simply because of being an adult: Eleanor Cameron:

I think it is this sense of restriction – of not feeling perfectly free to express all he knows to be true of teenage sexual feelings and the teenagers' deepest attitudes toward them – that so often pulls the quality of a writer's work for this age down to the level of the bland and superficial.

('McLuhan Youth and Literature', in Heins 1977: 113)

The main problem has generally been with 'realism' – usually equated with the less pleasant or socially acceptable aspects of realism. The movement towards political correctness has made matters more complex than they were in the days of H. Rider Haggard:

Personally, I hate war, and all killing … but while the battle-clouds bank up I do not think that any can be harmed by reading of heroic deeds or of frays in which brave men lose their lives.

What I deem undesirable are the tales of lust, crime, and moral perversion with which the bookstalls are strewn by the dozen.

(Rider Haggard 1926: 105)

At the start of a new century, it could be argued that the reverse pertains. Certainly the concept of truth-telling has shifted. One of the leaders of what might be called the 'ultra-realists' is Robert Cormier:

I don't think a happy ending should be one of the requirements of a children's book. Kids want their books to reflect reality. They know that the bully doesn't always get his comeuppance in the end.

(West 1988: 30)

I think there's a lot going on in today's world that we have a false view of. Television in particular is lying to us … We know life isn't always fair and happy. There are enough books with happy endings. I think there's room for the realistic novel about things that really go on in the world. I try to write a warning about what's waiting out there.

(Elkin *et al.* 1989: 13)

This is not a new idea. The artist Edward Ardizzone:

> I think we are possibly inclined, in a child's reading, to shelter him too much from the harder facts of life. Sorrow, failure, poverty, and possibly even death, if handled poetically, can surely all be introduced without hurt ... If no hint of the hard world comes into these books, I'm not sure that we are playing fair.
>
> ('Creation of a Picture Book', in Egoff *et al.* 1980: 293)

Or, as Lois Lowry observed when her book *The Giver* was censored:

> Pretending that there are no choices to be made – reading only books, for example, which are cheery and safe and nice – is a prescription for disaster for the young. Submitting to censorship is to enter [a] seductive world ... where there are no bad words and no bad deeds. But it is also the world where choice has been taken away and reality distorted. And that is the most dangerous world of all.
>
> (Apseloff 1996: 484)

Realism, in short, presents writers with a difficult problem. Here is Ursula Le Guin, one of the major fantasy and science-fiction writers of the twentieth century:

> I agree that children need to be – and usually want very much to be – taught right from wrong. But I believe that realistic fiction for children is one of the very hardest media in which to do it ... You get 'problem books'. The problem of drugs, of divorce, of race prejudice ... and so on – as if evil were a problem, something that can be solved, that has an answer, like a problem in fifth grade arithmetic. If you want the answer, you just look at the back of the book.
>   *That* is escapism, that posing evil as a 'problem' ...
>
> But what, then, is the naturalistic writer for children to do? Can he present the child with evil as an *insoluble* problem ... To give the child a picture of ... gas chambers ... or famines or the cruelties of a psychotic patient, and say, 'Well, baby, this is how it is, what are you going to make of it' – that is surely unethical. If you suggest that there is a 'solution' to these monstrous facts, you are lying to the child. If you insist that there isn't, you are overwhelming him with a load he's not strong enough yet to carry.
>
> ('The Child and the Shadow', Le Guin 1992: 64–5)

Children must be allowed an escape route. As Tove Jansson observed:

> There is a plethora of very fine children's books that mainly portray the writers' disappointments, phobias and depressions, tales of punishment, injustice and loneliness. But *one* thing he always owes his readers is a happy ending, some kind of happy ending. Or a way left open for the child to spin the tale further.
>
> (Weinreich 2000: 118)

Not only that, but 'realism' as a genre has become a site for fashionable angst. John Rowe Townsend noted in 'An Elusive Border':

I remember thinking how refreshing it would be to read a book about young people who enjoyed life, did well at school, had happy relations with their parents, and neither became nor made anybody pregnant. But fictionally, I suppose, that would be a dull life.

(Heins 1977: 49)

It would also be tactically difficult. Gillian Rubenstein:

It's partly a children's book convention that you write from the kids' point of view, so you cannot be entirely fair to the parents as well. If you are going to write about children of twelve and thirteen who have totally understanding and marvellous parents, there'll be nothing to write about.

(Nieuwenhuizen 1991: 243)

But parents, and other adults, are very sensitive, and this brings us to that constant problem of children's literature, censorship. A rationalist approach has been voiced by Joan Aiken in 'Between Family and Fantasy':

Exercising any degree of control over the kind of books written for or read by children is a highly doubtful policy ... What terrifies one child may seem merely comic to another, or may be completely ignored; one can't legislate for fear.

(Haviland 1980: 63)

This is all very well in theory, but writers who push at the edges of acceptability are confronted with practical censorship. Judy Blume:

Adults have always been suspicious of books that kids like. It seems as if some adults choose to forget what mattered to them when they were children ... Many adults do not trust children.

(West 1988: 11)

I think that a lot of adults in our society are uncomfortable with their own sexuality, and therefore their children's sexuality is a threat to them.

(Wintle and Fisher 1974: 315)

The most frightening thing about censors is their complete sense of self-righteousness.

(West 1988: 36)

One answer, adopted by the political novelist James Watson, is confrontation:

I'm particularly interested in noting where an accusation of bias is used – it says as much about the accuser as the person accused ... the very perception of impartiality is so soaked in ideological notions that there is no way to be impartial. So why pretend to be? If I'm accused of bias in my books – tough! I *am* biased – biased for certain value systems.

(Nettell 1989: 17)

While realism attracts much general attention, it is fantasy where children's literature has made such a major contribution that much authorial theoretical attention has been focused. Susan Cooper:

> In 'realistic' fiction, the escape and the encouragement come from a sense of parallel: from finding a true and recognisable portrait of real life. In these pages we encounter familiar problems, but they're *someone else's problems* ... Fantasy goes one stage beyond realism; requiring complete intellectual surrender, it asks more of the reader, and at its best may offer more. Perhaps this is why it is also less popular, at any rate among adults, who set such store by their ability to think.
>
> ('Escaping into Ourselves', in Hearne and Kaye 1981: 14, 15)

Jill Paton Walsh concurs:

> If a book has a dragon in it, then maybe one dismisses it as rubbish ... There are no dragons in the world, but there are ferocious, greedy and destructive keepers of gold-hoards. And there is greed in one's own soul. A work of fantasy compels a reader into a metaphorical state of mind. A work of realism, on the other hand, permits very literal-minded readings, even downright stupid ones ... Even worse, it is possible to read a realistic book as though it were not fiction at all.
>
> ('The Art of Realism', in Hearne and Kaye 1981: 38)

As Le Guin asked in the title of a famous paper, 'Why Are Americans Afraid of Dragons?' (Le Guin 1992: 34–40). The Brazilian author Bartolomeu Campos Queirós observed that 'Seems to me that fantasy is the only acceptable way of life' (*Bookbird* 1998: 29) and Terry Pratchett applied this view to children:

> So let's not get frightened when children read fantasy. It is the compost for a healthy mind. It stimulates the inquisitive nodes. It may not appear as 'relevant' as books set firmly in the child's environment, or whatever hell the writer believes to be the child's environment, but there is some evidence that a rich internal fantasy life is as good and necessary for a child as healthy soil is for a plant, for much the same reasons ... Like the fairy tales that were its forebears, fantasy needs no excuses.
>
> (Pratchett 1995: 5)

Writers have other matters to contemplate, from Paul Jennings's view that 'Some academics and judges on panels consider that a book has more substance if it is difficult to read' (Nieuwenhuizen 1991: 131) to Nadia Wheatley's dismissal of the classification of books as for adults or for children: 'wouldn't it be better to stop fussing about definitions of genre, and simply put a copy of each into two sections of the library?' (Nieuwenhuizen 1991: 299).

On the whole, they are optimistic about childhood, as is Mary Norton:

> Children nowadays are encouraged to invent, but still in ways devised by adults. 'Clear-up-that-mess' has destroyed many a secret world. As the Borrowers' house was destroyed by Mrs Driver. This particular incident, oddly enough, worries grown-ups far more than it does children. Children are used to repeated small destructions – in the name of punctuality or tidiness – and have learned to accept them. If raw materials are there to hand, they simply build again.
>
> (Crouch and Ellis 1977: 69)

Or, like Aidan Chambers, they are optimistic about the role that adults can take. Having cited Kafka's view that 'a book must be the axe which smashes the frozen seas' he goes on: 'the hands that best wield those axes will belong to sympathetic and knowledgeable adults who wield for themselves, with enormous pleasure and skill, axes of their own size and weight' (Chambers 1985: 33).

Children's authors have also written a great deal about the act of writing, a topic which seems to be of perennial interest to those who attend conferences. Interesting as those accounts can be, they are rarely generally applicable, and the ultimate anti-account, by William Mayne, might serve for all:

> After the idea was there I wrote the book, a statement that, though short, is completely adequate. There is nothing particularly interesting about writing a book. In fact, it is rather a bore for everyone, and generally spoils the idea that was there in the first place.
>
> (Crouch and Ellis 1977: 95)

Mayne stands for the child before the adult, and, one suspects, the writer before the critic: 'Adults can read my books if they like, it doesn't matter. I'm not interested in what they think' (Nettell 1990: 15).

As the highly original and award-winning novelist Jan Mark has observed, Mayne is right:

> Those of us who read Mayne when younger learned that there was no need to observe special requirements when writing for children. You may write exactly what you want to write, and in any way you see fit; the kind of freedoms taken entirely for granted by adult authors.
>
> (Mark 1996: 151)

Children's books are in a strong position at the beginning of the twenty-first century, and that position has been stated trenchantly by Philip Pullman, whose *His Dark Materials* trilogy (1995–2000) has had huge critical and popular success:

> I think the grand narratives aren't so much played out or exhausted in contemporary writing, as abandoned for ideological reasons, because they're felt to be somehow impure or improper. Maybe the whole thing is weakened by a fatal lack of ambition. This is what I find most irritating in my contemporaries among writers: lack of ambition. They're not trying big things. They're doing little things and doing them well.
>
> (Parsons and Nicholson 1999: 117)

Pullman might be thought to be a little generous here. Ann Fine, the second British Children's Laureate, has spoken trenchantly about current standards, and the ways in which critical judgements can be corrupted in the face of 'big-spend' marketing: 'Judgements can get confused ... It's only natural in a field full of nice people, who on the whole aren't full of themselves and deeply arrogant'; and she comes to an untheoretical and perhaps reactionary conclusion:

> There is an objective standard. Books can be judged. We must abandon this idiotic notion that, if something is universally appealing, it must have some fine quality about it ... The arts are shamelessly undemocratic. Publish these books by the score if you

like, but don't for a moment try to kid yourselves, or us, that they are good books, and everyone should be a whole lot more hesitant about giving them prizes.

(Fine 2003: 63–4, 65)

As the Austrian children's novelist Martin Auer implied in the epigraph to this chapter, writing for children should be a very serious business, and it is an encouraging thought, as Philip Pullman said in his acceptance speech for the British Carnegie Medal, that themes that are 'too large for adult fiction [can] only be dealt with adequately in a children's book' (Hunt and Lenz 2001: 122).

References

Adams, R. (1974) 'Some Ingredients of *Watership Down*', *Children's Book Review* 4, 3: 92–5.

Alexander, L. (1982) 'Sex, Violence, Passion, Misery and Other Literary Pleasures', *The Advocate* 1, 2: 65–70.

Apseloff, M. F. (1996) 'Lois Lowry: Facing the Censors', *Paradoxa* 2, 3–4: 480–5.

Ashley, B. (1986) 'TV Reality – the Dangers and the Opportunities', *International Review of Children's Literature and Librarianship* 1, 2: 27–32.

Bawden, N. (1987), 'Through the Dark Wood', in Harrison, B. and Maguire, G. (eds) *Innocence and Experience: Essays and Conversations on Children's Literature*, New York: Lothrop, Lee and Shepard, 68–75.

Bierman, V. (1991) 'Authorgraph No. 69: Anne Fine', *Books for Keeps* 69: 16–17.

Blishen, E. (1975) *The Thorny Paradise: Writers on Writing for Children*, Harmondsworth: Kestrel (Penguin).

Bookbird (1998) 'Special Issue: The Hans Christian Andersen Awards 1998', *Bookbird* 36, 3.

Byars, B. (1982) 'Writing for Children', *Signal* 37: 3–10.

Cameron, E. (1969) *The Green and Burning Tree*, Boston, MA: Atlantic, Little, Brown.

Carroll, L. (1973) *The Hunting of the Snark*, ed. Gardner, M., Harmondsworth: Penguin.

Chambers, A. (1985) *Booktalk. Occasional Writing on Literature and Children*, London: Bodley Head.

Clark, M. (1989) 'Authorgraph No. 54: Paul Zindel', *Books for Keeps* 54: 14–15.

Colvin, S. (ed.) (1911) *Letters of Robert Louis Stevenson*, Vol. 1, London: Methuen.

Cooper, S. (1990) 'How I Began', *The New Welsh Review* 2, 4: 19–21.

Crouch, M. and Ellis, A. (1977) *Chosen for Children*, 3rd edn, London: The Library Association.

Dickinson, P. (1970/1976) 'A Defence of Rubbish', in Fox, G., Hammond, G. and Jones, T. (eds) *Writers, Critics and Children*, New York: Agathon/London: Heinemann Educational.

Egoff, S., Stubbs, G. T. and Ashley, L. F. (eds) (1980) *Only Connect: Readings on Children's Literature*, 2nd edn, Toronto: Oxford University Press.

Elkin, J. *et al.* (1989) 'Cormier Talking', *Books for Keeps* 54: 12–13.

Fearne, M. (1985) *'Only the Best is Good Enough'. The Woodfield Lectures on Children's Literature, 1978–1985*, London: Rossendale.

Fine, A. (2003) 'So Many Books, So Little Time: The Patrick Hardy Lecture', *Signal* 100: 51–65.

Haviland, V. (ed.) (1974) *Children's Literature: Views and Reviews*, London: Bodley Head.

—— (ed.) (1980) *The Openhearted Audience: Ten Authors Talk about Writing for Children*, Washington, DC: Library of Congress.

Hearne, B. and Kaye, M. (1981) *Celebrating Children's Books*, New York: Lothrop, Lee and Shepard.

Heaton, C. (1988) 'On the Child's Side', *British Book News Children's Books*, June: 2–5.

Heins, P. (ed.) (1977) *Crosscurrents of Criticism. Horn Book Essays 1968–1977*, Boston: Horn Book.

Hunt, P. and Lenz, M. (2001) *Alternative Worlds in Fantasy Fiction*, London: Continuum.

Hunter, M. (1983) 'A Need for Heroes', *The Horn Book Magazine* 59, 2: 146–54.

Le Guin, U. (1992) *The Language of the Night: Essays on Fantasy and Science Fiction*, rev. edn, New York: HarperCollins.

Lewis, C. S. (1966) *Of Other Worlds*, London: Geoffrey Bles.

Mark, J. (1986) 'Children Writing', *Bookquest* 9, 2: 4–11.

—— (1996) 'The Way We Were', in Styles, M., Bearne, E. and Watson, V. (eds) *Voices Off. Texts, Contexts and Readers*, London: Cassell.

Meek, M., Warlow, A. and Barton, G. (eds) (1977) *The Cool Web: The Pattern of Children's Reading*, London: Bodley Head.

Metcalf, E.-M. (2002) 'Martin Auer', *Bookbird* 40, 2: 55–8.

Mills, C. (1992) 'Authorgraph No. 75: Chris Powling', *Books for Keeps* 75: 16–17.

Nettell, S. (1989) 'Authorgraph No. 58: James Watson', *Books for Keeps* 58: 17.

—— (1990) 'Authorgraph No. 63: William Mayne', *Books for Keeps* 63: 14–15.

Nieuwenhuizen, A. (1991) *No Kidding. Top Writers for Young People Talk about Their Work*, Chippendale, NSW: Sun (Pan Macmillan).

Nodelman, P. (1996) *The Pleasures of Children's Literature*, 2nd edn, White Plains, NY: Longman.

Parsons, W. and Nicholson, C. (1999) 'Talking to Philip Pullman: An Interview', *The Lion and the Unicorn* 23, 1: 116–34.

Philip, N. (1981) *A Fine Anger: A Critical Introduction to the Work of Alan Garner*, London: Collins.

Pratchett, T. (1995) 'Let There Be Dragons', *Books for Keeps* 83: 6–7.

Rider Haggard, H. (1926) *The Days of My Life*, Vol. 1, London: Longman.

Salway, L. (ed.) (1976) *A Peculiar Gift: Nineteenth Century Writings on Books for Children*, Harmondsworth: Kestrel (Penguin).

Steadman, R. (1990) 'What is a Child? ... and What is a Children's Book?', *Books for Keeps* 62: 25.

Townsend, J. R. (1971) *A Sense of Story. Essays on Contemporary Writers for Children*, Harmondsworth: Longman Young Books (Penguin).

Trease, G. (1964) *Tales out of School*, rev. edn, London: Heinemann.

Ure, J. (1989) 'Who Censors?', *Books for Keeps* 58: 19.

Weinreich, T. (2000) *Children's Literature – Art or Pedagogy?*, Frederiksberg: Roskilde University Press.

West, M. I. (1988) *Trust Your Children*, New York: Neal-Schuman.

—— (1990) 'Interview with Roald Dahl', *Children's Literature in Education* 21: 61–6.

Wintle, J. and Fisher, E. (1974) *The Pied Pipers: Interviews with the Influential Creators of Children's Literature*, London: Paddington Press.

Further reading

Carter, J. (1999) *Talking Books*, London: Routledge.

Chevalier, T. (ed.) (1989) *Twentieth-Century Children's Writers*, 3rd edn, Chicago and London: St James Press.

Commire, A. (ed.) (1971–) *Something about the Author: Facts and Pictures about Authors and Illustrators of Books for Young Children*, Vol. 1, Detroit, MI: Gale Research.

de Montreville, D. and Crawford, E. D. (eds) (1978) *Fourth Book of Junior Authors and Illustrators*, New York: H. W. Wilson.

de Montreville, D. and Hill, D. (eds) (1972) *Third Book of Junior Authors and Illustrators*, New York: H. W. Wilson.

Fuller, M. (1969) *More Junior Authors*, New York: H. W. Wilson.

Hildick, W. (1970) *Children and Fiction*, London: Evans Brothers.

Hopkins, L. B. (1974) *More Books by More People: Interviews with Sixty-Five Authors of Books for Children*, Englewood Cliffs, NJ: Scholastic.

Kingman, L. (ed.) (1965) *Newbery and Caldecott Medal Books 1956–65*, Boston, MA: Horn Book.

—— (ed.) (1975) *Newbery and Caldecott Medal Books 1966–75*, Boston, MA: Horn Book.

Kunitz, S. J. and Haycraft, H. (eds) (1951) *The Junior Book of Authors*, New York: H. W. Wilson.

Glossary

cohesion Cohesion refers to the ways in which sentences are linked together – by meaning, sound, words, or grammar.

deconstruction A theory and practice of reading (rather than a 'method' of criticism) which looks on texts as possessing infinite complex meanings rather than as being reducible to simple, 'static' meanings or interpretations. It looks, for example, at the 'blindnesses' or 'silences' of texts – the things that they do not say (or which they suppress). Deconstructive readings can, of course, be deconstructed themselves (infinitely).

dialectic Logical argument.

dialogical 'Double-voiced' language which responds to and is sensitive to the language and society around it (used by Mikhail Bakhtin); compare **monological** – 'single-voiced' language which operates in isolation, dominated, perhaps, by the aims of the writer.

discourse Broadly, communication; a communicative act, or series of acts.

efferent Moving outwards.

epistemological Dealing with knowledge and the theory of knowledge.

focalisation Sometimes taken to be the same as 'point of view' – the 'angle', viewpoint, or perspective from which or through which the story is told. The 'focaliser' may be the narrator (in a first-person narrative) or the person through whose eyes we see things (in first- or third-person narrative), usually the central character of a story.

formalism An early form of **structuralism**, which looked for recurrent patterns in texts.

'free' and 'bound' forms of speech Speech and thought can be presented in texts either 'directly', using inverted commas ('Hello!') or 'indirectly', where the speech or thought is 'reported' (How careless of them!). If there is no 'tag' (he said, she thought) the phrase is 'free'; if a tag is used ('Hello!', she said; How careless of them, she thought), the phrase is 'bound'. There is some disagreement among linguists as to the use of the terms, but broadly 'free' forms allow (or force) readers to use their imaginations; 'bound' forms allow authors more (potential) control.

gender Now widely taken to mean characteristics given to individuals through 'nurture', rather than the physical sex characteristics given by 'nature'.

gestalt psychology Believes that perceptions, reactions, etc., are gestalts: integrated perceptual structures conceived as functionally more than their parts.

hermeneutics Dealing with theories of interpretation.

historiography The writing of history.

isomorphic Linking the same forms.

Leavisite Strictly, following the critical ideas of F R. Leavis (1895–1978), an immensely influential Cambridge academic who was instrumental in shifting the emphasis of literary studies from history to the text. Leavis was broadly anti-theory, using close readings to produce judgements purporting to derive from the text, but actually lodged in a right-wing, if idiosyncratic, ideology. 'Leavisite' is now often used as a synonym for conservative and authoritarian (or alternatively, sensible) readings.

lexical set Words that are linked together by occurring within similar grammatical or cultural contexts (such as supposed gender characteristics), or forming 'natural groups' (like the months of the year); genres and individual authors will recurrently use similar lexical sets.

literary stylistics The application of 'objective', non-judgmental analytical techniques to the language of texts designed for 'non-functional' reading.

metafiction Self-conscious fiction, which draws attention to its fictiveness.

metonym An attribute standing for an object ('the stage' – the theatre).

polyphonic 'Having many voices' – texts which are not dominated by a single narrative or authorial authority (associated with Bakhtin).

postmodernism The idea that towards the end of the twentieth century there was a fragmentation of the certainties of culture, society and individualism in 'advanced' capitalist societies.

poststructuralism In reaction to the intended universality of **structuralism**, a criticism which questions all readings of texts (including its own) and emphasises instability and ambiguity.

pragmatics The study of language in context, in the sense of what it does, rather than what it is; intention and affect are important, rather than form.

psychological phenomenology Deducing what goes on in an author's mind from the text.

register Language used in a certain context or situation: there is, for example, language thought appropriate to, and therefore more likely to occur in, a church sermon, or on a football field, or in different literary genres.

semiotics The study of sign-systems.

structuralism Criticism which examines the patterns, codes, forms, conventions and structures of texts and larger cultural systems; generally descriptive rather than interpretative.

systemic analysis The analysis of language according to the system developed by Halliday, which sees language as a network involving choices which are influenced by context.

ur-narrative Primitive, original, theoretical or underlying narrative.

General Bibliography

This list is not inclusive of items which are in the chapter bibliographies.

Criticism, Theory and General Approaches

Ang, S. (2000) *The Widening World of Children's Literature*, Basingstoke and London: Macmillan.

Butts, D. (1992) (ed.) *Stories and Society: Children's Literature in its Social Context*, Basingstoke and London: Macmillan.

Clark, B. L. (2003) *Kiddie Lit. The Cultural Construction of Children's Literature*, Baltimore: Johns Hopkins University Press.

Coats, K. (2004) *Looking Glasses and Neverlands. Lacan, Desire, and Subjectivity in Children's Literature*, Iowa City: University of Iowa Press.

Egoff, S., Stubbs, G., Ashley, R. and Sutton, W. (eds) (1996) *Only Connect. Readings on Children's Literature*, 3rd edn, Toronto: Oxford University Press.

Fox, G. (ed.) (1995) *Celebrating Children's Literature in Education*, London: Hodder and Stoughton.

Hollindale, P. (1997) *Signs of Childness in Children's Books*, South Woodchester: Thimble Press.

Hourihan, M. (1997) *Deconstructing the Hero. Literary Theory and Children's Literature*, London: Routledge.

Jones, D. and Watkins, T. (eds) (2000) *A Necessary Fantasy? The Heroic Figure in Popular Children's Fiction*, New York and London: Garland.

Keenan, C. and Thompson, M. S. (eds) (2004) *Studies in Children's Literature 1500–2000*, Dublin: Four Courts Press.

Nikolajeva, M. (1996) *Children's Literature Comes of Age. Toward a New Aesthetic*, New York: Garland.

O'Sullivan, E. (2005) *Comparative Children's Literature*, London and New York: Routledge.

Styles, M., Bearne, E. and Watson, V. (eds) (1998) *The Prose and the Passion: Children and their Reading*, London: Cassell.

Wall, B. (1991) *The Narrator's Voice: The Dilemma of Children's Fiction*, Basingstoke and London: Macmillan.

Watson, V. (ed.) (2001) *The Cambridge Guide to Children's Books in English*, Cambridge: Cambridge University Press.

History and Bibliography

Alderson, B. (1986) *Sing a Song for Sixpence: The English Illustrative Tradition and Randolph Caldecott*, Cambridge: Cambridge University Press in association with the British Library.

Avery, G. (1975) *Childhood's Pattern: A Study of the Heroes and Heroines of Children's Fiction 1770–1950*, London: Hodder and Stoughton.

Bottigheimer, R. B. (1996) *The Bible for Children from the Age of Gutenburg to the Present*, New Haven, CT: Yale University Press.

Carpenter, H. (1985) *Secret Gardens: A Study of the Golden Age of Children's Literature*, London: George Allen and Unwin.

Demers, P. (1993) *Heaven Upon Earth. The Form of Moral and Religious Children's Literature to 1850*, Knoxville, TN: University of Tennessee Press.

Foster, S. and Simons, J. (1995) *What Katy Read. Feminist Re-Readings of 'Classic' Stories for Girls*, Basingstoke and London: Macmillan.

Goldthwaite, J. (1996) *The Natural History of Make-Believe*, New York: Oxford University Press.

Griswold, J. (1996) *The Classic American Children's Story. Novels from the Golden Age*, New York: Viking Penguin.

Hilton, M., Styles, N. and Watson, V. (eds) (1997) *Opening the Nursery Door. Reading, Writing and Childhood, 1600–1900*, London: Routledge.

Hunt, P. (ed.) 1995) *Children's Literature: an Illustrated History*, Oxford: Oxford University Press.

Kutzer, M. D. (2000) *Empire Children: Empire and Imperialism in Classic British Children's Literature*, New York: Routledge.

Opie, I. (1985/1988) *The Singing Game*, Oxford: Oxford University Press.

Opie, I. and Opie, P. (1951/1997) *The Oxford Dictionary of Nursery Rhymes*, Oxford: Oxford University Press.

—— (1959/2001) *The Language and Lore of Schoolchildren*, New York: New York Times Book Review.

Pickering, S. F. (1981) *John Locke and Children's Books in Eighteenth Century England*, Knoxville, TN: University of Tennessee Press.

—— (1993) *Moral Instruction and Fiction for Children, 1749–1820*, Athens, GA: University of Georgia Press.

Reynolds, K. (1990) *Girls Only? Gender and Popular Children's Fiction in Britain, 1880–1910*, Hemel Hempstead: Harvester Wheatsheaf.

——(1994) *Children's Literature in the 1890s and the 1990s*, Plymouth: Northcote House.

Richards, J. (ed.) (1989) *Imperialism and Juvenile Literature*, Manchester: Manchester University Press.

Thacker, D. C. and Webb, J. (2002) *Introducing Children's Literature from Romanticism to Post-modernism*, London and New York: Routledge.

Types and Genres

Agnew, K. and Fox, G. (2001) *Children at War. From the First World War to the Gulf*, London and New York: Continuum.

Auchmuty, R. (1992) *A World of Girls*, London: The Women's Press.

Auchmuty, R. and Wotton, J. (eds) (2000) *The Encyclopedia of School Stories*, Aldershot: Ashgate.

Blount, M. (1974) *Animal Land: The Creatures of Children's Fiction*, London: Hutchinson.

Cadogan, M. and Craig, P. (1976/2003) *You're a Brick, Angela!: A New Look at Girls' Fiction from 1839–1975*, Coleford, Bath: Girls Gone By Publishers.

Collins, F. M. and Graham. J. (eds) (2001) *Historical Fiction for Children: Capturing the Past*, London: Fulton.

Cook, E. (1976) *The Ordinary and the Fabulous*, 2nd edn, Cambridge: Cambridge University Press.

Dusinberre, J. (1987/1999) *Alice to the Lighthouse*, Basingstoke and London: Palgrave Macmillan.

Fisher, J. (1994) *An Index of Historical Fiction for Children and Young People*, Aldershot: Scolar Press.

Fisher, M. (1975) *Who's Who in Children's Books*, London: Weidenfeld and Nicolson.

—— (1976) *The Bright Face of Danger*, London: Hodder and Stoughton.

Gates, P. S., Steffel, S.B., and Molson, F. L. (2003) *Fantasy Literature for Children and Young Adults*, Lanham, MD: Scarecrow Press.

Horn, M. (ed.) (1999) *The World Encyclopedia of Comics*, Philadelphia: Chelsea House.

Kirkpatrick, R., Wotton, J. and Auchmuty, R. (2000) *The Encyclopedia of Boys' School Stories*, Aldershot: Ashgate.

Kuznets, L. R. (1994) *When Toys Come Alive: Narratives of Animation, Metamorphosis and Development*, New Haven, CT: Yale University Press.

Lurie, A. (2003) *Boys and Girls Forever. Reflections on Children's Classics*, London: Chatto and Windus.

Mellon, N. (1992) *Storytelling and the Art of Imagination*, Rockport, MA: Element.

Reynolds, K., Brennan, G. and McCarron, K. (2001) *Frightening Fiction*, London and New York: Continuum.

Richards, J. (1988) *Happiest Days: The Public Schools in English Fiction*, Manchester: Manchester University Press.

Styles, M. *From the Garden to the Street: 300 Years of Poetry for Children*, London: Cassell.

Sullivan, C. W. III (1989) *Welsh Celtic Myth in Modern Fantasy*, Westport, CT: Greenwood Press.

—— (ed.) (1999) *Young Adult Science Fiction*, Westport, CT: Greenwood Press.

Tatar, M. (1992) *Off With Their Heads! Fairy Tales and the Culture of Childhood*, Princeton, NJ: Princeton University Press.

Tucker, N. and Gamble, N. (2001) *Family Fictions*, London and New York: Continuum.

Tucker, N. and Reynolds, K. (eds) (1997) *Enid Blyton: A Celebration and Reappraisal*, London: National Centre for Research in Children's Literature.

Turner, E. S. (1975/1976) *Boys Will Be Boys*, 3rd edn, Harmondsworth: Penguin.

Warner, M. (1994) *From the Beast to the Blonde: On Fairytales and their Tellers*, London: Chatto and Windus.

Watson, V. (2000) *Reading Series Fiction: From Arthur Ransome to Gene Kemp*, London and New York: Routledge.

Watson, V. and Styles, M. (ed.) (1996) *Talking Pictures. Pictorial Texts and Young Readers*, London: Hodder and Stoughton.

Whalley, J. I. and Chester, T. R. (1988) *A History of Children's Book Illustration*, London: John Murray, with the Victoria and Albert Museum.

Contexts

Fox, C. (1993) *At the Very Edge of the Forest: The Influence of Literature on Storytelling by Children*, London: Cassell.

Oittinen, R. (2000) *Translating for Children*, London and New York: Garland.

Pinsent, P. (ed.) (1997) *Children's Literature and the Politics of Equality*, London: David Fulton.

Ravich, D. (2003) *The Language Police: How Pressure Groups Restrict What Students Learn*, New York: Knopf.

Applications

Bennett, J. (1991) *Learning to Read with Picture Books*, 4th edn, South Woodchester: Thimble Press.

Butler, D. (1980) *Babies Need Books*, Sevenoaks: Hodder and Stoughton.

Chambers, A. (2001) *Reading Talk*, South Woodchester: Thimble Press.

Gamble, N. and Yates, S. (2002) *Exploring Children's Literature*, London: Paul Chapman.

Melrose, A. (2002) *Write for Children*, London and New York: Routledge.

Styles, M., Bearne, E. and Watson, V. (eds) (1996) *Voices Off: Texts, Contexts, and Readers*, London: Cassell.

Wolf, S. A. and Brice Heath, S. (1992) *The Braid of Literature: Children's Worlds of Reading*, Cambridge, MA: Harvard University Press.

Childhood Studies

Curtis, J. C. and Curtis, M. (2001) *Play Today in the Primary School Playground: Life, Learning and Creativity*, Buckingham: Open University Press.

James, A., Jenks, C. and Prout, A. (1998) *Theorising Childhood*, Oxford: Polity Press.

James, A. and Prout, A. (eds) (1997) *Constructing and Reconstructing Childhood*, London: RoutledgeFalmer.

Jenkins, H. (ed.) (1999) *The Children's Culture Reader*, New York: New York University Press.

Kline, S. (1993) *Out of the Garden: Toys and Children's Culture in the Age of TV Marketing*, London: Verso

Maybin, J. and Woodhead, M. (2003) *Childhoods in Context*, Milton Keynes/Chichester: Open University Press/John Wiley.

Mills, J. and Mills, R. (eds) (1999) *Childhood Studies: a Reader in Perspectives on Childhood*, London: RoutledgeFalmer.

Montgomery, H., Burr, R., and Woodhead, M. (2003) *Changing Childhoods – Local and Global*, Milton Keynes/Chichester: Open University Press/John Wiley.

Sommerville, J. (1982) *The Rise and Fall of Childhood*, Beverly Hills, CA: Sage.

Woodhead, M. and Montgomery, H. (eds) (2002) *Understanding Childhood – an Interdisciplinary Approach*, Milton Keynes/Chichester: Open University Press/John Wiley.

Zornado, J. (2001) *Inventing the Child: Culture, Ideology and the Story of Childhood*, London and New York, Garland.

Index